ADVANCES IN HUMAN PERFORMANCE AND COGNITIVE ENGINEERING RESEARCH

ADVANCES IN HUMAN PERFORMANCE AND COGNITIVE ENGINEERING RESEARCH

Series Editor: Eduardo Salas

ADVANCES IN HUMAN PERFORMANCE AND COGNITIVE ENGINEERING RESEARCH

EDITED BY

EDUARDO SALAS

*Department of Psychology and Institute for Simulation & Training,
University of Central Florida, USA*

ASSOCIATE EDITORS:

CLINT A. BOWERS
Department of Psychology, University of Central Florida, USA

NANCY COOKE
Department of Psychology, New Mexico State University, USA

JAMES E. DRISKELL
Florida Maxima, USA

DIANNA STONE
Department of Management, University of Central Florida, USA

2001

JAI
An Imprint of Elsevier Science

Amsterdam – London – New York – Oxford – Paris – Shannon – Tokyo

ELSEVIER SCIENCE Ltd
The Boulevard, Langford Lane
Kidlington, Oxford OX5 1GB, UK

First edition 2001

Library of Congress Cataloging in Publication Data
A catalog record from the Library of Congress has been applied for.

British Library Cataloguing in Publication Data
A catalogue record from the British Library has been applied for.

ISBN: 0-7623-0748-X

⊚ The paper used in this publication meets the requirements of ANSI/NISO Z39.48-1992 (Permanence of Paper).
Printed in The Netherlands.

CONTENTS

LIST OF CONTRIBUTORS

Bradford S. Bell	Michigan State University, Dept. of Psychology
Clint A. Bowers	University of Central Florida
Kenneth G. Brown	University of Iowa
Gwendolyn E. Campbell	Naval Air Warfare Center Training Systems Division
Janis A. Cannon-Bowers	Naval Air Warfare Center Training Systems Division
Marvin S. Cohen	Cognitive Technologies, Inc.
Nancy J. Cooke	New Mexico State University
Douglas J. Gillan	New Mexico State University
Floyd Glenn	CHI Systems, Inc.
James M. Hitt	University of Central Florida
Steve J. Kass	University of West Florida
Florian Jentsch	University of Central Florida
Gary Klein	Klein Associates, Inc.
Steve W. J. Kozlowski	Michigan State University
K. Ronald Laughery	MicroAnalysis and Design, Inc.

Laura Militello	Klein Associates, Inc.
Morrell E. Mullins	Virginia Polytechnic Institute and State University
Eduardo Salas	University of Central Florida
Bryan B. Thompson	Cognitive Technologies, Inc.
Rebecca J. Toney	Michigan State University
Kim J. Vicente	University of Toronto
Daniel A. Weissbein	Michigan State University
Wayne Zachary	CHI Systems, Inc.

PREFACE

The complexity of the world of work continues to increase. Organizations need to employ the best and latest technology in order to remain competitive. They also demand more (and better) performance out of their operators, managers, technical personnel and executives. These need to have a complete repertoire of knowledge and skills, be safer, make less errors, be more productive, make better decisions and engage in teamwork. There is now an unprecedented interest by business, industry, government and the military to enhance human performance.

This volume launches a new series. A series that will focus on providing state-of-the-art chapters that advances our understanding of human performance in organizational systems as cognitive engineering principles are applied. Cognitive engineering is the application of cognitive science and psychology to understand the fundamental principles behind human cognition, actions and performance in supporting human-problem solving and maximizing overall performance. This is accomplished by applying theoretically derived and empirically validated engineering and psychological principles in the design of human-technology systems in organizations.

We envision this series serving as a forum where scientists and practitioners can engage in a dialogue to review, discuss, analyze and debate, the vast number of human performance issues that arise when individuals and groups interact with each other, the technology, the equipment and the organizational context. A number of disciplines contribute to our understanding of human performance in complex systems: human factors, computer science, industrial engineering, psychology (industrial/organizational, social, cognitive, military, engineering) organizational behavior, ergonomics and management. All bring theories, tools and approaches that help understand human performance in complex systems. And we hope this trend continues and those contributions can be highlighted in this series.

This volume contains eight chapters. First, Vicente reviews the history of the Electronics Department at Riso National Laboratory between the years of 1962–1979. He identifies some of the topics characterizing the Riso research in cognitive engineering and reviews some basic and applied problems. Finally, he discusses some implications for the cognitive engineering field.

ix

Next, Kozlowski et al. provides a theoretically based Adaptive Learning System (ALS) model that is fitting to meet the challenges of integrated-embedded training. Drawing from literature, the authors derive training design principles that are coherent with the model and suggest propositions and challenge to effectively integrate training in the workplace, and enhance adaptability. Then, Gillan and Cooke describe PRONET (Procedural Network), a method for summarizing, representing, and analyzing event sequences. A demonstration of the application of PRONET is then illustrated in two different conditions. Finally, the usefulness of PRONET is presented and future research suggested.

Klein and Militello in their chapter suggest some guidelines for conducting a Cognitive Task Analysis (CTA). The authors define CTA, discuss the criteria for success in a CTA project, and the CTA methods involved. The authors also discuss future research needs in the application of CTA. Zachary et al. reviews human performance modeling technologies that support and design the operation of complex systems. The authors provide a brief history of human performance modeling, establish a framework of modeling techniques, and present applications of human modeling techniques. Challenges and capabilities for future research are finally presented. Cohen and Thompson discuss the vital role of critical thinking in teamwork. The authors explore how members of military, business, and other organizations cope with uncertainty, change, and conflicting purposes. This chapter concentrates on the cognitive skills that individuals and teams need to function effectively in such organizations, and the methods needed for training those skills. Next, Bowers and Jentsch review commercial off the shelf (COTS) simulations for team research. Several criteria were used to evaluate each simulation. They included such factors as system requirements, independent variables that can be manipulated, dependent variables that can be observed, and other special considerations. They argue that technical aspects must be considered such as: fidelity of the simulation, to custom build or to acquire commercial off the shelf software and hardware, and the capability to network team tasks.

Finally, Hitt et al. discusses eight research paradigms for understanding human performance in a more complex and technologically advanced world. The selected topics are cognitive engineering, naturalistic decision making, human-centered design, simulation and training, virtual environment, automated systems, human factors in space exploration and international/cultural ergonomics. In addition to briefly discussing these paradigms, suggested future research directives are also provided.

In closing, we hope these chapters are interesting, useful and get us closer at understanding human performance in complex systems. Your feedback as well as your contributions is welcome.

Eduardo Salas
Series Editor

1. COGNITIVE ENGINEERING RESEARCH AT RISØ FROM 1962–1979

Kim J. Vicente

ABSTRACT

The purpose of this chapter is to contribute to ongoing discussions defining the future of cognitive engineering research by examining a part of its past. The intellectual history of one particular line of research, that of the Electronics Department at Risø National Laboratory, is reviewed. A number of influential studies, conducted between 1962 and 1979, are described. Among these are operational experience acquired from the introduction of a prototype digital console in a nuclear research reactor, two field studies of professional operators conducting representative tasks in representative settings (electronic trouble-shooting and conventional power plant control), and analyses of over 645 human error reports in the nuclear and aviation industries. Examples of the influence that the Risø work has had on basic and applied problems are reviewed. Also, some of the themes characterizing the Risø research in cognitive engineering are identified. These themes help define what cognitive engineering is, and what it might be concerned with in the future.

Advances in Human Performance and Cognitive Engineering Research, Volume 1, pages 1–57.

INTRODUCTION

Cognitive engineering is a comparatively new discipline. Consequently, it is useful to engage in efforts of self-examination to help define future research in this area. Just as it is important to reflect upon what we should be teaching our students (Woods, Watts, Graham, Kidwell & Smith, 1996) and the current state of our field (Endsley, Klein, Woods, Smith & Selcon, 1995), it is also useful to study where we have come from. This, in turn, can help us make more deliberate decisions about how to proceed in the future. In this chapter, I try to achieve this goal by presenting one history of cognitive engineering. I say "one" because there are many different histories that can be told, each from a different intellectual lineage stemming from one of the many people who contributed towards defining the discipline in the 1960s and 1970s (e.g. Bainbridge, Duncan, Johannsen, Leplat, Moray, Rouse, Sheridan, Stassen). The history presented here is that of the cross-disciplinary research group in the Electronics Department of Risø National Laboratory (a description of Risø is provided in the next section). This research team included Jens Rasmussen, Len Goodstein, Morten Lind, and Erik Hollnagel. Rasmussen was the group's conceptual leader (Rouse, 1988), so I will focus mainly on his publications, although these were undoubtedly influenced by others, especially Goodstein and Lind who worked at Risø since the 1960s. Hollnagel did not join the group until April of 1978 (Erik Hollnagel, personal communication, 1997).

Motivation

There are several reasons why it is important to present the history of this particular lineage. First, the Risø group has been very influential in defining the field of cognitive engineering. For example, Reason (1990) observed that some of the ideas arising from the Risø group have become "market standards" (p. xiii) in the cognitive engineering community. Moray (1988) stated that the Risø perspective is "nothing less than a paradigm shift" (p. 12) in the study of complex human-machine interaction. Second, despite this impact, the history of the Risø program is not very well known, except for the more focused analysis of Sanderson and Harwood (1988) and a very brief note by Vicente and Sanderson (1992). Many of the insights from this line of work were only published as technical reports that have not been widely available or read. As I will try to show, there is a great deal that can be learned from these old, obscure reports.

Because the more recent history of cognitive engineering is better known (e.g. Norman, 1981, 1986; Hollnagel & Woods, 1983; Rasmussen, 1986;

Rasmussen, Pejtersen & Goodstein, 1994; Vicente, 1999), this paper will focus on the period between 1962 and 1979. Figure 1 illustrates the key contributions published during this time that will be reviewed in this chapter. To add some

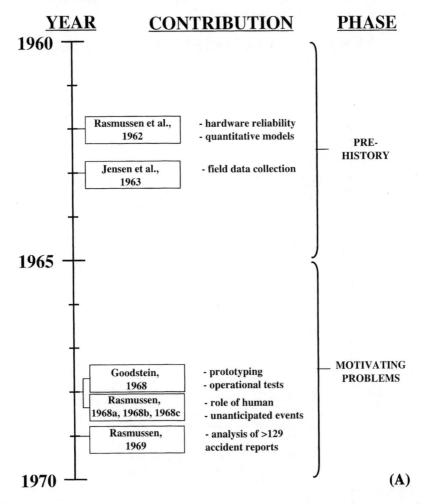

Fig. 1. A timeline of some key publications representing cognitive engineering research at Risø conducted between: (A) 1960–1970. (B) 1970–1980. There are two additional points on the timeline. Fischoff et al. (1978) seems to be the first publication to mention the phrase "cognitive engineering". Norman (1981) seems to be the first publication to describe cognitive engineering as a unique discipline.

context, two additional historical data points are represented on the timeline in
Fig. 1B: (1) the first time, that I know of, that the term "cognitive engineering"
appeared in print (Fischoff, Slovic & Lichtenstein, 1978, p. 343); and (2) the
first time that the term "cognitive engineering" was used in print to describe a
discipline with a unique set of characteristics (Norman, 1981).

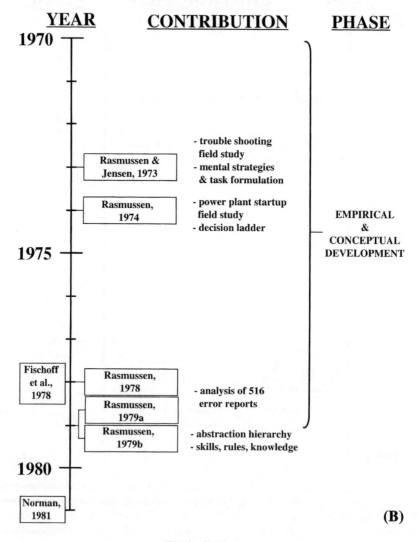

Fig. 1. Continued.

Caveats

Writing a chapter-length history of almost two decades of research conducted by a productive and influential group is bound to be a selective, and therefore, incomplete endeavor. To avoid any misinterpretations, it is important to make several caveats explicit. First, I have deliberately tried to present an intellectual history rather than a sociological one. Sociological histories of science are fascinating but they are notoriously subjective, presenting contradictory viewpoints caused by the biases introduced by the different participants. Consequently, I have based my account almost exclusively on scientific publications rather than on interviews with the researchers who participated in this history (although I have had contact with all of the participants listed earlier, beginning when I first worked at Risø in 1987–88). The benefit of this approach is that my historical account is backed up in detail by citations that can be verified by others. The disadvantage is that I have ignored the interpersonal dynamics that characterize all scientific activities (cf. Hull, 1988). Therefore, I have traded off comprehensiveness for verifiability.

Second, because I am relying on scientific publications as documentation, the sequence of ideas I present should not be confused with the sequence of thought processes that the participants actually engaged in while they conducted the research before publishing it. As Feynman (1966) observed:

> We have a habit in writing articles . . . to make the work as finished as possible, to cover up all the tracks, to not worry about the blind alleys or describe how you had the wrong idea at first, and so on. So there isn't any place to publish, in a dignified manner, what you actually did in order to get to do the work.

Thus, using the terms of philosophy of science, I am presenting a history of the context of justification, not a history of the context of discovery.

Third, I do not address the broader intellectual climate in which the Risø ideas evolved. An international community of researchers in human factors, psychology, systems engineering, biology, artificial intelligence, philosophy of science, and cognitive science influenced the Risø group (Morten Lind, personal communication, 1997). This broader influence is important and interesting, but I will not discuss it here.

Fourth, the fact that I have chosen to write a chapter about history does not mean that I believe that all of the important problems in cognitive engineering have been solved – far from it. We have barely scratched the surface on many key issues, and much important and challenging work remains to be done. However, as I will try to show in the remainder of the paper, taking this reflective look at the past might help us in directing our future research activities.

RISØ NATIONAL LABORATORY

Risø National Laboratory (or Research Establishment Risø, as it was first known) is a Danish government research laboratory that was created in 1956 at Roskilde Fjord, approximately 40 km from Copenhagen (see www.risoe.dk). Nielsen, Nielsen, Petersen and Jensen (1998) have documented the history of Risø, so I will borrow from their account in this section.

Niels Bohr, the Danish Nobel laureate in physics, served as the first chairman of the board. Risø was created "to realise Niels Bohr's visions of the peaceful use in Denmark of nuclear energy for electricity production and other purposes" (Nielsen et al., 1998, p. 1). Originally, six departments covering specific research disciplines were created: chemistry, physics, electronics, reactor engineering, health physics, and agricultural research (the organizational structure has since been changed many times, more recently to a project- and program-based form). Initially, there were approximately 100 employees, but this number grew to a peak of about 1,000 in 1988, and has hovered around 900 since then. Between 1956 and 1963, the appropriation act that supported the construction of offices, laboratories, and nuclear research reactors was funded at the level of 1.5 billion DKK (1995-value), which is equivalent to approximately $205 million USD, using today's exchange rate. Risø's annual operating budget has been approximately 450 million DKK (1995-value) for the last two decades (approximately $62 million USD-current value). The most remarkable statistic of all is that Risø's original goal of conducting research to support the implementation of electricity production via nuclear power was maintained for over a quarter of a century until it was decided that Denmark would not have any commercial nuclear power plants!

During its early history, Risø fostered an exceptionally unique environment for conducting research, perhaps because – from the very start – it was deliberately "shielded from direct political interference" (Nielsen et al., 1998, p. 4). Originally, the laboratory's funding came from the Danish Ministry of Finance, providing a vast supply of financial support. There was no requirement at all to bring in large research contracts from external funding agencies. For example, in the early 1970s, only 1% of Risø's income was obtained by conducting paid contract work for industry. Furthermore, there was no firm requirement to publish research results in academic journals (although some departments chose to do so). For example, much of the work of the Electronics Department described below was published in a series of green technical reports. Although Risø had collaborations with universities, its researchers were not required to teach classes, supervise graduate students, or take on extensive administrative responsibilities. Moreover, a great deal of discretion was provided to researchers: "Risø was given a flat organisational structure with a relatively small top management and a number of departments endowed with extensive freedom to plan and carry out their work" (Nielsen et al., 1998, p. 6). This approach was a realization of Bohr's "conception of science as an activity ill-fitted for tight planning" (Nielsen et al., 1998, p. 6).

Anyone familiar with contemporary academic or industrial research will recognize that these were extraordinary circumstances. All of this has changed, particularly in the last 10 years. Like almost all other research institutions around the world, Risø is now under extensive external scrutiny and intense economic pressure. Researchers are required to spend substantial amounts of time writing proposals to bring in large amounts of external funding. They are also required to engage in extensive project management activities that are associated with large research contracts. Furthermore, researchers often cannot afford to adopt long-term research goals, but instead are required to produce demonstrable short-term products. They are also required to document their productivity by publishing extensively in academic circles – the familiar doctrine of publish or perish. But during the period described in this chapter (1962–1979), none of these constraints were dominant. Although it is difficult to substantiate this claim with any certainty, I believe that it is not an accident that the research described in the remainder of this chapter was conducted at an institution with this type of unique research infrastructure.

PRE-HISTORY (1962–1963)

The first body of research to be reviewed is actually more accurately described as pre-history in that it was not directly concerned with issues that we readily recognize today as pertaining to cognitive engineering. Nevertheless, the activities of this period are relevant because they help explain the origins of the Risø research program in cognitive engineering.

Three research reactors were installed on site to support Risø's mission. The Electronics Department was responsible for the commissioning and safety certification of the instrumentation of the research reactors. And since the head of the Electronics Department (Jens Rasmussen) became chairman of the Risø Reactor Safety Committee, it should not be surprising to find that the Electronics Department's early efforts focused on analyzing the reliability of reactor equipment and instrumentation (Rasmussen & Timmerman, 1962; Jensen, Rasmussen & Timmerman, 1963). Note that the focus was strictly on examining hardware reliability, not human reliability, using probabilistic mathematical models and empirical data collection.

Analytical Models

The probability of equipment failure and the degree of redundancy required in backup safety systems to achieve the desired level of reactor safety were both investigated (Rasmussen & Timmerman, 1962). Figure 2 provides an example of the type of systems analysis that was conducted. The graph illustrates the probability of a spurious reactor shutdown due to a safe failure in the protection system. Different curves are plotted for various ratios of $n:m$, where:

$n =$ the number of instrumentation channel trips necessary for a reactor shutdown, and

$m =$ the number of independent channels in the instrumentation system measuring the same reactor variable.

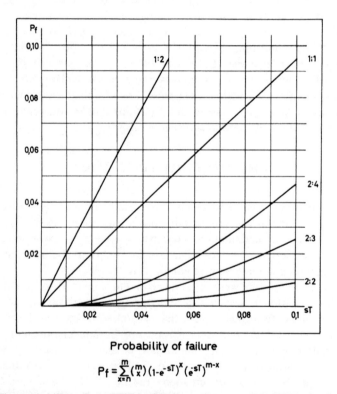

Probability of failure

$$P_f = \sum_{x=n}^{m} \binom{m}{x} (1 - e^{-sT})^x (e^{-sT})^{m-x}$$

Fig. 2. The probability of a spurious shutdown due to a safe failure in the reactor protection system as a function of time interval (Rasmussen & Timmerman, 1962). See text for description.

The results of this analysis showed that the failure rates depend on the degree of redundancy built into the instrumentation system. Additional analyses showed that the repair and test policies that are adopted for maintenance also have a large impact on instrumentation reliability.

Empirical Data Collection

In addition to analytical modeling of failure rates, considerable effort and attention was also paid to collecting empirical failure data under representative conditions (Jensen et al., 1963), a theme that would re-emerge in later work (see below). Failure data on the reactor instruments were collected at two of the research reactors (DR 2 and DR 3) over a two-year period, beginning in 1960. In addition, failure data on all of the research instruments constructed by the Electronics Department were collected over the same period. Figure 3 shows some of the data for the DR 2 instrumentation. The top part of the figure shows the number of components of various types, and the bottom part of the figure shows the distribution of failures observed during operation and maintenance. This work shows the preoccupation that researchers in the Electronics Department had in letting their research be guided by the characteristics of a practical problem, as determined by extensive data collection efforts conducted under complex, representative conditions. In this sense, this early work reveals a second theme that would continually re-emerge in subsequent phases of research.

Summary

This pre-history phase investigated the impact of hardware reliability on reactor safety using analytical models and empirical data collection. Two themes in this early phase would reappear in later work. First, the research direction was guided by a practical problem. Second, there was a strong emphasis on collecting data under representative conditions.

Although hardware reliability is not a central research concern in cognitive engineering, there is one passage in these early reports that foreshadows the consideration of human and organizational factors: "It is realized that the [probability] figures obtained are only approximate figures. Low figures, especially, must be used with great care, because the reliability in this case may be governed by factors not dealt with in this report" (Rasmussen & Timmerman, 1962, p. 31). In retrospect, this passage can be interpreted as indicating that hardware reliability may not be the primary bottleneck in improving reactor safety, and that other types of factors may contribute significantly to safety.

	Number of components							
	Number of instruments	Operation time x10³ h	Valves	Diodes	Fixed resistors	var. resistors	Condenser	Relay
Preamplifier	2	32	4		17		8	
Linear amplifier	2	30	17		62	2	3	
Power supply	2	29	9		20		6	1
Rate-meter	2	32	15		56	4	17	
Log. amplifier	1	15	10	4	36	3	10	
Scaler	1	15	28	2	184	7	75	1
Composite safety amplifier	4	58	17	2	101	7	6	5
Magnet amplifier	1	15	13		47	2	5	
Radiation-monitor power supply	1	18	4					
Radiation monitor	8	138	1					
Recorder		34	3					
Recorder		53	4					
Servo unit		15	4					

The failures are distributed as shown in table 7. Operation includes tests made by operators.

Distribution of Failures Found During Operation and Maintenance

	Operation	Maintenance	Total
Preamplifier	1	0	1
Linear amplifier	3	22	25
Power supply	0	2	2
Rate-meter	9	17	26
Log. amplifier	7	7	14
Scaler	1	10	11
Composite safety amplifier	28	35	63
Magnet amplifier	7	5	12
	56	98	154

Fig. 3. Some of the empirical data collected for the DR 2 instrumentation (Jensen et al., 1963). The top part of the figure shows the number of components of various types, and the bottom part of the figure shows the distribution of failures observed during operation and maintenance.

MOTIVATING PROBLEMS (1968–1969)

Some time during the 1960s, there was a qualitative shift of focus in the Risø program. The researchers realized that the reliability of complex systems, such as nuclear reactors, cannot be viewed from a strictly technical viewpoint without considering the human element in the system (Rasmussen, 1968a, b). It became apparent that the human operator played a key role in overall system reliability and safety, thereby lending credence to the earlier observation that low probability figures for instrumentation hardware must be interpreted with great caution because the bottleneck to safety and reliability may not be the instrumentation itself.

The next phase of research was directed at better understanding the interaction between designers, operators, automation, and instrumentation, and the converging impact that these have on overall system reliability. In retrospect, it was at this point that we can say that the Risø research program shifted into the purview of cognitive engineering proper. This work can be divided up into two categories, one consisting of an analysis of industrial accidents and another consisting of a design prototyping and field testing effort. As this section will show, this phase of research was directed at identifying significant, practical problems that would then serve to focus and motivate future research efforts.

Industrial Accident Analysis

Based on the work described in the previous section, the Risø researchers found that they could design redundant reactor safety systems with extremely high technical reliability. Yet, accidents still occurred. How could this be? To solve this mystery, an analysis of industrial accidents was conducted. This effort is similar to the human error analysis to be described later in the chapter.

The industrial accident analysis consisted of a review of 29 cases with major consequences to either plant or personnel in the nuclear domain during the period 1959 to 1965 and of 100 accidents in air transportation between 1959 and 1967 (Rasmussen, 1969). A number of conclusions were derived from this analysis, many of which have since been corroborated by more recent research. First, the accident analysis revealed that "most of the accidents are initiated during periods with non-routine operations (e.g. initial operation, experiments, maintenance)" (Rasmussen, 1969, no pagination). This observation is as valid today as it was 30 years ago (Leveson, 1995; Reason, 1990). Second, "accidents initiated by human maloperation amount to roughly three quarters of the total number of reported cases" (Rasmussen, 1969, no pagination). Again, little appears to have changed; human errors are frequently cited as being "responsible" for 60% to 80% of accidents in numerous domains (e.g. Perrow, 1984; Bogner, 1994). Third, "in nearly all cases the operators would have been able to make an appropriate decision and carry through the action if the actual state of the system had been known to them" (Rasmussen, 1969, no pagination). More recent studies have also empirically documented the importance of situation assessment in coping with potentially catastrophic events (Woods, 1984; Itoh, Yoshimura, Ohtsuka & Masuda, 1990). This finding is very important because it opens the door to the possibility of creating design interventions that can help operators prevent, or at least mitigate, industrial accidents.

Taken together, these findings pointed to the importance of designing to help operators adapt to the unanticipated. Rasmussen's (1969) accident analyses and subsequent analyses conducted by others (e.g. Perrow, 1984; Reason, 1990; Leveson, 1995) have consistently shown that accident-causing errors arise because operators are confronted with unfamiliar situations that had not been, or could not have been, anticipated by designers. As Rasmussen (1969) put it:

> In the design of automatic control systems for industrial process plants the designer has to realise that he cannot possibly foresee and analyse all relevant operational conditions of the plant; in certain circumstances he must rely upon an intelligent human operator for the identification and correction of abnormal plant behaviour (no pagination).

Thus, *designing for adaptation* becomes a critical concern in terms of improving safety. The design implications of this insight were described as follows:

> My conclusion is that the critical task of the display system will be to support the operator in the identification of his working conditions during abnormal periods such as periods of initial operation, start-up after major repairs or overhaul, or periods of technical failure. At such times the operator has to consider sets of data describing a great number of parameters; he has to judge the internal relations in such data sets to identify the abnormal state of the system, and parameters of no concern to him during normal operations may be of vital importance for this task. To fulfill this requirement, integrated analogue or graphic displays seem to be more appropriate than alpha-numeric displays (Rasmussen, 1969, no pagination).

To provide a sound, principled basis for achieving this challenging design objective, the Risø researchers used the insights they had developed to date to create a simple schematic model of operator performance. A diagram of this early model is presented in Fig. 4. Four separate categories of performance are depicted: (1) skilled, automatic response; (2) response to an unusual situation that is recognized based on previous experience and is thus dealt with using a familiar set of actions; (3) using a mental model of the plant to conduct an

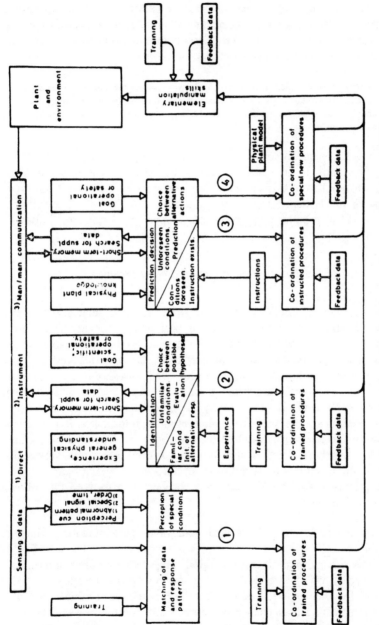

Fig. 4. A simple schematic model of operator performance (Rasmussen, 1969).

analytical evaluation of a situation that is unfamiliar to the operator but anticipated by the designer; (4) using a mental model of the plant to conduct an analytical evaluation of a situation that is both unfamiliar to the operator and unanticipated by the designer. Note that:

> this model is not intended to be a *psychological model* of the mental processes of an operator in a basic task, but a *functional model* to illustrate the general aspects of the operator's situation at a higher level as seen by the system designer (Rasmussen, 1969, no pagination, emphasis added).

This model is a precursor to the now well-known skills, rules, knowledge (SRK) taxonomy, to be described later in this chapter. The important design insight obtained from this model is that operators have different information processing needs depending on the situation, and that, to be effective, an interface must present information to support all modes of information processing.

Design Prototyping and Field Testing

Around the same time that the industrial accident analysis was being conducted, the Risø group designed a prototype, computer-based display system that was tested in the field (Goodstein, 1968). This display system, shown in Fig. 5, took the form of a console that was installed in a room adjacent to the traditional control room for DR 2, one of the research reactors at Risø. The prototype was limited in the sense that it did not actively control the reactor. Instead, it was merely designed to "shadow" the existing instrumentation system, collecting and presenting information in parallel with the traditional, analog, hard-wired control room. This parallel configuration allowed researchers to test a new unproven system under relatively realistic field conditions without compromising reactor safety.

The prototype was field tested for a number of years with the following objectives in mind:

- to investigate empirically critical questions pertaining to safety and reliability
- to explore the possibilities that a digital computer could offer in terms of an improved means of controlling and monitoring a process plant
- to acquire the experience and knowledge to specify and aid in the procurement of advanced instrumentation and control systems for various other experimental facilities at Risø

• to study the possibilities that a digital computer could offer in terms of human-machine-process plant communications.

The remainder of this subsection will focus on the latter objective.

The DR 2 prototype console shown in Fig. 5 had a number of interesting characteristics. One fascinating feature is the type of technology that

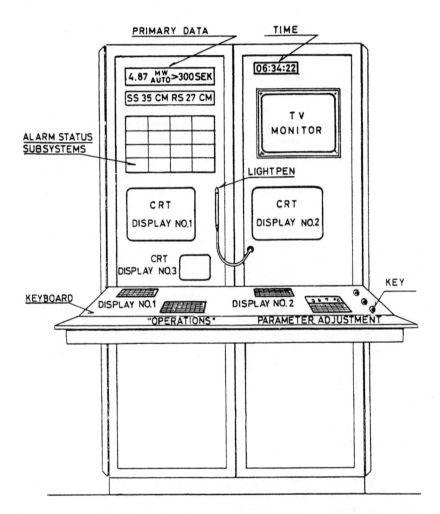

Fig. 5. An overview of the prototype, computer-based display console constructed for, and field tested at, the DR 2 research reactor (Goodstein, 1968).

researchers had to use to implement their design ideas. The display system was driven by a PDP-8 computer that had a ferrite core memory of 4K, and was connected to a back-up memory drum of 32 K. A Teletype was used for programmer communications and paper tape equipment was used as an input and output device. A light-pen and several keyboards were used by operators to interact with the console, and three small black and white CRTs were used to display information from the digital computer. In addition, there were several digital displays (e.g. to show the time of day). The display system was flexible in that it allowed operators to bring up different displays on the CRTs as a function of their current goals. Plant data were sampled at a rate of 1 Hz. Given the power of today's computer technology, it is hard to believe that any kind of prototype could be implemented with such comparatively primitive means.

Nevertheless, the DR 2 prototype was well ahead of its time in terms of the functionality that was embedded in it. Aside from the use of digital computers in a nuclear reactor – very advanced for the time – the display system also included: overview displays, emergent feature graphics, and display of higher-order functional information. Figure 6 illustrates a sample overview display that was implemented to monitor the overall status of the power measuring equipment. Higher-order functional information was presented by using the computational power of digital technology to derive thermal power from elemental measurements of temperature difference and reactor coolant flow. Moreover, the flexibility of digital technology was used to display the resulting higher-order functional information in a graphical pattern. Shut-down limits, automatic power set-back limits, and alarm limits were also shown, thereby showing the significance of the data by placing them in context. Although this display is primitive by today's standards, it embodies some of the key concepts that comprise contemporary approaches to interface design for complex, sociotechnical systems (Bennett & Flach, 1992; Vicente & Rasmussen, 1992; Wickens & Carswell, 1995; Woods, 1991).

Goodstein (1968) described an example of how the prototype display system was intended to be used by operators:

> In the event of an alarm, one of the CRTs will automatically identify in plain text the parameter(s) and their values which are affected. Given this start, the operator can call forth suitable representations of the status of the relevant sub-systems. These will help him to begin to generate a hypothesis about the primary cause as he compares parameters and relates them to his conception of how they should be. Effective coding of this information into sets of graphical patterns will hopefully counteract a known tendency for an operator to limit his attention to a very few (and probably incorrect group of) parameters in a critical situation where he lets his original hypothesis color the whole pattern of his future interpretation of the data he gets. With the CRT presentation, he is forced to look at a larger

set of data in order to use the light pen to call forth more detailed information about any
of the parameters shown (p. 556).

This passage shows the concerns that the researchers already had about the
impact of human-computer interface design on operators' cognitive processes,
and thus, human performance.

Operator interaction with this experimental prototype design was observed
over a number of years in the field. In today's language, we would say that this
phase of the Risø research program consisted of prototype building and
usability analysis in a naturalistic setting. These rich field observations served
as inputs to the direction of subsequent research.

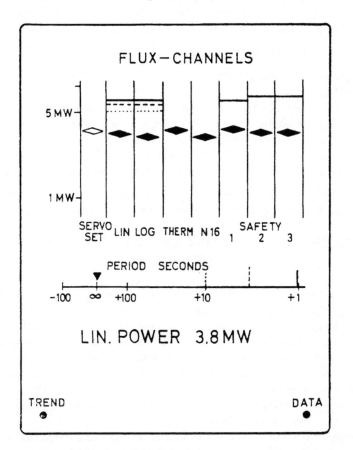

Fig. 6. An example display from the DR 2 prototype, computer-based display console
(Goodstein, 1968).

Summary

This second phase of research represented a turning point in the work conducted in the Electronics Department at Risø. By letting the characteristics of the problem shape the research focus in unexpected directions, investigators learned that human factors were critical contributors to safety and reliability; and by studying the demands imposed by this challenge under representative conditions, they learned that:

• industrial accidents tended to occur in situations that were both unfamiliar to operators and unanticipated by designers;
• human error was a contributing factor in 75% of the accidents reviewed;
• situation assessment was a particularly important cognitive activity.

Each of these insights had implications for designing safer systems:

• designing for human adaptation to the unanticipated was a critical design objective;
• it would be useful to have a functional model of operator performance so that the display of information could be tailored to the unique demands associated with each mode of operator information processing;
• graphical visualizations of higher-order functional information appeared to be a promising but unexplored means for improving human performance.

Despite the limited technology of the time, field tests of design prototypes were conducted to obtain operating experience under representative conditions.

EMPIRICAL AND CONCEPTUAL DEVELOPMENTS (1972–1979)

Following the shift from studying machine reliability to studying human-machine reliability, a number of empirical studies were conducted by the Risø group to provide a sound basis for helping designers create safer human-machine systems. A number of these studies turned out to be very important in that they led to conceptual developments that have influenced a great deal of cognitive engineering research. Ultimately, these concepts were integrated into *cognitive work analysis*, an integrated framework for the analysis, design, and evaluation of complex sociotechnical systems (Rasmussen, Pejtersen & Goodstein, 1994; Vicente, 1999).

In this section, the empirical studies that served as the foundation for these concepts are described. The development of four concepts will be reviewed: mental strategies, the decision ladder, the abstraction hierarchy, and the SRK taxonomy (for a more detailed, pedagogic review of each of these concepts, see Vicente, 1999).

Mental Strategies

Motivation
The earliest of these four investigations consisted of a field study of electronic trouble-shooting strategies (Rasmussen & Jensen, 1973). This research was motivated by a practical design question, namely: "How do we efficiently utilize the variety of ways to present information to a human operator – ways now offered by the computer controlled display systems that are used in many complex technical systems?" (Rasmussen & Jensen, 1973, p. 5). The schematic model outlined in Fig. 4 showed that operators process information in different ways, as a function of the situation. It would make sense, therefore, to try to understand the strategies (or mental processing routines) that operators may adopt so that the computer support can be directly tailored to support those strategies.

One might expect that the psychological literature could offer some insight into this problem, but Rasmussen and Jensen (1973) found that this was not the case. As a result, they wound up having to conduct some basic research (albeit in an applied setting) to overcome this gap in the literature. As they put it:

> The body of knowledge resulting from psychological experiments in clear-cut laboratory conditions dealing with well-defined and isolated aspects of human behaviour should be supplemented by studies of real life working conditions and of the mental procedures used by human system operators to make the laboratory results really useful (p. 5).

With the benefit of hindsight, we can see in this statement a precursor for the need to study naturalistic decision making (Klein, Orasanu, Calderwood & Zsambok, 1993; Zsambok & Klein, 1997).

Because they worked in an electronics department, Rasmussen and Jensen (1973) set out to understand the mental strategies used by professional technicians troubleshooting faults in electronic equipment. Their investigation was based on a verbal protocol methodology, despite the fact that such reports were considered to be overly subjective, and thus unreliable, by many psychologists. Rasmussen and Jensen chose this methodology because they found that it was the only way in which they could identify the mental strategies that the operators were using. A behavioristic study based solely on the overt behavior of the operators would not be satisfactory because the same behavior sequence could be generated by several, qualitatively different strategies. By asking operators to verbalize their thoughts, this ambiguity could be reduced, although there were penalties to pay in terms of the effort, precision, and objectivity associated with data analysis.

Methodology

This emphasis on representative conditions and cognitive processes was operationalized in the following experimental procedure. On the environment side, eight different types of instruments were included in the study, each having a particular fault. On the human side, six professional technicians participated in the study. A total of 45 cases were recorded, although the final detailed analysis comprised 30 cases. For each trial, the technicians were asked to "relax and tell what they were thinking, feeling and doing, and to express themselves in everyday terms including short hints in fast work sequences" (Rasmussen & Jensen, 1973, p. 8). The verbal protocols were captured on a tape recorder.

Interestingly:

> a record was immediately typed out and the man was asked to read it in the actual working position in front of the instrument to correct mistakes and supply supplementary information when he felt something was missing. At the same time the analyst had the first review of the record and a short talk with the man to clarify weak passages in the verbalization (p. 8).

The almost real-time transcription and review of verbal protocol data is an uncommon procedure, probably because of the cost that is required. However, the rationale provided by Rasmussen and Jensen suggests that this procedure has advantages in ensuring that the data are relatively comprehensive and interpretable by analysts.

At a general level, the data analysis effort involved a highly iterative, inductive process consisting of several steps. First, a preliminary coding scheme was developed and used to code the protocols. Second, the structure of the protocols was analyzed to see if it was well captured by the proposed coding scheme. Third, discrepancies were used to motivate changes to the coding scheme, and the entire process was conducted again. This inductive process required switching back and forth between the abstract and generic (i.e. the categories of strategies that could be used for coding purposes) and the concrete and the specific (i.e. the way in which these strategies were instantiated in the verbal protocol record in each case for a particular instrument).

At a more detailed level, a number of different techniques were adopted in parsing and coding the verbal protocol data. First, a set of elementary events describing the microstructure of the protocol sequences was developed (see Appendix A of Rasmussen & Jensen, 1973). The following are examples of some of the categories included in this classification scheme (the numbers refer to the code of the category):

05 – replace a component
21 – a procedure is planned and formulated
41 – conjectures and hypotheses are mentioned regarding the normal
    functioning
55 – data are recalled from previous measurements
61 – search in system to find measuring points or components
71 – individual test of data against normal data
82 – algebraic calculations
98 – confusion, cursing.

In addition, a taxonomy of the procedures and judgements that controlled the troubleshooting process was also developed. This taxonomy consisted of four general categories:

T: Trained routines, pattern recognitions
E: Experience (system knowledge obtained from previous cases)
U: Functional understanding
R: External system models or descriptions.

All of the verbal protocols were parsed using this coding scheme. Two types of computer print-outs were then generated to summarize the data for each trial. One format was a connectivity matrix showing first-order transitions between coding examples. An illustrative example is shown in Fig. 7. The second format

	A	B	C	D	E	F	G	H	I	J	K	L	M	N	O	P	Q	R	S	T	U	V	W
	22	14	10	-3	22	-4	-9	11	62	27	16	15	16	-9	--	21	-4	19	20	56	42	-5	48
A	-3	--	--	--	-4	--	--	--	-6	-2	--	--	-1	--	--	--	-1	-1	-4	--	--	--	--
B	--	--	-2	--	--	--	--	--	-9	-1	--	--	-1	--	--	-1	--	--	--	--	--	--	--
C	--	--	--	--	--	--	--	--	-8	--	--	--	-1	-1	--	--	--	--	--	--	--	--	--
D	--	-1	--	--	--	--	--	--	--	--	--	--	--	--	--	-1	--	-1	--	--	--	--	--
E	-2	--	--	--	--	-1	--	--	-6	-3	--	--	-1	--	--	-3	--	-6	--	-1	11	--	10
F	--	--	--	--	-1	-1	--	--	-1	--	--	--	--	-1	--	--	--	--	--	--	-3	-1	--
G	--	-1	-1	--	-1	--	-1	-2	--	--	--	--	--	--	--	-1	--	-1	-1	-1	-3	-1	-2
H	-1	-1	--	--	-1	--	-1	--	-1	-3	--	--	--	--	--	-1	--	-2	--	-2	-6	-2	--
I	--	--	-3	--	--	--	-1	-1	-4	-5	16	14	-9	-6	--	-1	-1	--	-1	21	-6	--	22
J	-3	-1	--	--	--	--	-1	-2	-8	-6	--	-1	-1	--	--	-2	--	-1	-1	-1	--	--	-1
K	--	-2	-1	--	--	--	--	--	-6	--	--	--	-1	--	--	-2	--	--	-4	-9	-2	--	-5
L	--	-2	-2	-1	-3	-1	--	-1	--	--	--	--	--	--	--	-1	--	--	-4	-8	-1	--	-6
M	-1	-3	--	--	-2	--	-1	--	-2	-1	--	--	--	--	--	-3	--	--	-2	-7	-7	--	-1
N	--	-2	--	--	--	--	-1	--	-2	--	--	--	--	--	--	-2	-1	--	-1	-5	-2	-1	--
O	--	--	--	--	--	--	--	--	--	--	--	--	--	--	--	--	--	--	--	--	--	--	--
P	-1	-1	--	-1	-4	--	--	-2	-5	-2	--	--	--	-1	--	--	--	-3	-1	-1	-1	--	--
Q	--	--	--	--	-2	--	-1	--	-1	--	--	--	--	--	--	--	--	--	--	--	--	--	-1
R	-6	--	--	--	-1	-1	--	-1	-3	-4	--	--	--	--	--	--	-1	-1	-1	--	--	--	--
S	-5	--	-1	--	-3	--	-2	-2	--	--	--	--	-1	--	--	-3	--	-3	--	--	--	--	--

Fig. 7. An example of the connectivity matrices used by Rasmussen and Jensen (1973) to analyze verbal procotols.

was a graphical read-out of the protocol statements ordered in temporal sequence. An annotated example is shown in Fig. 8 to illustrate the gist of the methodology. The graphical read-out format turned out to be more useful than the connectivity matrix because it made it easier for the analysts to locate and identify recurring routines in the data.

The identification of these recurring routines led the analysts to postulate certain strategies to account for the macro-structure in the verbal protocols. Each time a different strategy was identified, the entire protocol sequence had to be recoded according to the attributes of the newly postulated strategy. A graphical symbol was chosen for each strategy, and a set of codes was introduced to account for the parameters that were relevant for each strategy (see Appendix B of Rasmussen & Jensen, 1973 for the final set of coding categories). As mentioned above, this procedure was highly iterative, being repeated each time the analysts uncovered new insights in their data. Once a stable set of strategies was identified, the results from 30 trials were coded graphically. The resulting diagrams show the interconnections between the strategies for a particular trial and comments by the analysts to facilitate subsequent review. An example for one trial is shown in Fig. 9, again for illustrative purposes. A detailed explanation of the coding scheme is provided by Rasmussen and Jensen (1973).

Lessons Learned
Rasmussen and Jensen's (1973) field study led to methodological as well as empirical insights. Beginning with the former, some important lessons were learned regarding how best to analyze verbal protocol data collected under representative work situations. The following quotations give an idea of some of the methodological insights that were obtained:

> The task of finding the structure of nearly 50 verbal records made by several persons trying to locate individual faults in different types of systems, makes one realize how colorful real-life working conditions are and how much work is needed to carry through the analysis. An almost immediate experience is the danger that the analyst himself develops fixed routines in the analysis in order to be able to manage the classification of the multitude of situations. It proves imperative to have long breaks in the analyzing effort, to be able to relax from fixations and to return to the original material with an open mind. It also seems important to have several analysts criticizing each other's models of the structure in order to break fixations and to decide which differences in the classifications made by the different analysts result from weaknesses in the definition of the classes and which are due to differences in the interpretation of the records (p. 8).
>
> It is important for the analysts to have a background in engineering in order to be able to imagine themselves in the task situation, and thus have a clear understanding of the meaning of the manipulations and measurements. They can formulate *what* the man is doing, and thus find the structure of the information handling. On the other hand, some

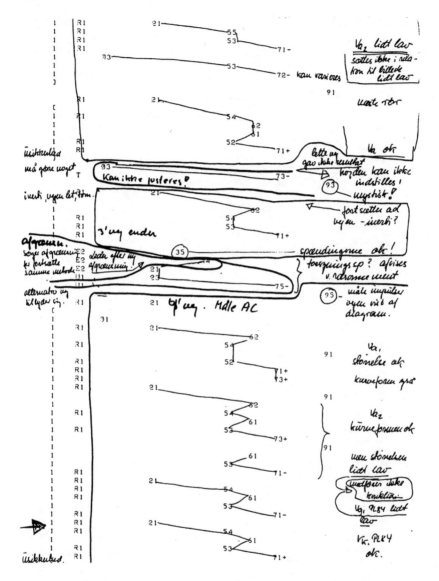

Fig. 8. An example of the graphical sequence read-out (with annotations) used by Rasmussen and Jensen (1973) to analyze verbal procotols.

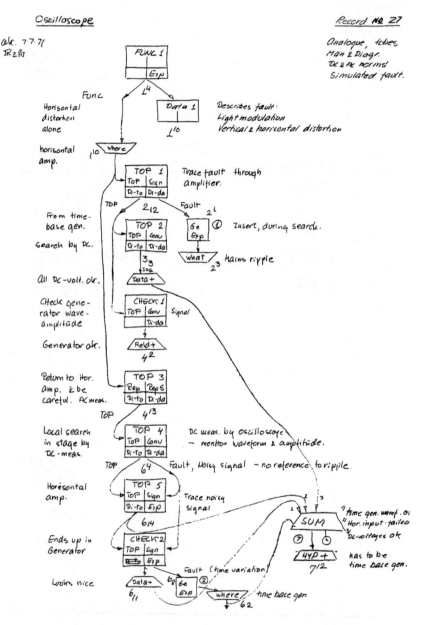

Fig. 9. An example of a coded verbal protocol record from one trial in the electronic troubleshooting field study conducted by Rasmussen and Jensen (1973).

knowledge of psychology is needed to explain *why* the man has chosen that particular approach and to formulate the goal and motivation which control the sequences found (p. 9, emphasis in original).

A very formalized analysis in which the procedure of the man is compared to a model covering all possible strategies is impracticable for real-life conditions, although it is a very effective tool in laboratory experiments with a smaller number of decisive parameters, as reported by Alan Newell (1966) (p. 9).

These hints provide a good starting point for anyone interested in analyzing verbal protocols under representative work situations.

In addition to these methodological lessons learned, a number of important empirical insights were also obtained from this field study. Perhaps the most important observation was that there can be several, quite different strategies that can be used to perform the very same task. As Rasmussen and Jensen (1973) put it, "the subroutines available to the men differ greatly along several characteristic dimensions, such as their generality, the complexity of the data handling procedure and the depth of system knowledge needed for support as well as the amount of observations used" (p. 48). This result can be appreciated by comparing the technicians' strategies with the more "intelligent" approach to troubleshooting – typical of a design engineer – that was advocated by both researchers and textbooks at the time that the study was conducted (the late 1960s). Briefly, the latter approach exploits knowledge of the functioning of the equipment being repaired so that an equipment-specific plan of attack can be developed. Typically, this knowledge would be acquired, in part, from a documentation manual for the equipment in question. A few carefully chosen measurements could be taken, and then integrated, using a carefully chosen reasoning sequence supported by an understanding of equipment functioning. This approach is elegant in that it requires only a few observations, is based on a detailed understanding of the equipment, and produces a logical chain of reasoning that extracts as much information as possible from each individual observation. Furthermore, it also has the benefit of uncovering an explanation for why the fault is producing the observed abnormal symptoms.

Rasmussen and Jensen (1973) found that the professional technicians participating in their study tended to adopt a very different approach to electronic troubleshooting. Rather than conduct a small number of observations, the technicians tended to conduct many observations in rapid sequence. Rather than extracting as much information as possible from each observation, the technicians tended to use each observation only to determine where to make the next observation. Rather than engage in elaborate, logical reasoning, the technicians tended to make very simple decisions, primarily whether each observation was good (i.e. normal) or bad (i.e. abnormal). Rather than exploit knowledge of the equipment to develop an equipment-specific plan of attack, the technicians tended to use generic methods that were generally independent of both the equipment and the fault. Finally, the technicians also sometimes exhibited a few shortcuts that could be interpreted as signs of laziness. For instance, sometimes they used a circuit diagram or a similar circuit as referents to determine the normal value for a particular observation rather than mentally deducing or remembering that value.

Given the stark contrast in the two approaches, it may seem natural to question the rationality of the technicians' strategies. Compared to the systematic, logical, and calculated engineers' approach, the technicians' approach appears to be very inefficient, ad hoc, and lazy. If nothing else, it is certainly very different from what the textbooks said the technicians should be doing.

Nevertheless, Rasmussen and Jensen (1973) found that the question of which approach was more rational – or better, more adaptive – could not be answered in isolation. Rather, the question could only be answered by considering two additional factors, namely the technicians' subjective task formulation and performance criteria (cf. Bruner, Goodnow & Austin, 1956). The *subjective task formulation* is the task that workers set for themselves. As these field study results show, the very same task can be approached in quite different ways. The engineers set out to develop an explanation for why the equipment exhibited the faulty responses. This is the reason why their approach put a premium on logical deduction. In contrast, the technicians formulated the troubleshooting task in quite a different way. They were merely interested in locating a fault in a piece of equipment that had previously been functioning properly (i.e. to find the root location of the discrepancy between normal and actual state). This explains why their approach was more pragmatic in nature.

The related construct of *performance criteria* was also very important in assessing the comparative adaptiveness of the two approaches to trouble-shooting. The engineers' and technicians' approaches emphasized a complementary set of criteria. Thus, which approach is more adaptive depends on the importance given to different performance criteria. For example, if the cost of observations is very high, then the engineers' approach may indeed be more adaptive. However, the professional technicians participating in this study worked in an environment where the cost of an observation was usually minimal. In addition, there was no intrinsic reward for using an approach that is more effortful. On the contrary, doing the job efficiently and effectively would suggest that minimizing computational effort would be more desirable. Furthermore, because the technicians' livelihood depended on repairing faulty equipment, it was important that they do so quickly, otherwise a backlog of repairs would begin to accumulate. Doing prompt work also meant minimizing the time spent reading manuals to gather equipment-specific knowledge. The technicians also faced many different faults on many different kinds of equipment on the job, so it would be adaptive to develop a diagnostic approach that was independent of those details. From these conditions, we can see that there is no advantage to using the "elegant" engineers' approach in this environment. The pragmatic approach exhibited by the technicians was consistent with a set of performance criteria that were adaptive, given the conditions under which the job was being performed. As Rasmussen and Jensen (1973) put it, "scanning a high number of observations by simple procedures is clearly preferred to the preparation of specific procedures worked out by studying or memorizing the internal functioning of the system" (p. 53).

This reliance on mental economy exhibited by expert operators is related to Klein's (1989) notion of recognition-primed decisions. Experts take advantage of their experience base to make decisions in a perceptual rather than analytical fashion. In Rasmussen and Jensen's (1973) field study, this observation was manifested in the following manner:

> Nearly 80% of the instances of fault evaluations found in our records are expressed as rapid statements and classified as recognition based upon general professional background or experience. Only about 20% of the evaluations indicate more careful reasoning based upon a mental model related to the internal functioning of the specific system (pp. 52–53).

This tendency has since been observed in a number of diverse application domains (Klein, 1989, 1997). Moreover, this finding takes on a more significant light when it is compared to the results obtained in traditional psychological laboratory experiments. Just as Klein found that expert decision makers rarely resort to the types of strategies identified by basic psychological research on decision theory, Rasmussen and Jensen found that their findings differed from those obtained from basic psychological research on problem solving: "rapid sequences of simple decisions based upon informationally redundant observations may be more characteristic of human problem solving than one would suspect from psychologists' great interest in complex, rational problem solving" (p. 58).

Another empirical insight obtained from this field study was that the technicians frequently shifted between strategies, both within and across problem solving episodes. These strategy switches were opportunistic in nature. As a result, it is very difficult to predict the exact sequence of cognitive steps that the technicians would take on any one trial because those steps are highly variable from one situation to the next. Therefore, at a very detailed level, there is not a great deal of structure across trials. Nevertheless, at a higher level of analysis, the technicians' cognitive activity is more structured because it draws upon a small number of stable strategy categories that can be instantiated in a very diverse set of ways for particular situations. In Rasmussen and Jensen's (1973) own words:

> although the complete procedure used in a specific case depends strongly upon the type of instrument and upon the actual fault, the procedures can be broken down into a sequence of subroutines [i.e. strategies], which can be grouped into typical classes (p. 48).

Thus, the electronic trouble-shooting field study was important because it showed that expert strategic behavior in a representative setting could be described systematically, despite its apparent complexity. These insights have important implications for the design of computer-based information systems that provide support tailored to the unique requirements of each strategy (Vicente, 1999).

The Decision Ladder

Motivation

The next conceptual development to be reviewed in this section was also motivated by the applied problem of how "to facilitate the matching of the formatting and encoding of data displays to the different modes of perception and processing used by human process controllers" (Rasmussen, 1974, p. 26). To provide a systematic approach to this design problem, it was necessary to engage in some conceptual modeling. More specifically:

> the work situation of the process operator necessarily has to be structured in some kind of generalized model and the tasks he is supposed to perform have to be identified and characterized in relation to his mental operations as well as to the system he operates (Rasmussen, 1974, p. 26).

Again, one might expect that the human factors or psychological literatures might offer some insight into this problem, but Rasmussen (1974) found that this was not the case. As a result, he again wound up having to conduct some basic research (albeit in an applied setting) to overcome a gap in the literature. As he put it:

> This is a difficult problem. Very often the process operator has a sequence of interacting activities which it is difficult to break down into identified sub-tasks without crude generalizations; the lengthy discussion in the literature of task taxonomy has not resulted in the structurization needed in our context. However, model or no model, display systems are designed all the time, and a crude model is better than no model, even if it is only useful for giving a preliminary break down of our engineering problem into sub-problems more manageable in interdisciplinary discussions (p. 26).

We can see in this statement the strongly pragmatic, problem-driven orientation that drove the Risø research program in cognitive engineering. In the remainder of this subsection, the study that was conducted to identify a way of structuring operators' activities to inform systems design will be described.

Methodology
This investigation also adopted a field study methodology. In this case, the application domain that was chosen was a conventional power plant. In particular, the startup process was observed over a period of approximately one week. The control room operators' activities were observed, and verbal protocols were collected. Thus, we again see the theme of collecting data about the behavior of experts under representative conditions emerge.

Rasmussen (1974) mentions that several different attempts were made to analyze these data, but no details concerning the analysis methods are given in his report. All we are presented with is the outcome of the research. As a result, our description of the methodology is necessarily brief.

Lessons Learned
Rasmussen began analyzing these verbal protocol data using a coding scheme like the one shown in Fig. 10 (J. Rasmussen, personal communication, April, 1987). This structure is very familiar to information processing psychologists (e.g. Wickens, 1992). It breaks down molar tasks into their constituent elemental information processing steps. Typically, these elemental steps are ordered in a linear sequence that progresses from perception to decision making to action. In this particular incarnation, there are eight elementary information processing steps. The sequence begins with a signal from the work domain that causes a need for activation or detection. This step is followed by observation of the work domain. Based on the data collected, an identification of the current state can be made. Next, this state identification can be interpreted to determine the consequences for the criteria of interest. Then, an evaluation can be made to determine which criteria are more important, and should therefore take precedence, for the present situation. Once this evaluation is made, the task to be pursued can be defined. Given this definition, a procedure for accomplishing the task can be formulated. Finally, the actions on the work domain can be executed.

Interestingly, this linear sequence model did not account for Rasmussen's (1974) field study findings. Expert behavior in a naturalistic setting was much

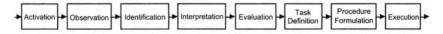

Fig. 10. An example of a linear information processing model of human activity (from Vicente, 1999).

more flexible, opportunistic, and economic than Fig. 10 would suggest. Rasmussen found that the information processing steps were rarely followed in sequence. Instead, these expert operators were frequently able to recognize situations, and as a result, take efficient shortcuts. For example, in very familiar situations, workers may know exactly what procedure they should be using merely by conducting a few observations. In those cases, the intervening information processing steps between Observation and Execution could all be bypassed. In addition, Rasmussen also noted that the flow of activity need not follow the left to right sequence specified in Fig. 10. Sometimes, it was possible for operators to move from right to left. For example, once the Task Definition step was completed, operators sometimes moved to the Observation step to determine if the plant was in the proper state to proceed with the required task.

Given these deviations from the normative linear sequence specified by the canonical information processing approach, Rasmussen (1974) made the following observation:

> the characteristic steps of a mental task – i.e. the sequence of steps between the initiating cue and the final manipulation of the system – can be identified as the steps a novice must necessarily take to a carry out the sub-task. Study of actual, trained performance may then result in a description of his performance [in] terms of shunting leaps within this basic sequence (p. 26).

Thus, the information processing approach identifies the steps that a novice would have to take to accomplish the task. Because Rasmussen observed experts (i.e. professional process control operators) in his study, he rarely observed this linear sequence. Instead, shortcuts and shunts were the norm rather than the exception.

Rasmussen (1974) proposed the decision ladder, shown in Fig. 11, as a means of capturing the opportunistic behavior exhibited by experts. By comparing Figs 10 and 11, we see that the decision ladder was created roughly by bending a linear sequence of information processing steps in half and adding shortcuts that connect the two sides of the ladder. There are two important insights embodied in the ladder. First, it is possible to parse a descriptive or normative timeline of human cognitive activities into a basic number of recurring decision tasks. Second, and more importantly, experts do not follow all of the information processing steps that a novice would perform. Instead, experts rely on their knowledge and experience and thereby exhibit direct shortcuts (or associations) that allow them to bypass several cognitive activities. These shortcuts account for the increased speed and reduced effort that are hallmarks of expert performance. A better intuitive feel for these insights can perhaps be obtained from the "unofficial" version of the decision

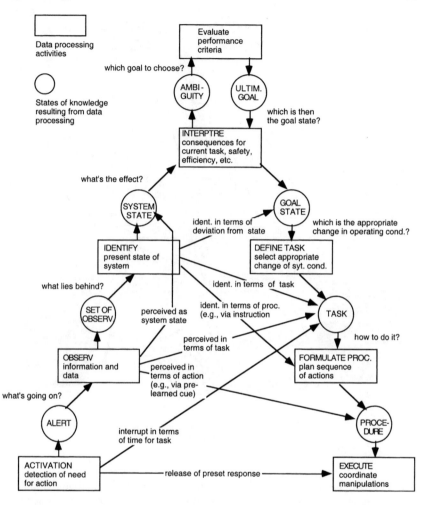

Fig. 11. The decision ladder (Rasmussen, 1974). See text for description.

ladder presented in Fig. 12. The flexible and mentally economic activities that were exhibited by the expert operators in this field study are shown very concretely in this diagram.

Rasmussen (1974) went on to use the categories identified in the ladder to derive implications for systems design. Different ways of supporting each category of information processing (or box) in the ladder were described. Note

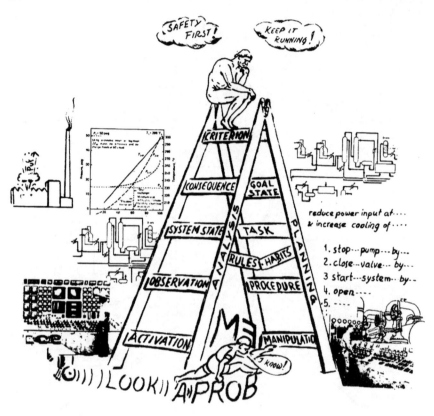

Fig. 12. The "unofficial" version of the decision ladder (Rasmussen, 1974). Compare with Fig. 11.

that this analysis addresses the problem that motivated this field study, namely how to match computer display coding to the way that an operator may solve a specific task. Interestingly, Rasmussen's analysis of design implications was documented in an unusual format that combined running text accompanied by quotes and diagrams in the margin of that text. Figure 13 provides an example for part of the discussion surrounding the Observation box in the ladder. Several instances of what are now known as emergent features displays (Bennett & Flach, 1992) are presented in the margin as examples of how to support this particular decision activity using computer-based support tools. The goal of such displays is "to present the available measurements and data in suitable sets and configurations allowing perception and processing at an conscious activities. However, at the same time it results in very selective attention, which does not leave the operator open to unexpected variations of the entire task situation. The extreme case is when the operator has a very high expectancy of the task to come; the external interrupt may then release an immediate preset response without any oonsideration of further information from the environment.

On the other hand, it should be realized that also the limited data capacity of higher level mental activities decreases the sensitivity and span of attention when operation moves to such higher levels in the sequence.

The large data processing capacity of the intuitive shunt paths is also needed during periods when the operator is constantly alert and monitoring plant operation to detect abnormalities. In our experience, the process operator may be left with a critical monitoring task, for instance during initial plant operation or periods following major repair or modifications. During such periods the plant may not be completely protected by the automatic monitoring system.

Detection of an abnormal situation takes place when man's environment deviates from the expected course and thus initiates his action. The operator has to know the "expected course", i.e. to have a reference frame defining the normal state. To have specified limiting values of individual variables is trivial, and is the way automatic alarm systems normally operate.

To follow or monitor a start up to see "if everything is normal" will rather be a check of plant structure and parameters by monitoring the constraints interrelating the displayed data. If he has to resort to higher level mental activities such as conscious identification and interpretation, his capacity, i.e. speed of operation will seriously decrease; he will become selective and his attention will then be focused upon preconceived hypotheses. The monitoring task consists instead of being open to the unexpected events.

To be open to unexpected events and not locked by preconceived ideas may imply that the data presented by the environment should be related to the subconscious dynamic model of the environment. If so the information displayed should be arranged in graphical patterns for which general subconscious . . .

Coekin, 1969:

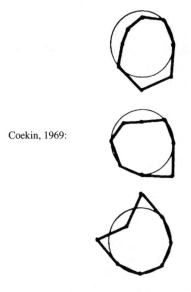

"A versatile representation of parameters for rapid recognition of total state."

Wohl, 1965:

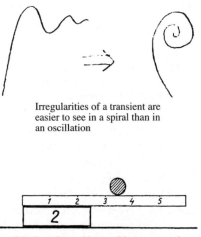

Irregularities of a transient are easier to see in a spiral than in an oscillation

Display of unstable condition suggested by P. Skanborg (internal report, 1972)

Fig. 13. An example of Rasmussen's (1974) discussion of systems design implications for each box in the decision ladder. This particular example illustrates several ways of supporting the Observation box in the ladder. Note the influence of visual thinking exhibited by the diagrams in the margin accompanying the main body of text.

appropriate level of information or data 'chunks'" (Rasmussen, 1974, p. 37). This presentation format clearly illustrates the importance of visual thinking in the development of these ideas, a theme that would emerge again in subsequent work (see below). The key point is that the decision ladder provided a systematic, structured basis for analyzing expert behavior in naturalistic settings so as to derive implications for systems design.

The Abstraction Hierarchy

Motivation
The electronic troubleshooting field study focused on mental strategies, or *how* operators do what they do (i.e. process criteria). In contrast, the decision ladder focused on information processing activities, or *what* operators do (i.e. product criteria). One important complementary research topic is to investigate the *object* of operators' strategies and activities (e.g. the electronic equipment itself in the case of the troubleshooting field study) in "task independent terms" (Rasmussen, 1979b, p. 46). What is the structure of the work domain (i.e. the physical system) that operators are working in, and how can that structure be organized in model formats that are compatible with what we know about human problem solving? The third study reviewed in this section was directed at these questions.

Once again, the basic research literature pertinent to this topic was found wanting:

> The internal representations of the environment used by human problem solvers has of course been studied by cognitive psychologists . . . and artificial intelligence groups . . . . In these cases however, very general representations have been discussed or emphasis has been laid on analysis of internal representations in well defined task situations, such as games or theorem proving which will not uncover the internal representations used for coping with the complexity of real-life tasks in man-made environments (Rasmussen, 1979b, p. 9).

Consequently, the Risø group was, yet again, forced to conduct basic research to address gaps in the literature that were relevant to the problems with which they were concerned.

As before, the eventual goal was very pragmatic in nature. The questions just described are important from a design perspective because it would be good to know what types of mental models would be useful for operators to have, if we are to design computer-based interfaces to support operator problem solving based on such models. Accordingly, "the hope [was] ultimately to develop a common and formalised morphology of models, which will serve an integrated approach to systems design" (Rasmussen, 1979b, p. 5). Thus, once more, we see the problem-driven nature of the Risø research program in cognitive engineering.

Methodology

This study involved a somewhat unusual methodology combining empirical investigation and theoretical analysis. The empirical portion was based on the two field studies described earlier. During the electronic troubleshooting field study (Rasmussen & Jensen, 1973) and the conventional power plant field study (Rasmussen, 1974), insights were obtained regarding the ways in which operators thought about the work domain with which they were interacting. Consequently, "the following categories of models are based on an attempt to characterize and formalize the models found to be of importance for technicians in diagnostic tasks in the control rooms and the workshops of industrial plants" (Rasmussen, 1979b, p. 8).

The theoretical portion of this investigation was based on a morphological analysis (Zwicky, 1967) that went well beyond the data that had been collected in those two field studies. An attempt was made to develop a taxonomy that would meaningfully structure the entire problem space of concern (i.e. mental models to support practical problem solving in complex systems). Thus, rather than directly modeling the available data in a strictly inductive fashion, an attempt was made to create a fundamental structure that could coherently organize these and many other data of interest in a top-down manner. This style of inquiry is rare in the behavioral sciences because it involves going well beyond existing data (Vicente, 1997). However, in more mature sciences, this type of theoretical development has led to very important and lasting insights (Holton, 1988).

Lessons Learned

One useful insight obtained from this study was a definition of the term *model*:

> A model is here defined as the internal representation of the properties or constraints in the environment which determine the interrelations among the data which can be observed from the environment. In mental activity, such models are used to predict future events and responses of the environment to human actions; to find causes for observed events; to determine proper changes in the environment to obtain desirable responses, etc. (Rasmussen, 1979b, p. 10).

More recent research on mental models has not always provided a definition of the phenomenon being investigated, making it difficult to obtain cumulative research progress.

The most important contribution to come out of this investigation was a deep insight into how operators represent complex systems during problem solving. Based on the aforementioned empirical and theoretical analyses, Rasmussen (1979b) proposed the abstraction hierarchy as a framework that can be used to represent complex systems at various levels of abstraction in a way that is consistent with the characteristics of human problem solving. The abstraction hierarchy is based on several important observations. First, when experienced operators are solving problems in the context of complex human-machine systems, they spontaneously adopt, and switch between, different models of the work domain in order to match the immediate task demands. Some of these models provide physical information whereas others provide functional information. Second, it is possible to represent engineering systems in a way that makes reference to purpose, thereby spanning material form and functional meaning. This is accomplished through the means-ends links between levels of the abstraction hierarchy. "Models at low levels of abstraction are related to a specific physical world which can serve several purposes. Models at higher levels of abstraction are closely related to a specific purpose which can be met by several physical arrangements" (Rasmussen, 1979b, p. 41). The result is a representation framework that bridges the gap between the technical and the psychological, thereby supporting goal-directed human problem solving.

Figures 14 and 15, both taken from Rasmussen's (1979b) technical report, illustrate some of these ideas. Note, once again, the role of visual thinking evidenced by the extensive use of diagrams. Figure 14 shows some examples of models of Physical Form, the lowest level in the abstraction hierarchy. As the diagrams indicate, this level of representation describes the work domain in terms of the spatial appearance and location of its constituent objects. Figure 15 shows some examples of models of Physical Function, a higher level in the abstraction hierarchy. As the diagrams indicate, the work domain components are represented in terms of their functional significance (e.g. a transistor) and their topological connections (e.g. circuit path) rather than their visual appearance (e.g. the cylindrical object) and spatial location (e.g. at the top of the circuit board). Figure 16 shows the results of the entire morphological analysis, consisting of a taxonomy of mental models at these and the remaining three levels of the abstraction hierarchy. Higher levels of the abstraction hierarchy are similar in that they provide additional languages for modeling the work domain, with each higher level providing more information about function and purpose while simultaneously providing less information about physical objects and equipment that are used to realize those functions and purposes. Different models will be useful at different times because each provides different insights into the structure and behavior of the work domain.

MODEL OF PHYSICAL FORM

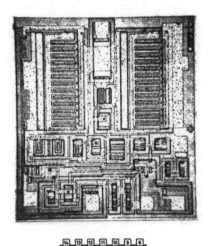

Fig, 1. Microphotography of integrated electronic circuit. Only the information on spatial arrangement of matter is significant to the general observer.

Fig. 2. Photography of traditional electronic circuit. To the uninformed observer this is a portrait of physical form. To observers with electronic background, this is hardly the case, as they probably will see a system of functional units - the picture presents a physical form structured in familiar objects or components.

Fig. 14. Examples of models of Physical Form (Rasmussen, 1979b).

Thus, to comprehensively support human problem solving, it is important that information at all levels of the abstraction hierarchy be presented to operators.

From a psychological perspective, one important property of the abstraction hierarchy is that higher levels are less detailed than lower levels. Shifting one's representation from a low, detailed level to a higher level of abstraction with less resolution makes complex work domains look simpler. In effect, this

MODEL OF PHYSICAL FUNCTION:
Components, States, and Events

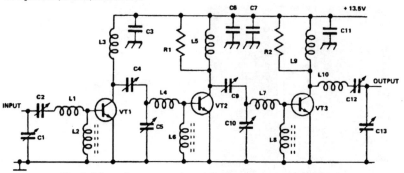

Fig. 6. Schematic representation of the functional structure of fig. 2.
Schematic diagrams interrelate symbols for components which,
to the professional observer, have well-known functional properties.

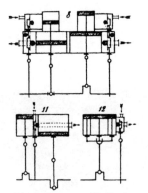

Fig. 7. Compare with fig. 4.

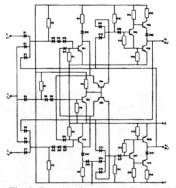

Fig. 8. Functional structure of cicuit of fig. 1. Together w
well-known component properties, it forms a model of
physical function.

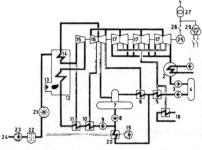

Fig. 9. Schematic diagram of fossil power plant.
When used, component properties are expressed
qualitatively; pumps circulate water, they can
stall etc., transistors amplify; diodes clamp voltages
etc., valves open and shut and fail to open, etc.

Fig. 15. Examples of models of Physical Function (Rasmussen, 1979b). Compare with
Figure 14.

MODEL CATEGORY	STRUCTURE	ELEMENTS	RELATIONS	DATA	ASPECTS OF MATERIAL REALITY IN THE SYSTEM	ASPECTS OF SYSTEM PURPOSE
FUNCTIONAL MEANING	Related to properties of environment	Physical variables, processes or objects of environments	As required by system's environment	Magnitude of variables or states of objects, processes	If present, only preserved in terms of limiting properties and assumption of rationality	Models expresses largely the requirements of the environment
ABSTRACT FUNCTION	Topology of overall causal structure of system	Abstract variables related to state in causal net	General laws, conservation laws; logic relations	Symbolic, quantitative variables; truth values; related to modeling language	Only causal structure preserved	Operating state of system with respect to purpose defines causal structure
FUNCTIONAL STRUCTURE	Network of relations ordered in sets, i.e., typical functions	Physical variables	Sets of physical laws and empirical relations; equations, graphs, tables related to typical functions and processes	Magnitude of variables	Physical processes and variables are represented	Typical elements of system purpose specify physical processes and function.
	Set of "objectivized" typical functions	Typical processes or functions	Potential for interaction between processes and functions	States of functions; events		
PHYSICAL FUNCTION	Sets of variables related to typical objects	Physical variables	Input/output relations of typical components, equations, graphs, tables	Magnitude of physical variables	Physical objects and related physical variables are represented	Typical elements of system purpose determine level of object formation and relevant variables or properties.
	Set of interacting objects or components	Typical components	Potential for interaction between objects	States of objects; events	Physical objects end their qualitative properties are represented	
PHYSICAL FORM	Lumped topographic map: "Landscape of typical objects"	Objects, technical components	Spatial distance	Form and spatial position of objects	Physical, material objects and their spatial relation	Elements of overall purpose determine object formation
	Distributed spatial maps	Fields of uniform surface or matter	Spatial arrangement	Location of fields of sense data; visual, tactile, auditive	Portrait-like map of material landscape	Purpose determines mode and resolution of recording senses

PURPOSE BASE-REASONS — MATERIAL BASE-CAUSES

Fig. 16. A morphology of mental models (Rasmussen, 1979b).

provides a mechanism for coping with complexity. Metaphorically, moving up one or more levels allows workers to "see the forest for the trees". Thus, part of the psychological relevance of the abstraction hierarchy is that it allows resource-bounded actors, as people are, to deal with work domains that would be unmanageable if they had to be observed by operators in full detail all at once. The abstraction hierarchy also derives psychological compatibility from the fact that it is explicitly purpose-oriented. The various levels in the hierarchy are linked by a structural means-end relation. This relationship provides a very important source of constraint that can be exploited by actors. Problem solving can be constrained by starting at a high level of abstraction, deciding which lower-level function is relevant to the current situation, and then concentrating on the sub-tree of the hierarchy that is connected to the function of interest. This type of problem solving is efficient because all work domain objects not pertinent to the function of current interest can be ignored.

As a result, an abstraction hierarchy representation supports goal-directed problem solving in a directed and computationally economic manner. It should allow actors to: (a) structure their overall problem solving process, (b) frequently start their problem solving activities at a higher level of abstraction to avoid detail, and (c) iteratively "zoom in" on lower levels of abstraction to selectively examine only those parts of the domain that are relevant to the goal or function of current interest. These predictions have been empirically confirmed by the field studies that motivated the development of the abstraction hierarchy:

> in the verbal protocols we have evidence that the ability of man to cope with the complexity of industrial environments, is due to his ability to shift his internal representation or mental model freely and effectively to match the immediate task demands (Rasmussen, 1979b, p. 35).

More recent studies have provided additional evidence to support this conclusion (e.g. Itoh et al., 1990; Vicente, 1996).

Since its original development, the abstraction hierarchy has been used as a basis for interface design and training program design (e.g. Itoh et al., 1990; Itoh, Sakuma & Monta, 1995; Vicente, 1996), thereby showing some progress on achieving the original aim of developing a framework that can provide an integrated basis for systems design.

The SRK Taxonomy

Motivation

The fourth and final investigation to be reviewed here (Rasmussen, 1978, 1979a) is unusual in the sense that it was not guided by a specific goal. While the topic of the investigation was human error, the study was rather exploratory in nature: "the aim of the note is solely to facilitate working group discussions within the Scandinavian NKA/KRU control room study project" (Rasmussen, 1979a, p. 1).

Methodology
In this case, the methodology adopted was a review of human error reports in the nuclear industry. Once again, the focus was on analyzing data on human behavior in representative conditions. More specifically, the licencee event reports compiled by *Nuclear Power Experience* were consulted in two phases. During the initial phase (Rasmussen, 1978), only the reports in the category of operator/technician errors during calibration, setting, and testing were included in the analysis. Note that the task of calibration is a well defined, proceduralized task. A preliminary review of the cases, revealed that the following phases of the task needed to be analyzed separately: (a) establishment of the test circuit; (b) the calibration act; and (c) restoration of normal operating condition of the system. In addition, a crude classification of the error types was developed: (a) omission of subtask or act; (b) errors in commission of subtask; (c) extraneous acts (i.e. acts affecting other systems). A total of 111 cases were analyzed in this phase.

The first phase of analyses had included "very few examples of human errors of a more complex nature, the majority being rather simple omissions and mistakes" (Rasmussen, 1979a, p. 1). Thus, a second analysis was conducted (Rasmussen, 1979a), based on several additional categories of licensee event reports that were thought to be linked with more complex errors: incorrect repair (40 cases); safety system affected (138 cases); alarm response errors (14 cases); equipment damage (13 cases); and operational problems (200 cases). Thus, a total of 405 additional cases were analyzed in this second phase, for a grand total of 516 human error reports. The patterns in both of these data sets were analyzed through the creation of tables that summarized the frequency of various types of events. An example of one of these tables is provided in Fig. 17.

Lessons Learned
One lesson – or perhaps, reminder – obtained from this study is that human error reports represent a biased source of data.

In general, reliable statistical information on human error rates related to different types of human errors is difficult to gather from this kind of event reporting. While the denominator problem of obtaining the actual frequency of error opportunities can be solved in principle, the reports do not actually give information on the total frequency of errors committed, but

	Various, not mentioned	Routine task on schedule	Routine task on demand	Special task on schedule	Ad hoc, improvization
Various	3	5	2	4	1
Absent-mindedness	1			1	1
Familiar association		2	1		3
Capability exceeded				1	
Alertness low	1	8			1
Manual variability, lack of precision	5	2		3	
Topographic, spatial orientation inadequate	1	4		4	1
Familiar routine interference					
Omission of functionally isolated act	11	25	4	13	3
Omission of administrative act	2	6	1	2	1
Omission; other		11		5	1
Mistakes, interchange among alternative poss.	1	9		1	
Expect, assume rather than observe	1	6		1	2
System knowledge insufficient		1	1		
Side effects of proc. not adequately considered		3		8	4
Latent causal cond. or relations not adequately considered		7	2	8	3
Reference data recalled wrong				1	

Fig. 17. An example of one of the data summaries comprising the human error report analyses conducted by Rasmussen (1978, 1979b).

rather the frequency of errors which are not immediately corrected by the operator himself. This means that the frequencies of different categories of errors found in the reports are heavily biased by the actual demands of the task. Clearly, human errors which lead to latent system faults or to effects which are not reversible by immediate counteraction will typically find their way to the reports (Rasmussen, 1978, p. 1).

The results presented below must be interpreted with these caveats in mind.

In addition to this methodological point, a number of empirical observations were also made (Rasmussen, 1978, 1979a). For example, the data showed that the highest error contribution was from omissions of steps in the procedure, especially steps that were supposed to be conducted during the last phase of a task. In addition, the importance of management factors to human error was also pointed out, albeit only in passing. A number of observations regarding the preconditions for the effective use of probabilistic risk analysis techniques were also made.

The most important product of this investigation, however, was conceptual rather than empirical in nature. The human error report analyses shed significant light on the psychological mechanisms that were responsible for human error in complex systems. There seemed to be qualitatively different types of errors, presumably caused by qualitatively different types of human behavior. This relationship was not documented in detail until later (Rasmussen, 1980), but it led Rasmussen (1979b) to propose the now well-known SRK taxonomy, illustrated in Fig. 18.

The SRK taxonomy postulates three qualitatively different ways in which people can interact with the environment: skill-based behavior (SBB); rule-based behavior (RBB); and knowledge-based behavior (KBB). Each level of cognitive control is based on a different type of internal representation, so it

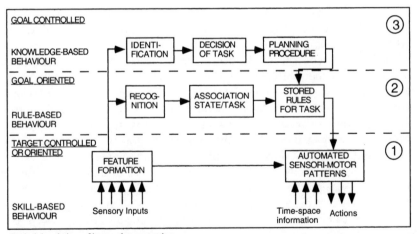

Typical descriptions of human data processing:

Level (3): Heuristic problem solving strategies, artificial intelligence models.

Level (2): Natural language models; decision tables; associative nets; fuzzy sets.

Level (1): Control theoretic models; bandwidth-gain-descriptions; sampling and queuing theory.

Fig. 18. The skills, rules, knowledge taxonomy of levels of cognitive control (Rasmussen, 1979b).

represents a different category of human performance. SBB consists of smooth, automated, and highly integrated patterns of action that are performed without conscious attention. A prototypical example is an automated psychomotor activity (e.g. walking) that is driven by a continuous perception-action loop. Action is usually based on feedforward (i.e. prospective), rather than feedback (i.e. reactive), control. That is, SBB typically consists of anticipatory actions, rather than waiting for the state of the world to change and only then reacting to it. Because it involves direct coupling to the environment, SBB is based on prototypical temporal-spatial patterns. Because it does not require conscious attention, SBB is not verbalizable.

RBB consists of stored rules derived from procedures, experience, instruction, or previous problem solving activities. Action is goal-oriented but goals are not explicitly represented. Workers may know the goals that the rules can achieve but they are not thinking about those goals when they are following the rules. Instead, goals can only be implicitly found in the structure of the rules. Typically, the rule will reflect the functional properties of the environment that constrain action. Thus, successful RBB can be explained in analytical terms by an observer, but such a description is a rational reconstruction that has no psychological validity. In the RBB mode, people are not reasoning; they are merely using familiar perceptual cues in the environment to trigger actions directly. In contrast with SBB, workers are usually aware of their cognitive activities at the RBB level, and thus, can verbalize their thoughts.

Finally, KBB consists of deliberate, serial search based on an explicit representation of the goal and a mental model of the functional properties of the environment. Thus, in contrast to RBB, in the KBB mode goals are considered explicitly rather than implicitly. Furthermore, KBB is slow, serial, and effortful because it requires conscious, focal attention. KBB is frequently, although not exclusively, used in unfamiliar situations where previous experience is no longer valid and a solution must be improvised by reasoning.

As shown at the bottom of Fig. 18, different types of human performance models can be mapped onto different levels of the SRK taxonomy. As such, the SRK distinction provides a taxonomy for models of human performance. Moreover, it can be used to derive useful implications for design as well (e.g. Vicente & Rasmussen, 1992).

Summary

This third phase of Risø research, focusing on empirical and conceptual developments pertinent to the practical problems identified in previous phases, was perhaps the most productive of all of those reviewed here. Many insights were obtained, covering a diverse number of topics, including: (a) methodologies for data collection and analysis; (b) empirical characteristics of expert behavior in naturalistic settings; (c) concepts useful for systems design in complex systems; and (d) metatheoretical approaches that are pertinent to the general pursuit of scientific knowledge.

Methodological Insights

Several insights regarding verbal protocol analysis were obtained:

- it is very useful to have almost real-time transcription of the protocols so that the analyst can fills gaps in the data and rectify misconceptions about the significance of the data;
- to avoid fixations on the part of the analyst, it is useful to take long breaks and to have multiple analysts critiquing each other's work;
- effective data analysis requires both psychological and domain knowledge;
- for protocols collected in the field, it is very difficult to create a formal coding scheme based on an exhaustive description of all possible strategies.

In addition, the inherent selection biases associated with the collection of human error reports in the field were noted.

Expert Behavior in Naturalistic Settings

Some of the characteristics of expert behavior in naturalistic settings were also obtained from the field studies:

- the very same task can be accomplished using different strategies, each with its own information requirements;
- experts exploit their knowledge base by relying heavily on recognition rather than on analysis, thereby allowing them to take shortcuts and omit steps that a novice would have to perform;
- experts frequently switch between strategies within the same problem solving episode, and at a detailed level, these shifts are opportunistic, and thus, essentially impossible to predict;
- whether cognitive activity is rational or not depends on the subjective task formulation and the performance criteria one adopts;
- operators use different mental models of the same underlying work domain during practical problem solving, and frequently switch between these models in the same problem solving episode;
- there are systematic, qualitative differences in human errors in complex systems.

These empirical observations were instrumental in the development of concepts that are useful for system design.

Concepts to Aid System Design
The key conceptual insights obtained during this period were as follows:

- despite its apparent complexity, it is possible to account for naturalistic expert behavior by identifying categories of information processing tasks and opportunistic shortcuts using the decision ladder, and categories of mental strategies for a particular task;
- knowledge of these categories can be used to design information support and presentation formats that are tailored to operators' cognitive demands;
- physical systems can be represented with respect to purpose using the abstraction hierarchy, thereby providing a bridge between the technical and the psychological;
- the abstraction hierarchy provides a set of representations that can be used to identify the information *content* that is needed to support human problem solving in complex systems;
- operators have qualitatively different levels of cognitive control that can be captured using the SRK taxonomy;
- the SRK taxonomy provides a set of distinctions that can be used to identify the information *form* that is needed to support human activity in complex systems.

Metatheoretical Insights
More broadly, the research conducted by the Electronics Department at Risø during this period showed that:

- a strongly pragmatic, problem-driven research orientation can be very productive if one's goal is to design better systems;
- it is possible to address applied problems of social significance while also making a contribution to the basic research literature;
- conducting research using experts in representative natural settings can lead to important empirical and conceptual insights, despite a lack of experimental control;
- visual thinking and documentation in science can complement verbal modes of thinking and documentation;
- morphological analysis can be useful in scientific discovery, despite going well beyond the data available at the time.

CONCLUSIONS

In this concluding section, I will discuss the contributions of the Risø research in cognitive engineering, some of its limitations, and finally, some implications that we can draw for the young discipline of cognitive engineering.

Contributions

The concepts and findings generated by the Risø program have had an exceptionally significant impact on both applied practice and basic research. Four instances of this influence are briefly reviewed here: (a) Westinghouse's conceptual design of an advanced control room for a next-generation nuclear power plant (Easter, 1987); (b) Toshiba's design and implementation of an advanced control room for a next-generation nuclear power plant in Japan (Itoh et al., 1990, 1995); (c) Reason's (1990) human error modeling framework; and (d) a novel psychological theory of expertise effects in memory recall (Vicente & Wang, 1998). Note that this list is far from exhaustive; other notable examples of the Risø program's influence could also be cited (e.g. Pejtersen, 1992; Norman, 1993, p. 257).

Westinghouse Control Room Design
Easter (1987) described the human factors engineering considerations that were factored into the design of Westinghouse's advanced control room for a next-generation nuclear power plant. The influence of the Risø work is cearly acknowledged in the very first sentence of the article: "By coupling the work of the Risø Laboratory in Denmark on human behaviour with new digital computation and display technology, Westinghouse has developed a totally new control room design" (p. 35). Easter then goes on to explain that, after the Three Mile Island accident in 1979, the nuclear industry acquired a better understanding of the cognitive demands faced by operators, especially during unfamiliar and unanticipated events.

In determining how to turn these demands into design requirements, Westinghouse adapted two concepts that had been developed by the Risø group. The abstraction hierarchy was adapted to represent the plant at both physical and functional levels of abstraction. These plant models were used to identify the information content that should be displayed in the control room design. The decision ladder was used as a model of operator decision making. It was used to determine how to tailor information presentation to various kinds of operator tasks, such as: detection; planning; action execution; and monitoring.

Easter (1987) goes on to describe the innovative solutions that emerged from these models, including the design of controls, displays, and alarms. The result is an integrated design solution whose characteristics can be traced back to the insights obtained from the abstraction hierarchy and decision ladder analyses. This design example provides an important instance of the Risø group's influence because it shows that the concepts described in this chapter can be applied to very complex problems in industry. This achievement is notable, given the difficulty that human factors engineering has traditionally had in transferring research results to applied problems (Meister, 1995).

Toshiba Control Room Design
The research described in this chapter has also influenced designers in the nuclear industry in Japan. Like Westinghouse, Toshiba also used concepts developed by Risø to design an advanced control room for their next generation plant. Toshiba's application appears to be the most thorough and faithful instantiation of the Risø framework for an industry-scale problem.

As described by Itoh et al. (1990), the abstraction hierarchy, decision ladder, and SRK taxonomy were all used to identify information requirements that could be used to design a control room that is compatible with the problem solving strategies used by operators. Two experiments were carried out to provide an empirical basis for some of the modeling work. Both experiments were conducting under very representative conditions, namely a full-scope nuclear power plant simulator.

The first experiment was conducted to identify the psychological mechanisms that that were responsible for operators' errors in responding to incidents and accidents. A total of 15 scenarios were included, covering a range from simple to multiple failure events. One crew consisting of four highly trained engineers experienced all of the scenarios. A wide variety of data were collected, including: video of operators' movements, dialogue between operators, operator control actions, alarm logs, plant status, guidance obtained from a decision support system, and post-experiment interviews. A total of 61 errors were identified and categorized using the decision ladder and the error mechanisms specified by the SRK taxonomy. One of the more important findings was that discrimination errors (e.g. failure to detect an emergency) and memory errors (e.g. failure to recognize a pattern in diagnosing an emergency) accounted for a large portion of the errors. These findings suggest that it would be useful to design interfaces that facilitate event discrimination and offload operators' memory (see below).

The second experiment was conducted to identify the envelope that operators used when problem solving within an abstraction hierarchy representation of the plant. In this case, there were only two scenarios, but both were relatively complex and unfamiliar, requiring KBB for effective performance. Again, there was one crew of four people, with the emphasis in this case being on the thought processes of the crew supervisor. The data collected were similar to that in the first experiment, with most of the emphasis being placed on verbal protocols in this case. The verbalizations were mapped onto an abstraction hierarchy representation of the plant to determine which models operators used during problem solving. The results indicated that operators used all levels of the abstraction hierarchy, switching between physical and functional models, thereby replicating the findings of the Risø group described earlier. Note that the existing control room design did not support all of these levels of abstraction. Thus, these findings were very helpful in identifying the information that should be built into an advanced control room design (see Fig. 5 on p. 101 of Itoh et al., 1990).

As Itoh et al. (1990) observed: "The findings obtained from these [two] analyses serve as a basis for developing design guidelines for man-machine interfaces in control rooms of nuclear power plants" (p. 102). This promise was fulfilled a few years later by Itoh et al. (1995), who described an advanced control room design that was built on the earlier analyses. The Risø concepts are very prominent in this application, with the abstraction hierarchy and the SRK taxonomy taking center stage. The Toshiba design provides operators with information at all levels of the abstraction hierarchy, thereby providing a normative external representation of the plant that can be used to support problem solving. This set of representations offloads memory because operators can see rather than recall the functional and physical structure of the plant. In addition, graphic visualizations of key relationships between variables are provided, including the first principles relations that are critical for coping with unanticipated abnormalities. As a result, the Toshiba design supports operator discrimination by creating visual patterns in the display that have a principled rather than an informal relationship to plant state and structure. These design concepts were instantiated to create a prototype advanced control room, thereby showing that the Risø concepts can be applied and implemented for a very large-scale industry problem.

Human Error
Reason's (1990) research on human error has had a significant influence in various disciplines, including systems engineering, human factors, and psychology. For the purposes of this chapter, the most interesting feature of his work is the extent to which it draws upon the work of the Risø group. One indication of this intellectual debt can be found in the acknowledgements to

Reason's book: "Jens Rasmussen, to whom this book is dedicated, has had a profound influence on the ideas expressed here, both through his writings and as a result of the many fruitful meetings he has convened (and generously hosted over the years) at the Risoe National Laboratory. His skill-rule-knowledge framework has justifiably become a 'market-standard' for the human reliability community the world over" (p. xiii).

Later in the book, we can see evidence of the influence that Reason (1990) enthusiastically acknowledged. Reason builds his typology of human errors onto the SRK taxonomy described earlier in this chapter, the rationale being that each level of cognitive control fails in different ways, leading to qualitatively different types of errors. This connection is strongest in Reason's Chapter 3, which shows in detail how his generic error-modeling system (GEMS) framework "is derived in large part from Rasmussen's skill-rule-knowledge classification of human performance" (p. 53). The GEMS framework was important because it showed that the previous classification of errors into two categories (i.e. slips and mistakes) was insufficient, and that there are in fact three qualitatively different types of errors (skill-based slips, rules-based mistakes, and knowledge-based mistakes), each with its own unique empirical signature (see his Table 3.3 on p. 69 for a summary, and pp. 68–95 for a detailed discussion).

Because Reason's (1990) ideas are so well-known in the cognitive engineering community, it may be difficult to see the significance of the SRK taxonomy as a catalyst for Reason's insights. Again, we can use Reason's words to show this enabling connection:

> At the time of greatest industry demand, the mid- to late-1970s, [there was] little or nothing in the way of an agreed theoretical framework for human error mechanisms. Rasmussen's skill-rule-knowledge classification has done an enormous service in filling this vacuum, both for the reliability engineers and for the psychologists. I hope that this book will carry this essential process some way further forward. Without an adequate and conceptually meaningful error classification and a workable theoretical infrastructure, there can be little or no principled basis to the business of human reliability quantification (p. 233).

Thus, the Risø work provided a critical foundation for Reason's (1990) important contributions. That Reason's work has, in turn, had such an influence reflects back positively on the significance of the Risø work.

Expertise Effects in Memory Recall

Part of the Risø framework, the abstraction hierarchy, has also had influence in what might appear to be a very distant and unrelated field, namely the basic psychology literature on expertise effects in memory recall that was stimulated by De Groot's (1946/1965) seminal work on chess expertise. In that recall experiment, four chess players of various levels of expertise were asked to reconstruct meaningful board positions after having been exposed to them for only a few seconds. De Groot found that the Master and Grandmaster level players performed this task with near perfect accuracy, whereas the performance of the lesser players was not nearly as impressive. In a subsequent experiment, Chase and Simon (1973) found that when the board positions consisted of randomly placed pieces, the recall performance of a Master plummeted so that it was not significantly different from that of a beginner, thereby indicating that the Master's superior performance on meaningful positions was not a result of better overall memory. This finding has had a tremendous impact on the expertise literature, leading to at least 51 studies using the same paradigm in at least 19 different domains of expertise (Vicente & Wang, 1998).

Vicente and Wang (1998) proposed a novel product theory of expertise effects in memory recall that accounts for many of the findings in this literature, including several that had not been accommodated by previous theories. Their *constraint attunement hypothesis* predicts that there will be a memory expertise advantage in cases where experts are attuned to the goal-relevant constraints in the material to be recalled, and that the more constraint available, the greater the expertise advantage can be. The abstraction hierarchy plays a critical role in this theory because it provides a principled basis for identifying the goal-relevant constraints in the environment in a way that is compatible with the characteristics of human problem solving. By modeling the environment in a psychologically-relevant way, the abstraction hierarchy provides a basis for empirically testing the claim that human expertise can be viewed as an adaptive process.

The empirical evidence in favor of the constraint attunement hypothesis is extensive and has been reviewed in detail by Vicente and Wang (1998). That a concept developed from problem-driven field studies of electronic trouble shooting and power plant control can make a contribution to curiosity-driven basic psychological theory is another indication of the scope of influence of the Risø research program in cognitive engineering.

In summary, it is very difficult to think of another line of research that has had such a demonstrable influence on practical problems in industry, basic theory in psychology, and basic research in cognitive science.

Limitations

Despite these notable contributions, there are still gaps in the Risø line of research. First, few of the concepts have been rigorously tested experimentally.

As the contributions reviewed in this chapter show, most of the early emphasis was on inductively developing concepts from field studies. The predictions that arise from these concepts were not directly tested through more controlled experimentation. More recently, examples of this type of research can be found in the literature (e.g. Vicente, 1996; Sharp & Helmicki, 1998; Reising, 1999; Burns, 2000a, b; Xu, Dainoff & Mark, 1999), but more are needed. Second, the generalizability of these ideas to different application domains needs to be evaluated further. Originally, the ideas were developed in the context of process control. Some attempts have recently been made to apply the same concepts to other domains, such as aviation (Dinadis & Vicente, 1999), engineering design (Rasmussen, 1990; Burns & Vicente, 2000), information retrieval (Pejtersen, 1992; Xu et al., 1999), medicine (Xiao, Milgram & Doyle, 1997; Hajdukie-wicz, Doyle, Milgram, Vicente & Burns, 1998; Sharp & Helmicki, 1998), and software engineering (Leveson, 2000). Nevertheless, more of this type of work needs to be done to evaluate the breadth of applicability of the Risø concepts. Finally, more effort needs to be devoted to making these concepts accessible to researchers and designers who were not involved in their development. A recent monograph takes a step in this direction (Vicente, 1999).

Implications for Cognitive Engineering

Because multifaceted contributions of the type discussed above are rare in human factors research, it is worthwhile speculating as to what characteristics of the Risø program may have led to this success. There are a number of themes that cut across the contributions reviewed in this chapter:

- the research started with a practical problem of social and economic relevance, not particular theories, methods, or generic academic curiosity
- the concepts developed were continually informed by, and focused by, very intensive analyses of data collected under representative conditions (field studies, operating experience, human error reports)
- early empirical results unexpectedly changed the original focus of the research (hardware reliability) to a new set of issues (supporting operator adaptation to novelty) that were found to be of greater relevance to the practical problem of interest.

This research strategy is markedly different from that adopted in most North American human factors research, which has focused primarily on well-controlled laboratory experiments (Meister, 1995). Perhaps, then, the methodological example offered by the Risø program can complement traditional human factors practices (cf. Vicente, 1997). Seeking out practical problems, analyzing them in the field, being sensitive to the results obtained, and changing the focus of the research as need be can help cognitive engineering make its mark, not only on applied practice, but on psychology and cognitive science as well.

Adopting this research strategy will not be an easy task, however, because it requires a particular type of infrastructure and institutional support. This may be the most important lesson we can learn from this historical review. As mentioned earlier, the research environment in the Electronics Department at Risø during the period covered in this paper was quite unique. Researchers were explicitly problem-driven rather than paradigm-driven; they had the luxury of being able to tackle research issues that were relevant to the problem at hand rather than research issues that were fashionable with funding agencies or journal editors and reviewers; they could afford to adopt a long-term rather than a short-term approach to their work; they could choose to adopt meaningful research methods that were very time-consuming and laborious rather than having to resort to methods that generated any kind of results efficiently; they could let the research findings dictate their next step rather than having to stick to the deliverables defined in a research contract; they had the time to focus and think uninterruptedly about their research rather than having to time-share most of their attention among a number of other activities such as administration, teaching, and proposal writing. A research setting with these characteristics is almost unheard of in contemporary society. Yet one could argue that these are ideal conditions for cognitive engineering research. If so, then perhaps the largest challenge facing our discipline may not be to do the appropriate research, but rather to create the conditions so that such research can be conducted.

ACKNOWLEDGMENTS

The writing of this chapter was sponsored by a research contract with the Japan Atomic Energy Research Institute (Dr. Fumiya Tanabe, Technical Monitor) and by grants from the Natural Sciences and Engineering Research Council of Canada. I would like to thank Dr. Tanabe and Dr. Kazuo Monta for their encouragement, Eduardo Salas for asking me to write the chapter and for providing a thorough review, and Cathy Burns, Jeff Caird, Klaus Christoffersen, Erik Hollnagel, David Hull, Greg Jamieson, Morten Lind, Neville Moray, Jens Rasmussen, Gerard Torenvliet, and David Woods for their comments on earlier versions.

REFERENCES

Bennett, K. B., & Flach, J. M. (1992). Graphical displays: Implications for divided attention, focused attention, and problem solving. *Human Factors, 34*, 513–533.

Bogner, M. S. (1994). Introduction. In: M. S. Bogner (Ed.), *Human Error in Medicine* (pp. 1–11). Hillsdale, NJ: Erlbaum.

Bruner, J. S., Goodnow, J. J., & Austin, G. A. (1956). *A study of thinking.* New York: Wiley.

Burns, C. M. (2000a). Putting it all together: Improving display integration in ecological displays. *Human Factors, 42*, 226–241.

Burns, C. M. (2000b). Navigation strategies with ecological displays. *International Journal of Human-Computer Studies, 52*, 111–129.

Burns, C. M., & Vicente, K. J. (2000). A participant-observer study of ergonomics in engineering design: How constraints drive design process. *Applied Ergonomics, 31*, 73–82.

Chase, W. G., & Simon, H. A. (1973). Perception in chess. *Cognitive Psychology, 4*, 55–81.

de Groot, A. D. (1946/1965). *Thought and choice in chess.* The Hague: Mouton.

Dinadis, N., & Vicente, K. J. (1999). Designing functional visualizations for aircraft system status displays. *International Journal of Aviation Psychology, 9*, 241–269.

Easter, J. R. (1987). Engineering human factors into the Westinghouse advanced control room. *Nuclear Engineering International, 32* (May), 35–38.

Endsley, M. R., Klein, G., Woods, D. D., Smith, P. J., & Selcon, S. J. (1995). Future directions in cognitive engineering and naturalistic decision making. In: *Proceedings of the Human Factors and Ergonomics Society 40th Annual Meeting* (pp. 450–453). Santa Monica, CA: HFES.

Feynman, R. P. (1966). The development of the space-time view of quantum electrodynamics. *Science, 153*, 699–708.

Fischoff, B., Slovic, P., & Lichtenstein, S. (1978). Fault trees: Sensitivity of estimated failure probabilities to problem representation. *Journal of Experimental Psychology: Human Perception and Performance, 4*, 330–344.

Goodstein, L. P. (1968). An experimental computer-controlled instrumentation system for the research reactor DR-2. In: *Application of On-Line Computers to Nuclear Reactors* (pp. 549–566). Halden, Norway: OECD Halden Reactor Project.

Hajdukiewicz, J. R., Doyle, D. J., Milgram, P., Vicente, K. J., & Burns, C. M. (1998). A work domain analysis of patient monitoring in the operating room. In: *Proceedings of the Human Factors and Ergonomics Society 42nd Annual Meeting* (pp. 1038–1042). Santa Monica, CA: HFES.

Hollnagel, E., & Woods, D. D. (1983). Cognitive systems engineering: New wine in new bottles. *International Journal of Man-Machine Systems, 18*, 583–600.

Holton, G. (1988). *Thematic origins of scientific thought: Kepler to Einstein* (Rev. ed.). Cambridge, MA: Harvard University Press.

Hull, D. L. (1988). *Science as a process: An evolutionary account of the social and conceptual developments of science.* Chicago: University of Chicago Press.

Itoh, J., Sakuma, A., & Monta, K. (1995). An ecological interface for supervisory control of BWR nuclear power plants. *Control Engineering Practice, 3*, 231–239.

Itoh, J., Yoshimura, S., Ohtsuka, T., & Masuda, F. (1990). Cognitive task analysis of nuclear power plant operators for man-machine interface design. In: *Proceedings of the ANS Topical Meeting on Advances in Human Factors Research on Man-Computer Interactions: Nuclear and Beyond* (pp. 96–102). La Grange Park, IL: American Nuclear Society.

Jensen, A., Rasmussen, J., & Timmerman, P. (1963). *Analysis of failure data for electronic equipment at Risø (Risø Report No. 38)*. Roskilde, Denmark: Danish Atomic Energy Commission, Research Establishment Risø.

Klein, G. A. (1989). Recognition-primed decisions. In: W. B. Rouse (Ed.), *Advances in Man-Machine Systems Research* (Vol. 5, pp. 47–92). Greenwich, CT: JAI Press.

Klein, G. (1997). The recognition-primed decision (RPD) model: Looking back, looking forward. In: C. E. Zsambok & G. Klein (Eds), *Naturalistic Decision Making* (pp. 285–292). Mahwah, NJ: Erlbaum.

Klein, G. A., Orasanu, J., Calderwood, R., & Zsambok, C. (1993). *Decision making in action: Models and methods*. Norwood, NJ: Ablex.

Leveson, N. G. (1995). *Safeware: System safety and computers*. Reading, MA: Addison-Wesley.

Leveson, N. G. (2000). Intent specifications. An approach to building human-centered specifications. *IEEE Transactions on Software Engineering, 26,* 15–35.

Meister, D. (1995). Divergent viewpoints: Essays on human factors questions. Unpublished manuscript.

Moray, N. (1988). Ex Risø semper aliquid antiquum: Sources of a new paradigm for engineering psychology. In: L. P. Goodstein, H. B. Andersen, and S. E. Olsen (Eds), *Tasks, Errors,and Mental Models: A Festschrift to Celebrate the 60th Birthday of Professor Jens Rasmussen* (pp. 12–17). London: Taylor and Francis.

Newell, A. (1966). *On the analysis of human problem solving protocols.* Paper presented at the International Symposium on Mathematical Methods in the Social Science. Rome, July 4–9, 1966.

Nielsen, H., Nielsen, K., Petersen, F., & Jensen, H. S. (1998). *Risø National Laboratory – Forty years of research in a changing society.* Roskilde, Denmark: Risø National Laboratory, Information Service Department. (www.risoe.dk/rispubl/risofacts/factpdf/risoehistory.pdf)

Norman, D. A. (1981). *Steps toward a cognitive engineering: System images, system friendliness, mental models (Tech. Rep.).* La Jolla, CA: UCSD.

Norman, D. A. (1986). Cognitive engineering. In: D. A. Norman and S. W. Draper (Eds), *User Centered System Design: New Perspectives on Human-Computer Interaction* (pp. 31–61). Hillsdale, NJ: Erlbaum.

Norman, D. A. (1993). *Things that make us smart: Defending human attributes in the age of the machine.* Reading, MA: Addison-Wesley.

Pejtersen, A. M. (1992). The Book House: An icon based database system for fiction retrieval in public libraries. In: B. Cronin (Ed.), *The Marketing of Library and Information Services – 2* (pp. 572–591). London: ASLIB.

Perrow, C. (1984). *Normal accidents: Living with high-risk technologies.* New York: Basic Books.

Rasmussen, J. (1968a). *On the reliability of process plants and instrumentation systems (Risø-M-706).* Roskilde, Denmark: Danish Atomic Energy Commission, Research Establishment Risø.

Rasmussen, J. (1968b). *Characteristics of operator, automatic equipment and designer in plant automation (Risø-M-808).* Roskilde, Denmark: Danish Atomic Energy Commission, Research Establishment Risø.

Rasmussen, J. (1969). *Man-machine communication in the light of accident records (S-1-69).* Roskilde, Denmark: Danish Atomic Energy Commission, Research Establishment Risø.

Rasmussen, J. (1974). *The human data processor as a system component: Bits and pieces of a model (Risø-M-1722).* Roskilde, Denmark: Danish Atomic Energy Commission.

Rasmussen, J. (1978). *Operator/technician errors in calibration, setting, and testing nuclear power plant equipment (N-17–78)*. Roskilde, Denmark: Risø National Laboratory, Electronics Department.

Rasmussen, J. (1979a). *Preliminary analysis of human error cases in U.S. licencee event reports (N-8–79)*. Roskilde, Denmark: Risø National Laboratory, Electronics Department.

Rasmussen, J. (1979b). *On the structure of knowledge – A morphology of mental models in a man-machine system context (Risø-M-2192)*. Roskilde, Denmark: Risø National Laboratory, Electronics Department.

Rasmussen, J. (1980). What can be learned from human error reports? In: K. D. Duncan, M. M. Gruneberg, & D. Wallis (Eds), *Changes in Working Life* (pp. 97–113). Chichester, England: Wiley, 1980.

Rasmussen, J. (1986). *Information processing and human-machine interaction: An approach to cognitive engineering*. Amsterdam: North-Holland.

Rasmussen, J. (1990). A model for the design of computer integrated manufacturing systems: Identification of information requirements of decision makers. *International Journal of Industrial Ergonomics*, 5, 5–16.

Rasmussen, J., & Jensen, A. (1973). *A study of mental procedures in electronic trouble shooting (Risø-M-1582)*. Roskilde, Denmark: Danish Atomic Energy Commission, Research Establishment Risø.

Rasmussen, J., & Timmerman, P. (1962). *Safety and reliability of reactor instrumentation with redundant instrument channels (Risø Report No. 34)*. Roskilde, Denmark: Danish Atomic Energy Commission, Research Establishment Risø.

Rasmussen, J., Pejtersen, A. M., & Goodstein, L. P. (1994). *Cognitive systems engineering*. New York: Wiley.

Reason, J. (1990). *Human error*. Cambridge, England: Cambridge University Press.

Reising, D. V. (1999). *The impact of instrumentation location and reliability on the performance of operators using an ecological interface for process control (Unpublished doctoral dissertation)*. Urbana, IL: University of Illinois at Urbana-Champaign.

Rouse, W. B. (1988). Ladders, levels and lapses; and other distinctions in the contributions of Jens Rasmussen. In: L. P. Goodstein, H. B. Andersen & S. E. Olsen (Eds), *Tasks, Errors and Mental Models: A Festschrift to Celebrate the 60th Birthday of Professor Jens Rasmussen* (pp. 315–323). London: Taylor and Francis.

Sanderson, P. M., & Harwood, K. (1988). The skills, rules, and knowledge classification: A discussion of its emergence and nature. In: L. P. Goodstein, H. B. Andersen & S. E. Olsen (Eds), *Tasks, Errors, and Mental Models: A Festschrift to Celebrate the 60th Birthday of Professor Jens Rasmussen* (pp. 21–34). London: Taylor and Francis.

Sharp, T. D., & Helmicki, A. J. (1998). The application of the ecological interface design approach to neonatal intensive care medicine. In: *Proceedings of the Human Factors and Ergonomics Society 42nd Annual Meeting* (pp. 350–354). Santa Monica, CA: HFES.

Vicente, K. J. (1996). Improving dynamic decision making in complex systems through ecological interface design: A research overview. *System Dynamics Review*, 12, 251–279.

Vicente, K. J. (1997). Heeding the legacy of Meister, Brunswik, and Gibson: Toward a broader view of human factors research. *Human Factors*, 39, 323–328.

Vicente, K. J. (1999). *Cognitive work analysis: Toward safe, productive, and healthy computer-based work*. Mahwah, NJ: Erlbaum.

Vicente, K. J., & Rasmussen, J. (1992). Ecological interface design: Theoretical foundations. *IEEE Transactions on Systems, Man, and Cybernetics*, SMC-22, 589–606.

Vicente, K. J., & Sanderson, P. M. (1992). On the origins of the skills, rules, knowledge framework: A brief comment on Dougherty (1990). *Reliability Engineering and System Safety, 36*, 181–182.

Vicente, K. J., & Wang, J. (1998). An ecological theory of expertise effects in memory recall. *Psychological Review, 105*, 33–57.

Wickens, C. D. (1992). *Engineering psychology and human performance* (2nd ed.). New York: Harper-Collins.

Wickens, C. D., & Carswell, M. (1995). The proximity compatibility principle: Its psychological foundation and relevance to display design. *Human Factors, 37*, 473–494.

Woods, D. D. (1984). Some results on operator performance in emergency events. In: D. Whitfield (Ed.), *Ergonomics Problems in Process Operations* (pp. 21–32). Birmingham, England: Institution of Chemical Engineers.

Woods, D. D. (1991). The cognitive engineering of problem representations. In: J. Alty and G. Weir (Eds), *Human-Computer Interaction in Complex Systems* (pp. 169–188). London: Academic Press.

Woods, D. D., Watts, J. C., Graham, J. M., Kidwell, D. L., & Smith, P. J. (1996). Teaching cognitive systems engineering. In: *Proceedings of the Human Factors and Ergonomics Society 40th Annual Meeting* (pp. 259–263). Santa Monica, CA: HFES.

Xiao, Y., Milgram, P., & Doyle, D. J. (1997). Planning behavior and its functional roles in the interaction with complex systems. *IEEE Transactions on Systems, Man, and Cybernetics, Part A: Systems and Humans, 27*, 313–324.

Xu, W., Dainoff, M. J., & Mark, L. S. (1999). Facilitate complex search tasks in hypertext by externalizing functional properties of a work domain. *International Journal of Human-Computer Interaction, 11*, 201–229.

Zsambok, C. E., & Klein, G. (1997). *Naturalistic decision making*. Mahwah, NJ: Erlbaum.

Zwicky, F. (1967). The morphological approach to discovery, invention, research and construction. In: F. Zwicky & A. G. Wilson (Eds), *New methods of thought and procedure* (pp. 273–297). Berlin: Springer-Verlag.

2. DEVELOPING ADAPTABILITY: A THEORY FOR THE DESIGN OF INTEGRATED-EMBEDDED TRAINING SYSTEMS

Steve W. J. Kozlowski, Rebecca J. Toney,
Morell E. Mullins, Daniel A. Weissbein,
Kenneth G. Brown and Bradford S. Bell

INTRODUCTION

The nature of work and organizations is changing. Over three decades ago, Terreberry (1968) observed that future organizational environments would evolve to become increasingly turbulent and unpredictable. As we prepare to enter the next millennium, that future is upon us. The dynamics and uncertainty associated with the constellation of external forces that impact organizations create pressures for innovation, flexibility, and adaptability. Adaptability as an individual, team, and organizational capability is increasingly critical to effectiveness.

The increasing rate of technological innovation, and the penetration of technology into all aspects of organizational operations, is changing the nature of work (Howell & Cooke, 1989). Work is increasingly complex, placing a high emphasis on cognitive skills and specialized expertise. It is increasingly mediated by computerized systems that link distributed experts together. From

Advances in Human Performance and Cognitive Engineering Research, Volume 1,
pages 59–123.

air travel, to medical diagnostics, emergency response, engineering design, and command and control, among many others, organizational functions that range from the mundane to esoteric are all dependent on teams of distributed experts operating via complex systems. Although teams are often co-located in time and space, the increasing connectivity of technology systems facilitates the creation of far-flung virtual teams that interact dynamically, but never actually meet face to face (Bell & Kozlowski, in press).

There are economic pressures for improved efficiency, cost-control, and effectiveness. Traditional training is typically conducted off-site. A substantial portion of training costs – upwards of 80% – is devoted to simply getting trainees to the site, maintaining them while there, and absorbing their lost productivity. Because off-site training is often decontextualized – that is, abstracted from the work setting – it also incurs potential problems of skill transfer that impede effectiveness.

This convergence of forces – environmental, technological, and economic – is driving a reconceptualization of the nature of training systems. Training is shifting from an inefficient, time consuming, and expensive enterprise to one that can be delivered efficiently, as needed, and just-in-time. It is shifting from an off-site single episode to a systematic series of learning experiences that are *integrated* in the workplace and *embedded* in work technology. It is shifting from a primary emphasis on retention and reproduction to a broader emphasis that also includes the development of *adaptive* knowledge and skills (Kozlowski, 1998). Training will not be a separate activity, but a continuous activity that is an integral part of the workplace and its systems. This reconceptualization of training systems is highlighted by three key terms in our title which constitute the theoretical and application focus of this chapter:

- *Integrate* – to form, coordinate, or blend into a functioning or unified whole;
- *Embed* – to enclose closely; to make something an integral part of;
- *Adapt* – to make fit; implies a modification according to changing circumstances;

(Webster's Ninth New Collegiate Dictionary, 1987).

Skill Demands in Complex Task Environments

Dynamic tasks necessitate adaptive skills. Many critical activities are accomplished by teams of distributed decision makers interacting through complex, technology-mediated systems. These task environments, which are characterized as dynamic decision making (DDM) situations, place high demands on the skills and capabilities of teams and their leaders. DDM tasks are shifting, ambiguous, and emergent, necessitating rapid assessment of the situation as it unfolds, diagnosis and prioritization of possible actions, and implementation of appropriate task strategies (Orasanu & Connolly, 1993). Modern systems present the decision maker with a wealth of raw information that must be distilled to its essentials, comprehended, and addressed under significant time pressure.

Complex task situations such as these place heavy demands on individual and team decision making (TDM), necessitating high levels of expertise to enable the strategic action and adaptability required for effective performance (Kozlowski, 1998). Although a substantial portion of the information processing required to assess the situation and take appropriate action can be augmented or automated, situation assessment and strategic action are largely the domain of the human decision maker. Effective utilization of these complex technology systems rests on the high level training, skills, and expertise of system operators.

Advanced technology necessitates high level skills. Technological advances will further augment decision-making systems. We can anticipate that the technology will accomplish more of the mundane vigilance and information processing tasks, and will also augment human decision making (e.g. decision aids, intelligent agents, coaches). Fewer people will be required to operate a system. However, the consequences of fewer operators include broader roles, greater responsibility, and increased criticality for each individual. This directly affects the configuration of abilities, knowledge, skills, and attitudes demanded of decision makers. Each team member in the system must now learn higher level skills, accomplish more tasks, and is more critical to the effectiveness of the team. Yet, the human decision maker will still be confronted by a dynamic, knowledge-rich task environment that demands rapid situation assessment and coordinated action. In effect, technological advances will make the skills of the human element *more*, rather than less, important. Thus, training requirements for adaptive, high-level skills and coordinated teamwork can be expected to *increase*, not decrease, as the sophistication and capabilities of technology improve.

Challenges for Training Design

The need for integrated-embedded training systems. Recent theory and research addressing DDM, TDM, and complex skill acquisition are clear that the cognitive and behavioral capabilities needed for effectiveness in these task environments are contextually based. Although these high level skills rest on more basic knowledge and skills that can be acquired in conventional training environments (i.e. the classroom), adaptive skills and team coordination fully develop and refine in the actual performance environment or in very close approximations to it. This means that training systems must either: (a) push training toward long-term exposure of intact teams to a wide variety of task situations in high fidelity, full mission simulations (i.e. extended off-site training), or (b) shift more training to the performance context, where tools, techniques, and methods to enhance acquisition of these key skills can be integrated with appropriate instructional support systems (i.e. contextualize training in the workplace, and embed it in work technology).

The development of promising new media and technologies for training, when combined with pressures to reduce costs associated with off-the-job training, reduce training time, and increase efficiency make option (b) the logical choice. By specifying the principles needed to operationalize inte-grated-embedded training systems, it will be possible to capitalize on an opportunity to enhance the flexibility and effectiveness of training for the next generation of advanced systems.

Application criteria. Developing integrated-embedded training systems that can reliably deliver the high-level adaptive skills presents several challenges. Such training systems must be able to enhance the acquisition of the high-level skills that underlie strategic action and adaptability. The training systems, and their associated instructional supports, must be developmental in order to shift the focus of skill acquisition as learning and performance improve. They must also be flexible enough to allow leaders to customize and adapt the training to deliver skills that are needed for current or anticipated situations (Kozlowski, Gully, Salas & Cannon-Bowers, 1996). Training systems must also offer ease of implementation, ease of use, and compatibility with advanced systems.

Theory and research objective. Although new training techniques and technologies offer the potential for flexibility, efficiency, and integration into the workplace, there is little theoretically-based guidance in the training and instructional design literatures that directly informs application. This is particularly relevant with respect to the challenges noted above. Without the foundation of a theoretically based and empirically grounded model, it is impossible to determine how to specify and utilize the potential capabilities of advanced technologies to provide integrated and embedded training.

The purpose of this research is to develop and evaluate theoretically based principles to guide the design of integrated-embedded training systems.

This chapter is organized into three sections to address our theoretical and research objective. We first provide an overview of our theoretical model, and explicate the logic underlying the application of the model to training design. In the second section, we provide a literature review of those research domains of substantive relevance to the theoretical model. The review provides the basis for the derivation of training design principles that are consistent with the theoretical model. The third section of the chapter identifies key leverage points in the model, and associated principles, that we believe hold the most research and application promise. Research propositions are posed and explicated. Finally, we close with a discussion of the contribution of our theory, and the research challenges that will have to be surmounted in order to effectively integrate training in the workplace, embed instructional tools in work systems, and enhance adaptability.

THEORETICAL MODEL

Background Assumptions
It is impossible to predict with certainty the specific training capabilities that can be embedded in the next generation of advanced systems. However, two training capabilities are likely to be prominent in whatever form the technology assumes: (1) the capability to selectively generate a variety of practice experiences (simulated and real), and (2) the capability to monitor trainee performance in real-time and to generate extensive, detailed, and specific information about the trainee's performance.

> *Thus, it is assumed that precise control of practice and feedback will be key attributes of advanced systems. The theoretical and research challenge is to determine the best ways to leverage the instructional potential of these training capabilities.*

Theoretical Model

Adaptive learning system. Recent research on learning, cognition, training design, and complex skill acquisition provides the theoretical underpinnings for our approach. We have developed a theoretically-based, application-oriented model formulated around the Adaptive Learning System (ALS), that is particularly well-suited to meet the challenges of integrated-embedded training. The ALS approach is designed to enhance the development of complex knowledge, learning strategies, and adaptive capabilities that are grounded in the performance context. ALS is based on a self-regulatory model of learning, motivation, and performance (Ames & Archer, 1988; Bandura, 1991; Karoly, 1993; Latham & Locke, 1991; Smith, Ford & Kozlowski, 1997).

Self-regulatory models have been shown to be particularly effective at enhancing learning for difficult and complex tasks (Bandura & Wood, 1989; Gist, Stevens & Bavetta, 1991; Karl, O'Leary-Kelly & Martocchio, 1993; Kozlowski, Gully, Brown, Salas, Smith & Nason, in press; Kozlowski, Gully, Smith, Nason & Brown, 1995; Kozlowski, Gully, Smith, Brown, Mullins & Williams, 1996; Martocchio, 1994; Martocchio & Dulebohn, 1994; Martocchio & Webster, 1992; Thomas & Mathieu, 1994). At its most elemental level, self-regulation involves monitoring the differences between goals and current states. Negative discrepancies induce self-evaluation and, depending on affective reactions and causal attributions, reallocation of attention and effort to move closer toward goal accomplishment.

The ALS is designed to selectively influence the self-regulatory process to influence learning and performance. It forms the core of our conceptual model shown in Fig. 1, and is comprised of three subsystems: (1) *Training Components* that encompass Training Design, Information Provision, and Trainee Orientation; (2) *Training Strategy*, which entails the construction of a training intervention from a combination of specific Training Components; and (3) the *Self-Regulation System* which entails the interconnections among Practice (Behavior), Self-Monitoring (Cognition), and Self-Evaluation/Reactions (Affect). Individual differences, such as cognitive abilities and dispositions, can interact with the ALS. The combination of individual differences and the ALS subsystems affect proximal training outcomes of learning and performance, which in turn influence distal outcomes of retention and adaptation.

Training Components consist of Training Design, Information Provision, and Trainee Orientation. *Training Design* refers to the nature of the information and practice (e.g. experiential exercises, simulation scenarios) to be used for training, including such features as their complexity, difficulty, degree of learner control, sequencing, and variability. *Information Provision* refers to the feedback provided to the trainee that influences their interpretation of *past* progress, and to the guidance provided that influences their preparation for *future* learning efforts. *Trainee Orientation* refers to motivational (e.g. training goals) and attributional frames that affect the way the trainee perceives the training experience. Thus, each Training Component represents a set of related instructional manipulations.

Training Strategy is the assemblage of specific training components that form a *Training Intervention*. That is, interventions are constructed from a combination of manipulations drawn from one or more of the Training Components. For example, the Training Intervention, *Sequenced Mastery Goals*, is a combination of sequenced complexity from Training Design,

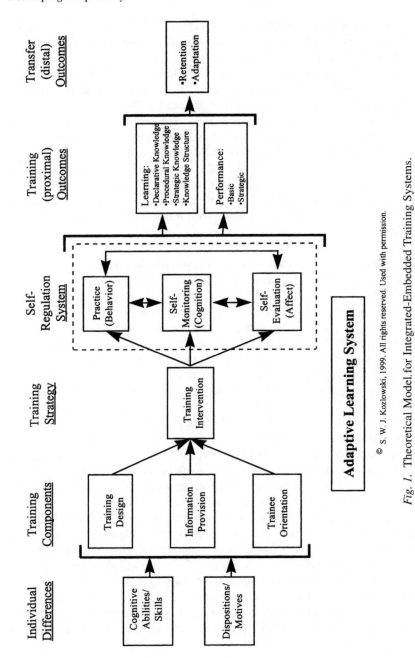

Adaptive Learning System

Fig. 1. Theoretical Model for Integrated-Embedded Training Systems.

mastery goals fromTrainee Orientation, and process feedback from Information Provision. Training Interventions are constructed to influence one or more of the foci of the Self-Regulation System.

The *Self-Regulation System* (SRS) is comprised of three foci. *Practice* entails the **behaviors** trainees exhibit as they interact with the training simulation or exercise, and is primarily influenced by Training Design features embedded in the intervention. *Self-Monitoring* represents the **cognitive** focus of the SRS that concerns trainee attention and reflection on their progress. It is primarily influenced by Information Provision. *Self-Evaluation/Reactions* represents the **affective** focus of the SRS. It reflects the emotional reactions trainees have to their learning and performance, and is primarily influenced by the Trainee Orientation. All three foci of the SRS are interlinked. The SRS is iterative and developmental over time, with impacts on learning, motivation, and performance.

Application logic of the ALS. The ALS leverages the SRS by impacting its underlying cognitive, behavior, and affective foci. The nature of this energization is determined by the combination of Training Components that comprise the Training Intervention. In operation, the model is predicated on trainees working toward training goals. Goals are either set by the training system as part of the intervention, or are determined by trainees themselves as the by-product of an intervention. Trainees monitor their progress toward goals during the training episode. Trainees determine progress by observing their behavior during practice and by interpreting specific feedback provided by the simulated task, exercise, or instructor. When learning complex tasks, trainees frequently fail to meet goals or self-set objectives. Negative discrepancies between goals and current performance prompt evaluation. Moderate negative discrepancies motivate additional attention and effort toward learning and performance. Large negative discrepancies will generally yield withdrawal.

Discrepancies also implicate affective reactions as trainees attempt to account for their progress, or lack thereof. Small negative discrepancies, indicating progress toward goals, will prompt the development of self-efficacy and attributions that enhance the self. Large negative discrepancies, indicating a lack of progress, will undermine the development of self-efficacy and prompt attributions that devalue the self. These affective reactions influence trainee motivation in the current and subsequent training episodes. Positive affect enhances motivation, learning, and performance, and provides resilience to the failures that are inherent in complex skill acquisition. Negative affect degrades motivation, and makes trainees prone to task withdrawal. Implications for training are self-evident.

Research focus. *The instructional logic of the ALS is predicated on selectively combining training components into an integrated intervention that allows the trainee to experience moderate negative discrepancies, and a sustained trajectory toward the accomplishment of training goals as they learn the critical knowledge and skills necessary for task effectiveness. The central research question for application of the ALS model concerns identifying combinations of training components that yield synergistic positive effects on the SRS, thus enhancing complex skill acquisition and adaptability.*

Feedback is a critical characteristic of instructional design, a central process in the SRS, and a key capability of the next generation of advanced systems. Thus, there is convergence from theory, research, and practice perspectives that the Information Provision Training Component must be a central feature of integrated-embedded training strategies. What form of feedback information, and how it is to be employed are key research issues.

Conventional research examining feedback effects on training and learning have tended to focus on its informational properties; that is, on the descriptive characteristics of feedback, including its amount, specificity, accuracy, frequency, consistency, and process/outcome orientation. Our literature review suggests that this descriptive focus is incomplete. Although it catalogs important informational properties of feedback, it neglects interpretive properties that may be more central to learning.

It is the interpretation of feedback that is most relevant to self-regulation, and hence a critical leverage point in the design of training interventions.

We have developed a typology of feedback shown in Fig. 2 that addresses this limitation. The foundation of the typology is provided by *Information Properties*, which includes Description as its primary property. Beyond that foundation, the typology includes three *Interpretation Properties*:

(1) Evaluation, (2) Attribution, and (3) Guidance.

Evaluation is **past** oriented, and concerns any manipulation that affects whether trainees perceive their performance as positive or negative. Normative feedback makes reference to the performance of others as a comparison standard. Velocity feedback is self-referenced against internal expectations for progress. Labeled feedback is simply a positive or negative sign provided by an external agent (i.e. the system, instructor, or leader) that is not referenced to an explicit standard. Evaluation affects the trainee's interpretation of **what happened**.

Attribution is also **past** oriented, and concerns any manipulation that affects the attributed cause of performance. Locus references internal (e.g. ability, effort) or external (e.g. luck, task difficulty) causes. Stability references whether causes are malleable or fixed. Controllability references whether the causes of performance can be influenced by the trainee. Attribution affects the trainee's interpretation of *why it happened*.

Guidance is *future* oriented, and concerns any manipulation that directs future cognition, behavior, and/or affect. Behavioral guidance directs the trainee about what actions to do next. Cognitive guidance directs the trainee

Information Properties

Description

- specificity
- amount
- frequency
- accuracy
- consistency (with goals)
- process/outcome orientation

Interpretation Properties

Evaluation

- normative (other-referenced)
- velocity (self-referenced)
- labeled positive/negative (unreferenced)

Attribution

- internal/external locus
- stable/unstable
- controllable/uncontrollable

Guidance

- behavior
- cognition
- affect

Fig. 2. Typology for ALS Information Provision.

about what to think, such as using metacognitive strategies or to focus on particular practice strategies. Affective guidance directs the trainee to exercise emotional control with respect to his or her reactions to practice feedback. Guidance provides an interpretation of *what next*.

LITERATURE REVIEW: DESIGN PRINCIPLES FOR INTEGRATED-EMBEDDED TRAINING

The theoretical model was constructed to be a comprehensive conceptual framework for deriving principles for integrated-embedded training. The following review provides a description of the literature supporting our theoretical rationale, and a conceptual foundation for several research avenues represented by the principles derived from the model. The review is organized to follow the major segments of the model shown in Fig. 1: Individual Differences, Training Components, the Self-Regulatory System, and Training Outcomes.

Individual Differences

Cognitive Individual Differences
Different levels of cognitive and metacognitive abilities and skills are brought to the training setting by each trainee. These individual difference variables can have important effects on training and transfer outcomes, although they are often ignored in research on training design. Therefore, training research has and should continue to explore ways to design training interventions so as to make the best use of trainees' cognitive abilities and skills. These individual differences should be considered when making decisions concerning the design of training.

Cognitive ability. The general cognitive ability of trainees can have an important effect on both learning and performance outcomes of training. First, and well-documented, is that general cognitive abilities have demonstrated predictive validity for training performance (Ree & Earles, 1992; Schmidt, Hunter, Outerbridge & Goff, 1988). Based on this evidence, researchers have advocated that different kinds of training should be developed and targeted at trainees of different ability levels (Kanfer, 1996; Kanfer & Ackerman, 1989). This notion of tailoring training to abilities is particularly relevant to integrated-embedded training, because such systems have the potential to be adaptive to the different ability levels of the trainees. The adaptability could be in the form of the type of training given (Kanfer, 1996; Kanfer & Ackerman, 1989), the type of feedback provided (Podsakoff & Fahr, 1989), or the type of guidance provided (Bell, 1999). Training can also be designed to reduce the demand for cognitive ability (Goska & Ackerman, 1996).

Learning outcomes are also hypothesized to be affected by a trainee's cognitive ability. All things being equal, trainees with high cognitive ability would be expected to learn more and in a shorter period of time than trainees with low cognitive ability. This is because attentional resources – which are largely determined by cognitive ability – are central to the skill acquisition process (Ackerman, 1992; Kanfer & Ackerman, 1989; Norman & Bobrow, 1975). Different attentional resources are necessary at different stages of skill acquisition (Ackerman, 1992; Kanfer & Ackerman, 1989; Norman & Bobrow, 1975). Flexibility for different stages of skill acquisition is also feasible with integrated-embedded training. For example, incorporating specific error-prone events to prompt learning (e.g. scenario-based training; Cannon-Bowers, Burns, Salas & Pruitt, 1998) requires more cognitive resources at certain stages of training (Ivancic & Hesketh, 1995), and should therefore be used only at those stages of training for which they would be useful to trainees.

Some authors suggest that trainees should be made aware of their cognitive abilities (Garcia & Pintrich, 1994), and should be taught self-regulation strategies that correspond to their level of understanding and ability (Carver & Scheier, 1982). For example, a trainee who is having trouble with mastering basic aspects of a complex task should be encouraged to self-regulate at the level of the task, rather than focusing on more comprehensive goals or normative information that draws attention to the self level. This notion is particularly relevant to considerations of the role of the self-regulation system in learning.

Metacognitive skills. Metacognition is often conceptualized as "thinking about thinking." This ability to think about – choose, monitor, and adapt – cognitive strategies can also affect training outcomes. For example, a person working on a task may not only be thinking about performing the task, which is a cognitive skill, but may also be thinking about how her performance is progressing toward a goal, what strategies are being used or need to be used to improve performance, and how she feels about her performance, which are meta-cognitive skills. Although metacognitive skills may be conceptualized as a trainable component of the self-regulatory process, many researchers have examined metacognitive skills as primarily an individual difference variable. Some individuals bring to training high metacognitive awareness, or strong skills, and others have low metacognitive awareness, or weak skills (Ridley, Schutz, Glanz & Weinstein, 1992; Schraw & Dennison, 1994; Swanson, 1990). Schraw and Dennison (1994) and Swanson (1990) demonstrate that metacognitive skills are distinct from general cognitive ability and task knowledge. Swanson also suggests that metacognitive skill is more predictive of training performance than is general cognitive ability. Such metacognitive skills may include trainees' use of mnemonics, mental repetition, mental models, summarizing, synthesizing, and familiarizers (associating new information with information you already know) to aid them in monitoring their learning process.

Several studies indicate that the use of metacognitive skill can be fostered by other variables. First, metacognitive skill is related to learning orientation; a strong mastery orientation entails the use of metacognitive skills (Ames & Archer, 1988; Ford, Smith, Weissbein, Gully & Salas, 1998; Schraw, Horn, Thorndike-Christ & Bruning, 1995). Second, metacognitive skill is related to goal setting; self-set goals are more effective for trainees with high metacognitive skills (Ridley et al., 1992). Third, motivation and encouragement should help trainees use their current level of metacognitive skill (Brief & Hollenbeck, 1985; Garner, 1990). Although metacognitive skills may vary across trainees, it may also be possible to train, influence, or leverage the use of metacognitive skills by increasing motivation (e.g. Garner, 1990) or influencing the SRS. The effectiveness of training metacognitive skills can be evaluated by our model, because the effects of individual differences on metacognitive skill can be distinguished and controlled. This will be discussed in more detail when we address the self-regulation system.

Integrated-embedded training will allow training to be adapted to many different combinations of variables. For example, self-regulation that is encouraged can be varied according to the level of understanding or ability of trainees (Carver & Scheier, 1982), either on an individual basis or with respect to their point of progress through the training program. This could be accomplished by providing different types of feedback which would focus trainees to self-regulate at different levels. Other metacognitive skills that facilitate adaptability may also be accommodated within integrated-embedded training systems. Examples of derived ALS principles relevant to trainee cognitive abilities are listed in Table 1.

Motives and Dispositions

Goal orientation. Goal orientation is the extent to which individuals prefer mastery or performance goals. Individuals with a learning orientation are more likely to adopt mastery goals focused on improving skills and increasing competence (Elliot & Dweck, 1988; Boyle & Klimoski, 1996; Duda & Nicholls, 1992). Learning-oriented individuals believe that their abilities are

Table 1. ALS Design Principles: Cognitive Abilities and Skills.

Citation	Principle
	Cognitive Ability
Bandura (1991) Dweck (1986)	Trainees should be encouraged to believe cognitive ability is a skill that can be developed to better maintain motivation and more likely adopt mastery goals.
Ivancic and Hesketh (1995)	High ability trainees should be encouraged to make errors during training, as they have the attentional capacity to reflect on and learn from them.
Kanfer (1996)	High ability trainees should be provided with motivation control skill training later in training to maintain high performance levels when the task becomes less challenging.
	Low ability trainees should be provided with emotional control skill training early in training to prevent interference of on-task effort from negative thoughts.
Kanfer and Ackerman (1989)	High ability trainees should be encouraged to engage in self-regulatory activities to improve performance, because they have more attentional resources to devote to both task performance and self-regulation
	Low ability trainees should be encouraged to engage in goal-setting activities later in training to improve performance.
Podsakoff and Farh (1989)	Trainees of both high ability and high self-efficacy should be provided with negative feedback to improve performance.
Ree and Earles (1992)	Trainees should be chosen on the basis of their cognitive ability, because general cognitive ability is a better predictor of training performance than specific abilities such as metacognitve ability.
	Metacognitive Skills
Garcia and Pintrich (1994)	Trainees should be encouraged to become aware of their own knowledge and strategies in both motivational and cognitive domains to improve performance and transfer.
Swanson (1990)	Trainees should be encouraged to develop metacognitive skills, because metacognitive skills are a better predictor of training performance than general cognitive ability.
Ford et al. (1998)	Trainees should be encouraged to develop metacognitive skills, because their use during training will enhance learning, performance, and self-efficacy.

malleable and are characterized by positive affect, increased motivation, constructive self-instruction, and active self-monitoring (Dweck, 1986, 1989; Dweck & Leggett, 1988).

Performance-oriented individuals possess a different set of concerns. Rather than developing competence, they are concerned with demonstrating competence to themselves or others. Motives of performance-oriented individuals include wanting others to think they are smart or to simply do better than others around them (Meece, 1994). Performance-oriented individuals believe that their abilities are fixed. They seek situations in which they can demonstrate their competence, and tend to avoid novel situations where their competence is unknown or in question (Dweck, 1986, 1989). It has been suggested that an orientation toward performance tends to suppress the metacognitive and cognitive processes that are stimulated by the adoption of a learning orientation (Schraw et al., 1995).

Goal orientation has several motivational implications that are relevant to deriving instructional principles. First, initial motivation is dependent in large part on the goal orientation trainees bring with them to the training environment; learning oriented trainees are more motivated to learn than performance-oriented individuals (Archer, 1994). Learning-oriented individuals tend to maintain motivation during training, provided successful performance is construed by trainees as a skill that can be improved (Bandura, 1991). Finally, learning-orientation can interact with the training technique to increase intrinsic motivation (Nordstrom, Wendland & Williams, 1995). For example, trainees with a learning orientation who are given Error Management Training (in which trainees are taught to use errors constructively) will likely gain more from the training than will performance-oriented trainees.

The theoretical underpinnings of goal orientation as an individual difference focus on the individual's implicit theory of intelligence. Individuals either believe that intelligence is malleable, and can be improved through effort, or they believe that it is a fixed quantity and people must simply deal with what they possess (Dweck, 1986). Belief in the malleability of intelligence maps to a learning orientation. On the other hand, a view of intelligence as immutable is more closely related to a performance orientation. Care must be taken in the design of training, since individuals who believe intelligence to be immutable are less efficacious (e.g. Martocchio, 1994), and may be more likely to withdraw (either physically or psychologically) from the training when faced with failure (Ivancic & Hesketh, 1995). Indeed, much of the research on goal orientation and learning has treated it as a situational state by manipulating trainee beliefs about the malleability of their ability, but has done so without controlling for the goal orientation traits (e.g. Martocchio, 1994).

Trait self-efficacy. Self-efficacy is usually conceptualized as a domain-specific belief in one's competence (Bandura, 1991). High self-efficacy has been found to be associated with increased performance, with the relationship moderated by the complexity of the task (Bandura & Cervone, 1983, 1986). An alternative perspective is one that treats efficacy as a more global construct, where individuals have a general belief in their capability to handle any situation that might arise (Scherer, Maddux, Mercadante, Prentice-Dunn, Jacobs & Rogers, 1982; Eden & Zuk, 1995). It might be argued that people enter any situation, even a novel one, with varying degrees of confidence in their abilities to handle whatever problems may confront them (Mathieu, Tannenbaum & Salas, 1992). It is reasonable to expect that those individuals who feel more confident in their ability to respond to such situations will show the same type of effects, at a general level, that have presented themselves in the self-efficacy literature. However, the meaningfulness of a trait conceptualization of self-efficacy is questionable, particularly when we consider how to distinguish such a notion from more general self-image. Because of this ambiguity, our use of the term "self-efficacy" will throughout this paper refer to the domain-specific conceptualization that is more theoretically appropriate. Discussions of task-specific self-efficacy as a training outcome are addressed in subsequent sections of this chapter.

Locus of control. As with the theory of intelligence discussed above, individuals vary in the extent to which they attribute control of occurrences to themselves (internal locus of control) or to their environments (external locus of control). Individuals with an internal locus of control, who perceive themselves to have some control over the training environment, will maintain their motivation better than will those with an external locus of control (Noe & Schmitt, 1986).

Obviously, trainee motives and dispositions are critical to skill acquisition. Not only do they provide direct influences on outcomes (Dweck & Leggett, 1988), they may also interact with the training program to influence outcomes of interest (Ivancic & Hesketh, 1995; Martocchio, 1994). Some examples of derived ALS principles relevant to trainee dispositions are compiled in Table 2.

Training Components

Information Provision
Information Provision is that component of training typically referred to as feedback. It is composed of information the training system provides to the trainee for use in the self-regulation process. The information provided may have many different properties, which can be generally categorized along two

Table 2. Training Design Principles: Trainee Motives and Dispositions.

Citation	Principle
	Mastery/Performance Orientation
Archer (1994)	Trainees with high mastery orientations rather than high performance orientations should be chosen for training if trainees need to be highly motivated prior to beginning the training.
Boyle and Klimoski (1996)	Trainees with high performance orientations should be pushed to adopt mastery goals during training, to acquire more declarative knowledge.
Duda and Nicholls (1992)	Trainees with high mastery orientations should be chosen for training if one of the goals of training is to increase collaboration among trainees.
Ivancic and Hesketh (1995)	Trainees with high performance orientations (or entity views of intelligence) should not be provided with error-filled training because they are less capable at handling negative feedback.
	Trait Self-Efficacy
Karoly (1993)	Trainees with high self-efficacy should be given feedback, particularly when performing poorly, as they will be likely to increase their effort.
Mathieu et al. (1993)	Trainees with high self-efficacy at the outset of training are likely to maintain high levels of efficacy throughout the training.
	Locus of Control
Noe and Schmitt (1986)	Trainees with an internal locus of control are likely to maintain motivation throughout training.

lines: properties which are purely informative (providing descriptive information), and properties which are interpretive (providing additional characterization of the information, which may have motivational or metacognitive consequences). These characteristics are illustrated in Fig. 2. This section describes these information and interpretive properties and literature relevant to deriving principles to guide the provision of information during training.

Information properties. Information properties of feedback provide trainees with knowledge of learning or performance results. Thus, this aspect of feedback is often termed "knowledge of results." All feedback has at least some of this descriptive property, and is characteristic of the traditional notion of feedback. The descriptive feedback simply relates to the trainee what behaviors they did or did not exhibit, what concepts or facts they did or did not learn, and what results they did or did not achieve. Description is a behavior-oriented property. Most conceptualizations of feedback end here, providing a categorization of types of descriptive feedback including its specificity, amount, frequency, accuracy, consistency, and process/outcome orientation. These different types of descriptive feedback are briefly described and illustrated below.

Feedback presented to trainees can differ with respect to the specificity, or detail, of the information. For example, in a complex decision-making task, "You made many decisions," would represent a more general feedback statement, whereas, "You made 28 decisions in 8.5 minutes of practice," would be a much more specific feedback statement. In general, researchers seem to agree that specific feedback is preferable to general feedback (Earley, Northcraft, Lee & Lituchy, 1990; Lindsley, Brass & Thomas, 1995; Wofford & Goodwin, 1990), particularly when goals are specific and when task strategies are being learned (Earley et al., 1990).

Feedback can also differ with respect to the amount or quantity of information presented to trainees. If trainees are performing five different behaviors, feedback could be presented for only the most important behavior or all five behaviors. Amount of feedback may also be related to the specificity of the feedback, in that more specific feedback necessarily entails a greater amount of feedback be given than does very general feedback.

The frequency with which trainees are presented the information is another way in which feedback can vary. Feedback can be presented at one time only (i.e. at the end of training), after every performance episode, or after every minute of the performance episodes. To maximize retention and transfer, feedback should not be given excessively (Schmidt & Bjork, 1992); however, to maximize self-efficacy, feedback should be given frequently (Gist & Mitchell, 1992). These conflicting recommendations may be resolved by evaluating which goals are more important to the training – raising efficacy or improving retention and transfer. Mikulincer (1989) suggests that less feedback be provided during early stages of skill acquisition, particularly when trainees are prone to interfering thoughts following negative feedback. Some authors stress the importance of the timeliness of the feedback (Lindsley et al., 1995) particularly when developing a strong procedural knowledge base (Anderson, 1987). This simply means that feedback information should be presented contiguous to the performance episode rather than at a later time, further removed from the performance episode.

The accuracy of feedback information presented to trainees can vary as well. For example, feedback can represent the trainee's actual learning and performance, or the trainee might receive fabricated feedback. This is usually provided to achieve some expected motivational gain. Researchers indicate that, in the interest of long term gains, feedback should be accurate so that trainees will know what task behaviors need improvement (Hunter-Blanks, Ghatala, Pressley & Levin, 1988; Lindsley et al., 1995). Podsakoff and Farh (1989) suggest that feedback should be credible; credibility can be established by demonstrating some evidence for the authenticity of the feedback. Feedback which is perceived as credible will have greater effect on trainee behavior. However, positive feedback does have benefits of increasing self-efficacy, which increases resilience. Therefore, a trainer might choose to provide a trainee with positive evaluative feedback that is technically not accurate (e.g. "you are doing very well"), particularly when the trainee is learning a complex task that results in substantial negative feedback (e.g. many mistakes, low scores) during the initial stages of skill acquisition.

Feedback presented to trainees can differ with respect to how consistent the information is with the trainee's goals. Just as a trainee can have either mastery or performance goals, the feedback can be tailored so that it provides information on the trainee's progress toward either mastery or performance improvement. For example, feedback consistent with mastery goals would inform the trainee as to what concepts and/or facts have or have not been learned; feedback consistent with performance goals would inform the trainee as to what level of performance, relative to the goal, has been achieved. Feedback consistency is important with respect to any goals; it is not limited to mastery and performance goals. So if a goal were for a trainee to perform faster, speed information should be given.

Finally, feedback presented to trainees may differ with respect to whether the information is process oriented or outcome oriented. Generally, process feedback concerns how a trainee is using information or how behaviors are performed; outcome feedback describes how well that information is used or those behaviors are performed. If there are three behaviors associated in combination with an outcome, process feedback would provide information concerning how well the three behaviors were exhibited, whereas outcome feedback would only provide information related to achievement of the outcome. It is recommended that process feedback be provided when task strategies are being learned (Earley et al., 1990), so that trainees can learn to modify and improve the strategies. Process feedback regarding errors should be provided when building a procedural knowledge base, but withheld when trainees are learning how to handle errors (Anderson, 1987).

One of the challenges of using descriptive feedback in training is determining the optimal combination of feedback types at different points in the learning process. Alternatively, training can be designed to influence the interpretation trainees apply to the information, as discussed in the following section.

Interpretation properties. Descriptive feedback provides raw information; interpretation is a psychological process that extracts meaning from the information. This psychological interpretation of the meaning of feedback is central to self-regulatory processes, but is typically uncontrolled in training. However, it is possible to augment feedback to provide an interpretive direction or prompt. Thus, from a theoretical perspective, it is a key leverage point in our model. The three primary ways of manipulating the interpretive properties of feedback include: *evaluation* – providing a point of reference with which to compare the feedback information; *attribution* – prompting potential causal explanations for the feedback information; and *guidance* – providing direction for future actions, thoughts, and/or feelings. Another way to frame these three interpretive properties is that they explain (respectively); *what happened, why it happened, and what should happen next.*

Evaluation is the interpretation property that involves a comparison of descriptive feedback to a reference point. Such comparative information may have substantial impacts on the subsequent training and performance behavior of the trainee. For example, trainees performing poorly should be given negative evaluative feedback when performing simple tasks, but not when performing complex tasks. For simple tasks, negative evaluative feedback will lead to increased effort and performance; for complex tasks it may lead to reduced effort and performance (Karoly, 1993). The literature suggests three categories of evaluative feedback – normative feedback, velocity feedback, and labeled feedback – which differ with respect to how the feedback sign is established.

Normative feedback compares a trainee's performance to a social standard, in that it provides information about the trainee's relative standing with respect to a reference group. Those with whom the trainee's performance is compared may include other trainees, others who have performed the task before, etc. It has been suggested that social comparison information will best allow trainees to develop accurate perceptions of their own ability levels (Fahr & Dobbins, 1989). However, there are some reasons to exercise caution when using normative feedback. Kluger and DeNisi (1996) report that such normative feedback encourages trainees to pay attention to themselves and draws attention away from the task, which may result in performance decreases. Field

(1996) determined that normative feedback provided during early skill acquisition was beneficial for high ability trainees in improving performance, but for low ability trainees undermined self-efficacy and produced negative self-reactions.

Velocity feedback is self-referenced, in that the trainee's performance is compared only with her or his own prior performance on the task. The trainee is then able to gauge the rate of progress at which a performance goal is being reached. This feedback is termed "velocity" because it is analogous to the physical concept of change in distance over time (Carver & Scheier, 1990; Hsee & Abelson, 1991; Kluger & DeNisi, 1996). Such self-referenced feedback has not been frequently examined in research.

Labelled feedback is not referenced to self-performance or the performance of others, but is referenced to an unspecified standard and carries either a positive or a negative label. If a trainee's performance exceeds the standard, it carries a positive label. If a trainee's performance falls below the standard, it carries a negative label. Labelled feedback may be provided by a trainer, leader, test, or other delivery agent. This "labelled" property of evaluative feedback has been investigated in numerous studies and is associated with a variety of findings. Such findings may also apply to feedback which is not expressly labelled as positive or negative when presented to the trainee, but the trainee interprets the normative or velocity feedback to be positive or negative. The most basic of these findings is that positive feedback may help increase learning (Martocchio & Webster, 1992). However, such a broad statement should be viewed with some caution; other research indicates conditions under which this assertion may or may not hold true (Kluger & DeNisi, 1996).

Some authors indicate that trainees learning tasks with differing levels of complexity will respond differently to the positive or negative label of the feedback. Negative feedback will be motivating to trainees learning simple tasks, whereas positive feedback may lead to complacency or overconfidence. For trainees learning complex tasks, negative feedback will likely be demotivating, whereas positive feedback will benefit trainees (Karoly, 1993; Waldersee & Luthans, 1994). Thus, under difficult or complex task conditions, initially poor performance may be labelled as moderately negative. Trainees given such an interpretation will be more likely to maintain effort and less likely to abandon the goal than trainees given large negative discrepancies as feedback (Bandura & Cervone, 1983).

Self-efficacy may also have a moderating effect on how trainees respond to the feedback label. Following negative feedback, trainees with low self-efficacy may suffer further decreases in self-efficacy, and subsequently reduce effort and performance. Low self-efficacy trainees will maximize self-efficacy and task performance when provided with positive feedback (Karl et al., 1993; Kluge & Demisi, 1996). When a goal of training is to enhance self-efficacy, positive feedback should be provided (Karl et al., 1993; Latham & Locke, 1991; Martocchio & Webster, 1992).

When trainees are using behaviors, routines, and/or strategies that are ineffective, specific negative feedback will allow trainees to learn how to correct their performance (Garner, 1990; Wofford & Goodwin, 1990). However, trainees who are in a long term training program should not be given continual negative feedback, or they will be likely to decrease motivation and performance, and may abandon the goal (Waldersee & Luthans, 1994).

Attribution. This interpretation property involves the cause to which a trainee attributes descriptive feedback. Such attributional information may have substantial impacts on the subsequent training and performance of the trainee. The three dimensions of attributional causality presented here – locus, stability, and controllability – are consistent with the constructs proposed by Weiner (1985).

A trainee may view feedback resulting from an internally influenced cause, such as ability and/or effort, or an externally influenced cause, such as luck and/or task difficulty. A trainee may additionally view feedback as resulting from a stable cause, such as ability and/or task difficulty, or an unstable cause, such as effort and/or luck. It should be noted that these examples were somewhat arbitrarily chosen; some trainees may perceive ability to be a stable trait, while others perceive it as not stable, but malleable (see the Individual Differences section). Similarly, perceptions of task difficulty may or may not necessarily be stable; as one becomes proficient on a novel task it is perceived to be less difficult. Thus, providing trainees with negative feedback that suggests performance resulted either from external or unstable causes may help to preserve trainee self-efficacy and effort toward future performance attempts (Silver, Mitchell & Gist, 1995).

Finally, a trainee may view feedback as resulting from a controllable cause, such as effort, or a cause which is beyond her or his personal control, such as luck. Feedback which encourages trainees to attribute performance to controllable factors may lead to an increase in trainees' self-efficacy and effort (Martocchio & Dulebohn, 1994).

Guidance. Guidance is an interpretation property that involves giving a trainee direction regarding future actions that should be taken for improvement. Guidance can be thought of as a kind of proactive "feedforward" mechanism, as opposed to "feedback." Such guiding information may have substantial impacts on the subsequent training and performance of the trainee. For example, providing trainees with information about their current level of achievement and advisement about what they need to do to attain the goal will allow them to learn more efficiently and will help prevent premature goal termination (Tennyson, 1980, 1981).

The form of guidance can be behavioral, cognitive, or affective. Guidance can describe what behaviors a trainee should next engage in and what strategies might be employed in order to best achieve the learning or performance goal (e.g. Earley et al., 1990). Guidance can also describe what a trainee should think about and how to think about it in order to best achieve the goal. This type of guidance particularly makes use of metacognition to help trainees improve their learning strategy and/or performance. One example is the work on judgments of learning and feelings of knowing by Nelson, Dunlosky, Graf and Narens (1994). Another example is the work by Bell on adaptive guidance (Bell, 1999; Bell & Kozlowski, 1999). Finally, what emotions the trainees might next encounter and how to best handle that affect may also be provided by interpretive information (Bell, 1999). Emotional control skill training (e.g. Kanfer, 1996) which builds such skills can be useful.

While there is considerable coverage in the literature on topics that concern the informational properties of feedback provision, much less has been examined with respect to the interpretive nature of feedback. We propose that it is these interpretive properties which provide the best means of manipulating feedback during training in order to affect the self-regulation process. Interpretive feedback can convey information to trainees that evaluates how they are doing, suggests attributable causes, and guides their future actions. Selected ALS principles relevant to information provision are shown in Table 3.

Training Design
Training is generally conducted off-site, in a classroom, decontextualized from the performance environment. New technologies and increased connectivity enhance the potential for distance learning, web-based training, and simulation systems to integrate training in the work context and to embed instructional capabilities into work technology (Schreiber, 1998). Although the future holds great promise for the development of training that can be delivered – literally – "just-in-time" by an intelligent tutor or agent, much current emphasis for pushing training into the workplace is focused on the use of simulation. Simulations can often be run on the same systems in which trainees perform, or in low physical fidelity systems that nonetheless capture the essential psychological fidelity of the task (Kozlowski, 1998).

Table 3. ALS Design Principles: Information Provision (Feedback).

Citation	Principle
	Information Properties
Anderson (1987)	Feedback about errors should be provided immediately if the goal is to develop rapidly a strong procedural knowledge base; Feedback about errors should be withheld if the goal is to prompt learning of how to identify and handle errors.
Earley et al. (1990) Wofford and Goodwin (1990)	Feedback about strategies and practice behaviors should be specific, particularly when feedback is negative, to facilitate the acquisition, practice, and improvement of appropriate strategies and behaviors. Specificity will avoid ineffective strategy or behavioral changes.
Gist and Mitchell (1992)	Feedback should be provided frequently to facilitate the development of self-efficacy during training for a complex task.
Lindsley et al. (1995) Podsakoff and Farh (1989)	Feedback about training performance should be accurate and credible, regardless of the positive or negative sign of that feedback, to facilitate long-term development of self-efficacy and competency.
	Interpretation Properties
	Evaluation
Bandura and Cervone (1983)	Trainees should be encouraged to believe (whenever possible) that substantial negative performance discrepancies are moderate discrepancies, to maintain effort and avoid goal abandonment.
Field (1996)	Normative feedback should not be provided to low ability trainees during early stages of skill acquisition, to avoid decreasing self-efficacy and increasing negative self-reactions.
Karl et al. (1993)	Positive performance feedback should be provided to increase self-efficacy of trainees.
Karoly (1993) Waldersee and Luthans (1994)	Negative evaluation (or corrective) feedback should not be provided to trainees learning a complex task, to avoid reductions in effort and performance; Positive evaluation feedback should not be provided to trainees learning a simple task, to avoid decreases in effort and performance.
	Attribution
Martocchio and Dulebohn (1994)	Feedback should encourage trainees to attribute performance to controllable factors, to maintain self-efficacy and effort.
	Guidance
Tennyson (1981) Tennyson, Tennyson and Rothen (1980)	Guidance should be provided to trainees in learner control environments to prevent premature termination of effort directed toward learning.
Tennyson (1980) Tennyson and Buttrey (1980) Santiago and Okey (1992)	Guidance should be provided to trainees in learner control environments to appropriately sequence their effort and attention, and to facilitate the acquisition of critical knowledge and skills.

One of the major advantages in using simulations is that the characteristics of the simulation (i.e. task) can be tailored to the needs of the trainer and trainees. Although the task is often taken as given in training research, aspects of the task or information in the training materials have been found to have important psychological consequences for learning. Task characteristics such as sequencing, complexity, variability, workload, and built-in errors, used appropriately, can impact the depth or speed of knowledge acquisition. Many of these task, simulation, or instructional characteristics can be determined by the trainer and thus become an important part of the design to the intervention. Often the implications of relevant task characteristics are not considered, and they may interfere with the success of training interventions. However, when task characteristics are taken into consideration during the design of training, these characteristics can be a leverage point for maximizing the efficiency and effectiveness of integrated-embedded training. Research findings on task characteristics are reviewed below.

Sequencing. Sequencing refers to the order in which training material is presented. Research has indicated that sequence and pacing of training is critical to building long term retention of skills, and the improvement of stable knowledge structures (Kozlowski et al., 1995, 1996, in press; Schmidt & Bjork, 1992). For example, Reigeluth, Merrill, Wilson and Spiller (1980) suggest that to build stable knowledge structures, training material should be elaborated from simple to complex starting with a familiarizer or analogy, and the most important topic should be presented first. Furthermore, not only does the difficulty of the material affect the optimal sequencing, but in some cases the subject matter being trained should influence the sequence of training. For example, to train learning skills, primary learning strategies should be presented prior to supporting strategies (Dansereau, Brooks, Holley & Collins, 1983). Likewise, research suggests that strategy training should be reserved for later portions of training programs, since in early skill acquisition cognitive capacity is reserved for task accomplishment (Etelapelto, 1993). Thus, the difficulty and type of material being presented can have implications for determining the best sequencing of material.

Complexity. Like sequence, the complexity of material has implications for learning. Task complexity has been defined as the number, interrelationship, or dynamics of task components (Wood, 1986). Complex tasks can be difficult to learn, which may demotivate the trainee causing them to become distracted, lose self-efficacy, and even withdraw from the task. Fortunately, several authors have suggested ways to prevent such problems. Research suggests that trainees learning complex tasks should be encouraged to monitor their rate of progress rather than performance itself (Carver & Scheier, 1990). Monitoring progress reduces the potential to experience large discrepancies between one's current performance and the goal level. Monitoring progress focuses the trainee on improvement, thereby maintaining self-efficacy. As learning and performance progresses to a point where the trainee has some initial success and understanding of the task, goal setting can be used to maintain appropriate amounts of goal-performance discrepancy (Carver & Scheier,1990; Kanfer & Ackerman, 1989).

The complexity of the task also has implications for the use of feedback. Trainees should not be given negative feedback when performing poorly on complex tasks, as this may reduce effort and performance (Karoly, 1993). Instead, trainee self-efficacy should be fostered when learning complex tasks to increase motivation. Trainees should be encouraged to take a satisfaction perspective, meaning they should focus on their improvement or progress toward their goal to avoid low self-efficacy. Although maintaining efficacy is vital for complex tasks, on simple tasks self-efficacy alone cannot be relied upon as a motivator. Boredom or too much self-satisfaction can lead trainees to decrease effort on simple tasks. Therefore, trainees on simple tasks should be encouraged to take a dissatisfaction perspective, setting more challenging goals to provide a discrepancy between their performance and their goal which will maintain interest. Likewise, for simple tasks negative or corrective feedback can be used for those performing poorly to increase performance, whereas positive feedback can actually inhibit performance (Bandura & Cervone, 1986; Karoly, 1993; Salomon, 1984; Waldersee & Luthans, 1994).

In addition to the motivational implications, task complexity may impact the type of intervention that will be optimal for learning, particularly where goals are concerned. Difficult, specific goals may cause learning difficulty for trainees on tasks with many different strategies. Guidance in strategy selection should accompany goals in such tasks (Earley, Connolly & Ekegren, 1989). Presenting goals early in training may be useful for encouraging performance on low complexity tasks. For complex tasks, goals should be delayed until skill strategies have developed or proceduralization has begun (Earley, Lee & Hanson, 1989; Kanfer & Ackerman, 1989). Proximal subgoals which break the task into smaller parts should be used on cognitively complex tasks to increase initial self-efficacy and persistence (Kozlowski et al., 1995, 1996, in press; Stock & Cervone, 1990). Error training, which is discussed later in this section, may be increasingly beneficial as tasks become increasingly difficult (Frese, Brodbeck, Heinbokel, Mooser, Schleiffenbaum & Thiemann, 1991; Ivanicic & Hesketh, 1995).

Variability. Variability is the third type of task characteristic shown to have implications for learning. Variability is the degree to which the training task provides some variety in relevant characteristics of the training stimulus. Baldwin (1992) has demonstrated that providing variability in the training scenarios and model competency improved the generalizability of behaviors learned in training. Ohllson (1996) suggests that variability of the training situation is important because training should provide sufficient practice for trainees to learn the links between the goal, the situation, and the appropriate action. Finally, Schmidt and Bjork (1992) present evidence that stimulus variability may decrease short term performance, but is critical for long term retention and transfer.

Workload. Several authors have found the degree of cognitive workload related to learning and performance. Workload is the degree of attention or activity required to perform a task and may be related to learning. Workload is primarily a function of other decisions made about the task, such as the sequencing and complexity of the task. Early in skill acquisition complex, consistent tasks are resource limited, meaning increased attention and effort should yield increased performance. Later in skill acquisition, consistent tasks become data limited and increased devotion of attentional resources will not yield better performance (Norman & Bobrow, 1975; Kanfer & Ackerman, 1989). Therefore, maintaining a trainee's full attention and effort early on will be critical for learning, but later the trainee may be unable to increase performance simply by devoting more effort.

Trainees should be able to make at least some consistent progress during training. Extremely high workload, difficult or unsolvable problems can result in anxiety that undermines effort and attention (Mikulincer, 1989). Errors should only be encouraged if the learner has the attentional capacity to reflect on and learn from them (Ivancic & Hesketh, 1995).

Errors. Errors, while typically thought of as problematic in learning, can serve important functions for learners. Although we often think of errors as something to eliminate during training, research indicates that including errors in certain circumstances may aid in learning and retention. Many authors have examined when it is appropriate to include errors in training design (Frese & Altman, 1989; Frese et al., 1991; Ivancic & Hesketh, 1995; Lord & Levy, 1994; Nordstrom et al., 1995). If errors occur frequently in the transfer domain, trainees should be encouraged to make errors in training in order to learn error management strategies and develop their knowledge or mental model of the task system. This is particularly true for trainees with a tendency to make errors (Frese & Altman, 1989; Frese et al., 1991; Lord & Levy, 1994; Nordstrom et al., 1995). Some researchers suggest that trainees should not be restricted from making mistakes. Tasks that do not allow trainees to commit errors limit their ability to learn by exploring (Frese et al., 1991).

The type of skill being trained may determine whether explicitly "building in" errors is appropriate. Errors are especially important if the goal of training is to develop problem-solving, hypothesis testing, or other cognitive skills (Ivancic & Hesketh, 1995). When training procedural skills, training should not include errors in some instances (Ivancic & Hesketh, 1995), although some suggest that trial and error training may be appropriate (Prather, 1971).

Using errors to improve learning is not simply a matter of including them or not including them; how the training system uses the errors and incorporates them into instruction is critical to making them useful. Simple heuristics should be provided to the learner to counter the common notion that errors are a sign of weakness or stupidity, and trainees should be taught that errors can serve a positive role in learning (Frese & Altman, 1989; Frese et al., 1991). Encouraging errors is best done in the middle of training so as not to overwhelm trainees. In addition, easily interpretable feedback should be provided by the instructor or task if errors are used as part of training (Frese & Altman, 1989). Informative task environments are needed for error management training to allow the trainee to correctly diagnose the problem and make the error attribution necessary for learning (Ohllson, 1996). When using error training, feedback should be immediate and directed at specific behaviors (Anderson, 1987; Wofford & Goodwin, 1990). If the goal of training is to enable trainees to handle errors in transfer, then feedback regarding errors may be withheld to allow learners to identify errors, although this may sacrifice some speed of procedural knowledge development (Anderson, 1987).

Clearly, incorporating errors into training can have motivational consequences that can affect learning. Nordstrom et al. (1995) suggest that error management training and goals can be used to increase motivation and lower frustration associated with errors in the transfer environment. Individual differences in capability to handle negative feedback or learning orientation should be considered before employing error training, particularly early in training (Ivancic & Hesketh, 1995; Kuhl & Koch, 1984). Trainees may be encouraged to attribute errors to variable causes that can be overcome to maintain self-efficacy in the face of goal-performance discrepancies (Thomas & Mathieu, 1994).

Recent research has also suggested that not only can errors be added into training, but in some cases it is useful to give the trainee control over their own training processes to varying degrees (Tennyson, 1980; 1981). This has been referred to as providing learner control over training. However, Tennyson's work has indicated that the learner, given control, needs information to avoid over-estimating how well they have learned and to inform them about actions to take to maximize learning. Learners with control over time-on-task or sequence of instruction should be provided with information about their learning and predicted needs to avoid premature termination of the training. Given proper information, learners can decide when they have learned material and eliminate unnecessary learning trials. Thus, learners should be given control plus some advisement or feedback in order to make training efficient (Tennyson, 1980, 1981).

Rather than advisement, some research suggests that learners on a new task should either start with some prior knowledge of the training domain or begin with initially structured training before being given control. Learners with some prior conceptual knowledge about the task are in a better position to make decisions about their learning and may learn more efficiently given some control over the medium, pace, sequence, or practice in training. Learners lacking conceptual knowledge about the task should have their initial learning structured more than those with some prior learning (Gay, 1986). This reinforces the importance of training sequence, particularly when control is to be given to the trainee.

In summary, there are a variety of characteristics to be considered in training design when the focus is on leveraging learning effectiveness. It is an unfortunate fact, however, that training design, particularly simulation design, is more often directed by a desire to achieve realism, rather than a desire to enhance learning. Selected ALS principles relevant to training and simulation design are listed Table 4.

Trainee Orientation
Trainee orientation reflects the motivational goals that trainees adopt with regard to the training task, simulation, or practice. Research in both organizational and educational psychology has emphasized the distinction between mastery or *learning goals*, where trainees seek to improve their knowledge and skills, and *performance goals*, where trainees are concerned with demonstrating their competence (Ames & Archer, 1993; Archer, 1994; Farr, Hofmann & Ringenbach, 1993). Although conceptualized as an individual difference (Dweck, 1986), research has frequently treated this as a manipulable situational variable. Current evidence suggests that situational and dispositional influences are independent and additive (Archer, 1994; Kozlowski et al., 1995, 1996, in press). Individual differences in goal orientation were discussed earlier in this section of the chapter.

Table 4.   ALS Design Principles: Training and Simulation Design.

Citation	Principle
	Sequencing
Etelapelto (1993)	Trainees should not be provided strategy instruction until later in training, to facilitate basic skill development during early stages of training.
Reigeluth et al. (1980)	Training material should be elaborated so that instruction proceeds from general to detailed, and from simple to complex.
	Complexity
Carver and Scheier (1990)	Trainees learning a complex task should be encouraged to monitor their rate of progress (rather than just their performance), to reduce dissatisfaction, as complex tasks may produce large performance discrepancies.
Earley et al. (1990)	Trainees learning complex tasks should not be given goals until later in training, when the individual develops effective strategies; Trainees learning simple tasks should be provided with goals early in training.
Stock and Cervone (1990)	Trainees learning complex tasks should be provided with proximal subgoals that break the task into smaller parts, to increase self-efficacy and persistence.
	Workload and Variability
Mikulincer (1989)	Trainees presented with extremely difficult problems that appear unsolvable should be assisted in making some consistent progress during training to avoid anxiety and abandonment of effort.
Schmidt and Bjork (1992) Ellis (1965)	Variability in practice trials should be provided during training to maximize retention and transfer.
	Errors
Frese and Altmann (1989) Nordstrom et al. (April, 1995) Prather (1971)	For domains where errors are a frequent part of the transfer environment, trainees should be encouraged to make errors in training so they can learn to develop tolerance for errors, how to handle errors, and to experience lower frustration. Errorless training may lead to effective training performance but decrements in transfer performance.
Frese et al. (1991)	For difficult tasks, trainees should be encouraged to make errors in training to increase transfer.
Ivancic and Hesketh (1995)	Trainees should be encouraged to make errors in training in order to develop problem-solving or hypothesis-testing skills.

While learning and performance goals are not mutually exclusive (i.e. a trainee can be oriented to both mastery and performance; Button, Mathieu & Zajac, 1995), there are a number of training components that affect whether trainees focus on one goal more than the other. These situational factors can be divided into two categories: Instructional goals and general training frames. Instructional goals are the explicit directions provided to trainees. General training frames are cues or prompts given to trainees regarding the training, the task, or their ability that can be conveyed purposivefully (i.e. by explaining that the task is extremely difficult) or unintentionally (i.e. by implying that trainees do not have the ability to perform successfully).

Instructional goals. Goal orientation can be influenced by explicit instructions presented to trainees. Instructions suggest the behaviors and actions trainees should engage in during training, and in this sense identify the goals trainees should strive to achieve. Generally speaking, goals can either emphasize performance or learning.

Performance goals have been studied extensively over the last 20 years. Locke and Latham (1990) review years of research and literally hundreds of studies demonstrating the benefits of difficult and specific performance goals. Trainees given performance goals outperform trainees given no goals, "do your best" goals, or general goals. Research suggests this effect is strongest when trainees are committed to a goal that they have the ability to accomplish, and when the task is simple and provides clear feedback (Latham & Locke, 1991).

In the training context, two of these moderators present ubiquitous problems. First, training is often for complex, rather than simple tasks. Second, trainees generally do not begin training with the ability to accomplish performance goals or objectives on these complex tasks – that is, after all, the purpose of training. Research clearly indicates that the benefits of performance goals are attenuated on complex tasks, and that performance goals can even result in performance decrements (Cervone, Jiwani & Wood, 1991; DeShon & Alexander, 1996; Earley et al., 1989; Earley, Connolly & Lee, 1989; Huber, 1985; Wood, Bandura & Bailey, 1990). Further, performance decrements are even worse for individuals with low ability (Kanfer & Ackerman, 1989).

Some authors have used this research to conclude that goals should not be used early in skill acquisition (Kanfer & Ackerman, 1989; Kanfer, Ackerman, Murtha & Dugdale, 1994). Other authors have suggested modifications to performance goals that may improve their usefulness in training contexts. For example, Earley and colleagues have demonstrated that supplementing performance goals with strategy guidance can offset the difficulties created by goals on complex tasks (Earley et al., 1989).

While strategy training is one potential solution to the problems created by performance goals in training, the educational literature suggests learning problems will continue as long as trainees are oriented toward performance. Archer (1994) and Dweck (1986, 1989) suggest that performance goals, as compared to learning goals, lead to maladaptive learning patterns. In their research, students following performance goals tended to avoid challenging tasks, exhibit negative feelings following performance, and use surface strategies during task engagement (for a review see Dweck, 1986). Thus, students who follow performance goals learn less and exhibit greater dissatisfaction than trainees who pursue learning goals. This finding is supported by recent organizational research that suggests it is not goals per se that result in decreases in complex task performance, but the way in which performance goals frame the task (DeShon & Alexander, 1996; DeShon, Brown & Greenis, 1996). As a result, training research should consider alternative goals, such as learning goals, that can be employed in training complex tasks. For simple or well-learned tasks, however, research clearly indicates the usefulness of performance goals to increase motivation and subsequent performance.

Research suggests that trainees will learn more when given *learning goals* than when given performance goals. This effect occurs through a number of mechanisms. First, trainees pursuing learning goals make better use of learning strategies (Ames & Archer, 1993; Archer, 1994; Garner & Alexander, 1989; Nolen & Haladyna, 1990; Pintrich & DeGroot, 1990; Schraw et al., 1995). Second, attributions that encourage sustained effort following failure are stimulated (Ames & Archer, 1993; Archer, 1994; Elliot & Dweck, 1988). When negative feedback is received, effort is maintained by leading trainees to interpret their failures as caused by external but controllable factors, or to internal strategies that are controllable (e.g. Curtis, 1992). Either of these attributions help trainees maintain self-efficacy in spite of negative feedback. Supporting these research findings, Kozlowski and colleagues (1995, 1996, in press) demonstrate that learning goals enhance self-efficacy and metacognitive coherence during training, and improved retention and adaptability during transfer. The third benefit of learning goals is that positive attitudes toward learning are facilitated (Archer, 1994). These attitudes can facilitate later learning efforts as well as a positive attitude toward the task being trained. Finally, Duda & Nicholls (1992) add that learning goals can increase cooperation among trainees.

As noted earlier, performance goals and learning goals are not mutually exclusive, and consequently the effects of performance goals are not the opposite of the effects for learning goals. Rather, the difference between these goals is best captured by the outcome that they encourage trainees to pursue. Learning goals encourage the *development* of knowledge and skill, while performance goals encourage the *demonstration* of current levels of knowledge and skill. These differences affect the self-efficacy and attributions of trainees, which in turn influence the practice behaviors and self-monitoring activity employed by trainees.

The negative effects of performance goals seem to apply most during the earliest stages of skill acquisition, when trainees have not developed the knowledge and skill necessary to perform effectively. Ultimately, both goals are critical to success in organizations, but at different times. Early in skill acquisition, learning goals are critical for building skill and self-efficacy. When individuals have the requisite skill and self-efficacy, performance goals can be applied to maintain interest and motivation on task (Kanfer, 1996).

Research by Winters and Latham (1996) provides some support for this assertion. These authors demonstrated that on simple tasks performance goals were beneficial; but on complex tasks, learning goals resulted in better final performance. It is reasonable to suggest that, after the complex task was well learned, performance goals would maintain performance levels more than learning goals. A similar position is asserted in the educational literature where Wentzel (1991) suggests effective school performance requires individuals to pursue both types of goals. With regard to team development, leaders and trainers are advised to provide learning goals during early stages of skill acquisition, and move toward performance goals as skills become better learned (Kozlowski, Gully, McHugh, Salas & Cannon-Bowers, 1996).

General training frame. Learning and performance orientations can be induced by training instructions that do not focus explicitly on goals or objectives to be accomplished. Research indicates that general statements made by trainers can influence the orientation that trainees take toward the training task. For purposes of improving training outcomes, researchers have focused on eliciting learning orientations. A few of the dominant methods that have been used to create learning orientations can be organized into three categories: (1) framing training in terms of long-term outcomes and success, (2) encouraging trainees to be satisfied with training successes, and (3) persuading trainees that they have the ability to succeed.

First, framing training in terms of long-term outcomes and success can induce a learning orientation. Curtis (1992) suggests that training which emphasizes long-term benefits of training will increase motivation to learn the material and, ultimately, learning. Similarly, Meece (1994) suggests that training which emphasizes self-improvement and the usefulness of information provided in training will encourage the adoption of a learning orientation.

Second, a learning orientation can be induced by encouraging trainees to be satisfied with effective performance, discounting poor performance as due to strategy or task difficulty rather than ability. For example, Bandura (1991) reviews research that suggests self-satisfaction for performance success in complex tasks can serve to increase self-efficacy and increase future on-task effort.

Third, persuading trainees that they have the ability to perform effectively can induce a learning orientation. Meece (1994) emphasizes that trainers can push trainees to adopt learning orientations by instilling the belief that they can accomplish the goals of training. Miller, Behrens, Greene and Newman (1993) suggest that persistence, positive affect, and self-regulation can be encouraged by increasing trainee self-efficacy. Similarly, Martocchio (1994) demonstrates that training which emphasizes the malleability of ability can increase self-efficacy. In this experiment, increased self-efficacy led to greater learning.

In summary, the way trainees are oriented toward training can influence their self-regulatory processing. Sometimes by design, and often inadvertently, training systems and trainers create a press toward performance rather than an orientation toward learning. The literature indicates, however, that a mastery or learning orientation is more effective for enhancing skill acquisition for complex tasks. Selected ALS principles relevant to trainee orientation are shown in Table 5.

Self-Regulatory System

Overview

From a training perspective, the self-regulatory system can be conceptualized as possessing three components. These components – practice behaviors, self-monitoring, and self-evaluation/reactions – map onto those behavioral, cognitive, and affective aspects of performance that trainees regulate throughout the learning process. This conceptualization allows us to attend to all those domains in which trainee self-regulation might reasonably be expected to impact training outcomes.

While a trichotomization of self-regulation is useful, it must be kept in mind that the dimensions are not completely separable. "Doing," "thinking," and "feeling" all affect each other and we are not asserting that any one has primacy. All three are engaged concurrently, such that whenever a trainee has an experience which stimulates her to practice more, she will simultaneously

Table 5. ALS Design Principles: Trainee Orientation.

Citation	Principle
	Instructional Goals
Ames and Archer (1993)	Mastery or learning goals should be presented to increase metacognitive behavior such as self-monitoring and self-instruction.
Boyle and Klimoski (1996)	Mastery orientations should be fostered by creating successful early training experiences or by presenting mastery goals, in order to facilitate persistence, task interest, and task satisfaction.
Dweck and Leggett (1988)	Mastery orientations should be fostered during training to discourage internal attributions about failure and negative affect, to encourage greater focus of attentional resources, and to increase performance.
Nolen and Haladyna (1990)	Mastery orientations should be fostered by emphasizing learning and independent thinking and presenting mastery goals early in training.
Schunk (1994)	Performance goals should be presented under conditions of task engagement, on short-term or easy tasks, or for rapid task completion.
	General Training Frame
Bandura (1991)	Trainees should be encouraged to be self-satisfied with the attainment of subgoals as well as end-goals, to foster a mastery orientation and retain motivation throughout skill acquisition.
Curtis (1992)	Trainees should be encouraged to focus on long-term outcomes and success, to avoid task withdrawal due to initial difficulty and failure.
Meece (1994)	Trainees should be encouraged to believe they can accomplish a goal by emphasizing self-improvement, discovery of new information, and the usefulness of learning material, in order to facilitate the adoption of a mastery orientation.

become more cognizant of and reflective about her practice behaviors, and will likely experience some change in her efficacy as the result of task experience.

In its broadest sense, the self-regulatory system is likely greater than the sum of its parts. However, we must study the parts in order to make meaningful assertions about the learning-related consequences of self-regulatory activities, and ultimately how we can leverage different aspects of this activity to attain particular outcomes. With that in mind, we turn our attention to the three components of the self-regulatory system.

Although self-regulation has been recognized as crucial in the educational and instructional design literatures for years (e.g. Flavell, 1979), it is only recently that its applicability to the organizational training literature has been noted (e.g. Gist & Mitchell, 1992; Kanfer & Ackerman, 1989). For the purposes of training, self-regulation can be divided into three general domains: *practice*, the behaviors individuals engage in during training to improve their skills; *self-monitoring*, the focus of cognitive attention and effort, and the reflection on one's progress toward desired objectives as part of the skill-building process; and *self-evaluation/reactions*, which includes the affective, emotional, and motivational consequences self-regulation. The literature on each of these will be reviewed to clarify their relevance to instructional design, and the effects of each on critical training outcomes as well as the overlap of each with the other two components will be discussed.

Practice
Within the training context, one of the most obvious tools available to trainers is practice. Practice is central in simulation-based training, since having trainees practice the skills that are the target of training serves the purpose of making the skills more "real" to the trainees, rather than leaving them in the abstract, lecture-based domain. Practice also gives trainees the opportunity to learn the links among the goal, the situation, and the appropriate action, provided the task environment is informative (Ohllson, 1996). The benefits of practice are numerous, and a few findings from the literature bear particular note. Practice increases transfer performance (Goska & Ackerman, 1996) and allows the trainee to develop automaticity on consistent aspects of the task, which thereby frees up attentional resources (Lord & Levy, 1994). As a result, trainees can do more things and handle more difficult situations than they might have otherwise. Finally, depending on the type of practice encouraged, it can increase the retention of information from training (Hastie, 1984), can increase persistence (Forsterling, 1985), and can increase the positive affect of trainees (Carver & Scheier, 1990).

It should be clear that practice is important. The question then becomes, what specific recommendations with respect to practice and self-regulation can be identified from the literature? One area in which the literature makes recommendations with respect to trainees' practice behaviors is that involving hypothesis-testing and error-making. Frese and Altmann (1989), for example, put forth the notion that trainees should be encouraged to actively develop their own hypotheses and explore different problem solutions during training. Engaging in this type of hypothesis-testing activity during practice presumably engages the trainees more fully in the task domain, thereby making the lessons more salient.

Moreover, an orientation toward experimentation on the part of trainees is evident in the literature recommending the use of errors as practice tools. Errors are discussed at great length in other sections of this chapter, but some findings are of particular relevance to our discussion of practice. For instance, Lord and Levy (1994) put forth the counterintuitive notion that trainees should be encouraged to make errors during training, as these stimulate and enhance learning. Frese and Altmann (1989) echo this recommendation, and further specify that errors may be most effective as learning tools if they occur near the middle of the training process. In that way, the trainees are not overwhelmed with information, but still have a chance to practice error management strategies.

Ivancic and Hesketh (1995) add an important caveat to the literature on errors. Building errors into training, they claim, is only beneficial if the goal of training is the development of problem-solving or hypothesis-testing skill, in which case the errors facilitate transfer. In cases where procedural skills are being trained, the use of errors is less advisable as it can lead to learning of incorrect behaviors.

It may be surprising that most of the design principles relevant to practice behaviors relate to their impact on the self-monitoring/evaluation aspects of self-regulation. The importance of self-monitoring becomes clear when we realize the following: When trainees are encouraged to consider the activities they engage in during practice, and to use their time in practice to actively improve their skills, they undergo a process of active improvement during which their focus on the task is greatest (Smith et al., 1997). We will therefore discuss those principles relevant to self-monitoring first.

The work of Carver and Scheier (1982, 1990) points out the importance of the trainees' focus during practice sessions. If trainees focus on their own behavior while practicing and use their assessments of that behavior as guideposts to help them evaluate whether developmental goals are being met, they will become more generally efficient at self-regulation (Carver & Scheier, 1982; Karoly, 1993). Practice can be further enhanced by asking the trainee to make judgments of learning, which can help trainees determine which practice behaviors might be most beneficial (Nelson et al., 1994). Monitoring activity can be taken a step further during practice; trainees can be instructed, as part of their practice regimen, to visualize possible courses of action that represent positive behavior scenarios. This can lead to positive expectancies with respect to the task as well as increase positive affect (Carver & Scheier, 1990).

Turning our attention to the impacts of practice on the self-reactions domain (self-efficacy and attributions), Martocchio and Webster (1992) discuss an interesting issue in their work on cognitive playfulness among trainees. Trainees who approach their tasks with a cognitively "playful" attitude, under which they are willing to experiment with the task situation and "play" with it, tend to perform better on the training task than those who lack such an attitude. Practice behaviors can also be driven by the attributions trainees make during training. Hastie (1984) tells us that the processing and retention of critical information are increased if trainees make attributions about their own behavior while practicing. Along the same lines, Forsterling (1985) suggests that teaching proper attributional techniques, with respect to the causes of failure and success, can increase performance on and persistence with the trained task.

Finally, practice allows the trainee time to become familiar with the task domain, which can help them avoid potentially maladaptive efficacy-performance spirals. In such a situation, due to a lack of familiarity with the task, the trainee performs badly, his self-efficacy goes down and he becomes demotivated, and he subsequently performs even worse reifying the downward spiral (Lindsley et al., 1995). Selected ALS principles relevant to practice are illustrated in Table 6.

Practice is the behavioral element of the self-regulation system, yet as we have seen, it is difficult to separate operationally from affective self-regulation (practicing making appropriate attributions) and cognitive self-regulation (monitoring behavior and evaluating progress). When we tell individuals to practice doing either of these, we are asking them to engage in a behavior, so that the primary impact of such a manipulation will be behavioral. This serves to highlight the warning we gave earlier: Whenever a manipulation targets the self-regulation system, we must be certain that the primary impact will occur in the appropriate domain. It is very easy to imagine a training program designed to increase self-monitoring which simply increases the amount of practice and doesn't provide any new skills with respect to monitoring the self. How can we best train self-monitoring? This is an issue we take up in the next section.

Self-Monitoring
Self-monitoring is the cognitive component of the self-regulation system. It involves the allocation of attentional resources to a task (in this instance, to the training task) and to tracking discrepancies between current performance and goals, as well as the capacity to continually determine whether one's learning strategy is appropriate and, if not, how to change it. The literature on self-

Table 6. Design Principles: Self-Regulation System.

Citation	Principle
	Practice (Behavior)
Goska and Ackerman (1996)	Trainees should be given the opportunity to practice critical skills in order to increase transfer performance.
Ivancic and Hesketh (1995)	Trainees should not be encouraged to make errors when learning procedural skills, as it may impede the acquisition of correct behaviors.
Lindsley et al. (1995)	Trainees should be given time to become familiar with the task to avoid maladaptive downward efficacy-performance spirals in transfer.
Lord and Levy (1994)	Trainees should be provided as much practice as possible during training to develop automatic control processes and reduce attentional demands.
Nelson et al. (1994)	Trainees' idiosyncratic "judgments of learning" should be used to reallocate study and practice time to the most difficult trials or items, in order to make learning most efficient.
Ohllson (1996)	Trainees should be provided enough practice to learn the links between the goal, the situation, and the appropriate action.
	Self-Monitoring (Cognition)
Bandura (1991)	Trainees should be encouraged to closely self-monitor progress, to increase the likelihood of setting progressive goals for performance improvement.
Carver and Scheier (1982) Karoly (1993)	Trainees should be encouraged to monitor their own behavior and performance during training, to enhance the self-regulation process and increase progress toward the goal.
Flavell (1979)	Trainees should be provided instruction in cognitive monitoring skills, to learn and perform better in complex task environments.
Harris (1990)	Trainees should be encouraged to self-monitor their use of strategies during training, rather than be provided with strategies, to increase performance.
Kanfer and Ackerman (1989)	Trainees should not be encouraged to self-regulate during early skill-acquisition stages that involve the development of declarative knowledge, to avoid the diversion of attentional resources that would lead to decreases in performance.
Lord and Levy (1994)	Trainees should be encouraged to establish reference values for their tasks, to more easily maintain attention.
Schunk (1990)	Trainees should be encouraged to engage in self-observation during training, to better monitor their progress and increase motivation.

Table 6.   Continued.

Citation	Principle
	Self-Evaluation/Reactions (Affect)
	Self-Efficacy
Bandura (1991) Kanfer and Ackerman (1989)	Trainees should be provided self-efficacy enhancing training experiences to encourage their setting higher goals and maintaining more effective self-regulatory activities.
Carver and Scheier (1990)	Trainees should be encouraged to visualize possible courses of action as positive behavior scenarios, to enhance positive expectancies and affect.
Gist and Mitchell (1992)	Trainees should be provided with information that allows a complete understanding of the task's attributes, complexity, environment, and how all of these can be controlled, in order to enhance trainees' self-efficacy.
Schunk (1990)	Trainees should be provided with proximal goals during training, to enhance self-regulation and self-efficacy.
	Attributions
Bandura and Wood (1989) Bandura (1991) Martocchio and Dulebohn (1994)	Trainees should be encouraged to believe their environment and performance are controllable, to maintain effort and motivation, and to increase self-efficacy and performance.
Forsterling (1985) Thomas and Mathieu (1994)	Trainees should be encouraged to attribute causes of failure to unstable, external, and/or controllable causes to avoid reduction of self-esteem, self-efficacy, and/or motivation.
Quinones (1995)	Trainees should be discouraged from attributing negative feedback to ability factors, to enhance self-efficacy.
Schunk (1990)	Trainees should be encouraged to make internal attributions for training successes to enhance self-efficacy.

monitoring has burgeoned in recent years as the self-regulation system has come to be viewed as increasingly central to understanding learning, motivation, and performance. Self-monitoring is viewed as the central element of self-regulation (Karoly, 1993). Not surprisingly, the literature supports this position based on the finding that self-monitoring does, in fact, increase self-regulatory behaviors (Carver & Scheier, 1982). How can self-monitoring be leveraged to enhance learning and adaptability for complex tasks? We first examine the direct impacts of self-monitoring on training outcomes, and then consider its relationship with other self-regulation components, particularly self-evaluation.

Flavell (1979) asserted the notion that instruction in cognitive monitoring skills would help individuals not only to learn better – because of the increased attention they pay to their own cognition – but also to perform better in complex task environments. This basic idea has been expanded by more recent research. For example, Carver and Scheier (1990) note the importance of monitoring not only the behaviors individuals perform, but the progress they make toward their goals. It makes little sense, after all, to believe that individuals will learn better if they observe only static elements of their behavior, instead of paying attention to their own development and using that development to guide their future activities.

Such monitoring requires attentional resources, as many researchers have pointed out. Ivancic and Hesketh (1995) note that some forms of monitoring are only appropriate once individuals have sufficient attentional capacity to reflect on and learn from their experiences. This reiterates Kuhl and Koch's (1984) finding that self-monitoring activities should be discouraged early in training if learning and performance are to be maximized. Kanfer and Stevenson (1985) went a step further, pointing out that the extent to which self-monitoring interfered with future learning and performance might be dependent on the complexity of the task, with more complex tasks producing greater interference. Kanfer and Ackerman (1989) provide some evidence to support this notion, noting that early in training much of the critical development is in the form of building a declarative knowledge base; self-monitoring activities seem much more relevant and less intrusive after declarative knowledge has been developed.

All of these variables together – the timing of self-monitoring, the sequencing of the training, and the complexity of the material to be learned – determine the effectiveness of self-monitoring. Therefore, the process of teaching trainees to self-monitor should not be taken lightly. When trainees are instructed to do so, it is critical that the monitoring not only be appropriate for their stage of cognitive development with respect to training, but also that their self-monitoring activities be evaluated to ensure that they are monitoring the proper aspects of their behavior and reaching the proper conclusions (Goska & Ackerman, 1996). One area in which such concerns are especially salient centers around the goals of training.

In considering goals, several factors have potential influence on the occurrence and utility of self-monitoring. For instance, the adoption of a learning goal has been found to increase self-monitoring behaviors (Ames & Archer, 1988). This should come as no surprise, since the essence of the learning goal encourages the continual monitoring of the trainee's progress toward mastering the material.

Bandura (1991) provides some interesting material with respect to goals and self-monitoring. For instance, he points out that encouraging self-monitoring can lead trainees to set progressive goals for performance improvement. He also notes that goals which are set too high can lead to dysfunction in the self-regulation system. This is thought to occur because of the dissonance brought about by the act of setting goals that are based on monitoring of one's performance and then not successfully reaching those goals. This interaction between goals and self-monitoring keeps the impact of goals from being as clear-cut as might otherwise be the case, but the recommendations from the literature still make it possible to design training that uses both goals and self-monitoring to their fullest effect.

Other variables must be taken into account as well when considering the interaction of goals and monitoring. The ability of trainees to self-set goals may allow their attention to be more easily maintained (Lord & Levy, 1994), thereby increasing their capacity to self-monitor. Characteristics of the task may also influence the effectiveness and utility of self-monitoring. For maximally beneficial monitoring, proximal, difficult goals should be used (Schunk, 1990), with easy goals offered early in training and more challenging goals offered later in training (Bandura & Wood, 1989). As with issues of attentional resources, the use of goals and their impacts on the self-monitoring portion of the self-regulatory process are complex. The selected principles for self-monitoring included in Table 6 represent one way to approach these complex issues.

The development and use of strategies within the training context may represent the pinnacle of self-monitoring behaviors. Individuals who are capable of understanding the task to such a degree that they can develop task strategies, implement those strategies, evaluate their strategies, and finally alter their strategies to better fit the requirements of the task are undoubtedly those who will be able to best adapt the skills gained in training to the transfer environment. Not only does strategy use allow for more efficient implementation of procedural skills, it has also been shown to be a critical factor in maximizing on-task learning (Pintrich & DeGroot, 1990).

Not surprisingly, strategy development and use is intricately tied to training goals. The work of Earley and colleagues has made this relationship very clear. Earley, Wojnaroki and Prest (1987) found that providing specific goals increases the amount of planning activity (strategizing) that goes into the task, in order to improve performance. Expanding on this notion, Earley, Northcraft,

Lee and Lituchy (1990) found that the provision of challenging, specific goals promoted higher quality strategy use and performance when combined with specific feedback. Their most specific finding was that if the development and use of strategies are one of the goals of training, then specific goals and specific feedback provide the most direct and powerful way to improve strategies. However, Earley, Lee and Hanson (1990) found that if a task has highly complex components, it may be beneficial to withhold goals from trainees until after effective strategies have been developed. For integrated-embedded training, then, it may be most useful to allow individuals a chance to practice with novel task scenarios and develop some strategies prior to giving them the specific goals and specific feedback that will allow them to tailor their strategies to their most effective level.

The main issues with respect to self-monitoring seem to be (1) trainees' limited attentional resources, (2) characteristics of the goals and the goal situation the trainees are faced with, and (3) the extent to which trainees develop and use strategies. These are primarily cognitive issues, and as we already noted the relationship between cognitive and behavioral components of the self-regulatory system, we must now note the relationship between the cognitive and affective subsystems.

The relationship between self-monitoring and self-evaluation – the affective, emotional, motivational aspects of the self-regulatory system – is complex. Bandura (1991) found that self-monitoring activities were most effective when trainees had high self-efficacy for the task. Harris (1990), on the other hand, found that self-monitoring could be used to improve self-efficacy, and Miller et al. (1993) found that levels of self-monitoring can be raised by encouraging high self-efficacy among trainees. The fact that these subsystems interact in such a complicated manner has been noted as potentially problematic in the literature (e.g. Mitchell, Hopper, Daniels, George-Falvy & James, 1994). The tie between the cognitive and affective domains is further strengthened by Russell and McAuley (1986), whose work on attributions demonstrates a link between the way trainees think about their training experiences and the affective or evaluative reactions they have to them. More consideration of attributions, as well as other evaluative domains, is made in the next section of this chapter.

Self-Evaluation/Reaction
As was mentioned at the outset of this section, there should be no implied primacy among the three components of the self-regulation system. Self-efficacy and causal attributions – the two primary aspects of what we define as self-evaluation and self-reaction – are just as important to effective

self-regulation during training as are self-monitoring and practice, though each will be important at different points in the training process and may be targeted by different types of training interventions. In fact, Mitchell et al. (1994) point out that the importance of self-efficacy itself will vary across times within training, being most important at the early stages of training and less so as training progresses.

The literature makes it clear that self-efficacy and attributions are important to self-regulatory processes. We first review the evidence for the importance of self-efficacy and attributions to the self-regulation system, then discuss how to raise self-efficacy, and conclude with a discussion of how to encourage attributions that sustain efficacy and persistence in the training environment. Selected principles relevant to self-evaluation are shown in Table 6.

The case for the importance of self-efficacy is made most succinctly by Kanfer and Ackerman (1989), who note that the presence of task-relevant self-efficacy is absolutely essential if self-regulatory activities are to be engaged or maintained. Miller et al. (1993) echo this finding, reporting that self-regulation can be increased by encouraging high self-efficacy among trainees. While the Miller and colleagues study focuses primarily on post-training self-regulation, it is reasonable to expect manipulations designed to increase self-efficacy during training would have the same impact on self-regulation during training that the authors reported post-training. In fact (and as was mentioned earlier), Bandura (1991) offers a replication of the finding that increasing self-efficacy increases self-regulation.

The importance of attributions to self-regulation is similarly established. Martocchio and Dulebohn (1994) report that attributions about past experiences can have an impact on trainee expectations for success and failures, which could reasonably be expected to impact the quality and quantity of self-regulation they engage in relevant to training. As such, the authors suggest that attributional retraining may be needed, presumably to prevent inappropriate self-regulations from taking place. Hastie (1984) also points out that the likelihood trainees will process and retain information from training will depend in part on the attributions they make relevant to their training experiences.

Raising self-efficacy. With the importance of efficacy and attributions to the self-regulation system thus established, we now turn our attention to the question of how to raise trainee self-efficacy. Bandura and Wood (1989) offer two methods by which self-efficacy may be raised. The first, providing trainees with easy goals, has the benefit of not requiring a great deal of attentional resources, thereby allowing trainees to spend their time developing effective strategies. More useful, perhaps, is teaching trainees that they have control over their performance in training, since success in an environment where they perceive themselves in control will obviously increase their sense of self-efficacy.

Schunk (1990) recommends using different aspects of the training environment to influence self-efficacy. Goals should be proximal in order for self-efficacy to be built with respect to the task, as distal goals make it too difficult for the trainee to see the relationship between his or her behavior and the ultimate outcome. Stock and Cervone (1990) agree that goals should be proximal, but recommend breaking goals down into proximal subgoals to better enable their completion.

In addition, Schunk (1990) argues that goals should be specific, to allow the trainees to have a solid referent when they make later efficacy judgments. The question "Did I do what I was supposed to?" is much easier to answer if the goal is specific than when the goal is nebulous. Winters and Latham (1996) support this finding, noting that specific goals increase the use of task strategies in addition to raising self-efficacy. Finally, as was discussed earlier in the section on Information Provision, Schunk (1990) puts forth the notion that feedback should be provided if self-efficacy is to be built, since without some feedback about performance it is impossible for the trainee to make judgments regarding his or her capability to perform the trained task. Karoly (1993) notes that feedback has the added benefit for participants already high in self-efficacy of increasing the effort they are willing to expend on the training task.

Gist and Mitchell (1992) note several ways to enhance self-efficacy that differ from the somewhat micro-level concerns voiced above. First, they argue that trainees need as much information as they can get about the task to ensure maximum efficacy. The more information that is available to trainees, the better they will be able to gauge their progress on the task. Second, Gist and Mitchell argue that if self-efficacy for the task is a critical outcome of training, the training should be designed with care to tap all the requisite knowledge, skills, and abilities for the task; if any are left out, trainees will note the deficiencies and blame themselves when such blame may not be wholly appropriate. A final concern Gist and Mitchell voice is that trainees who are supposed to build self-efficacy on the task be given information in training that improves their understanding of the behavioral, analytical, or psychological performance strategies for the task. Here again, we see the link among the components of the self-regulation system.

A final set of recommendations for raising self-efficacy deals directly with the affective experience of training for the trainees. Carver and Scheier (1990) recommend that trainees be taught to engage in "positive visualizations" about the task, in order to increase their self-efficacy. Efficacy is built in this manner by setting up positive expectancies and general positive affect with respect to the task. Quiñones (1995) makes a similar recommendation, noting that it is possible to boost trainee self-efficacy by framing training as "advanced" – that is, training designed to further existing skills. It should be clear that trainees who leave training believing they have gained "advanced" skills will report higher self-efficacy than will those who believe they have gained only basic competencies with the task.

Encouraging attributions. Encouraging appropriate attributions is also important with respect to the affective aspects of the self-regulatory system, since the attributions trainees make about the causes of their performance can impact what they attend to, what they practice, and how motivated they are for future training and transfer sessions. The principles relevant to attributions are fairly simple, but their importance cannot be overemphasized.

Forsterling (1985) recommends that in order to maintain motivation, trainees should be taught to attribute causes of failure to unstable, external, or controllable causes. A fine line must be drawn here, as too many external attributions may lead the trainee to a condition of learned helplessness in which he or she does not believe anything can be done to prevent failure. One way to deal with this issue is broached by Ivancic and Hesketh (1995), who recommend attributing the causes of failure to unstable situational influences. Because situational influences vary significantly, learned helplessness is an unlikely response unless the same failure conditions are found across a variety of situations. The reader will note that these issues are important in light of the literature on error-based training which was reviewed earlier.

A final way to deal with failure attributions is put forth by Thomas and Mathieu (1994), who note that the external causes of failure should not only be treated as variable, but also as things that the trainee can overcome. In this way, changes in self-efficacy as a result of failure will be minimized, as the trainee is being told, "You didn't succeed because of something out of your control – but with further training, you can handle situations like this just fine."

Leveraging Self-Regulation Through Training

Our model conceptualizes a Training Strategy as an intervention that is created through the combination of training components (Training Design, Information Provision, and Trainee Orientation; see Fig. 1). By combining different aspects of these components, the training system and trainer can influence different aspects of the self-regulatory system.

Initially, several linkages should be obvious. Training and simulation design characteristics, for example, should most strongly affect practice behaviors, since the design of the task will directly influence what behaviors are required by the task. Similarly, the information provided to trainees should have its most direct impact on the self-monitoring (cognitive) portion of the self-regulatory system, and the trainee orientation (motivation) variables should be most directly relevant to efficacy and attributions, the evaluative and affective portion of the self-regulatory system.

What is less apparent is what we have tried to make explicit throughout this section. Impacts of a training component on any given part of the self-regulatory system will never be solely on a single aspect of self-regulation. Training design elements (such as the sequencing of the material presented) will direct what behaviors the trainee practices, but will also affect what cognitive processes he or she monitors (by directing attention) and should also be expected to affect self-efficacy (by providing direction in skill building which the trainee can use to gauge his progress). However, the self-regulatory activities that are not directly in line with the training component are going to be less focal to the trainee, and will not constitute a substantial portion of his or her self-regulatory activities. We can therefore use the training components as levers to engage the self-regulatory process, in that they have the potential to guide which type of self-regulatory activity becomes the trainees' primary focus. Combinations of training components, then, can be designed such that multiple aspects of the self-regulatory system are called into play, which has the potential to create more active, aware, and reflective learners.

A caveat must be noted, however, with respect to combinations of training components. The complementarity of the components must be ensured, or problems in the self-regulatory system may result. By complementarity, we simply mean that the training components must be consistent with one another, and not lead to conflicting or contradictory types of self-regulatory processes within the three domains of self-regulation.

Training Outcomes

Traditional methods of designing training systems use a behaviorist approach that emphasizes correct performance. In fact, training programs often place too much emphasis on achieving performance-related goals (Farr et al., 1993). This focus on producing observable improvements in behavior has led to a narrow conceptualization of learning and training outcomes (Ford & Kraiger, 1995). We take an explicitly multi-dimensional perspective (Kraiger, Ford & Salas, 1993), identifying differences between learning and performance-oriented training outcomes which are proximal to completing training, and between these proximal outcomes and more distal transfer outcomes such as retention and adaptation.

Proximal outcomes. Proximal training outcomes are learning outcomes that arise directly from training and are exhibited immediately at its completion. These outcomes can be broadly divided into two categories: (1) Learning, and (2) Performance. The differences between these two reflect a basic distinction between more abstract cognitive indicators of learning and behavioral manifestations of that learning.

Learning outcomes include the cognitive outcomes of declarative knowledge, procedural knowledge, strategic knowledge, and knowledge structure suggested by Ford and Kraiger (1995) and Kraiger et al. (1993). Ford and Kraiger (1995) conceptualize learning outcomes as beginning with basic factual or declarative knowledge (what), which is then organized and compiled into procedural knowledge (how), and then with greater experience becomes strategic knowledge (which, when, and why). *Declarative knowledge* represents comprehension of basic task features and concepts, and is a prerequisite for skilled performance. *Procedural knowledge* is the knowledge of how to perform critical tasks. While procedural knowledge is often considered to be directly reflected in successful performance outcomes, there are abstracted measures available which assess whether key portions of a skill have been successfully learned (e.g. Royer, Carlo, Dufresne & Mestre, 1996). These abstract manifestations of skill should be distinguished from actual performance, which is measured and defined by the nature of the task rather than by the component skills to be learned. *Strategic knowledge* represents the knowledge necessary for situational assessment, prioritization, and trade-offs. Finally, *knowledge structure* reflects trainees' awareness of the links among important task features and outcomes. Knowledge structure has been associated with expert-novice differences, with experts possessing more stable and coherent structures (e.g. Schvaneveldt, 1990). Knowledge structure has been treated as a form of mental model representation.

Performance is the ability to successfully complete the behavioral requirements outlined by training objectives. We have found it useful to distinguish between basic performance and strategic performance. *Basic performance* captures the information processing and decision making aspects of the task domain. These aspects of performance are essential foundation elements of successful performance, but they are also superficial and routine aspects of the task domain. *Strategic performance* involves the more complex behavioral routines that underlie adaptability to the dynamics of DDM task environments.

Thus, strategic performance is a broader construct that encompasses situational awareness, prioritization of actions, and the implementation of task strategies.

Distal outcomes. Each of the outcomes explained above is expected to affect a trainee's ability to use trained skills on tasks that occur following training. Transfer from training settings back to work settings is characterized by the dimensions of maintenance and generalization (Baldwin & Ford, 1988). *Retention* refers to the maintenance of learning outcomes over time, and is a prerequisite to transfer. For the purposes of integrated-embedded training that occurs in settings that are similar if not identical to the performance settings, generalizability refers to the *adaptability* of skills to new configurations of environmental stimuli rather than to new settings (Kozlowski, 1998; Kozlowski, Gully, Nason & Smith, 1999).

We conceptualize adaptability as the generalization of trained knowledge and skills to new, more difficult, and more complex task situations.

RESEARCH IMPLICATIONS AND DIRECTIONS

Our conceptual model provides multiple avenues for training research that has the goal of developing adaptive capabilities. Based on our literature review and on our research on complex skill acquisition, we can identify Training Design and Trainee Orientation components that we believe exhibit high promise and should be included in the construction of interventions. For Training Design, theory and research are clear that the complexity of knowledge and skills to which trainees are exposed should be sequenced, and that training experiences should vary in complexity. Thus, sequencing and variability of complexity (Wood, 1986) are key Training Design components in our research. For Trainee Orientation, performance and mastery training frames, in combination with training goals, have been shown to have differential effects on the practice, self-monitoring, and self-evaluation/reactions aspects of the SRS. Thus, training goals are examined as an integral aspect of our training strategy. Our research indicates that interventions representing the combination of these Training Components enhances the quality of practice, self-monitoring, and self-evaluation/reaction (Bell, Mullins, Toney & Kozlowski, 1999; Brown & Kozlowski, 1997; Brown, Mullins, Weissbein, Toney & Kozlowski, 1997; Kozlowski et al., 1995; 1996, in press; Mullins, Brown, Toney, Weissbein & Kozlowski, 1998; Mullins, Kozlowski, Toney, Brown, Weissbein & Bell, 1999).

As noted at the onset, we believe that the interpretation properties of feedback provide the most promising new direction for training research.

Indeed, improving our scientific knowledge of how to best employ the information provision aspects of advanced technology systems is critical to integrated-embedded training design. Thus, this Training Component comprises the primary focus of new research. A brief overview of the directions for new research is provided below.

Sequenced descriptive feedback and goal-feedback consistency. Principles of training design generally assume that descriptive feedback should be specific, accurate, frequent, consistent, and process oriented. The next generation of advanced systems will be able to deliver descriptive feedback with these properties in prodigious amounts. The questions are: what information, how much of it, and in what sequence? For example, too much descriptive feedback may limit attentional resources needed for learning, diverting it to less important aspects of performance (Schmidt & Bjork, 1992), and may overwhelm the trainee with a mass of raw information. In contrast, more limited descriptive feedback that is sequenced to match current levels of skill development may better focus trainee attention on more proximal and attainable learning goals, thereby enhancing self-regulation that leads to skill acquisition (Stock & Cervone, 1992). Which is the better way to manage the provision of descriptive feedback? Furthermore, feedback is likely to be most useful when coupled with appropriate instructional objectives. Thus, this effect is likely to be enhanced when sequenced feedback is consistent with mastery versus performance instructional goals; that is, goals that emphasize learning objectives versus goals that emphasize achieving specific performance levels.

> *Proposition 1a:* Sequenced mastery feedback will enhance learning, performance, and adaptability when coupled with mastery goals. The effects of coupling mastery feedback with performance goals are unclear. Sequenced mastery feedback may shift attention away from performance goals toward mastery goals, enhancing learning, or they may interfere with learning, thereby adversely affecting training performance and transfer.

> *Proposition 1b:* Sequenced performance feedback will boost training performance when coupled with performance goals. Such feedback is generally expected to be less effective for trainees given mastery goals, although prior research indicates that mastery goals coupled with performance feedback is an effective training strategy.

Evaluative feedback. Positive evaluative feedback tends to build self-efficacy (Karl et al., 1993), which leads to the setting of higher goals and increased trainee self-regulation (Bandura, 1991), as well as to motivation toward performance improvement (Bandura & Cervone, 1983). Negative evaluative feedback, tends to undermine self-efficacy (Karl et al., 1993), thereby leading to reduced effort and performance (Karoly, 1993). These effects have prompted some to suggest that training should always provide positive evaluative feedback to prevent negative outcomes. However, the effects may be more complex. Too much positive feedback can raise self-efficacy so much that it may actually hinder learning. That is, when self-efficacy is "artificially boosted" by positive feedback trainees may conclude that they have mastered the material and may reduce attention and effort before they have actually done so. Thus, feedback that is consistently positive may cause trainees to miscalibrate their mastery of the task domain and reduce their self-regulation prematurely.

Our model suggests that moderate negative discrepancies are most effective for prompting self-regulation and motivation once trainees have acquired basic task knowledge. Thus, we propose that positive feedback will be most useful very early in skill acquisition when trainees have yet to master basic task information. By providing positive feedback early when the trainee makes many simple errors, efficacy is boosted and motivation is maintained. As trainees master basic aspects of the task domain, the greater effort needed to learn more complex aspects of the task can be enhanced by moderately negative feedback. At this point, their self-efficacy will provide resilience to the potentially detrimental effects of negative feedback, while the discrepancy between the training goal and current proficiency will prompt attention and effort. This suggests that evaluative feedback should be sequenced from moderately positive to moderately negative across the skill acquisition process (Toney & Kozlowski, 1999).

Proposition 2: Positive evaluative feedback during early skill acquisition that transitions to moderately negative feedback in later acquisition will promote better self-regulation, learning, and performance than feedback that is consistently positive or negative.

Attribution. Research indicates that trainee attributions of causality can have impacts on their affective states, future expectations, and the behaviors they engage in during training (Forsterling, 1985; Curtis, 1992). In general, when good performance is attributed to oneself, motivation, learning, and performance improve over time. When bad performance is attributed to oneself, the effects are negative. Indeed, in order to protect the self, bad performance is more often attributed to external, stable, and uncontrollable factors, justifying withdrawal from the task. Attributional interpretations occur naturally. Because complex tasks engender many trainee errors, particularly early in skill acquisition, uncontrolled attributional processes have the potential to under-mine self-regulation, learning, and performance.

From a ALS training perspective, trainees whose causal attributions that are internal, malleable, and controllable, will exhibit better learning and perform-ance than trainees whose causal attributions are external, stable, and uncontrollable. Moreover, attributions interact with evaluative feedback. Internal attributions accompanied by positive feedback will result in better learning and performance than internal attributions associated with negative feedback. Finally, trainees will tend to make many more errors early in training, and relatively fewer after they have acquired basic skills. Thus, external attributions (e.g. task difficulty) early in training when feedback is mostly negative can protect the self, whereas internal attributions later in training (e.g. ability, effort, task strategies) can enhance the motivation to improve performance.

Proposition 3: Early in skill acquisition, attributional feedback should be external, stable, and uncontrollable (e.g. task difficulty). As basic skills are acquired, attributional feedback should shift to internal, malleable, and controllable in order to promote learning and performance.

Guidance. Feedback is informative about past behavior, but is not diagnostic about what the trainee should do, think, or feel next. Indeed, it is a major challenge for trainees is to figure out what sort of practice behavior, metacognition, and emotional control is most appropriate for improvement. Intelligent tutors and other adaptive algorithms that attempt to monitor trainee development and guide the next steps in the learning process have demonstrated potential to enhance learning for *static* knowledge domains. For example, when left on their own to interpret how much more practice was needed to memorize information, trainees tended to terminate practice prematurely (Tennyson, 1980, 1981). On the other hand, the literature also suggests that many "adaptive algorithms" are relatively simplistic. The programs merely exhort the trainee to practice more, relative to trainees who have control over their practice time. The trainees who practice more, do learn more, but do so inefficiently (Tennyson, 1980, 1981). Moreover, there is little theoretical or practical gain from the finding that more practice yields better learning.

Embedded adaptive guidance orients the trainee toward what to *think* about next (self-monitoring of attention during study and practice), and what to *do* next (behavioral practice). This intervention combines the cognitive and behavioral aspects of guidance, as it is virtually impossible to influence one without also influencing the other. As the trainee masters basic knowledge and skills, the guidance adapts to their level of acquisition and instructs them to focus attention and effort on increasingly advanced knowledge and skills in the task domain. Embedded adaptive guidance is intended to influence the focus of trainee attention and relevance of practice behavior. Thus, this form of guidance is not intended to get the trainee to practice *more*, rather it is intended to get the trainee to practice *better* (Bell & Kozlowski, 2000).

Our model also suggests that affective guidance may complement the instructional effects of cognitive/behavioral guidance. One of the primary challenges of training design for complex tasks is that trainees often perform poorly during the initial stages of skill acquisition. Performance that fails to meet the trainee's – often unrealistic – expectations undermines self-evaluations, and can ultimately lead to significant reductions in motivation to learn (Bandura, 1991; Kanfer & Ackerman, 1989). Affective guidance is expected to help trainees to maintain emotional control and to bolster self-evaluations in the face of early task difficulties. It is not an instructional intervention per se, but rather a support that is intended to work in concert with cognitive/behavioral guidance.

Proposition 4: Behavioral/cognitive guidance will lead to a more relevant sequencing of individuals' effort and attention (practice and self-monitoring), improve the acquisition of strategic knowledge and performance, and enhance adaptability. Affective guidance will lead to more overall effort and a less withdrawal.

DISCUSSION

Pushing Training Systems into the Workplace
We began this chapter by noting the convergence of forces – environmental, technological, and economic – that are creating both pressures and opportunities to rethink the logic of training system design. Training needs to be able to accomplish more learning, more quickly, more often, more flexibly, and more effectively. The nature of training is changing from a single episode, off-site, inflexible, decontexualized, time and resource intense activity to a multi-episode, flexible, contextualized, time and resource efficient system. It is changing from a focus on learning basic skills and reproducing skills in the workplace to a focus on learning basic, strategic, and adaptive skills that generalize beyond training (Kozlowski, 1998). The key to this shift in the nature of training is the enhanced capability to build training into the workplace; to *integrate* it into the work context and *embed* it in work technology. This capability is predicated on advanced computer technologies and connectivity.

Our purpose is to promote this revolution in training through the development of a theoretically based and practically relevant model that can guide the application of these technologically based training capabilities. The simple fact of the matter is that we have many potentially useful instructional tools available, and relatively few well-developed instructional models to guide their combination and application in this training revolution. The purpose of our model is to fill that gap.

Theoretical Contributions

There are two primary theoretical contributions of our approach: (1) The provision of a common theoretical mechanism to integrate the effects of a wide range of instructional tools and techniques; and (2) The provision of a comprehensive conceptual framework to guide the design of training research, application, and evaluation.

Theoretical mechanism. We use a single theoretical mechanism to integrate the effects of a broad range of potential instructional tools and techniques. By providing a common theoretical mechanism for their effects, our model can address the likely effects that accrue from the combination of several constructs or tools. This is particularly important from an applied perspective as well, because training interventions are rarely singular constructs. Training interventions are molar combinations of multiple constructs or tools. Our model provides a conceptual foundation to guide that combination.

The training design literature has traditionally been technique oriented. Many observers have noted this tendency toward faddism; training design has often focused excessive attention on the tools and media that deliver training (e.g. Campbell, 1971; Goldstein, 1980). The remarkable capabilities and features inherent in advanced systems have the potential to fall into the faddism trap. Features like intelligent tutors that can step in to assist the novice in basic comprehension, or intelligent agents that can guide more experienced decision makers to consider all options, or web-based training systems that can be accessed anytime, anyplace, and for anything, are fabulous *tools* – but they are merely tools with instructional potential. The key is to know how those tools can be systematically combined and applied to accomplish instructional objectives.

The creation of these tools and techniques is linked to the capabilities of technology. The tools in and of themselves do not have common theoretical underpinnings that can guide their application. That is where the model we have developed makes its contribution. It provides a classification for different kinds of training tools and techniques, which can then be located as training design, information provision, or trainee orientation components. More importantly, the model provides a *common theoretical process* for under-standing the likely impact of the techniques. Variants of the self-regulation model have proven remarkably useful for guiding research on the basic processes of learning, motivation, and performance. By linking the component categories to critical aspects of the SRS – practice behavior, self-monitoring, and self-evaluation/reaction – we provide a common theoretical mechanism for understanding the likely effects of specific instructional constructs or tools, and the expected effects of combining the tools or constructs into more molar interventions. This is a substantial conceptual advance over the single tool approach that typifies research on training design.

Guiding research, application, and evaluation. The model provides a compre-hensive conceptual framework for capturing factors relevant to integrated-embedded training design at the individual level of analysis. That is, the model encompasses the domains of individual differences, training components and strategy, self-regulation, proximal outcomes of learning and performance, and distal outcomes of retention and transfer. Thus, it provides a foundation for understanding the interaction of individual differences with training strategies. This can help guide the development of training strategies that adapt to the abilities and dispositions of the trainee. It provides a foundation for constructing multidimensional training outcomes that are relevant to enhancing the important outcomes of long-term retention and adaptive capabilities. It can guide research, application, and evaluation.

Although our model is intended to be comprehensive, it is focused primarily at the individual level of analysis; self-regulation and the means to influence it are formulated around individual level psychological processes. Additional issues will need to be incorporated into our theoretical framework as we shift attention to the team level, and the unique challenges that accrue when we consider emergent and collective phenomena (Kozlowski & Klein, 2000). For example, teams create a context for individual learning and performance, and must be explicitly considered in the design of training systems (Kozlowski & Salas, 1997). Moreover, teams are not necessarily uniform and additive collectives that can be treated as simple aggregates of individuals. Indeed, some theorists assert that teams progress through a developmental process that proceeds across levels – from individuals, to dyads, to the team network – as well as time (Kozlowski et al., 1999). Although we have not explicitly incorporated team level considerations in the current model, other theoretical work provides a basis for extending key aspects of our conceptualization to the team level (Kozlowski, Gully, McHugh, Salas & Cannon-Bowers, 1996; Kozlowski, Gully, Salas & Cannon-Bowers, 1996; Kozlowski et al., 1999).

Moreover, theory and research to extend key aspects of the model to the team level are currently underway (DeShon, Milner, Kozlowski, Toney, Schmidt, Wiechmann & Davis, 1999; Kozlowski & DeShon, 1997).

Summary and Conclusion

The ALS is a theoretically driven approach to the design of integrated-embedded training systems that is highly flexible and offers ease of implementation. It operates by exerting leverage on foci of the self-regulation system, which recent research has demonstrated to be central to learning and performance for difficult, complex, and dynamic tasks. The training strategy incorporated in the ALS constructs instructional interventions by combining specific training components that affect different aspects of the SRS. By designing synergistic combinations, instructional interventions can be tailored to the developmental progress of trainees and can enhance learning, performance, and adaptability.

Our research will target those training components that offer the greatest practical and theoretical potential for improving complex skill acquisition, and the enhancement of adaptive capabilities. By building on existing principles of training design (e.g. mastery goals, sequencing), and examining promising new ideas (e.g. information, interpretation) that are likely to be key capabilities of the next generation of advanced technology systems, the research is expected to yield new principles of training design uniquely suited for the design of integrated-embedded training systems.

ACKNOWLEDGMENTS

This research was supported by the Naval Air Warfare Center Training Systems Division (N61339-96-K-0005), S. W. J. Kozlowski, Principal Investigator. We offer special thanks for the advice, support, and assistance provided by Katrina E. Ricci and Janis A. Cannon-Bowers. The views, opinions, and findings expressed in this report are those of the authors and do not necessarily reflect the views of any organization.

REFERENCES

Ackerman P. L. (1992). Predicting individual differences in complex skill acquisition: Dynamics of ability determinants. *Journal of Applied Psychology*, 77, 589–614.

Ames, C., & Archer, J. (1988). Achievement goals in the classroom: Students' learning strategies and motivational processes. *Journal of Educational Psychology*, 80, 260–267.

Anderson, J. R. (1987). Skill acquisition: Compilation of weak-method problem solutions. *Psychological Review*, 94, 129–210.

Archer, J. (1994). Achievement goals as a measure of motivation in university students. *Contemporary Educational Psychology, 19*, 430–446.

Baldwin, T. T. (1992). Effects of alternative modeling strategies on outcomes of interpersonal-skills training. *Journal of Applied Psychology, 77*, 147–154.

Baldwin, T. T., & Ford, J. K. (1988). Transfer of training: A review and directions for future research. *Personnel Psychology, 41*, 63–105.

Bandura, A. (1991). Social cognitive theory of self-regulation. *Organizational Behavior and Human Decision Processes, 50*, 248–287.

Bandura, A., & Cervone, D. (1983). Self-evaluative and self-efficacy mechanisms governing the motivational effects of goal systems. *Journal of Personality and Social Psychology, 45*, 1017–1028.

Bandura, A., & Cervone, D. (1986). Differential engagement of self-reactive influences in cognitive motivation. *Organizational Behavior and Human Decision Processes, 38*, 92–113.

Bandura, A., & Wood, R. (1989). Effects of perceived controllability and performance standards on self-regulation of complex decision making. *Journal of Personality and Social Psychology, 56*, 805–814.

Bell, B. S. (1999). *The effects of guidance on learning and training performance in a complex training simulation*. East Lansing, MI: Michigan State University, Masters Thesis.

Bell, B. S., & Kozlowski, S. W. J. (2000, April). Guiding individuals through training: The effects of behavioral and cognitive guidance in a complex training environment. In: S. W. J. Kozlowski (Chair), *Developing Complex Adaptive Skills: Individual- and Team-Level Training Strategies*. Symposium presented at the 15th Annual Conference of the Society for Industrial and Organizational Psychology, New Orleans, LA.

Bell, B. S., & Kozlowski, S. W. J. (in press). *Virtual teams: Implications for leadership. Groups and Organization Management*.

Bell, B. S., & Kozlowski, S. W. J. (1999). *The effects of cognitive, behavioral, and affective guidance on basic, strategic, and adaptive performance*. (Final Report 3.1; Contract No. N61339–96-K-0005). Orlando, FL: Naval Air Warfare Center Training Systems Division.

Bell, B. S., Mullins, M. E., Toney, R. J., Kozlowski, S. W. J. (1999, April). Goal orientation: Elaborating the effects of state and trait conceptualizations. In: S. L. Fisher & J. M. Beaubien (Chairs), *Goal Orientation: Expanding the Nomological Network*. Symposium conducted at the 14th Annual Conference of the Society for Industrial and Organizational Psychology, Atlanta, GA.

Boyle, K. A., & Klimoski, R. J. (1995). *Toward an understanding of goal orientation in the training context*. Paper presented at the Tenth Annual Conference of the Society for Industrial and Organizational Psychology, Orlando, FL.

Brief, A. P., & Hollenbeck, J. R. (1985). An exploratory study of self-regulating activities and their effects on job performance. *Journal of Occupational Behaviour, 6*, 197–208.

Brown, K. G., & Kozlowski, S. W. J. (1997, April). *Self-evaluation and training outcomes: Training strategy and goal orientation effects*. Paper presented at the 12th Annual Conference of the Society for Industrial and Organizational Psychology, St. Louis, MO.

Brown, K. G., Mullins, M. E., Weissbein, D. A., Toney, R. J., & Kozlowski, S. W. J. (1997, April). Mastery goals and strategic reflection: Preliminary evidence for learning interference. In: S. W. J. Kozlowski (Chair), *Metacognition in Training: Lessons Learned from Stimulating Cognitive Reflection*. Symposium conducted at the 12th Annual Conference of the Society for Industrial and Organizational Psychology, St. Louis, MO.

Campbell, J. P. (1971). Personnel training and development. *Annual Review of Psychology, 22,* 565–602.

Cannon-Bowers, J. A., Burns, J. J., Salas, E., & Pruitt, J. S. (1998). Advanced technology i scenario-based training. In: J. A. Cannon-Bowers & E. Salas (Eds), *Decision Making Under Stress: Implications for Training and Simulation* (pp. 365–374). Washington, DC: APA Books.

Carver, C. S., & Scheier, M. F. (1982). Control theory: A useful conceptual framework for personality-social, clinical, and health psychology. *Psychological Bulletin, 92,* 111–135.

Carver, C. S., & Scheier, M. F. (1990). Origins and functions of positive and negative affect: A control-process view. *Psychological Review, 97,* 19–35.

Cervone, D., Jiwani, N., & Wood, R. (1991). Goal setting and the differential influence of self-regulatory processes on complex decision-making performance. *Journal of Personality and Social Psychology, 61,* 257–266.

Curtis, K. A. (1992). Altering beliefs about the importance of strategy: An attributional intervention. *Journal of Applied Social Psychology, 22,* 953–972.

Dansereau, D. F., Brooks, L. W., Holley, C. D., & Collins, K. W. (1983). Learning strategies training: Effects of sequencing. *Journal of Experimental Education, 51,* 102–108.

DeShon, R. P., & Alexander, R. A. (1996). Goal setting effects on implicit and explicit learning of complex tasks. *Organizational Behavior and Human Decision Processes, 65,* 18–36.

DeShon, R. P., Brown, K. G., & Greenis, J. L. (1996). Does self-regulation require cognitive resources? Evaluation of resource allocation models of goal setting. *Journal of Applied Psychology, 81,* 595–608.

DeShon, R. P., Milner, K. R., Kozlowski, S. W. J., Toney, R. J., Schmidt, A., Wiechmann, D., & Davis, C. (1999, April). The effects of team goal orientation on individual and team performance. In: D. Steele-Johnson (Chair), *New Directions in Goal Orientation Research: Extending the Construct, the Nomological Net, and Analytic Methods.* Symposium conducted at the 14th Annual Conference of the Society for Industrial and Organizational Psychology, Atlanta, GA.

Duda, J. L., & Nicholls, J. G. (1992). Dimensions of achievement motivation in schoolwork and sport. *Journal of Educational Psychology, 84,* 290–299.

Dweck, C. S. (1986). Motivational processes affecting learning. *American Psychologist, 41,* 1040–1048.

Dweck, C. S. (1989). Motivation. In: A. Lesgold & R. Glaser (Eds), *Foundations for a Psychology of Education* (pp. 87–136). Hillsdale, NJ: Lawrence Earlbaum Associates.

Dweck, C. S., & Leggett, E. L. (1988). A social-cognitive approach to motivation and personality. *Psychological Review, 95,* 256–273.

Earley, P. C., Connolly, T., & Ekegren, G. (1989). Goals, strategy development, and task performance: Some limits on the efficacy of goal setting. *Journal of Applied Psychology, 74,* 24–33.

Earley, P. C., Connolly, T., & Lee, C. (1989). Task strategy interventions in goal setting: The importance of search and strategy development. *Journal of Management, 15,* 589–602.

Earley, P. C., Lee, C., & Hanson, L. A. (1990). Joint moderating effects of job experience and task component complexity: Relations among goal setting, task strategies, and performance. *Journal of Organizational Behavior, 11,* 3–15.

Earley, P. C., Northcraft, G. B., Lee, C., & Lituchy, T. R. (1990). Impact of process and outcome feedback on the relation of goal setting to task performance. *Academy of Management Journal, 33,* 87–105.

Earley, P. C., Wojnaroki, P., & Prest, W. (1987). Task planning and energy expended: Exploration of how goals influence performance. *Journal of Applied Psychology, 72*, 107–114.

Eden, D., & Zuk, Y. (1995). Seasickness as a self-fulfilling prophecy: Raising self-efficacy to boost performance at sea. *Journal of Applied Psychology, 80*, 628–635.

Elliott, E. S., & Dweck, C. S. (1988). Goals: An approach to motivation and achievement. *Journal of Personality and Social Psychology, 54*, 5–12.

Ellis, H. C. (1965). *The transfer of learning*. New York: Macmillan.

Etelapelto, A. (1993). Metacognition and the expertise of computer program comprehension. *Scandinavian Journal of Education Research, 37*, 243–254.

Farr, J. L., Hofmann, D. A., & Ringenbach, K. L. (1993). Goal orientation and action control theory: Implications for industrial and organizational psychology. In: C. L. Cooper & I. T. Robertson (Eds), *International Review of Industrial and Organizational Psychology* (pp. 193–232). New York: John Wiley & Sons.

Farh, J. L., & Dobbins, G. H. (1989). Effects of comparative performance information on the accuracy of self-ratings and agreement between self- and supervisor ratings. *Journal of Applied Psychology, 74*, 606–610.

Field, K. A. (1996). *Effects of the form of feedback on performance, self-competency judgments, and affective reactions*. Thesis submitted to the University of Minnesota.

Flavell, J. H. (1979). Metacognition and cognitive monitoring: A new area of cognitive-developmental inquiry. *American Psychologist, 34*, 906–911.

Ford, J. K., & Kraiger, K. (1995). The application of cognitive constructs and principles to the instructional systems model of training: Implications for needs assessment, design, and transfer. In: C. L. Cooper & I. T. Robertson (Eds), *International Review of Industrial and Organizational Psychology* (pp. 1–48). New York, NY: John Wiley & Sons.

Ford, J. K., Smith, E. M., Weissbein, D. A., Gully, S. M., Salas, E. (1998). Relationships of goal orientation, metacognitive activity, and practice strategies with learning outcomes and transfer. *Journal of Applied Psychology, 83*, 21–233.

Forsterling, F. (1985). "Attributional retraining: A review". *Psychological Bulletin, 98*, 495–512.

Frese, M., & Altmann, A. (1989). The treatment of errors in learning and training. In: L. Bainbridge & S. A. R. Quintanilla (Eds), *Developing Skills with Information Technology* (pp. 658–682). New York: Wiley.

Frese, M., Brodbeck, F., Heinbokel, T., Mooser, C., Schleiffenbaum, E., & Thiemann, P. (1991). Errors in training computer skills: On the positive function of errors. *Human-Computer Interaction, 6*, 77–93.

Garcia, T., & Pintrich, P. R. (1994). Regulating motivation and cognition in the classroom: The role of self-schemas and self-regulatory strategies. In: D. H. Schunk & B. J. Zimmerman (Eds), *Self-Regulation of Learning and Performance: Issues and Educational Applications*. Hillsdale, NJ: Erlbaum.

Garner, R. (1990). When children and adults do not use learning strategies: Toward a theory of settings. *Review of Educational Research, 60*, 517–529.

Garner, R. & Alexander, P. A. (1989). Metacognition: Answered and unanswered questions. *Educational Psychologist, 24*, 143–158.

Gay, G. (1986). Interaction of learner control and prior understanding in computer-assisted video instruction. *Journal of Educational Psychology, 78*, 225–227.

Gist, M. E., & Mitchell, T. R. (1992). Self-Efficacy: A theoretical analysis of its determinants and malleability. *Academy of Management Review, 17*, 183–211.

Gist, M. E., Stevens, C. K., & Bavetta, A. G. (1991). Effects of self-efficacy and post-training intervention on the acquisition and maintenance of complex interpersonal skills. *Personnel Psychology, 44*, 837–861.

Goldstein, I. L. (1980). Training in work organizations. *Annual Review of Psychology, 31*, 229–272.

Goska, R. E., & Ackerman, P. L. (1996). An aptitude-treatment interaction approach to transfer within training. *Journal of Educational Psychology, 88*, 249–259.

Hsee, C. K., & Abelson,R. P. (1991). Velocity relation: Satisfaction as a function of the first derivative of outcome over time. *Journal of Personality and Social Psychology, 60*, 341–347.

Harris, K. R. (1990). Developing self-regulated learners: The role of private speech and self-instructions. *Educational Psychologist, 25*, 35–49.

Hastie, R. (1984). Causes and effects of causal attribution. *Journal of Personality and Social Psychology, 46*, 44–56.

Howell, W. C., & Cooke, N. J. (1989). Training the human information processor: A review of cognitive models. In: I. L. Goldstein (Ed.), *Training and Development in Organizations* (pp. 121–182). San Francisco: Jossey-Bass.

Huber, V. L. (1985). Effects of task difficulty, goal setting, and strategy on performance of a heuristic task. *Journal of Applied Psychology, 70*, 492–504.

Hunter-Blanks, P., Ghatala, E. S., Pressley, M., & Levin, J. R. (1988). Comparison of monitoring during study and during testing on a sentence learning task. *Journal of Educational Psychology, 80*, 279–283.

Ivancic, K., & Hesketh, B. (1995). Making the best of errors during training. *Training Research Journal, 1*, 103–125.

Kanfer, F. H., & Stevenson, M. K. (1985). The effects of self-regulation on concurrent cognitive processing. *Cognitive Therapy and Research, 9*, 667–684.

Kanfer, R. (1996). Self-regulatory and other non-ability determinants of skill acquisition. In: P. M. Gollwitzer & J. A. Bargh (Eds), *The Psychology of Action: Linking Cognition and Motivation to Behavior* (pp. 404–423). New York, Guilford Press.

Kanfer, R., & Ackerman, P. L. (1989). Motivation and cognitive abilities: An integrative/aptitude-treatment interaction approach to skill acquisition [Monograph]. *Journal of Applied Psychology, 74*, 657–690.

Kanfer, R., Ackerman, P. L., Murtha, T., & Dugdale, B. (1994). Goal setting, conditions of practice, and task performance: A resource allocation perspective. *Journal of Applied Psychology, 79*, 826–835.

Karl, K. A., O'Leary-Kelly, A. M., & Martocchio, J. J. (1993). The impact of feedback and self-efficacy on performance in training. *Journal of Organizational Behavior, 14*, 379–394.

Karoly, P. (1993). Mechanisms of self-regulation: A systems view. *Annual Review of Psychology, 44*, 23–52.

Kluger, A. N., & DeNisi, A. (1996). The effects of feedback interventions on performance: A historical review, a meta-analysis, and a preliminary feedback intervention theory. *Psychological Bulletin, 119*, 254–284.

Kozlowski, S. W. J. (1998). Training and developing adaptive teams: Theory, principles, and research. In: J. A. Cannon-Bowers & E. Salas (Eds), *Decision Making Under Stress: Implications for Training And Simulation* (pp. 115–153). Washington, DC: APA Books.

Kozlowski, S. W. J., & DeShon, R. P. *A network-based approach to team situational awareness, coordination, and adaptive performance.* Air Force Office of Scientific Research (F49620–98–1–0363). April 1998 to December 2000.

Kozlowski, S. W. J., Gully, S. M., Brown, K. G., Salas, E., Smith, E. A., & Nason, E. R. (in press). Effects of training goals and goal orientation traits on multi-dimensional training outcomes and performance adaptability. *Organizational Behavior and Human Decision Processes*.

Kozlowski, S. W. J., Gully, S. M., McHugh, P. P., Salas, E., & Cannon-Bowers, J. A. (1996). A dynamic theory of leadership and team effectiveness: Developmental and task contingent leader roles. In: G. R. Ferris (Ed.), *Research in Personnel and Human Resource Management* (Vol. 14, pp. 253–305). Greenwich, CT: JAI.

Kozlowski, S. W. J., Gully, S. M., Nason, E. R., & Smith, E. M. (1999). Developing adaptive teams: A theory of compilation and performance across levels and time. In: D. R. Ilgen & E. D. Pulakos (Eds), *The Changing Nature of Work Performance: Implications for Staffing, Personnel Actions, and Development* (pp. 240–292). San Francisco: Jossey-Bass.

Kozlowski, S. W. J., Gully, S. M., Salas, E., & Cannon-Bowers, J. A. (1996). Team leadership and development: Theory, principles, and guidelines for training leaders and teams. In: M. Beyerlein, D. Johnson, & S. Beyerlein (Eds), *Advances in Interdisciplinary Studies of Work Teams: Team Leadership* (Vol. 3, pp. 251–289). Greenwich, CT: JAI Press.

Kozlowski, S. W. J., Gully, S. M., Smith, E. M., Brown, K. G., Mullins, M. E., & Williams, A. E. (1996, April). Sequenced mastery goals and advance organizers: Enhancing the effects of practice. In: K. Smith-Jentsch (Chair), *When, How, and Why Does Practice Make Perfect?* Symposium conducted at the 11th Annual Conference of the Society for Industrial and Organizational Psychology, San Diego, CA.

Kozlowski, S. W. J., Gully, S. M., Smith, E. A., Nason, E. R., & Brown, K. G. (1995, May). Sequenced mastery training and advance organizers: Effects on learning, self-efficacy, performance, and generalization. In: R. J. Klimoski (Chair), *Thinking and Feeling While Doing: Understanding the Learner in the Learning Process*. Symposium conducted at the 10th Annual Conference of the Society for Industrial and Organizational Psychology, Orlando, FL.

Kozlowski, S. W. J., & Klein, K. J. (2000). A multilevel approach to theory and research in organizations: Contextual, temporal, and emergent processes. In: K. J. Klein & S. W. J. Kozlowski (Eds), *Multilevel Theory, Research and Methods in Organizations: Foundations, Extensions, and New Directions* (pp. 3–90). San Francisco, CA: Jossey-Bass.

Kozlowski, S. W. J., & Salas, E. (1997). An organizational systems approach for the implementation and transfer of training. In: J. K. Ford, S. W. J. Kozlowski, K. Kraiger, E. Salas, & M. Teachout (Eds), *Improving Training Effectiveness in Work Organizations* (pp. 247–287). Mahwah, NJ: Lawrence Erlbaum Associates.

Kraiger, K., Ford, J. K., & Salas, E. (1993). Application of cognitive, skill-based, and affective theories of learning outcomes to new methods of training evaluation. *Journal of Applied Psychology, 78*, 311–328.

Kuhl, J., & Koch, B. (1984). Motivational determinants of motor performance: The hidden second task. *Psychological Research, 46*, 143–153.

Latham, G. P., & Locke, E. A. (1991). Self-regulation through goal setting. *Organizational Behavior and Human Decision Processes, 50*, 212–247.

Lindsley, D. H., Brass, D. J., & Thomas, J. B. (1995). Efficacy-performance spirals: A multilevel perspective. *Academy of Management Review, 20*, 645–678.

Locke, E. A., & Latham, G. P. (1990). *A theory of goal setting and task performance*. Englewood Cliffs, NJ: Prentice-Hall.

Lord, R. G., & Levy, P. E. (1994). Moving from cognition to action: A control theory perspective. *Applied Psychology: An International Review, 43*, 335–367.

Martocchio, J. J. (1994). Effects of conceptions of ability on anxiety, self-efficacy, and learning in training. *Journal of Applied Psychology, 79*, 819–825.

Martocchio, J. J., & Dulebohn, J. (1994). Performance feedback effects in training: The role of perceived controllability. *Personnel Psychology, 47*, 357–373.

Martocchio, J. J., & Webster, J. (1992). Effects of feedback and cognitive playfulness on performance in microcomputer software training. *Personnel Psychology, 45*, 553–578

Mathieu, J. E., Tannenbaum, S. I., & Salas, E. (1992). Influences of individual and situational characteristics on measures of training effectiveness. *Academy of Management Journal, 35*, 828–847.

Meece, J. L. (1994). The role of motivation in self-regulated learning. In: D. H. Schunk & B. J. Zimmerman (Eds), *Self-regulation of Learning and Performance: Issues and Educational Applications* (pp. 25–44). New Jersey: Erlbaum.

Mikulincer, M. (1989). Cognitive interference and learned helplessness: The effects of off-task cognitions on performance following unsolvable problems. *Journal of Personality and Social Psychology, 57*, 129–135.

Miller, R. B., Behrens, J. T., Greene, B. A., & Newman, D. (1993). Goals and perceived ability: Impact on student valuing, self-regulation, and persistence. *Contemporary Educational Psychology, 18*, 2–14.

Mitchell, T. R., Hopper, H., Daniels, D., George-Falvy, J., & James, L. R. (1994). Predicting self-efficacy and performance during skill acquisition. *Journal of Applied Psychology, 49*, 506–517.

Mullins, M. E., Brown, K. G., Toney, R. J., Weissbein, D. A., & Kozlowski, S. W. J. (April, 1998). Individual differences, self-efficacy, and training outcomes. In: S. M. Gully & J. E. Mathieu (Chairs), *Individual Differences, Learning, Motivation, and Training Outcomes*. Symposium conducted at the 13th Annual Conference of the Society for Industrial and Organizational Psychology, Dallas, TX.

Mullins, M. E., Kozlowski, S. W. J., Toney, R. J., Brown, K. G., Weissbein, D. A., & Bell, B. S. (1999, April). *Adaptive performance: Mastery versus performance goals and feedback consistency.* Paper presented at the 14th Annual Conference of the Society for Industrial and Organizational Psychology, Atlanta, GA.

Nelson, T. O. (1996). Consciousness and metacognition. *American Psychologist, 51*, 102–116.

Nelson,T. O., Dunlosky, J., Graf, A., & Narens, L. (1994). Utilization of metacognitive judgments in the allocation of study during multitrial learning. *Psychological Science, 5*, 207–213.

Noe, R. A., & Schmitt, N. (1986). The influence of trainee attitudes on training effectiveness: Test of a model. *Personnel Psychology, 39*, 497–523.

Nolen, S. B., & Haladyna, T. M. (1990). Personal and environment influences on students' beliefs about effective study strategies. *Contemporary Educational Psychology, 15*, 116–130.

Nordstrom, C. R., Wendland, D., & Williams, K. B. (1995). "To err is human": An examination of error management training. Poster presented at the Tenth Annual Conference of the Society for Industrial and Organizational Psychology, Orlando, FL.

Norman, D. A., & Bobrow, D. G. (1975). On data-limited and resource-limited processes. *Cognitive Psychology, 7*, 44–64.

Ohllson, S. (1996). Learning from performance errors. *Psychological Review, 103*, 241–262.

Orasanu, J., & Connolly, T. (1993). The reinvention of decision making. In: G. A. Klein & J Orasanu (Eds), *Decision Making in Action: Models and Methods* (pp. 3–20). Norwood, NJ: Ablex Publishing Corp.

Pintrich, P. R., & DeGroot, E. V. (1990). Motivational and self-regulated learning components of classroom academic performance. Special selections: Motivation and efficacy in education: Research and new directions. *Journal of Educational Psychology, 82,* 33–40.

Podsakoff, P. M. & Farh, J. (1989). Effects of feedback sign and credibility on goal setting and task performance. *Organizational Behavior and Human Decision Processes, 44,* 45–67.

Prather, D. C. (1971). Trial-and-error versus errorless learning: Training, transfer, and stress. *American Journal of Psychology, 84,* 377–386.

Quiñones, M. A. (1995). Pretraining context effects: Training assignment as feedback. *Journal of Applied Psychology, 80,* 226–238.

Ree, M. J., & Earles, J. A. (1992). Intelligence is the best predictor of job performance. *Current Directions in Psychological Science, 1,* 86–89.

Reigeluth, C. M., Merrill, M. D., Wilson, B. G., & Spiller, R. T. (1980). The elaboration theory of instruction: A model for structuring instruction. *Instructional Science, 9,* 195–219.

Ridley, S. D., Schutz, P. A., Glanz, R. S., & Weinstein, C. E. (1992). Self-regulated learning: The interactive influence of metacognitive awareness and goal-setting. *Journal of Experimental Education, 60,* 293–306.

Royer, J. M., Carlo, M. S., Dufresne, R., & Mestre, J. (1996). The assessment of levels of domain expertise while reading. *Cognition and Instruction, 14,* 373–408.

Russell, D. & McAuley, E. (1986). Causal attributions, causal dimensions, and affective reactions to success and failure. *Journal of Personality and Social Psychology, 50,* 1174–1185.

Salas, E., Cannon-Bowers, J. A., & Kozlowski, S. W. J. (1997). The science and practice of training: Current trends and emerging themes. In: J. K. Ford, S. W. J. Kozlowski, K. Kraiger, E. Salas, & M. Teachout (Eds), *Improving Training Effectiveness in Work Organizations* (pp. 357–368). Mahwah, NJ: Lawrence Erlbaum Associates.

Santiago, R. S., & Okey, J. R. (1992). The effects of advisement and locus of control on achievement in learner-controlled instruction. *Journal of Computer-Based Instruction, 19,* 47–53.

Scherer, M., Maddux, J. E., Mercadante, B., Prentice-Dunn, S., Jacobs, B., & Rogers, R. W. (1982). The self-efficacy scale: Construction and validation. *Psychological Reports, 51,* 663–671.

Salomon, G. (1984). Television is "easy" and print is "tough": The differential investment of mental effort in learning as a function of perceptions and attributions. *Journal of Educational Psychology, 76,* 647–658.

Schmidt, F. L., Hunter, J. E., Outerbridge, A. N., & Goff, S. (1988). Joint relation of experience and ability with job performance: Test of three hypotheses. *Journal of Applied Psychology, 73,* 46–57.

Schmidt, R. A., & Bjork, R. A. (1992). New conceptualizations of practice: Common principles in three paradigms suggest new concepts for training. *Psychological Science, 3,* 207–217.

Schraw, G., & Dennison, R. S. (1994). Assessing metacognitive awareness. *Contemporary Educational Psychology, 19,* 460–475.

Schraw, G., Horn, C., Thorndike-Christ, T., & Bruning, R. (1995). Academic goal orientations and student classroom achievement. *Contemporary Educational Psychology, 20,* 359–368.

Schunk, D. H. (1990). Goal setting and self-efficacy during self-regulated learning. *Educational Psychologist, 25,* 71–86.

Schreiber, D. A. (1998). Organizational technology and its impact on distance training. In: D. A. Scheiber & Z. L. Berge (Eds), *Distance Training: How Innovative Organizations are Using Technology to Maximize Learning and Meet Business Objectives* (pp. 3–18). San Francisco: Jossey-Bass.

Schvaneveldt, R. W. (1990). *Pathfinder associative networks: Studies in knowledge organization.* Norwood, NJ: Ablex.

Silver, W. S, Mitchell, T. R., & Gist, M. E. (1995). Responses to successful and unsuccessful performance: The moderating effect of self-efficacy on the relationship between performance and attributions. *Organizational Behavior and Human Decision Processes, 62,* 286–299.

Smith, E. M., Ford, J. K., & Kozlowski, S. W. J. (1997). Building adaptive expertise: Implications for training design. In: M. A. Quinones & A. Dudda (Eds), *Training for a Rapidly Changing Workplace: Applications of Psychological Research* (pp. 89–118). Washington, DC: APA Books.

Stock, J., & Cervone, D. (1990). Proximal goal-setting and self-regulatory processes. *Cognitive Theory and Research, 14,* 483–498.

Swanson, H. L. (1990). Influence of metacognitive knowledge and aptitude on problem solving. *Journal of Educational Psychology, 82,* 306–314.

Tennyson, R. D. (1980). Instructional control strategies and content structures as design variables in concept acquisition using computer-based instruction. *Journal of Educational Psychology, 72,* 225–232.

Tennyson, R. D. (1981). Use of adaptive information for advisement in learning concepts and rules using computer assisted instruction. *American Educational Research Journal, 18,* 425–438.

Tennyson, R. D., & Buttrey, T. (1980). Advisement and management strategies as design variables in computer-assisted instruction. *Educational Communication and Technology Journal, 28,* 169–176.

Tennyson, C. L., Tennyson, R. D., & Rothen, W. (1980). Content structure and instructional control strategies as design variables in concept acquisition. *Journal of Educational Psychology, 72,* 499–505.

Terreberry, S. (1968). The evolution of organizational environments. *Administrative Science Quarterly, 12,* 590–613.

Thomas, K. M. & Mathieu, J. E. (1994). Role of causal attributions in dynamic self-regulation and goal processes. *Journal of Applied Psychology, 79,* 812–818.

Toney, R. J., & Kozlowski, S. W. J. (1999, April). Shifting feedback from positive to negative: Benefits of evaluative feedback on learning and training performance. In: S. M. Gully & S. W. J. Kozlowski (Chairs), *Learning to Fail or Failing to Learn? The Role of Errors, Failures, and Feedback in Learning Environments.* Symposium conducted at the 14th Annual Conference of the Society for Industrial and Organizational Psychology, Atlanta, GA.

Waldersee, R., & Luthans, F. (1994). The impact of positive and corrective feedback on customer service performance. *Journal of Organizational Behavior, 15,* 83–95.

Webster's Ninth New Collegiate Dictionary. (1987). Springfield, MA: Merriam-Webster.

Weiner, B. (1985). An attributional theory of achievement motivation and emotion. *Psychological Review, 92,* 548–573.

Wentzel, K. R. (1991). Social competence at school: Relation between social responsibility and academic achievement. *Review of Educational Research, 61,* 1–24.

Winters, D. & Latham, G. (1996). The effect of learning versus outcome goals on a simple versus a complex task. *Group and Organization Management.*

Wofford, J. C., & Goodwin, V. L. (1990). Effects of feedback on cognitive processing and choice of decision style. *Journal of Applied Psychology, 75,* 603–612.

Wood, R. E. (1986). Task complexity: Definition of the construct. *Organizational Behavior and Human Decision Processes, 37*, 60–82.

Wood, R., Bandura, A., & Bailey, T. (1990). Mechanisms governing organizational performance in complex decision-making environments. *Organizational Behavior and Human Decision Processes, 46*, 181–201.

3. USING PATHFINDER NETWORKS TO ANALYZE PROCEDURAL KNOWLEDGE IN INTERACTIONS WITH ADVANCED TECHNOLOGY

Douglas J. Gillan and Nancy J. Cooke

ABSTRACT

Research on human cognition in complex tasks, such as interacting with advanced technology, requires the development and validation of new methods. This paper describes PRONET, a method for summarizing, representing, and analyzing event sequences. The first section outlines how the PRONET method can be applied to any sequence of events, with lessons learned from previous applications of the method. The second section presents demonstrations of the application of PRONET. In the first demonstration – a computer-based simulation of operant training – the PRONET analysis and representation clearly shows the change in the behavior of the simulation produced by changes in reinforcement contingencies, but also shows interesting aspects of behavior that were not affected. In the second demonstration – involving transfer of word processing skill – network-related and performance measures showed the expected pattern of positive transfer. In addition, the network of the far transfer participant suggested that she used task knowledge to search for conditions that would permit the correct action. Two previously-published examples showed the usefulness of the PRONET method in characterizing

Advances in Human Performance and Cognitive Engineering Research, Volume 1,
pages 125–161.
ISBN: 0-7623-0748-X

a hybrid event sequence consisting of environmental conditions and behavioral actions and a sequence of events from a team.

INTRODUCTION

The cognitive revolution has reached an uneasy middle age. Cognitive psychology replaced behaviorism as the dominant area of experimental psychology in the late 1960s. But, like so many of the revolutions in the '60s, cognitive psychology has failed to live up to the sparkling promise of its early days. Although some cognitive psychologists have claimed that cognitive theory and research has uncovered the workings of the mind (e.g. Pinker, 1997), that same research and theory has led to very limited applications (for more on this critique, see Gillan & Schvaneveldt, 1999). If psychologists really understood the workings of the mind, it seems likely that the applications in such areas as education and training, the design of interfaces to advanced technologies, and testing and measurement would be overwhelmingly success-ful. Although certain demonstration programs in applying cognitive principles in education have shown promise (for examples, see Mayer, 1999), it is hard to imagine even the most optimistic cognitive psychologist claiming over-whelming success in applications.

Cognitive processes reveal themselves through behavior. In laboratory-based research, cognitive scientists typically measure such simple features of behavior as response time, accuracy of the response, or the type of a response. However, as cognitive engineers examine complex behavior in fields of practice, these simple measures may not accurately reflect the behavior. In other words, to study cognition in the wild (e.g. Hutchins, 1996), we must first create and validate new methodological approaches. These new methods must represent the complex behavior in a way that accurately reflects the behavior, and that also makes the data comprehensible and useful for making inferences about the cognitive processes underlying the behavior.

Interactions between people and advanced technologies, such as computers, provide a domain that is rich in both situated cognition and data recording capabilities. For example, usability tests frequently record behavioral events like keystrokes, mouse clicks, and errors that occur as a user interacts with software. In addition, recording and analysis of complex behavior can be useful in a variety of other cognitive engineering applications, including cognitive task analysis, training program development, and the design of cognitive aids. Complex behavioral data during productive tasks can be captured with relative ease in the work context for that task, using either videotapes of a user's interaction and commercially available or custom-built software for coding user responses (e.g. Owen, Baecker & Harrison, 1994) and/or data logging software that automatically records the events and times and stores them in a computer file (e.g. Hammontree, Weiler & Hendrich, 1995). Usability tests often collect the data unobtrusively as the video camera and/or event logging software run in the background while the user performs his or her tasks. In addition, event logging software enables usability testers to perform evalua-tions either in a controlled laboratory setting or in the user's environment. Unfortunately, analysis of the event records derived either from videotapes of user interactions or log files typically involves only a transcription of selected key segments, thereby relegating the bulk of the data and the potential wealth in latent information to the "archives" where it will remain until "needed". As a consequence, data remain unexamined that: (1) cognitive researchers might examine to study how users think during complex. productive tasks, and (2) cognitive engineers might examine as part of their applied work (for example, usability engineers could use the data to improve user interfaces).

Why does this unfortunate loss of information occur? Cognitive engineers ignore the bulk of the event logs because of immense difficulties associated with analyzing the data. Approaching the analysis of a record of behavioral data raises a myriad of questions: What is the most meaningful level of detail at which to parse the sequence of events? How can the very large event stream be summarized? How similar or different are two event logs? What aspects of the data are most critical for interface design considerations? Such questions, coupled with the more typical problems that arise when dealing with very large and complex data sets, make any extensive analysis of event logs seem insurmountable.

Recently, researchers have begun to develop methods designed to answer some of the questions raised above. An emerging area known as ESDA (exploratory sequential data analysis) has fostered the development of techniques and tools to facilitate the analysis of data that arise from sequences of events (Sanderson & Fisher, 1994). In particular, ESDA techniques focus on making complex sequential data understandable through summarizing and statistically treating the data (for examples, see Bakeman & Gottman, 1997; Bakeman & Quera, 1995; Gottman and Roy, 1990), as well as, in some cases, presenting that summary in a visual format (for examples, see Cooke et al., 1996; Rauterberg, 1993, 1996). The ideal approach to dealing with complex sequential data would appear to be one that provided: (1) a statistical analysis to simplify and regularize the data, as well as (2) a way to perform inferential tests, and (3) an easy to interpret visual representation of the behavior. PRONET (Cooke et al., 1996) summarizes sequential event data based on creation of a matrix of transitions between events and the application of the

Pathfinder algorithm (Schvaneveldt, 1990) to the matrix. The output of the Pathfinder algorithm applied to the event transition matrix can be presented in a visual format – a network with events represented as nodes and event transitions represented as links between nodes (for examples of other network-producing methods that could be applied to behavioral sequences of user interactions, see Guzdial, 1993; Reisig, 1992; and Millen, Schriefer, Lehder & Dray, 1997). In addition, the Pathfinder algorithm reduces the data by eliminating certain links and the resulting network can be characterized or compared to other networks by means of inferential statistical tests.

Because the PRONET approach meets the criteria outlined above – statistical treatment to simplify and provide inferential tests and a network format for presenting the behavioral sequence data, PRONET appears to be a promising method for analyzing event log file data. Accordingly, this paper provides readers with a detailed description of the method behind PRONET so that anyone wishing to make use of PRONET can do so. In addition, we review several very different demonstrations that show the capabilities of PRONET. The first demonstration analyzes behaviors of a digital entity in a computer-based simulation used in training (Graham, Alloway & Krames, 1994). A second detailed demonstration is a more usual case of humans using complex technology, specifically, a human transferring her skill in using a novel version (to her) of a well-learned word processing application. The other demonstrations that we review – all of which examine the behavior of humans' interactions with advanced technology – are covered in less detail because their detailed descriptions are available in previous publications. These varied demonstrations show an important feature of PRONET – the flexibility in which researchers, educators, or designers might apply it.

PRONET: PROCEDURAL NETWORKS

In this section we provide a detailed description of PRONET, a method for summarizing and representing sequential event data. The sequence of events may be human or animal behavior, machine events, or environmental events. PRONET represents the event sequence in terms of a network of nodes (the events) and links (based on the transitions between events) similar to the result of Markov analysis or a Petri net representation; however, the PRONET approach differs from Markov and Petri net representations in that the Pathfinder network scaling algorithm (Schvaneveldt, Durso & Dearholt, 1989; Schvaneveldt, 1990) – the statistical basis for the PRONET method – provides a statistical method for selecting certain sequences of behaviors to maintain in the network and other sequences of behavior to eliminate (see Cooke & Gillan,

1999, for a review of these methods). Pathfinder analyzes a set of pairwise proximities as a node-link structure. Below, we outline the general procedure for PRONET (for more details, see Cooke et al., 1996; and Cooke & Gillan, 1999).

Collecting, Coding, and Organizing the Data

The PRONET method can be conducted with any type of sequential data. In the context of an interaction between a human and technology, data will most likely take the form of user, system, and environmental events. The data ma also be collected by a variety of means, including videotaped behavior, think-aloud verbal reports, eye movements, gestures, or event logging software.

Encoding the events, the most difficult and time-consuming aspect of PRONET, involves transforming the continuous stream of raw event data into a series of discrete categorized events. In order to enhance data summary, categories should be fewer in number than actual unique events. Decisions about event categories are important and highly dependent on the purpose of the data analysis. As is illustrated in some of the demonstrations described in this paper, more than one encoding scheme may make sense. Accordingly, an important factor in selecting a coding scheme is the question asked of the data. Cooke et al. (1996) proposed six heuristics to aid in developing the coding scheme:

- Minimize the number of event categories in order to reduce data and allow more observations per node.
- Preserve distinctions that are meaningful for the goals of analysis.
- Consider ignoring or merging into one category events that are uninteresting or less important than other events.
- Consider merging events into a single category if they always co-occur.
- If an event does not change across encoded protocols, then there is no need to represent that event as a node.
- Generate an event taxonomy and iterate on a subset of the data in order to decide on the appropriate level of abstraction.

Following encoding, PRONET requires the series of discrete categorized events be transformed into a co-occurrence or event transition matrix. In this matrix, the rows and columns represent events, and entries in the matrix represent the frequency with which the event in the column followed the event in the row. Although raw co-occurrence frequencies can be submitted to Pathfinder, they do not take into account differences in the absolute frequency with which single events occurred. For that reason, we recommend the use of conditional transition probabilities.

A PRONET analyst will need to make several decisions about these transitions. PRONET also permits analysts to define events as a string of behaviors of any size and to examine transitions of events that follow one another with any size lag. The nature of the task or the characteristics of the users may provide good reasons to consider some of these higher-order transitions. In the event that transitions of several varying lags are used, they may be combined in a proximity matrix, but it may make sense to weight them differently. For instance, longer lags could be given less weight than shorter lags. In addition, the analyst should consider eliminating spurious transitions – including those that occur between subtasks or that consist of an event that occurs independent of the preceding event.

Applying Pathfinder to the Transition Matrix Data

Following the creation of an event transition matrix, a PRONET analyst would next apply the Pathfinder algorithm to the data. The Pathfinder network scaling technique (Schvaneveldt, Durso & Dearholt, 1989; Schvaneveldt, 1990) is a statistical method for structural modeling, much like cluster analysis (Johnson, 1967) and multidimensional scaling (Kruskal & Wish, 1978). These structural modeling methods translate pairwise proximity estimates for a set of items (collected as relatedness ratings, co-occurrence of sorted items, or recall order) into either a spatial or graphical configuration. PRONET has two special characteristics: (1) the items are events, including behavior produced by a human, a nonhuman animal, or a non-living system such as a computer that can generate events, and (2) the proximities among events are based on transition frequencies or probabilities between event pairs.

The various structural modeling methods reveal the latent structure in the proximity data. The methods differ from one another in terms of the representational format and assumptions underlying the method of generating the representation. Pathfinder assumes that the proximity estimates reflect information about distance in a network structure.

Pathfinder links represent relations, and a weight associated with the link and derived from the original proximity data reflects the strength of the relation. In contrast, the nature or meaning of the relation is unidentified. Links can also be directed if proximity estimates are asymmetrical, as one typically finds in proximities derived from event transitions. Nodes can also be unconnected if the estimates between an item and all other items fail to exceed a minimum strength criterion set by the experimenter.

A completely connected network can be used to represent (without any data reduction) the original proximities. One of the benefits of the Pathfinder algorithm, however, is in its data reduction properties. The algorithm eliminates various links in order to reduce the data and facilitate comprehension of the resulting network. Basically, if a link exceeds the minimum strength criterion set by the experimenter, it is included by the algorithm if the minimum distance path (chain of one or more links) is greater than or equal to the distance indicated by the proximity estimate for that pair.

Two parameters, r and q, determine how network distance is calculated and therefore, affect the ultimate density of the network. The parameter r is based on the Minkowski r metric (Dunn-Rankin, 1983) so that, when r equals infinity, path distance is equivalent to the maximum weight along the path. The parameter q specifies the maximum number of links allowed in a path. The KNOT software[1] which implements the algorithm, sets default values for r and q of infinity and number of items -1, respectively. The default values (i.e. $r=$ infinity; $q=$ number of items -1) result in networks of minimum complexity. Further, when $r = infinity$, only ordinal assumptions of the proximity data are required. Decreasing the q value results in networks of greater complexity, which may be undesirable when dealing with complex event data – the networks will be sufficiently complex with the default parameters. However, the value of r may be set at 1 or 2 to reflect that probabilities as the proximity measure have ratio properties. When $r=1$ the path distance is computed by summing the link weights along a specific path; when $r=2$, the path length is computed as the Euclidean distance. Setting r to either value will likely result in a more complex network, but may seem warranted from a measurement perspective.

When the data analyzed using Pathfinder are event transition frequencies or probabilities, they can be treated as similarities by the algorithm with high frequencies corresponding to high similarity. It is also necessary to identify the data as asymmetrical. Finally, the analyst has the opportunity to specify a minimum cutoff for frequencies or probabilities. Transitions with frequencies or probabilities below this cutoff will not be represented as links in the network. This step actually eliminates quite a few of the transitions that would otherwise be linked. Other links will later be eliminated by the distance rule associated with the Pathfinder algorithm and described above. As the complexity of the network (i.e. number of links) increases, the number of indirect paths between two nodes increases, leading the Pathfinder algorithm to eliminate direct paths that are "less efficient", thereby resulting in greater relative data reduction.

The output of Pathfinder is a list of nodes and weighted links, as well as the network representation in which events are represented as nodes. Directed links indicate transitions that occur between nodes. Readers should keep in mind that a path of two or more links is not an indication that that sequence of three or more events ever occurred contiguously. On the other hand, each consecutive pair of linked events has occurred together at least once.

Nodes may fail to be connected for three reasons. If nodes A and B are not linked in a PRONET network, (1) event A may not have ever been followed by event B in the observed sequence, (2) event B may have followed event A but at such a low probability that it was eliminated by the cutoff criterion, or (3) the probabilities in an indirect path between the two events (e.g. between A and C and C and B) were enough higher than in the direct path between A and B that the direct path was eliminated.

Pathfinder has several features that make it well-suited to the analysis of sequential data found in behavioral records. First, it is more flexible than other scaling techniques in that the output of Pathfinder is not constrained to hierarchical configurations as is the case for most clustering techniques. Second, Pathfinder can represent asymmetric relations which are characteristic of sequential event data. Finally, various empirical results have supported the psychological validity of Pathfinder representations (Cooke, Durso & Schvane-veldt, 1986; Cooke, 1992).

Interpreting the PRONET Network
Once a completed network is in hand, an analyst can make use of several procedures, both qualitative and quantitative, for interpreting the results. A qualitative interpretation entails examining each network in terms of nodes, links, and overall structure. Nodes that are disconnected from the rest of the network indicate omitted or infrequent events. This information is often very informative in the design of advanced technology (e.g. underused menu options or commands in a computer interface).

Links between nodes provide an indication of procedures that the user undertakes in accomplishing tasks. When events that are environmental or system-initiated are included, if-then or production rules can be derived from cases in which a system-event and user-event are strongly linked. In addition, chains of interconnected events and cycles may also be worthy of further examination. Finally, highly central nodes that are connected to many other nodes provide an indication of centrality or importance of events in the procedure. For example, in developing a computer-based training system, a highly central event involving access to help would suggest that the trainee found the system difficult to use. In examining the overall structure of the network, analysts should look for subnetworks (a set of events with multiple within-set links). Distinct subnetworks that have few connections to the rest of the network indicate events that occur together, as in a subsystem, but that do not typically occur with events outside of the subsystem.

A PRONET analyst might use the following heuristics to aid in the interpretation of the networks:

- Network nodes correspond to events that occurred during a session.
- Each node is associated with a frequency (the number of times it was executed in the session or series of sessions). Frequencies can be categorized and coded for graphical presentation. Node frequency provides an indication of events that never occurred or occurred a great deal. This information is very useful for determining software functions never used or used often.
- Links between nodes in the network have a spatial direction which corresponds to the temporal ordering of the events during the session. This means that links can go in one or both directions. The direction indicates the order in which the two events (nodes) occurred in the interaction.
- Links are also associated with a weight indicating the strength of the link. Strong links are those for which the sequence occurred frequently or with high conditional probability.
- Sequences that occur frequently provide information about the user's typical strategies for the task.
- Networks can be examined for events that are linked to specific other events of interest to identify the events that precipitated a problem.
- Networks can be examined to identify events that are highly central (i.e. linked to several other events). This can indicate the importance of that event.
- The software will also provide quantitative indices representing the similarity of two or more networks (shared nodes, links, etc.).

At a quantitative level, the output of Pathfinder can be analyzed in a number of ways. Node frequency is not represented in the output, but is available in the transition matrix. It is possible to graphically represent this value, however, by making frequent nodes larger or darker. Other values that are available include number of links and weights of links. These values can be examined within a single network or they can be compared across networks. The KNOT program also contains a similarity measure, based on the proportion of shared links in two networks ranging from 0 (complete dissimilarity) to 1 (identity), which provides a quantitative value describing the similarity between two network structures (Goldsmith & Davenport, 1990). This measure can be used to compare procedural networks of behavior associated with two different interfaces, two different training programs, or two different experience levels. Behavior can also be assessed by comparing an individual network to a referent structure which may represent some ideal behavior or the behavior of an experienced user.

PRONET DEMONSTRATIONS

Demonstration I: Computer-Based Simulation of Operant Training

The first demonstration examines an aspect of advanced technology – a computer-based simulation of operant conditioning called Sniffy the Rat (Graham, Alloway & Krames, 1994). For this demonstration, we used PRONET to summarize the simulation itself by examining Sniffy's behavior at five phases during typical operant training of a bar press response. The value of analyzing this simulation includes: (1) the limited set of behaviors in the simulated operant training situation provides a straightforward demonstration of PRONET; (2) the changes in behavior during operant training were programmed into the simulation; as a consequence, they are predictable and reliable, so that if PRONET is a valid analytical tool, the resulting networks should reflect those changes; and (3) the demonstration illustrates the use of PRONET to summarize sequences of computer-generated events, and as a method for validating computer-based simulations.

Method

The method used for this demonstration of PRONET mirrored the description above. We observed and recorded seven behaviors produced by Sniffy, the computer-based simulation of a rat, during five sessions. The Sniffy simulation shows a rat in an operant conditioning chamber (i.e. Skinner box) that has a bar for pressing, a light, a water spout, and a food hopper which appear to be at the far end of the chamber. The seven behaviors were: (1) sniffing the environment, (2) scratching itself, (3) standing in any place in the simulated operant conditioning chamber other than when standing was part of a bar press response, (4) licking itself, (5) drinking water from the water spout shown as part of the simulation, (6) pressing the bar shown, and (7) eating food from the hopper. This was the entire behavioral repertoire of Sniffy. The limited number of unique behaviors made the use of Sniffy well suited for the present demonstration. However, we do not claim that the results of our demonstration are generalizable to real rats receiving real operant training.

The five sessions represent 20 minute segments of different phases of typical operant training. Table 1 summarizes the five sessions. The first session involved observing Sniffy in an untrained state for 20 minutes. The simulation was set up so that Sniffy had received no prior training. Pressing on the bar (either by Sniffy or by the user moving the cursor over the bar and clicking on the mouse button) resulted in delivery of a food pellet (in the simulated world). However, Sniffy had not been given any experience with this contingency. Prior

Table 1. The Five Sessions Used in the Analysis of the Sniffy the Rat Computer-Based Simulation.

	Session 1	Session 2	Session 3	Session 4	Session 5
Type of Training	Untrained	CRL	VR-10	Early Extinction	Late Extinction
Training Procedure	No shaping of bar press received. Food given after every bar press.	Shaping of bar press previously given. Food given after every bar press.	Food given after every 10th bar press, on average.	No food after bar presses.	No food after bar presses.

to the second session, we shaped Sniffy to press the bar using successive approximations of the desired response. Also prior to the second session, the Sniffy simulation was run for 30 minutes on a continuous reinforcement (CRF) schedule. Thus, the second session involved 20 minutes of observing and recording Sniffy's responses, following the shaping and 30 minutes of CRF experience.

Before the third session, the Sniffy simulation was gradually extended to a Variable Ratio 10 (VR10) reinforcement schedule (i.e. on average Sniffy would receive one pellet of food for every 10 bar presses). The training involved giving Sniffy experience with a Fixed Ratio 2 (FR2), FR3, FR5, FR7, FR9, and FR10, prior to giving her 50 minutes of experience with a VR10 schedule. During the third session, we observed and recorded Sniffy during the last 20 minutes of that VR10 training. During the two extinction sessions, Sniffy had the link between bar press and food delivery eliminated. In fact, no response by Sniffy or the experimenters could produce the delivery of food. In Session 4 (Early Extinction), we observed and recorded Sniffy's behaviors for the first 20 minutes of the Extinction procedure. Then, prior to Session 5 (Late Extinction), the simulation was run for 2 hours under conditions of extinction. Session 5 consisted of the next 20 minutes of extinction training. To create each session, we gave Sniffy the experience described, then saved the simulation as a unique file. Thus, this demonstration involved observing five different Sniffy files, one for each phase of Sniffy's training.

The sequences of the seven responses generated during the five phases of operant conditioning were used to create transition matrices and conditional probability matrices as described in the previous section. Then, the Pathfinder algorithm was applied to the conditional probability matrices to generate network solutions.

Results

Figure 1 shows the PRONET solutions for each of the five stages of operant training. In the graphic representations of each network, the frequency of each response is coded by the size of the network node (i.e. the box), the thickness of the lines making up the box, and a number in the box. The conditional probability of a transition from one response to the next served as the basis for the link weights which are coded by the thickness of the lines and the number

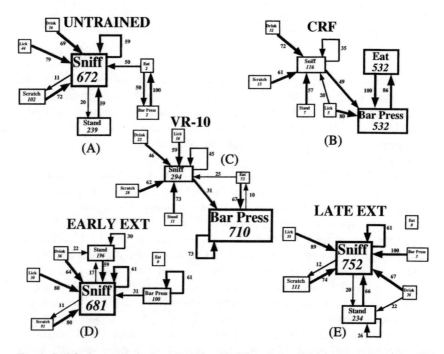

Fig. 1. Pathfinder networks based on the conditional transition matrices from the five session of operant training in Demonstration I – Pretraining, continuous reinforcement, variable ratio 10, the first 20 minutes of extinction, and the final 20 minute of extinction. The frequency of each behavior is represented by the size of the nodes, the thickness of the lines for the box, and numbers within the box; the level of conditional probability is represented by the thickness of the lines linking nodes and the number next to the line (which is $100 \times$ the conditional probability).

next to the line (which is 100 times the conditional probability). In each network, links with a weight less than 10 were eliminated.

Examining the PRONET network from the Pretraining session (Fig. 1A) shows that sniffing was the primary response prior to training, with bar pressing and eating being rare. All of the responses were very likely to be followed by sniffing except for bar pressing. Then, once delivery of food was made contingent on pressing the bar in the CRF session (Fig. 1B), the frequency of bar pressing and eating increased dramatically, with the bar pressing typically followed by eating which was always followed by pressing the bar. The frequencies of sniffing, standing, and scratching all decreased, whereas licking and drinking did not decrease as precipitously. Sniffing was still more likely response to follow all of the other behaviors than eating or bar pressing. In the VR10 session (Fig. 1C), bar pressing became the dominant response, and pressing the bar was very likely to be followed by more bar pressing. As would be expected from a VR10 schedule of reinforcement, bar pressing was followed by eating with a conditional probability of 10%. Compared to the CRF session, the frequency of sniffing increased, but remained much lower than in Pretraining. Scratching, standing, licking, and drinking remained at low levels. As during the Pretraining and CRF sessions, behaviors other than bar pressing were likely to be followed by sniffing. Even eating had a fairly sizable conditional probability of being followed by sniffing during this session.

During the first 20 minutes of extinction (Fig. 1D), Sniffy greatly decreased bar pressing, with corresponding increases in sniffing, standing, and scratching. Drinking and licking remained at low levels. Because this was an extinction session, eating did not occur. As in the previous sessions, behaviors were likely to be followed by sniffing. The major exception was bar pressing – a bar press was most likely to be followed by another bar press, a remnant of the VR10 training. Later in extinction (Fig. 1E), bar pressing had returned to a very low frequency, with sniffing, standing, and scratching returning to their high levels observed in pretraining. As in all sessions, most responses were most likely to be followed by sniffing.

The PRONET networks of the five phases of Sniffy, the virtual rat's operant training show that the operant contingencies modified Sniffy's behavior – bar pressing and eating became the dominant responses during CRF training, with bar pressing gaining sole dominance during VR10 training. This pattern of change in behavior is typical of operant conditioning and is evident in the cumulative record that accompanies the simulation. Thus, the results of this demonstration support the validity of the PRONET method.

The PRONET analysis also reveals the changes in the frequency and likelihood of other behaviors as bar pressing increased. As bar pressing increased in both frequency and in the likelihood of being the response to follow eating, sniffing, or a previous bar press, the frequency of other types of behavior decreased, with the bulk of the decrease coming from sniffing, standing and scratching. The frequencies of licking and drinking did not change as much throughout the five sessions. Another aspect of the behavior in the simulation that was not very sensitive to the reinforcement contingencies was the likelihood of a transition to sniffing following any response. Most responses tended to be followed by sniffing (except for those directly involved in the reinforcement contingency, bar pressing and eating) in all five sessions. These findings show that PRONET can reveal the relations among the entire set of events in a sequence.

If Sniffy had been a live rat rather than a simulated one, sniffing around a chamber could be interpreted as an exploratory behavior. Thus, the propensity for a rat to sniff frequently in the Pretraining session and to return to sniffing after engaging in any other behavior would suggest that the rat had a general purpose procedure, "If behavior A is completed, then explore". A researcher observing a real rat whose behavior resulted in PRONET networks like the ones in the five sessions here might reasonably infer that this exploration procedure remained intact throughout the five sessions. To continue to have a strong exploration procedure despite the contingency between bar pressing and reinforcement and the consequent increase in bar pressing and decrease in the frequency of sniffing in the CRF and VR10 sessions would seem to be unexpected. That is to say, this aspect of the simulation appears to have low face validity. Thus, in addition to showing that the PRONET networks provide simplified and interpretable summaries of a sequence of behaviors, this analysis points out another valuable use of the PRONET method – to evaluate sequences of the behavior of computer-based simulations.

Demonstration II: Transfer of Procedural Knowledge

Users of technology often must transfer knowledge of how to use a system from one task environment to another. For example, a user who learns to use a word processing application in an office will try to use the same application for tasks at home. In today's world of multiple applications and computer platforms, users may also have to transfer between computer systems. For example, an experienced user of Microsoft Word for Windows might have to use WordPerfect or Word for the Macintosh. Can PRONET networks help researchers identify the procedures that underlie successful transfer, thereby giving guidance to designers so that they can develop interfaces that make it easier for users to transfer knowledge?

Method

The participants in this study were students at New Mexico State University: one of whom had limited computer experience (hereafter referred to as the Baseline participant), one who had extensive experience with Microsoft Word for Windows and with Microsoft Windows 95 (hereafter referred to as the Windows-to-Windows Transfer participant), and one who had extensive experience with Microsoft Word for the Macintosh, but had no prior experience with Word for Windows and little experience with Microsoft Windows (hereafter referred to as the Mac-to-Windows Transfer participant). The research task required the participants to use Windows95 and Word for Windows 7.0 to type a business letter. A scenario was given to them which specified the requirements of the letter, including specific margins and font type, creation of two tables, pagination requirements, and the purpose of the letter and basic contents. In addition, we asked the participants to save the letter, print it, create a new folder, and move the letter to the new folder. We recorded the users' actions both by videotaping and by use of a specially-designed program for logging Windows events. During the task time (approximately 35 minutes) the test coordinator observed the participant via the TV monitor in a room adjacent to the testing room. Once a participant had completed the task, the test coordinator replayed sections of the video for that participant and asked him or her to provide a retrospective verbal report. In general, the test coordinator focused on aspects of the task that seemed problematic for the participant and areas in which the participant's goals or intentions had to be clarified. These data were collected largely to supplement the log file and video data. The retrospective report required approximately 15 minutes.

The behavioral sequence data were treated as described in the section that outlines the PRONET procedure above. Here we will detail the unique steps in data treatment for this research. We first coded each event for each participant based on the output from the event logging software, the associated videotape of a participant's interaction, and, when necessary, the retrospective verbal protocol. Because certain issues concerned with user cognition and with usability may focus more on the user's purpose or goals (i.e. the functional level), whereas other issues may center more on the actions that the user performed (i.e. the operational level), we decided to employ coding schemes to correspond to each of these levels. These levels of abstraction mirror the keystroke and functional level models used in GOMS analysis (Card, Moran & Newell, 1983). Because of the relative ease of interpretability, the data from the high level coding are presented in this report. Next, we transformed each coded event sequence into a frequency matrix in which events were represented along the rows and columns, then into conditional probability matrices. Finally, these conditional transition probabilities were analyzed using the Pathfinder algorithm with the default parameters of $q = n - 1$, and $r = \infty$. (In these analyses we did not consider transitions that occurred less than 10% of the time.)

In addition to analyzing the data from the participants, we developed a task analysis of the letter writing task. The task analysis was used to generate an optimized sequence of behaviors which was then analyzed using PRONET. The result was an optimized network of behaviors for the task that served as a comparison for the networks from the human participants.

Results

In addition to the PRONET analysis, we measured two aspects of performance: the time to complete the task in minutes, and the quality of the final product (assessed by the mean judgment of three blind judges on a scale of 1 = poor to 10 = good). The Windows-to-Windows participant was the fastest, taking 30 minutes to complete the task, with the Mac-to-Windows participant requiring 37 minutes and the Baseline participant taking 48 minutes. The quality of the participants' letters were rated as 7.3, 8.3, and 5.0, respectively. The better performance by the Mac-to-Windows participant than the Baseline participant indicates positive transfer in this task. In fact, the quality of the letter produced was slightly better for the Mac-to-Windows participant than even the Windows-to-Windows, further supporting the idea of positive transfer from Microsoft Word on the Macintosh to Word for Windows.

Another way to compare the three participant's behavior as they used Word for Windows to write the letter is to look at the similarity between each of their PRONET networks and the optimized network based on the task analysis. Table 2 compares the networks in terms of network similarity, based on the proportion of shared links and difference between the observed and expected number of links in common. Network similarity takes into account the total number of links in the networks whereas the difference between the observed and expected number of links in common does not. Also, the difference between observed and expected links or between the observed and expected similarity tends to be more sensitive than the raw link and similarity measures. The absolute values in Table 2 are low because (1) a relatively open-ended task with many possibilities for different actions produces a low proportion of shared events between any two individuals, resulting in low overall similarities between the individuals' networks, and (2) the measure used here was the amount by which the observed similarity *exceeded* the expected similarity.

Table 2. Observed – Expected Network Similarity Measures for Each Participant Compared to the Optimized Performance Based on Task Analysis (Higher Values Indicate High Similarity.

	Observed-Expected Network Similarity	Observed-Expected Links in Common
Baseline	0.01	0.36
Windows-Windows	0.10**	4.19
Mac-Windows	0.03*	1.82

* $p < 0.05$; ** $p < 0.01$) and Observed – expected links in common for each participant compared to the optimized performance (higher values indicate more links in common) in Demonstration II.

Having many paths to reach a given outcome typically produces differences across users in terms of which actions were executed and the frequency of the transitions between actions. As a consequence, the resulting networks differ a great deal in their node composition – actions that were never executed by a participant will not occur as a node in the network and, as a consequence that node cannot be linked to any other node. However, the data agree with the other performance measures in that they show higher similarity between the optimized performance and the two experienced users than between the optimized performance and the baseline user, with the highest similarity by the Windows-to-Windows participant.

Examining the specific structures of each network can be most useful for interpretation and for identifying specific procedural knowledge that a user may have (or gaps in procedural knowledge). Figures 2–4 shows the high-level functional networks for each user during the session in which they created a letter using Word for Windows. In the networks, nodes indicate events occurring in the participant's interaction with the computer and are coded by shape to indicate the event category (from the coding scheme) and by size, border thickness, and pattern to indicate the frequency of the event. Links indicate that one event followed another in a sequence in the order indicated by the arrows. The thickness and dashedness of the lines provides an indication of link strength which is based on the conditional probability of that particular transition.

Figure 2 shows the high-level network from the analysis of the Baseline user's behavior. The network consists of 14 nodes and 26 links that summarize 14 functions which occurred a total of 255 times with 34 unique transitions between functions. The PRONET analysis produced a simple network. The

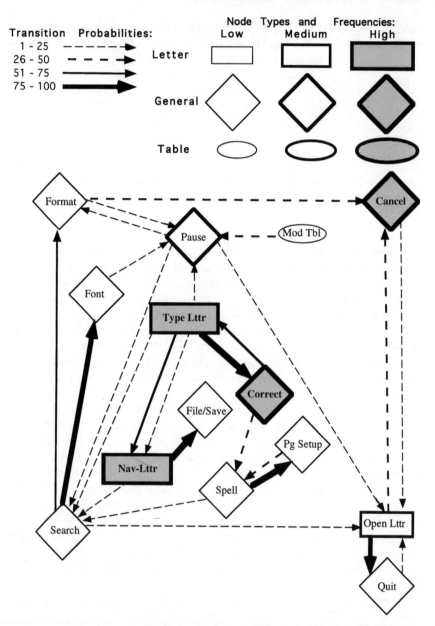

Fig. 2. Pathfinder network based on the conditional transition matrix for the Baseline participant in Demonstration II. The shading of the nodes represents the type of behavior; the size of the node indicates the frequency of the behavior; and the thickness and dashedness of the lines linking nodes represents the level of conditional transition probability.

network indicates that this participant created the table without using the software's table-creating capabilities, nor did she use Help to find out how to access those capabilities. One explanation of this pattern of behavior would be that she did not know that Word has special purpose functions for creating tables. In addition, Correct, Pause, and Search are central to the Baseline user's network: (1) Type Lttr connects strongly with all three functions; and (2) Pause and Search have numerous links with other functions. The centrality of pausing and searching suggest that this participant frequently stopped to think about what to do next and to find information and, further, that these interruptions were not confined to one type of function, but were more universal. The pattern of the Baseline user's network – with much pausing, searching, and correcting, as well as the failure to use the relevant table-creating functions – are consistent with a low level of experience with computers and help explain her poor performance.

Figure 3 shows the high-level network, consisting of 22 nodes and 33 links, from the Windows-to-Windows user's transition probability data (representing the data from 22 functions which occurred a total of 183 times with 69 unique transitions). Several key features of the network stand out. First, the functions related to the letter tend to be interconnected and can be seen in the upper half of the large network. Several general functions are linked to the letter-related functions, but not the table-related functions – Close, Save, Page Setup, Page Break, Spell Check, Quit, Pause, and Search. Perhaps the most interesting of these are Pause and Search. This participant appears to have paused to compose the letter (the Pause -Type Lttr link), and in deciding whether to save or quit the file. Searching occurred as she typed and navigated through the letter. In addition, she searched in order to find how to open the table. The functions related to the table, found in the bottom half of the network, also tend to be interconnected and not directly connected to those for the letter. The general functions linked exclusively to table-related functions – including Select, Copy, Cut, and Paste – indicate that she reused (or attempted to reuse) parts of the table to a greater extent than she did parts of the main body of the letter. Finally, the general function, Correct, bridges between the letter- and table-related functions. Note however, that Correct is linked only to typing the letter among the letter-related functions, but is linked to typing, navigating, and modifying the table. The small highly interconnected subnetwork of Correct, Mod Tbl, Nav-Tbl, and Type Tbl suggests that this user made many corrections as she created the table. This network is consistent with a user knowledgeable about basic word processing, but not at creating tables as part of the word processing application.

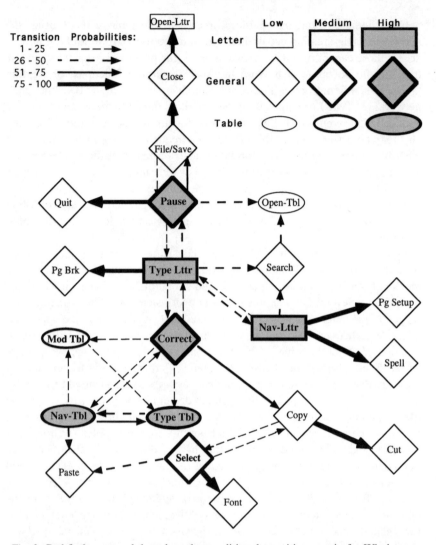

Fig. 3. Pathfinder network based on the conditional transition matrix for Windows-to-Windows participant in Demonstration II. The shading of the nodes represents the type of behavior; the size of the node indicates the frequency of the behavior; and the thickness and dashedness of the lines linking nodes represents the level of conditional transition probability.

The PRONET network for the Mac-to-Windows user (Fig. 4) consists of 25 nodes and 46 links (reduced from 25 functions which occurred a total of 172 times in 71 unique transitions between functions). The network has a degree of segregation between letter-related and table-related functions, with Typing, Navigating, and Modifying the Table grouped in a small subnetwork that also contains Correct and Select. Typing the letter is contained in a cycle with Correct, Cut, and Paste, and also links to Page Break, Page Setup and Spell Check. However, the other letter-related functions – Open Lttr and Nav Lttr – are not linked directly to Type Lttr. For the Mac-to-Windows user, corrections were preceded by typing, either in the letter or the table, and, not surprisingly were often followed by more typing. In addition, corrections were followed by selecting text, cutting text, or modifying the table. This user engaged in a relatively large amount of searching, with Search as perhaps the central node of her network. One explanation for the pattern of behavior revealed by the network – widespread connections with Correct and Search, but appropriate use of functions – might be related to her previous experience with Word for the Macintosh, rather than with the Windows95 version used in this study. Both versions of Word allow the participant to perform most of the same functions by means of similar procedures. However, in Word for Windows, certain specific command names and the menu layout differ from Word for the Macintosh. Thus, this user appears to have had to engage in a substantial amount of searching, but typically located the appropriate function.

The behavior of the Mac-to-Windows user in this complex transfer task suggests she played an active role in transfer. Briefly, this user may have engaged in a substantial amount of searching because she knew what she wanted to do and had some idea of how to do it, but had to find a way to do it. In contrast, cognitive theories of transfer of training (cf. Polson, Muncher & Englebeck, 1986; Singley & Anderson, 1989) typically assume that: (1) task knowledge involves procedures consisting of rules that specify that when a condition is met, an action will be produced, and (2) transfer is based on the common procedures between the training and transfer tasks. To account for the behavior of the Mac-to-Windows participant, one might assume: (1) that she had organized knowledge (or mental models) about both the task and the system with which she had experience, and (2) that the task of creating a letter activated her task knowledge which led to the activation of her system knowledge (e.g. Gillan, 1997). She then may have used both types of knowledge to guide an active search for conditions that would permit the specific actions to accomplish her goals. The suggestion that a user knows the action to perform and searches for the condition that will permit that action to occur reverses the condition-action sequence found in common elements

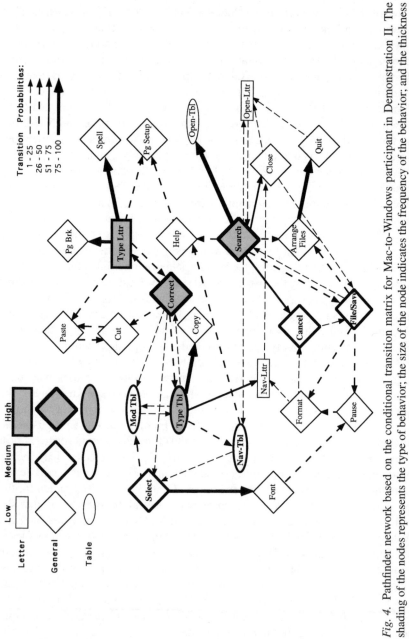

Fig. 4. Pathfinder network based on the conditional transition matrix for Mac-to-Windows participant in Demonstration II. The shading of the nodes represents the type of behavior; the size of the node indicates the frequency of the behavior; and the thickness and dashedness of the lines linking nodes represents the level of conditional transition probability.

theories. This observation of the specific behaviors during transfer occurred because the PRONET method permitted a detailed examination of a user's behavior in a situation closely modeled after a real-world task; in contrast, most research on transfer only records performance measures like response time and errors.

SELECTED EXAMPLES OF PRONET ANALYSIS OF COMPLEX BEHAVIORAL SEQUENCES

In addition to the two demonstrations above, previously-published studies have applied the Pathfinder algorithm to event sequences as humans interact with technology. Like the above demonstrations, these studies support the thesis of this paper that PRONET networks provide a valid and useful representation of sequences of events in human-machine interaction research and design. They also illustrate an important aspect of the PRONET method – that it can be applied across a wide variety of situations and events, making it a valuable tool for investigations both in and out of the laboratory. Below we review two examples from these previously-published studies that used the PRONET approach in ways not shown in the demonstrations above. In the first study below, Cooke et al. (1996) created networks consisting of both environmental events (the information displayed by a computer) and human behaviors in response to those displays. In the second study, the researchers (Vortac, Edwards & Manning, 1994) developed networks based on the behavior of teams as well as on individual's behavior.

Cooke et al. (1996) used PRONET to compare the behavior of student subjects as they acquired the ability to troubleshoot faults in the payload deployment and retrieval system (PDRS) of the Space Shuttle remote manipulator system (i.e. the robotic system in the shuttle) in a simulation. (The PDRS is used in deploying and stowing the manipulator arm in the Shuttle.) The simulation – a simplified version of an actual NASA mission control system – required that the user read information from a screen to identify a fault and to take action to correct the fault. The system cycled through the four stages of the PDRS – deploying a positioning mechanism, releasing latches, latching the latches, and stowing the positioning mechanism. The participants' task was to monitor the display, detect if a fault had occurred, identify the fault from a set of 13 possible faults, decide on the cause of the fault out of seven possible causes, and select a corrective action from 14 possible actions. At the end of each stage, the participant received feedback that specified if the troubleshooting decisions were correct and, if not, showed the correct alternative.

The participants' behavioral sequences were encoded into discrete events with a screen event as an antecedent condition and each participant response as the consequent action(s). Thirty-seven different screen configurations served to denote separate conditions; actions corresponded to the 36 potential selections that the participant could make with a mouse click. Cooke et al. (1996) applied the Pathfinder algorithm to matrices of transitions between the 73 events (37 conditions and 36 actions) for three sessions as the participants learned to perform the troubleshooting task. In addition, based on an analysis of the task, the researchers determined the ideal sequence of behaviors and, based on it, developed an ideal PRONET network for this complex task. They reasoned that, if participants acquired new procedural knowledge during the 12 hours of training, then their networks should come to resemble the ideal network as correct links replace incorrect links.

Cooke et al.'s (1996) analysis of the Pathfinder networks showed systematic changes as predicted – more correct links, fewer incorrect links, and an increasing similarity between the participants' networks and the ideal network. In addition, the measure of similarity of the participants' networks with the ideal network (a measure called the C value) correlated highly with participants' performance during the complex task: r's of 0.86 with the percentage of correct fault identification, 0.58 with the percentage of correct diagnoses, and 0.58 with the percentage of correct actions taken. These high positive correlations indicate that as the participants' networks became more similar to the ideal, their performance improved.

Figures 5 and 6 show the Pathfinder networks from Sessions 1 and 3, respectively, redrawn from one of Cooke et al.'s (1996) participants. (The links that match those of the ideal network are shown by the solid lines, whereas the links that don't have a corresponding link in the ideal network are dashed. In addition, due to the visual complexity of the figures, we chose not to display the link weights.)

The networks are complex, but by focusing on specific aspects of the two networks, they can become interpretable. For example, look at the diagnosis of fault nodes (labeled with DI). By determining the nodes that link with the diagnosis nodes (that is, that have go from a condition node [C], an action node [A], or from an identification of fault node [ID] to the diagnosis node), we can see the final step before a fault diagnosis. In Session 1, the network shows 17 links into diagnosis nodes, with 10 matching the ideal network and 7 not matching a link from that network. In contrast, in Session 3, the network shows 13 links into diagnosis nodes, with 11 matches to the ideal network and 2 non-matches. This observation suggests that, in this task, increased accuracy in

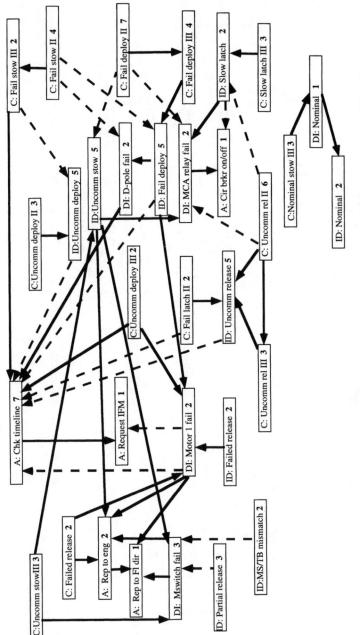

Fig. 5. Pathfinder network for Subject A during the first 2-hour training session with a PDRS simulation. Event frequencies are represented by the bold numbers in the box. The solid lines correspond to links shared with the ideal network; dashed lines correspond to links not shared with the ideal network. The letters within the node boxes indicate the type of event: C = condition, A = action, ID = identification of fault, DI = diagnosis of fault. (Figure adapted from Cooke et al., 1996.)

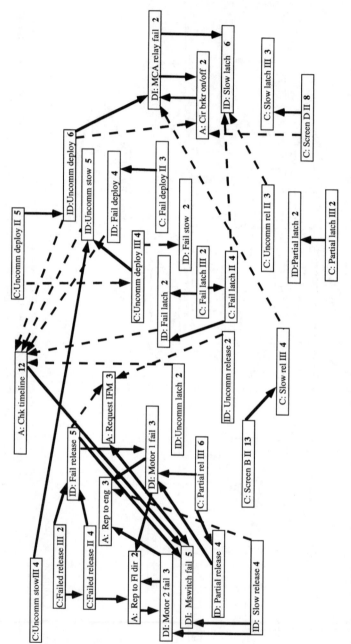

Fig. 6. Pathfinder network for Subject A during the third 2-hour training session with the PDRS simulation. Event frequencies are represented by the bold numbers in the box. The solid lines correspond to links shared with the ideal network; dashed lines correspond to links not shared with the ideal network. The letters within the node boxes indicate the type of event: C = condition, A = action, ID = identification of fault, DI = diagnosis of fault. (Figure adapted from Cooke et al., 1996.)

procedural knowledge is based largely on the loss of incorrect links or procedures (see also Anderson, 1983).

The second illustrative example comes from research on air traffic controllers by Vortac et al. (1994). One of the goals of the research was to use a Pathfinder network based on the frequencies of transitions between behaviors to study modules of cognitive processes and their relation to automation. Vortac et al. (1994) used the term module to mean a set of cognitive processes that frequently co-occur and have formed a single unit of cognition. Two important characteristics of a module are: (1) that the entire module has a single triggering event, rather than having separate triggers for each component cognitive process, and (2) effort is required if the module needs to be broken apart or fractionated. These modules resemble Anderson's (1983) construct of composed procedures – a set of procedures that becomes a unit due to repeated co-occurrence – and Hayes-Roth's (1977) construct of a cogit. One major concern of Vortac et al.'s (1994) was that implementing automation in a system should not disrupt any cognitive modules that the system operators had developed. That is, when introducing a new automated system, the underlying processes of the module or actions related to the module should not be distributed between operators or between the system and the operator.

In their research with air traffic controllers, Vortac et al. (1994) used Pathfinder networks to identify possible cognitive modules. They set the following criteria for this identification: (1) transitions between behaviors should occur frequently; (2) these transitions should be in close temporal proximity; (3) these transitions should occur in multiple situations; (4) the triggering event(s) should be both identifiable and reliable; (5) in a team task, one individual performs the actions related to the module, the actions are not distributed across the team. Thus, in order to apply these criteria, Vortac et al. (1994) recorded the behaviors of both individuals on two person teams, and then compared Pathfinder networks derived from individuals' behavior to networks derived from the team's behavior. In recording team behavior and deriving the Pathfinder network for this study, Vortac et al. (1994) kept track of the identity of the team member who produced the response. (However, researchers using Pathfinder to create a network of team behaviors could ignore the individual's identity. Given Vortac et al.'s goals in this study, being able to associate team actions with the actor was important.)

By comparing the individual and team networks, Vortac et al. (1994) found one set of behaviors that met the criteria for a cognitive module in a high fidelity simulation of controlling en route air traffic. The behaviors of verifying the information on a paper flight progress strip (FPS) or changing that information (what the researchers labeled as WRITE) were linked in the

Pathfinder networks for both individuals and teams with behaviors for manipulating the FPS (e.g. moving it between posting boards in the ATC control area, sequencing a set of FPS's in a posting board, or removing the FPS) (what the researchers called MANIP). The co-occurrence of these two types of behavior was frequent, the two behaviors occurred close together in time, the transition between behaviors occurred across scenarios of varying complexity, from simple to complex. The sequence of WRITE – MANIP was triggered reliably by events related to transitions in flight control sectors, such as the initial contact with a sector. The sequence was also triggered, but somewhat less reliably, by a controller command to an aircraft. Finally, on a team, whichever individual engaged in a WRITE behavior, that same individual performed the subsequent MANIP behavior. The focus on FPS-relevant behaviors was important because the FPS system was being planned to be replaced by a computer-based and somewhat automated system. Vortac et al.'s (1994) results indicate that the new design of the FPS system should not distribute the WRITE and MANIP tasks between the human operator and the automated system.

GENERAL DISCUSSION

The demonstrations and examples described above show PRONET to be useful in summarizing, representing, and analyzing a diverse set of sequences of behavior – from a simulation of simple operant training of a bar press response (perhaps the most studied paradigm in all of experimental psychology), to using a word processor, to learning to diagnose faults in a Space Shuttle subsystem, to air traffic control. Aspects of the networks produced by the PRONET method were to some degree unsurprising. For example, the networks in the operant training sessions reflected the dramatic changes in behavior produced by changing the reinforcement contingencies. Likewise, the increasing similarity of networks to an ideal in the PDRS fault diagnosis learning task across the three sessions, and the closer similarity of experienced participants' networks to an ideal than an inexperienced participant in the transfer task all would be expected. So, a skeptic might say, "So what? PRONET just shows me what I already know". However, part of validation of a method involves demonstrating that the method can show you the expected results. Imagine, for example, if PRONET couldn't show the changes in behavior during operant training or showed greater similarity to an ideal sequence of behaviors for a novice than for an experienced word processor – the method would rightly be judged as lacking. In addition, are there other methods that have been demonstrated to have the kind of range that PRONET has demonstrated in the three demonstrations above. A cumulative record could show the same increased bar pressing during operant training, but wouldn't show the effects seen in the more complex tasks; response time or accuracy measures would show the same performance effects during complex task training or transfer, but might not capture the full picture of operant training.

In the introduction, we criticized the standard measures used in cognitive psychology as being too simplistic to reflect the complexity of a sequence of behavior during a productive task in the work context. How did PRONET fare on that account? In the simple operant task, the PRONET networks revealed that several of the responses and most of the transitions between responses were not especially sensitive to the changes in reinforcement contingency. That is, the frequencies of drinking and licking did not decrease much as bar pressing became the dominant response, and the probability of a transition to sniffing remained high for most responses throughout the various sessions. This pattern of results would not have been noticeable with a cumulative record or response time measures. Similarly, the pattern of behavior of the Mac-to-Windows user in the transfer demonstration that suggested that she was searching for the system-appropriate way to implement an action could be observed in the network. Measures like the overall task completion time or number of errors would have glossed over this observation. The importance of this observation is that it suggests that transfer involves an active learner, similar to the active nature of learners during acquisition (see Carroll, 1990).

Benefits and Costs of PRONET

An important criterion on which to evaluate any approach to data analysis focuses on the amount of effort required to perform the analyses in relation to the informational benefits that one gets from the analyses. The PRONET analysis reduced long and complicated streams of behavior to a network representation of those data that can be displayed on a single page. For example, the three participants analyzed in the transfer demonstration took between 30 and 45 minutes to complete the task and in doing so generated between 5300 and 10,500 lines of log file code recorded by the software. Any systematic analysis of this code, whether by the PRONET approach or any other system, would have to deal with this amount of data. Thus, although collection of data by automatically recording a user's behavior during a task either by videotaping or creating a computer log data file requires essentially no effort by researchers, any use of those data will be effortful. With PRONET, the path elimination feature inherent in the Pathfinder algorithm suggests that, as the complexity of the original data increases, the opportunity for path elimination also increases, thereby proportionally reducing the number of transitions in the network. Thus, the amount of data reduction makes it possible to collect large amounts of usability data in the field, while the methods of data reduction in PRONET may even make it advantageous to collect large amount of data.

An additional benefit of PRONET is its flexibility. The analyses in this paper looked only at first order transitions (lag of 1). That is, we counted the sequence of A→B→C as one increment in the frequency of co-occurrence matrix for A→B, and one for B→C, but none for A→C. This latter case would be examined only if higher order transitions were included. In addition, we decided to delete from the networks any transitions that occurred less than 10% of the time. Although these decisions were not arbitrary, other approaches might be taken. The use of higher order transitions, examining multistep units of behavior (e.g. A–B–C instead of A–B and B–C), and various cutoffs for considering transitions as links could also be examined using PRONET.

If the effort to use PRONET were reduced, then the benefits of using PRONET – reduction in data and the increase in its interpretability and utility – would more strongly outweigh the cost in effort. The researchers spent most of their time on the projects described in the demonstrations encoding the behavioral data (e.g. chunking lines of log file code into categories that could be represented in a Pathfinder network as nodes). Although this process was effortful, the amount of time and effort is misleading because the encoding had to be done by hand and the coding scheme had to be enhanced concurrent with some of the encoding. The encoding process could be automated, for example, if the log file software recorded the data in a previously-developed coding scheme that was formatted by a PRONET tool for subsequent analysis by the Pathfinder algorithm. The PRONET tool would take the output after each session and use it to increment transition frequencies in an $N \times N$ matrix where N represents the number of different events. Once the matrix was updated, the original log file data could be deleted, leaving behind only the frequency matrix.

A Research and Development Agenda

PRONET provides one method among several that have been developed in the behavioral and information sciences over the past 30 years for summarizing and visualizing event sequences. These methods include Markov modeling (e.g, Guzdial, 1993), lag sequential analysis (e.g. Sackett, 1978; Bakeman &

Gottman, 1997), Petri nets (Elwert, 1996; Palanque & Bastide, 1996; Petri, 1980; and Rauterberg, 1993, 1995), and process discovery and validation (Cook & Wolf, 1995, 1997). Each of these methods could be useful in helping cognitive researchers and user interface designers, as the demonstrations described above show PRONET to be (see also Gillan & Cooke, 1998). Thus, one goal of future research should be to validate these methods for use in the study of cognitive systems in context. These methods should be examined using event sequence data from complex, productive tasks in the work context to determine: (1) the relation between the output of each method and performance measures, such as task completion time and task accuracy; (2) the degree to which each method represents the event sequence in a simplified and interpretable form, and (3) the ability for researchers to perform additional analyses on the output of each method.

A reasonable hypothesis is that the various methods – PRONET, Petri nets, Markov modeling, lag sequential analysis, and process discovery and validation – will be differentially useful as a function of the type of events, characteristics of the sequence, or the environmental conditions in which the events occurred. Thus, another goal for future research should be to identify the conditions under which each method would be most useful as a tool for representing and analyzing event sequences.

For PRONET to be more than simply a research instrument and to provide timely and useful information in typical task contexts, additional development will be required. Ideally, a system with the following characteristics will need to be developed: (1) the ability for the researcher, designer, or analyst to define the level of behavior to be recorded at the keystroke or functional level; (2) automatic recording of behaviors in sequence (much like a log data file); (3) organizing the sequence of behaviors in a transition matrix and a transition probability matrix, with the ability for the researcher, designer, or analyst to specify the lag size, and (4) automatic application of the Pathfinder algorithm, with the ability to set the r and q parameters. Such a system would allow the researcher, designer, or analyst to simply set the parameters, then after a session of user interaction, to examine the Pathfinder network. In the absence of such a system, much time and effort is required to prepare the data for analysis. However, we recognize that many important issues need to be addressed before this ideal system could be developed – primary among these is developing either: (1) an interface that permitted the researcher to specify functional categories and to map those categories onto keystroke level events, or (2) an intelligent system that could identify a set of keystroke level responses that would constitute a functional level category.

Guidelines for System Designers Using PRONET

Perhaps the most important point for designers to keep in mind is that conducting and interpreting a Pathfinder analysis, whether of a sequence of behaviors or similarity ratings of a set of concepts, requires the acquisition of a substantial amount of skill. One cannot acquire that level of skill simply by reading a summary paper like this. Rather, that skill probably can be acquired best through practice with the method, reflection about the usefulness of the analysis, and feedback concerning the quality of the output of the analysis. Thus, we encourage potential users of PRONET to make use of the method initially to analyze tasks with a limited set of behaviors, like those in Demonstration I above, and tasks for which the analysis is not critical to the success or failure of a product. In addition, we caution first-time users of the method to expect that their early networks may be difficult to interpret; but with practice in the various elements of the PRONET approach, an analyst's skill will increase, leading to interpretable network representations of even complex behavioral sequences.

One key to applying PRONET successfully is in selecting the task. For example, complex, multifaceted work – such as work consisting of unrelated, concurrent tasks – would be less likely to produce useful networks than would more integrated tasks motivated by a single goal. Also, as we found with the operant conditioning and word processing demonstrations, the level of the task performer's skill will influence the network. Thus, a designer interested in the changes in behavior during skill acquisition should compare PRONET networks from users at various levels of experience. However, a designer interested in examining steady state behavior would be served best by collecting behavioral sequences from only more experienced users.

A second aspect to which PRONET users should attend is the level of analysis of the behavior. Our study of transfer of word processing knowledge that produced the data described in Demonstration II above provides a case in point. In analyzing the task, we parsed the behavioral sequences at two levels – a microscopic level (what Card et al., 1983, called "the keystroke level") and a more macroscopic level (Card et al.'s "functional level"). We undertook this dual analysis with the thought that the microscopic level analysis would be close to the level of the interface elements (e.g. the menu items and screen icons), whereas the macroscopic behaviors would be closer to the level at which the word processing participants conceived of the their work. Thus, to examine transfer of procedural knowledge, the functional level seemed to be a better choice. The key to deciding on the level at which to parse the behavior for PRONET is, first, to know how you plan to use the data.

Third, PRONET users should decide on which lag(s) between behaviors will be most meaningful to analyze. Typically, most analysts will examine the lag 0 sequence (i.e. temporally adjacent responses). However, analysts in certain complex situations might find it enlightening to look at sequences of behaviors separated by one or more responses. For example, a task in which environmental events A and B (e.g. two different computer-sent messages) both produced the same immediate response (acknowledgment of receipt of the message), but produced reliably different second responses (e.g. initiating process X vs. terminating process Y) would produce more meaningful networks with an analysis at a lag of 1 than at a lag of 0. Given that the recording of the sequence of behaviors can be examined to produce a transition matrix at lag $= 1$ or lag $= 2$ as easily as lag $= 0$, analysts may want to perform multiple analyses, each with a different lag value. Another option (done by in the research by Vortac et al., 1994, that we describe above) is to weight transitions of various lags differentially, then to combine the weighted transitions. Decreasing the weight as the temporal distance between behaviors increased would usually be the most useful approach.

A fourth important choice in applying PRONET is the selection of the r and q parameters in Pathfinder, which help to determine the density of the network. The simplest Pathfinder network will be produced with the settings of $r =$ infinity and $q =$ the number of behaviors $- 1$. However, as analysts acquire more ability, an approach to consider would be to create network of varying densities by varying the settings of r and q.

Fifth, the interpretation of the network will be essential to the success of the PRONET analysis. PRONET provides a representation of a sequence of events, but the representation by itself has no meaning. The meaning that can be derived from the analysis comes from a clear understanding of your objectives in performing the analysis. In the absence of a concrete and well-formed goal, the likelihood of a PRONET network producing insight into user behavior is low. Given a clearly stated goal of the analysis, making use of interpretive heuristics (previously described in the above section, PRONET: Procedural Networks) should improve the quality of the interpretation. Briefly, those heuristics focused on extracting meaning from the elements of the network at various levels. Each link and the nodes that it connects represent a temporal relation between two events; the links with the highest weights would be those that had the highest probability of occurring. An environmental event leading to a behavioral event with a high link weight may reveal a user's procedural knowledge. Identify certain key events (especially those that might indicate an error or a problem) and find the events that consistently lead to or follow from those key events. Examine the network for events that have many connections because these will likely be central events (e.g. a choice point). The nodes and links may also be organized in structures, such as a chain of events (which would indicate a linear event sequence) or a subnetwork of tightly interconnected nodes (which might help you to identify a user-defined subtask).

In closing, we now have computer and videotaping technologies that permit us to collect massive amounts of observational data. Unfortunately, our development of data analytic tools has not kept pace with the data collection abilities. Ultimately, we need to be able to mine these data so that we can extract information about user's perceptual and cognitive processes. Progress in science and engineering depends on the development of good new methods. However, mass adoption of poor methods slows progress in science and engineering. The discipline of human factors in general, as well as the subdiscipline of human-computer interaction, have been willing to adopt new methods. Many of the new methods have at least been validated; positive examples of such methods include GOMS (e.g. Card, Moran & Newell, 1983) and cognitive walkthroughs (e.g. Polson, Lewis, Rieman & Wharton, 1992). Unfortunately, in other cases, the methods have been adopted without any assessment. We believe that researchers and practitioners in human factors should be as willing to evaluate the methods that they use as they are to evaluate user interfaces. In their classic paper, Gould and Lewis (1985) suggest that collecting user data is a key to successful usability engineering. We would amend that recommendation in two ways – that designers collect and *analyze* user data that is *usable and interpretable* for design.

NOTE

1. Pathfinder programs (i.e. KNOT) have been written in Pascal, C, Lisp, and APL. Various version of the program run on the IBM PC, Apple Macintosh, and SUN Microsystems computers. Information on obtaining programs is available from Interlink, Inc., P.O. Box 4086 UPB, Las Cruces, NM 88003–4086.

ACKNOWLEDGMENTS

The authors thank Microsoft for support of the research described in Demonstration II and for providing the software necessary for that study. Technical, logistic, conceptual, and design assistance was provided by Preston A. Kiekel, Shane Melton, Krisela Rivera, and Doug Reynolds.

REFERENCES

Anderson, J. R. (1983). *The architecture of cognition*. Cambridge, MA: Harvard University Press.

Bakeman, R., & Gottman, J. M. (1997). *Observing interaction: An introduction to sequential analysis* (2nd ed.). Cambridge: Cambridge University Press.

Bakeman, R., & Quera, V. (1995). *Analyzing interaction: Sequential analysis with SDIS and GSEQ*. Cambridge: Cambridge University Press.

Card, S., Moran, T., & Newell, A. (1983). *The psychology of human-computer interaction*. Hillsdale, NJ: L. Erlbaum.

Carroll, J. M. (1990). *The Nurnburg funnel: Designing minimalist instruction for practical computer skill*. Cambridge, MA: MIT Press.

Cook, J. E., & Wolf, A. L. (1995). Automating process discovery through event-data analysis. *Proceedings of the 17th Annual ICSE 'Conference on Software Engineering* (pp. 73–82). New York: ACM.

Cook, J. E., & Wolf, A. L. (1997). Controlling product evolution through process validation. *Proceedings of the ICSE '97 Workshop on Process Modeling and Empirical Studies of Software Evolution* (pp. 23–27). New York: ACM.

Cooke, N. J. (1992). Predicting judgment time from measures of psychological proximity. *Journal of Experimental Psychology: Learning, Memory, and Cognition, 18*, 640–653.

Cooke, N. J., Durso, F. T., & Schvaneveldt, R. W. (1986). Recall and measures of memory organization. *Journal of Experimental Psychology: Learning, Memory, and Cognition, 12*, 538–549.

Cooke, N. J., & Gillan, D. J. (1999). Representing human behavior in human-computer interaction. In: A. Kent & J. G. Williams (Eds), *Encyclopedia of Computer Science* (pp. 283–308). New York: Marcel Dekker.

Cooke, N. J., Neville, K. J., & Rowe, A. L. (1996). Procedural network representations of sequential data. *Human-Computer Interaction, 11*, 29–68.

Dunn-Rankin, P. (1983). *Scaling methods*. Academic Press: San Diego.

Elwert, T. (1996). Continuous and explicit dialogue modeling. *Conference on Human Factors in Computing Systems CHI'96 Conference Companion*. New York: ACM.

Gillan, D. J. (1997). The three psychologies of human-computer interaction. *Proceedings of the Human Factors and Ergonomics Society 41st Annual Meeting* (pp. 385–389). Santa Monica, CA: HFES.

Gillan, D. J., & Cooke, N. M. (1998). Making usability data more usable. *Proceedings of Human Factors and Ergonomics Society 42th Annual Meeting* (pp. 300–304). Santa Monica, CA: HFES.

Gillan, D. J., & Schvaneveldt, R. W. (1999). Applying cognitive psychology: Bridging the gulf between basic research and cognitive artifacts. In: F. T. Durso, R. Nickerson, R. Schvaneveldt, S. Dumais, M. Chi & S. Lindsay (Eds), *The Handbook of Applied Cognition* (pp. 4–31). Chichester, England: Wiley.

Goldsmith, T. E., & Davenport, D. M. (1990). Assessing structural similarity of graphs. In: R. W. Schvaneveldt (Ed.), *Pathfinder Associative Networks: Studies in Knowledge Organization* (pp. 179–195). Norwood, NJ: Ablex.

Gottman, J. M., & Roy, A. K. (1990). *Sequential analysis: A guide for behavioral researchers*. Cambridge: Cambridge University Press.

Graham, J., Alloway, T., & Krames, L. (1994). Sniffy, the virtual rat: Simulated operant conditioning. *Behavior Research Methods, Instruments, & Computers*, *26*, 134–141.

Guzdial, M. (1993). Deriving software usage patterns from log files. *GVU Center Technical Report No. 93–41*. Atlanta, GA: Georgia Institute of Technology.

Hammontree, M., Weiler, P. and Hendrich, B. (1995). PDA-based observation logging. In: *Human Factors in Computing Systems Chi '95 Conference Companion*. New York: ACM.

Hayes-Roth, B. (1977). Evolution of cognitive structures and processes. *Psychological Review*, *84*, 260–278.

Hutchins, E. (1996). *Cognition in the wild*. Cambridge, MA: MIT Press.

Johnson, S. C., (1967). Hierarchical clustering schemes. *Psychometrika*, *32*, 241–254.

Kruskal, J. B., & Wish, M. (1978). *Multidimensional Scaling,*. Beverly Hills, CA. Sage.

Mayer, R. E. (1999). Instructional technology. In: F. T. Durso, R. Nickerson, R. Schvaneveldt, S. Dumais, M. Chi & S. Lindsay (Eds), *The Handbook of Applied Cognition* (pp. 551–569). Chichester, England: Wiley.

Millen, D. R., Schreifer, A., Lehder, D. Z., & Dray, S. M. (1997). Mind maps and causal models: Using graphical representations of field research data. In: *Human Factors in Computing Systems CHI'97 Conference Companion* (pp. 265–266). New York: ACM.

Owen, R. N., Baecker, R. M., & Harrison, B. (1994). Timelines, a tool for the gathering, coding, and analysis of temporal HCI usability data. In: *Human Factors in Computing Systems Chi '94 Conference Companion*. New York: ACM.

Palanque, P. and Bastide, R. (1996) Temporal aspects of usability: Time modeling in Petri nets for the design of interactive systems. *SigCHI Bulletin*, *28*, 43–46.

Petri, C. A. (1980). Introduction to general net theory. In: W. Bauer (Ed.), *Lecture Notes in Computer Science: Net Theory and Applications* (pp. 1–21). Berlin: Springer-Verlag.

Pinker, S. (1997). *How the mind works*. New York: Norton.

Polson, P. G., Muncher, E., & Englebeck, G. (1986). A test of a common elements theory of transfer. In: M. Mantei & P. Obeton (Eds), *Human Factors in Computing Systems CHI'86* (pp. 78–83). New York: ACM.

Rauterberg, M. (1993) AMME: An automatic mental model evaluation to analyze user behavior traced in a finite, discrete state space. *Ergonomics*, *36*, 1369–1380.

Rauterberg, M. (1995). From novice to expert decision behavior: A qualitative modeling approach with Petri Nets. In: Y. Anzai, K. Ogawa & H. Mori (Eds), *Symbiosis of Human and Artifact: Human and Social Aspects of Human-Computer Interaction* Vol. 2 (pp. 449–454). Amsterdam: Elsevier.

Rauterberg, M. (1996) *The AMME Manual: A Petri net based analyzing and modeling tool kit for log files in human-computer interaction*. Technical Report CC-5-96, Work and Organization Psychology Unit, Swiss Federal Institute of Technology, Zurich, Switzerland.

Reisig, W. (1992). *A primer in Petri net design*. Berlin: Springer-Verlag.

Sackett, G. P. (1978). Measurement in observational research. In: G. P. Sackett (Ed.), *Observing Behavior* (Vol. 2): *Data collection and analysis methods* (pp. 25–43). Baltimore: University Park Press.

Sanderson, P. M., & Fisher, C. (1994). Exploratory sequential data analysis: Foundations. *Human-Computer Interaction*, *9*, 251–317.

Schvaneveldt, R. W. (Ed.) (1990). *Pathfinder associative networks: Studies in knowledge organization*. Norwood, NJ: Ablex.

Schvaneveldt, R. W., Durso, F. T., & Dearholt, D. W. (1989). Network structures in proximity data. In: G. H. Bower (Ed.), *The Psychology of Learning and Motivation: Advances in Research and Theory* (Vol. 24, pp. 249–284). New York: Academic Press.

Singley, M. K., & Anderson, J. R. (1989). *The transfer of cognitive skill.* Cambridge, MA: Harvard University Press.
Vortac, O. U., Edwards, M., & Manning, C. (1994). Sequences of actions for individual and teams of air traffic controllers. *Human-Computer Interaction, 9,* 319–343.

4. SOME GUIDELINES FOR CONDUCTING A COGNITIVE TASK ANALYSIS

Gary Klein and Laura Militello

ABSTRACT

Cognitive Task Analysis (CTA) attempts to explain the mental processes involved in performing a task. These processes include the knowledge, skills and strategies that are needed to accomplish the task functions. The criteria for success in a CTA study are: making a useful discovery about the cognitive skills being studied; being able to communicate the discovery to the users (i.e. those who will need to use the CTA for design); and having a meaningful impact on the eventual design.

Currently, a wide variety of CTA methods are being used. As we learn how to define the cognitive demands presented by a task/situation, we hope we will be able to map CTA methods onto these demands, so that we can more efficiently select and apply the appropriate methods. This should result in more efficient studies, and greater user satisfaction. It should also help move the field of CTA into becoming more of a technology.

INTRODUCTION

Information technologies are affecting more and more work domains. These technologies place higher demands on cognitive skills such as decision making, planning, and maintaining situation awareness. For these reasons, human

Advances in Human Performance and Cognitive Engineering Research, Volume 1,
pages 161–199.
ISBN: 0-7623-0748-X

factors professionals are increasingly turning to Cognitive Task Analysis (CTA) methods to design better decision support systems, to design better human-computer interfaces, and to design better training programs. Although several CTA methods are rooted in laboratory techniques for studying cognition, many were developed to address applied needs. The value of CTA methods is to enable the investigator to "get inside-the-head" of the person performing the task, and to understand the strategies and skills that are used.

The goal of this chapter is to suggest some guidelines for conducting CTA projects. We hope that these will be helpful at several different levels. We want to enable the organizations sponsoring CTA studies to determine what to expect from a CTA study, and to estimate the success of a study that has been commissioned. We also hope that these guidelines will be useful for practitioners carrying out CTA studies, to better plan the way that methods are selected and applied. The guidelines we present have emerged from our own CTA projects; we have conducted more than 50 such studies in the past 15 years, and have collaborated on several dozen more (see Klein, 1998, for a description of many of these efforts). In addition, we have learned a great deal from colleagues in other organizations who have performed CTA projects that we consider to be highly successful.

CTA methods may be useful because they offer researchers the opportunity to understand the way people make key judgments and decisions, interpret situations, make perceptual discriminations, solve problems, generate plans, and use their cognitive skills to carry out challenging tasks. When a CTA project helps us appreciate how cognitive skills are used, we can do a better job of supporting these processes, and of removing barriers to them. CTA methods can therefore help practitioners improve the performance of complex tasks that have a strong cognitive component.

Traditional task analysis methods were not explicitly designed to address the subtle, cognitive aspects of task performance. That is why CTA methods can be useful to develop: better training programs, better human-computer interfaces, better decision support systems, better selection procedures, better accident investigations.

Training for tasks that require judgment and decision making is an example of an area of application. Seamster, Redding and Kaempf (1997) point out that cognitive skills require unique methods for assessment as well as for training; training methods that were designed to teach procedural skills do not have the flexibility to handle cognitive skills. The growing use of information technology has resulted in systems that place more cognitive demands on the operators, and the effect is that CTA methods are becoming more important for helping system operators learn how to manage the flow of data and information.

For application in system design, the cognitive engineering approach depends heavily on CTA methods (e.g. Andriole & Adelman, 1993; Essens, Fallesen, McCann, Cannon-Bowers & Dorfel, 1995; Rasmussen, Pejterson & Goodstein, 1994; Woods, 1993). The use of CTA in cognitive engineering studies is one way to factor the users' cognitive requirements into a design.

The increased interest in CTA methods also raises some questions, such as what counts as a CTA study (the boundaries are not very clear), and whether people were examining cognitive task requirements before there was CTA (clearly they were). One of our goals for this chapter is to suggest criteria that might help to reduce these types of confusion. If a research team labels its work as a CTA project, simply because their interviews included two or three general questions about cognition, without getting at the decision strategies employed by the operators, then we might experience some concern about whether this was really a example of CTA. Similarly, an effort that carefully probed the ways operators were interpreting data to arrive at judgments would seem to count as a CTA project, even if the investigators never used that term. The methods that the researchers use to elicit and analyze and represent their data are more important than the labels they attach to the work.

This chapter presents some criteria for what counts as a successful CTA project. We have illustrated these criteria with some examples. We recognize that not everyone will agree with our position, and if that disagreement can turn into informed debate, then that would also be useful.

The organization of the chapter is as follows. The first section presents a brief overview of the progress that CTA has made during the past decade. The second section considers several definitions of CTA. We next present our view of what counts as a successful CTA project. Then we contrast CTA with Behavioral Task Analysis. The next section offers a theoretical perspective for CTA based on aspects of expertise. Then we list some of the most common CTA methods and discuss criteria for selecting CTA methods. Finally, we offer some research directions for further examination of CTA methodology.

PROGRESS IN CTA

In the United States, CTA methods are relatively new. In contrast, European human factors and ergonomics professionals have long been examining cognitive processes. The reason for this divergence is the influence of behaviorism in the U.S., through the work of J. B. Watson and B. F. Skinner. As the dominant paradigm for almost half a century, behaviorism discouraged

U.S. researchers from studying cognition, and the practioners who grew out of this tradition were likewise uncomfortable with examining mental events. The European tradition was more favorable for the study of cognitive processes.

The cognitive revolution in the U.S. took hold during the late 1960s, with the publication of work such as Neisser's book, Cognitive Psychology (1967). The journal of the same name published its initial issue in 1968, and the European journal "Cognition", began in 1972. Although this movement changed the climate for basic research, it did not influence the application of human factors methods.

The field of artificial intelligence created the initial demand to "get inside-the-head" of experts. Artificial Intelligence researchers became active in the period after WWII, and the work of Newell and Simon (e.g. 1972) opened up another perspective on studying cognition, by trying to build computational models of thought. In the late 1970s, Artificial Intelligence researchers put more emphasis on the content of thought, to go along with the algorithms and heuristics that had been studied. The researchers started building expert systems. This work proceeded by eliciting from experts the rules that they followed in performance complex tasks. Hayes-Roth, Waterman and Lenat (1983) presented a comparison of different expert system approaches, to make the technology more accessible to computer scientists. The expert systems framework took Artificial Intelligence out of the laboratory, and into applications.

One of the bottlenecks in building expert systems was in eliciting these rules, in order to fully capture the expertise. The knowledge elicitation proved to be time-consuming and difficult. A new specialty was born, the knowledge engineer, whose job it was to find out how the experts performed their cognitive tasks.

The emergence of knowledge engineering was key to the evolution of CTA. The knowledge engineers created a demand for new and effective methods of getting inside the heads of experts. Because expert systems were intended to replace subject matter experts, it was important to capture the subtle aspects of expertise along with the more obvious rules. The practical goal of expert systems developers was to describe the basis for expertise for specific tasks. This is the same program that we find today for CTA.

The development of expert systems has not flowered in the ways that were expected. One reason may be that rule-based accounts of expertise are too simplistic and too brittle. Today, the leading artificial intelligence proponents have turned to neural nets and genetic algorithms to capture expertise without having to do any knowledge engineering.

However, the legacy of knowledge engineering continued in the field of human factors. Once the methods of knowledge engineering were demonstrated for building expert systems, the applications to other domains were obvious. If it was possible to describe how experts were performing cognitively complex tasks, then these descriptions could also be used for designing intelligent tutoring systems, and for designing training programs. The descriptions could be used in developing new computer systems, and particularly in helping human factors professionals handle the challenges of human-computer interface design. A further impetus to develop CTA methods came from military organizations interested in gaining a better understanding of decision making. The Army Research Institute initiated a program to study decision making in natural settings. In 1989 the Navy followed suit, after the U.S.S Vincennes shootdown of a commercial airliner, and began its program of research on Tactical Decision Making Under Stress (TADMUS), as described by Cannon-Bowers and Salas (1998). These efforts funded additional development of CTA methods. There are several other factors that contributed to the development of CTA methods, including the exploration of cognitive aspects of instruction. Currently, the human factors community is showing an increased level of interest in CTA. A special issue of the journal *Human Factors* (to be edited by Woods and Hoffman) is one example; a special issue of *Ergonomics* is another example. There have been several recent books (Gordon, 1994; Kirwan & Ainsworth, 1993; Klein, 1998; Klein, Orasanu, Calderwood & Zsambok, 1993; Seamster, Redding & Kaempf, 1997; Vicente, 1999; Zsambok & Klein, 1997; Schraagen, Chipman & Shalin, 2000) and articles/reports (Cooke, 1994; Essens et al., 1995) that are partially or entirely focused on CTA. The annual meetings of the Human Factors and Ergonomics Society usually include one or more workshops and sessions on CTA.

The rapid growth of interest and methods offers an opportunity to step back and consider some underlying themes in the field of CTA. This may be a useful time to examine questions such as what constitutes a CTA study.

DEFINITIONS OF COGNITIVE TASK ANALYSIS

To define CTA, it may be useful to first consider the three terms "cognitive," "task," and "analysis." The idea of a *cognitive* investigation is to study the mental processes of the individuals. This does not mean that there are "non-mental" or "non-cognitive" tasks, but rather that the effort is aimed at processes such as decision making, situation awareness, judgment, problem detection, attention management, and so forth. The contrast to a *cognitive* investigation would be an investigation of the steps that a person was supposed to follow in performing a task, and the explicit cues initiating and terminating each step. A *cognitive* investigation would look to see if the cues were all straightforward, or if some were subtle, and others were dependent on context and on the interpretation of the situation. The *cognitive* processes would include the strategies that were used, the skills (such as perceptual discriminations) that had been acquired, and the knowledge (including rich mental models) that was necessary.

The focus on "task" is also important. A CTA investigation is about how people perform *tasks* in natural settings. The *tasks* can be work related, such as generating a weather forecast, predicting the spread of a fire, or noticing signs of infection in a neonate. The *tasks* can fall outside of work, as in shopping in a supermarket or driving. But in all cases, the interest is in how people are performing *tasks* in natural settings, as opposed to basic research tasks.

The third term is "analysis," and this signifies an attempt to extract meaning from the data gathered, to provide an *explanation*. In many situations, researchers can ask subject matter experts questions such as what they were noticing, why they selecting a certain option, how they interpreted the new information. These questions obviously get at cognitive processes for specific tasks. But the questions do not constitute an *analysis*. Similarly, generating a list of important cognitive processes in performing a task (e.g. scanning the data, drawing inferences, storing information) does not constitute an *analysis*. The CTA still needs to explain how these processes are accomplished in the specific domain studied. An *analysis* implies a planful approach for examining the data gathered, identifying cognitive strategies, and representing these as a comprehensive explanation, so that others can learn how the task was done.

Together, the three parts of CTA can be defined as: A set of methods to elicit, explain, and represent the mental processes involved in performing a task. This definition of CTA is reasonably consistent with other definitions that have been offered. Redding (1989) has defined CTA as determining the mental processes and skills needed to perform a task at high proficiency levels, and the changes that occur as skills develop. This seems to be a reasonable definition. It frames the CTA as an investigation into mental processes and skills, and it emphasizes expertise that has either been achieved or is being developed. One quibble is that this definition should include knowledge, along with skills. A second quibble is that many CTA projects do not capture changes during skill acquisition, although these are certainly useful. A third quibble is that CTA is also appropriate when a task is not performed at high proficiency level. CTA is applicable at the novice level (e.g. an investigation of novice drivers (Klein, Vincent & Isaacson, 2001). In addition, it can be productive to contrast the strategies of experts and novices, as a way of learning more about the expertise needed for proficient performance. Nevertheless, for most applications, CTA is directed at trying to understand the cognitive skills, knowledge, and strategies needed to achieve high proficiency levels. In addition, CTA studies often try to identify the barriers to attaining or applying cognitive skills. Thus, in helping to design training programs, human-computer interfaces, and decision support systems, the intent is to help people develop and exercise expertise.

Essens et al. (1995) describe the *product* of a CTA as "a task-specific cognitive model including hypotheses about cognitive performance" (p. 43). This is consistent with Redding's definition. It means that the CTA needs to result in an understanding of how a person is thinking and judging and sizing up situations. However, this definition raises the question of what counts as a model, a topic that can sometimes be contentious. The concept of a model in this definition seems to correspond to the concept of an explanation in our definition.

Militello, Hutton, Pliske, Knight and Klein (1997) have defined CTA as the description of the cognitive skills needed to perform a task proficiently. This follows Redding's concern with capturing expertise, and with clarifying the value added of experience.

Roth, Woods and Pople (1992) state that "A Cognitive Task Analysis depends on two mutually-reinforcing activities: an analysis of the cognitive demands imposed by the world that any intelligent agent would have to deal with (a model of the cognitive environment); and an empirical investigation of how practitioners, both experts and less-skilled individuals, respond to the task demands (performance models)" (p. 1195). This extends Redding's framework, to describe the challenges posed by the world in which a person is acting. To be useful, a CTA must connect with the constraints of the world, particularly constraints in the task environment. Some researchers (e.g. Vicente, 1999) argue that the exploration of these constraints is itself a useful form of analysis, and perhaps even a starting point for the cognitive exploration. We agree with Roth et al. and with Vicente about the importance of tying the cognitive analysis to the constraints of the situation. The importance is reflected in the term "task," because the investigation must capture the situational constraints in specifying the task that is being studied.

Gordon and Gill (1997) have claimed that CTA is most suited for cognitively complex tasks with an extensive knowledge base, complex inferences and judgment, in a complex, dynamic, uncertain, real-time environment. We agree. However, we have found that it is possible to perform effective CTA studies even when the tasks are not dynamic, or highly complex, as in studies of the strategies used by consumers. Designers of consumer products need to understand consumer decision making regarding the purchase and use of products. This understanding is critical and very difficult to obtain without CTA methods. These CTA studies may not be as dramatic as studies of pilots, but they can still be informative and useful.

One way to clarify the definition of CTA is to provide counter-examples, describing what CTA is *not*. These counter-examples include:

- basic research into cognition
- a prescription about how people should be thinking
- a behavioral task analysis
- a list or diagram of cognitive tasks that could be added to a curriculum.

CTA is not research into the nature of basic cognitive processes. Certainly, a basic research investigation could include CTA methods; our assertion is that basic research into cognition does not automatically qualify as a CTA study. Because of the difficulty of setting up controlled conditions, few studies of basic cognitive processes investigate the types of tasks performed in natural settings. Traditional cognitive research does not attempt to determine the cognitive demands imposed by the world (whether the world of a pilot, a nuclear power plant operator, a nurse, or a supermarket shopper) and does not attempt to empirically determine the way people respond to these demands. We do not imply that traditional laboratory studies are unimportant. On the contrary, the insights provided by basic research about cognitive processes such as attention, working memory, categorization, and decision making can be valuable for developing better CTA methods and for interpreting results. Moreover, some basic research programs (e.g. Meyer & Kieras, 1997) have important implications for applied projects. And the findings that emerge from such research can be incorporated into CTA efforts. However, our claim is simply that basic cognitive research studies that do not investigate how people perform natural tasks are not examples of CTA.

One way to think about this distinction is that there is a difference in the goals of CTA projects and basic research studies. CTA projects attempt to explain phenomena. These phenomena, such as how a military pilot adjusts to unexpected enemy air defenses, how a shopper selects a product, how a baggage screener notices a problem in just a few seconds, cannot be explained in terms of steps or rules to be followed. There is more to the story, and that is the part that CTA seeks to fill. In contrast, basic research attempts to test theories. Even when basic researchers study natural settings, their focus is on the theories, and the hypotheses drawn from these theories.

CTA is not a prescription about how people *should* be thinking, using normative theory. The focus of CTA is on learning what people actually do, what they actually know. This is very different from analyzing what they should be doing and setting up a condition to demonstrate that they did not follow an optimal procedure. While studies focusing on optimal procedures can sometimes be informative, often they depend on being able to eliminate complicating contextual factors. Optimization becomes very difficult to measure in natural contexts (e.g. Klein, 2000). But once the context is limited, the basis for expertise is also limited. In contrast, the goal of a CTA project is to learn more about expertise, and particularly to discover facets of cognitive skill that had not previously been recognized. It is only after the cognitive processes of proficient performers are understood that CTA researchers have a basis for suggesting how decisions and judgments should be made.

CTA is different from behavioral task analysis. This distinction has been mentioned earlier, and will be discussed in greater detail in a later section.

The output of a CTA study should go beyond a list or diagram of cognitive tasks. The listing of tasks does not constitute an analysis or explanation. One concern here is that the researchers will generate a list or diagram of cognitive tasks as if these tasks should be added to the existing training requirements. When this happens, one of the worst features of behavioral task analysis (a non-integrated listing of tasks) is made even less palatable by piling cognitive tasks onto behavioral ones.

CRITERIA FOR SUCCESS IN CTA PROJECTS

We can distinguish three criteria for success of a CTA effort. A project needs to make an important *discovery*, it needs to *communicate* this discovery, and the communication needs to result in a meaningful *impact*.

Discovery

What counts as an important discovery? For a CTA project to be counted as successful, this means that the CTA team has learned something new and important about key judgments and decisions. The CTA team has identified judgments and decisions and other cognitive demands about which the sponsors or potential users were unaware, the strategies used to make the decisions, or the patterns used to make the judgments. The discoveries can be about strategies of making decisions, as in the determination that highway engineers use different strategies to make different types of decisions (Hammond, Hamm, Grassia & Pearson, 1987). The discoveries can be about patterns of cues, as in CTA efforts to define how nurses detect sepsis in infants (Crandall & Getchell-Reiter, 1993), or how nurses detect necrotizing enterocolitis (Militello & Lim, 1995). Other examples include identifying the information-seeking strategies used by skilled weather forecasters (Pliske, Klinger, Hutton, Crandall, Knight & Klein, 1997); describing the decision strategies of fireground commanders (Klein, Calderwood & Clinton-Cirocco, 1986); discovering how milk delivery personnel are able to rapidly and accurately prepare the right number of containers (Scribner, 1985); determining how Micronesians are able to navigate long distances without navigational equipment (Hutchins, 1983); and describing how anesthesiologists adapt to the new cognitive and physical demands created by the introduction of a physiological monitoring system (Cook & Woods, 1996).

Figure 1 shows a range of outcomes that could emerge from a CTA study, from the enumeration of cognitive functions, through the dissection of these functions, and up to the generation of an explanation of how the function is accomplished. At a minimum, a CTA investigation should identify the cognitive functions that are required. This would include describing the types of judgments and decisions that are needed. However, just listing these types of judgments is usually not enough. The potential users are likely to examine the list and comment that there is nothing on it that is surprising, or useful.

Figure 2 presents an example, taken from the domain of aircraft operation. The key types of decisions are presented, but they are not unpacked. We see where the tough decisions are, but we can only guess about the type of expertise needed to make each of them. This should be the starting point for the CTA study, not the conclusion. In Fig. 2, further analysis might show that

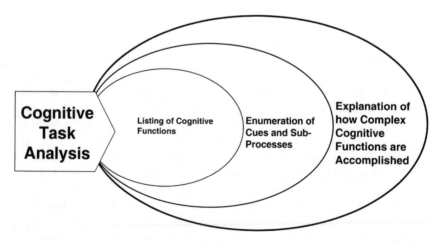

Fig. 1. Range of Outcomes for CTA Projects.

2.1.1 Perform normal takeoff operations

2.1.2 Perform takeoff roll procedures

     2.1.2.1   Position aircraft on runway centerline and stop

     2.1.2.2   If required, transfer control of aircraft

     2.1.2.3   If required, comply with standard policy for transfer of aircraft control

     2.1.2.4   Select HDG HLD on MCP

     2.1.2.5   Set WX radar for takeoff

     2.1.2.6   Release brakes and set takeoff thrust

     2.1.2.7   Advance power on both engines

     2.1.2.8   PF call for EPR

     2.1.2.9   PNF select EPR on MCP

     2.1.2.10 Engage auto-throttle in EPR mode as engines are accelerating through 1.1 EPR

     2.1.2.11 Comply with standard policy for takeoff and go/no go decision

     2.1.2.12 Maintain directional control

     2.1.2.13 Monitor engine and flight instruments

           13.1 If abnormality exists, Captain decides and initiates Rejected Takeoff

     2.1.2.14 Complete standard callouts for takeoff conditions

     2.1.2.15 Comply with Standard Policy for Takeoff Flight Path Control Techniques

           15.1 Recognize unstable flight path condition and be prepared to execute immediate recovery

Fig. 2. Portion of Task Analysis for Aircraft Takeoff.

several of these functions can be performed more effectively by training on a few skills, such as building up a better sense of typicality.

Returning to Fig. 1, the next level of discovery is to describe the cues and patterns and strategies that go into the judgments. Table 1 presents a list of cues taken from Crandall and Getchell-Reiter (1993) who studied nurses in neonatal intensive care units. These are the cues that the nurses had learned to recognize as possible precursors of sepsis. At the time of the research, approximately half of these cues had not appeared in the medical or nursing literature. Therefore, the cataloging of cues was an important discovery in its own right. The nurses initially had believed that they could not generate any explanations for how they were making an early detection of sepsis, and it took hard work, using the Critical Decision Method to probe specific incident accounts, in order to obtain this list.

The most exciting discoveries in a CTA study are those that result in an explanation or insight regarding the way a cognitive function is performed. Most CTA studies do not achieve this outcome, but we believe it should be established as a criterion for success. Thus, Smith, Ford and Kozlowski (1997) used simulated malfunctions to study pilot reactions, and showed in detail the differences in mental models that resulted in effective versus ineffective troubleshooting. Cook, Woods, Walters and Cristoffersen (1996) studied medical evacuation personnel and went beyond the surface features of the task to describe the underlying decisions regarding tradeoffs between resources; this resulted in a better design for a decision support system. Crandall and Getchell-Reiter (1993) did not leave their analysis at the listing shown in Table 1. They described how nurses used patterns of cues. The detailing of these nursing decisions was arranged in the context of specific incidents that could be used for training. Klein et al. (1986) described the decision-making strategies of firefighters as a recognition-primed decision model.

Studies such as these demonstrate how a CTA study can result in an explanation for a phenomenon that previously was not well understood. These

Table 1.   Indicators of Sepsis.

Indicator	Identified in medical literature		Number of cases in which expert nurses checked for indicator
	Yes	No	
Unstable temperature	X		3
Hypothermia	X		2
Elevated temperature	X		
Feeding abnormality	X		4
Abdominal distention	X		5
Increased residual	X		2
Vomiting	X		
Lethargy	X		8
Irritability	X		
Color changes	X		9
Respiratory distress	X		4
Apnea	X		6
Cyanosis	X		2
Tachypnea	X		
Seizures	X		
Jaundice	X		
Purpura	X		
Bradycardia		X	7
Unresponsive		X	5
Poor muscle tone		X	5
Perfusion or mottling		X	2
Edema		X	2
"Sick" eyes		X	2
Clotting problems		X	2

explanations can be valuable for the sponsors and potential users of the research, and the findings often will contribute to our basic understanding of expertise and decision making in field settings.

Communication

What counts as effective communication of the discovery? Representation of findings can be more difficult than knowledge elicitation. Successful communication occurs when the CTA team provides the potential user of the findings with an understanding that is sufficiently vivid so that the user can take the cognitive processes into account in designing an intervention. The CTA representation is attempting to generate the response, "Now I see how they are really doing that job." If the project is a collaborative effort, and the person who performed the CTA is part of a design team, she/he can represent the user's perspective during the design process, and representation may not be as important. However, if the CTA results are handed off, then it becomes critical for the recipients (i.e. system developers, instructional designers, etc.) to appreciate the operators' cognitive skills. In many cases, operators are themselves unable to articulate their own strategies (e.g. Nisbett & Wilson, 1977) and the designers of systems or training may not be skilled at inferring these strategies. Therefore, the role of the CTA is essential as an advocate for the subtle cognitive skills that must be supported if the task is to be performed effectively.

An example of effective communication comes from some work by Cook et al. (1996), in their study of the process of medical evacuation in military operations. Cook et al. went beyond the existing list of tasks and functions, and portrayed the medical evacuation personnel using a problem space. Inside that space was a region in which the resources (for slots on aircraft) were greater than the demand. For that region, there was little benefit for trying to optimize the solutions. In a second region of the problem space, the resources were less than demands. Here, the job was less about configuration and prioritizing than it was about negotiating for more resources, or for permission to postpone service. The third region was marked by uncertainty about whether the resources were sufficient to meet demand. Here, the system operators would need help in finding efficient configurations. The immediate task for the operators was to determine which region of the problem space they were in. This approach to representation was very useful for the system designers to help them understand the needs of the operators.

Impact

What counts as having an impact? When the CTA findings are put into action, this criterion is achieved. CTA projects are initiated for a purpose, and the intended users of the findings usually know how they want to apply the results. The goal of the study may be to help the users change the way they design a product or a system, or to revise the way they are training people, or even to confirm the users' current practices so that they can press on rather than continuing to gather more data. Sponsors may find uses for basic research types of CTA studies seeking to identify strategies of decision making, problem solving, planning, or situation awareness.

In the domain of air traffic control (Redding & Seamster, 1994) a comprehensive CTA of aviation training was conducted, resulting in a redesign of the Federal Aviation Administration's controller training curriculum. In the domain of avionics troubleshooting (Gott, Pokorny, Kane, Alley & Dibble, 1996) an extensive CTA of expert troubleshooting skill was conducted. The U.S. Air Force is in the process of developing an intelligent tutor based on this CTA. A second system developed along these lines (Pokorny, personal communication, 1997) is an expert system for supplementing personnel policy administrators in the U.S. Air Force. The resulting system is currently in beta test.

It is generally difficult to measure the eventual value of an intervention. Evaluation of impact generally involves gathering longitudinal data and taking into account intervening variables, neither of which are trivial tasks. For most CTA projects, funding ends at the time the intervention is introduced. Nevertheless, it is possible to obtain some data on the impact of the intervention that was based on CTA findings.

Another example of impact comes from the work of Di Bello and her colleague (e.g. Di Bello, 1997; Di Bello & Spender, 1996). Their work was with maintenance technicians in the transportation industry, to help improve the use of new information technology tools. Most of these tools, for scheduling, workflow, spares management, and so forth, are rejected in the workplace. A primary reason for this rejection is that the workers themselves do not have confidence in the tools, or understand how to apply them. Di Bello conducted a CTA study to understand how bus mechanics were scheduling their work. The CTA method consisted of observation and interview using two simulations. The first simulation presented a mechanic with a set of actual work orders and requested that the mechanic review these and generate a schedule for performing repairs. The second simulation presented a mechanic with longitudinal data on a single bus, to see what inferences the mechanic could derive. Di Bello and Spender found that the less effective mechanics lacked a mental model for seeing patterns in the longitudinal data, and were therefore forced into a reactive profile (repairing what came in) as opposed to a proactive stance to anticipate problems and prevent them. These findings were translated into a training program using a fleet of 30 buses in a low-fidelity simulation to enable the mechanics to see the limitations of their reactive strategy, and to realize the value of anticipating problems. With their shift in mental models the mechanics were able to appreciate how the new software scheduling program provided them with the data they needed. Evaluation data showed that prior to the training, 70% of the mechanics were categorized as showing a reactive mental model (versus 30% who showed a proactive mental model). After the training, the ratio had reversed, and 70% of the mechanics showed a proactive mental model for anticipating problems and preventing them.

Klinger and Militello (in preparation) modified the human-computer interface for Airborne Warning and Control System (AWACS) weapons directors. The CTA study showed how the weapons directors were losing situation awareness because of memory limitations. Each time the weapons directors looked away from the screen (to operate switches), they needed time to re-orient because all the icons on the screen had moved. In addition, the operators had difficulty keeping track of key icons such as high threats or assets such as tankers for aerial refueling. The human-computer interface solutions were straightforward (marking the key icons, using an on-screen menu to double for the most common switch actions). A laboratory study using high-fidelity simulators indicated that the redesigned interface resulted in a significant improvement in performance. In addition, the redesigned interface was selected to be incorporated in the next modification cycle for the AWACS weapons directors' workstations.

Andriole and Adelman (1993) provide some additional examples of cognitive engineering projects that resulted in improved performance. These studies show that it is possible to measure impact, but this is done most easily during the development of pilot programs or prototypes.

What does *not* count as a successful CTA study? Often reports of CTA projects include pages of tables and matrices reporting data in exhaustive detail, demonstrating the amount of effort expended, but these reports do not communicate discoveries. If CTA methods are to be judged useful, they must produce discoveries that are useful to the sponsoring organization. Careful data collection and exhaustive reporting are not a substitute for learning and describing something new and important about the way specialists think about key tasks. We recognize that there are projects in which a detailed reporting of data is required, or in which pithy summaries of discoveries are not possible, but the criterion for success can be whether or not the findings were used to help the sponsoring organization make a change, and to describe how the findings contributed to the change.

COGNITIVE TASK ANALYSES VERSUS TRADITIONAL TASK ANALYSIS

We can distinguish between CTA and more traditional task analysis methods that focus on behaviors. (We will refer to the latter as behavioral task analysis.) CTA studies address the cognitive requirements for a task, whereas behavioral task analyses focus on the observable behaviors and cues. It is possible to perform a behavioral task analysis, to develop task sequence diagrams, and to specify the initiating and terminating conditions for sub-tasks, without considering cognitive issues of how the cues are recognized, how the sub-tasks are interpreted, or how the situational interpretation affects the strategies selected. One of the strengths of behavioral task analysis is its emphasis on the objective nature of the data: explicit tasks and sub-tasks, specific and unambiguous cues, and clear criteria for terminating one step and initiating the next. These advantages are achieved by steering clear of the ambiguous, context-bound issues that are central to CTA.

Kirwan and Ainsworth (1993) do not present a sharp distinction between CTA and behavioral task analysis. They define task analysis as "the study of what an operator (or team of operators) is required to do, in terms of actions and/or cognitive processes, to achieve a system goal. Task analysis methods can also document the information and control facilities used to carry out the task" (p. 1). Kirwan and Ainsworth describe more than 40 different task analysis approaches, including several CTA methods. We have chosen to accentuate the distinction between CTA and behavioral task analysis because of our concerns that a cognition-free behavioral task analysis may provide a misleading account.

Some would argue that skilled task analysts are already doing many of the things that are discussed in the CTA literature, so CTA does not offer anything new. We agree that there are many experienced practitioners of behavioral task analysis whose practices include ways of probing subject matter experts to capture different types of cognitive skills. Therefore, behavioral task analysis may not preclude CTA. Nevertheless, we see a distinction. Traditional task analysis usually does not call for probes of cognitive processes, and rarely provides guidance in conducting such probes. Hence, the methods themselves do not necessarily lead to the capture of the cognitive aspects of skilled performance. CTA may be seen as complementary to traditional task analysis

– a way to enrich the accounts of how the steps of a task are performed. But the two, CTA and behavioral task analysis, are different. CTA methods provide tools for investigating cognitive elements in the context of real-world constraints and affordances of the tasks.

In our experience, CTA efforts can benefit from having previous behavioral task analysis data to describe explicit functions that need to be performed. Similarly, we believe that many behavioral task analyses can benefit from having CTA data to clarify how the work is actually being accomplished. Otherwise, there is a risk that behavioral task analyses may distort the picture of performance. Traditional task analysis seeks to decompose tasks into smaller elements, and to generate orderly hierarchical accounts.

The way in which the Instructional Systems Development process has been traditionally applied is a prime example of such an approach. Although the process has been successfully applied in describing highly proceduralized tasks, the resulting representation can oversimplify cognitively loaded tasks. This strategy of hierarchical decomposition does not provide a systematic means to capture and explore the important cognitive skills that may underlie tasks and subtasks identified. Often the resulting representation is a series of steps with no explanation of the cognitive strategies needed to accomplish the steps satisfactorily.

The interpretation of a task list is that if one follows the steps identified, the task should be accomplished. However, for cognitively loaded tasks, subject matter experts often do not follow those steps, and are not following any steps at all (Klein, 1978). In these cases, traditional task analysis may result in a partial and potentially misleading account of performance. The requirement in an Instructional System Development project to write testable objectives for skills generates further pressure to decompose a task into small steps that can easily be checked off or assessed via multiple choice questions. The steps may have little psychological reality, but are a means to permit objective evaluation. When this goes too far, the so-called steps of the task are not accurate descriptions of proficient performance. Here, CTA can provide a more accurate account of how specialists move beyond the rule-based level of performing complex tasks.

Thus, we argue that CTA studies have the challenge of describing the decision-making, judgment, and problem-solving strategies used to perform tasks. The descriptions can elaborate on existing task descriptions. DeMaio, Parkinson, Leshowitz, Crosby and Thorpe (1976) studied instructor pilots who were taught a rigid procedure for visually scanning flight instruments. Eye movement data revealed that the instructor pilots did not themselves follow the procedure, and were better able to detect anomalies than the students. One risk of behavioral task analyses is that they can promote the rigid adherence to inefficient practices, such as over-learning a scanning strategy, rather than developing the associations and patterns that would permit rapid attention to the flight instruments that were most relevant. One of the promises of CTA is to allow us to break loose from the official procedures, and discover the bases for expertise within a domain.

FRAMING CTA EFFORTS AROUND ASPECTS OF EXPERTISE

At some point in the future, we may be able to work from a theoretical account that would guide the application of CTA methods. The availability of an overarching perspective would help to develop CTA into a technology: determining the boundary conditions of different CTA methods, evolving guidelines for selecting CTA methods to match the features of the situation, deriving formats for reporting findings, establishing metrics for evaluating the degree of success of the CTA effort, preparing training programs for using CTA methods, and setting standards for practice.

We are not close to that point, and we may find that it is not necessary. Behavioral task analysis methods have proliferated and have been applied without a theory of the task. Practices in designing human-computer interfaces have improved without theory. The maturation of practice can be sufficient to achieve progress, without requiring a top-down direction.

Moreover, the prospects for theory are not great. A theoretical account might have to cover the nature of expertise, the functional distinctions between types of tasks, constraints in the world of practice, and the features of the cognitive processes themselves. We are not close to having a comprehensive theory in any one of these areas, let alone an integration of all of them.

An additional distinction can be made regarding the assumptions behind the method. Thus, some methods have emerged from rule-based information processing accounts of cognition, whereas others are linked to phenomeno-logical descriptions of cognition, still others can be traced to ethnographic techniques, and others to systems engineering approaches. Therefore, the conceptual background regarding the field of psychology may have to be taken into account.

Therefore, the ambition of deriving a taxonomy of CTA methods may be premature. Attempts to develop such a taxonomy have faltered, as the analysts found that the initial distinctions and characteristics of CTA methods carried little force for directing which methods should be used under what conditions. We can now see that a taxonomy would require that we know how to characterize tasks and situations, in order to recommend which technique to use for what type of project. A taxonomy would require the theoretical accounts listed at the beginning of this section.

Despite these problems, we do not claim that efforts at theory building should be suspended until all of the components are firmly in place. The attempt to develop theory, and to derive taxonomies, allows us to mark our understanding of CTA methods, and to make this understanding explicit to ourselves and to others. Moreover, the attempt to formulate theory regarding CTA may help to clarify what is needed from a theory of expertise, or a theory of cognitive processes.

To attempt some contribution to theory building, we will describe our current perspective on the aspects of expertise that practitioners try to capture using different CTA methods. By examining some standard sources on cognition (Barsalou, 1985) and expertise (Chi, Glaser & Farr, 1988; Ericsson, 1996; Ericsson & Smith, 1991), we have compiled a sample of important aspects of skilled performance of complex tasks. We have also realized that it may be useful to distinguish between aspects of expertise that reflect what a person knows, and the ways that people can apply the knowledge. This distinction is presented in Table 2.

Our belief, based on a literature review and on experience conducting CTA projects, is that we can identify a small set of different types of knowledge that experts have. They have a set of associations (e.g. Sloman, 1996, on associative inferences versus rule-based inferences; also see Simon, 1956, on pattern learning) which include the judgment of what is *typical* in a situation. And this type of knowledge permits experts to quickly spot anomalies that are departures from typicality. Experts have formed *mental models* which are usually causal frameworks explaining how things happen. And this type of knowledge permits experts to mentally simulate what will happen in the future, based on the current configuration of events and states. It also permits experts to discover workarounds when a plan is blocked, using their mental models of how to introduce changes to lead to a desired effect. Experts have learned a great many *routines* for getting things done, and this permits them to make rapid decisions. Experts have learned to make *perceptual discriminations*. And this enables them to see things that novices cannot detect. Finally, experts have learned a great deal of *declarative* information. However, CTA studies usually do not try to capture this type of knowledge because it is so vast, and because it is fairly accessible without any special CTA techniques. Therefore, declarative knowledge is not included in Table 2.

The match between skills and knowledge is obviously more complex than shown in Table 2. Thus, the ability that experts have to make perceptual

Table 2.   Aspects of Expertise to be Captured by CTA Studies.

Knowledge: What you have to know	*Skills*: What you can do with that knowledge
Typicality (patterns)	Spot anomalies
Mental models (causal dynamics)	Assess situations
Routines	Perform workarounds
Perceptual discriminations	Mental simulation of past and future (expectancies, time horizons, prioritizations, attention management, and synthesizing information)
	Achieve rapid decision making, detect affordances in a situation, apply heuristics, and detect problems

discriminations can help them spot anomalies and also detect early signs of problems. We consider the breakout in Table 2 to be a potentially useful step for preparing to do a CTA study. It may be useful to consider what types of knowledge and cognitive skills the CTA should emphasize, and even to reflect on the CTA approach that might be well suited for that type of knowledge or skill.

Some tasks depend on the ability to make fine discriminations between similar cues and patterns. Shanteau (1992), Klein and Hoffman (1993), and others have described how specialists have better *perceptual skills* in a domain than novices. We suggest that perceptual discriminations are challenging in a CTA study because they are difficult for subject matter experts (SMEs) to describe. However, by having subject matter experts relate an actual incident, the cues and discriminations may be more easily accessed from memory.

Some tasks depend heavily on being able to understand the causes and interactions in a situation. Specialists appear to use their experiences and feedback to build up a richer map of the causal connections. Therefore, to capture the basis of their expertise, we need to clarify the nature of their *mental models* (for a basic overview of mental models, see Rouse and Morris (1986)). However, mental models are notoriously difficult for SMEs to describe. One strategy that has worked for us is to use a simulation that requires the SME to perform a workaround, because in this context the causal influences emerge more easily.

One reason we prefer to use an incident-based method such as the Critical Decision Method is that it seems well-suited for capturing perceptual discriminations, and also because the incidents can be probed in a way that requires workarounds ("but what would you have done if . . ."), thereby reflecting aspects of the SME's mental model. In addition, the incidents also describe some of the skills that are based on expert knowledge (e.g. incidents involving rapid decisions, or early problem detection).

Some tasks are dynamic and time pressured and depend on quick reactions to fleeting events. Specialists are able to control their attentional capacities more skillfully than novices are (e.g. Gopher, Weil, Bareket & Caspi, 1988; Hanish, Kramer & Hulin, 1991). For dynamic tasks, it may be necessary to learn how this *attentional control* is developed and manifested.

Specialists often need to learn *typicality*, in the form of domain-specific prototypes, so that they can recognize typicality, and with that, can recognize anomalies (see the work of Logan, 1988).

Some tasks require people to *synthesize*, to go beyond the evidence given, to draw out inferences and make projections. Specialists appear to have available more heuristics, not in the technical sense of strategies for searching through problem spaces, but in the general sense of having more informal rules and more "tricks of the trade." They know shortcuts and context-specific rules of thumb and *routines* that are often not documented. They can rely on mental simulations (Klein & Crandall, 1995) to project trends and to build explanations.

Specialists may not have "better" memories, as shown by research on chess players (e.g. de Groot, 1946/78, 1986; Holding, 1985). Their strength is in being able to use better strategies for the management of working memory and for long-term storage and retrieval (e.g. Ericsson, 1996). Therefore, we may want to study their strategies for *memory management*. The control of working memory appears related to workload management. The control of long-term memory is important because most domains require specialists to acquire a great deal of declarative knowledge. Therefore, it can be useful to study how specialists obtain this knowledge, how they organize it, and how they retrieve it from long-term memory.

Many tasks require people to monitor themselves and adjust their performance in line with perceived difficulties. The literature on *metacognition* documents important skill development (Means, Salas, Crandall & Jacobs, 1993; Metcalfe & Shimamura, 1994; Smith et al., 1997). It can be useful to find out what strategies experts are employing in order to gauge how well they are doing, and how to adjust to conditions.

If we can use CTA to understand the way competent performers employ these cognitive processes, and particularly if we can determine the way they differ from novices and from mediocre performers, then the effort can have important benefits. The goal of a CTA is to help us to move beyond the behaviors, and into the mental activities of the skilled worker. The goal is also to teach us what the person with expertise is really thinking about. Table 2 simply lists some of the types of knowledge and skills that contribute to expertise. A useful explanation would take the CTA findings and clarify how SMEs perform a task. We discussed this earlier when we examined the nature of discoveries emerging from CTA projects.

Doubtless, the list of aspects of expertise that is presented in Table 2 can be expanded and reorganized. Our intent is *not* to provide a definitive account of the cognitive facets of expertise. We are simply trying to show that there *are* different facets, and that an effort to study the cognitive aspects of task performance can draw on these and other processes. If a task does not present any of these types of challenges, then there is probably little reason to conduct a CTA. For example, a study (Kaempf, Thordsen & Klein, 1991) of Army soldiers in charge of setting up communications gear did not generate any discoveries about their strategies or tacit knowledge. We believed that they did not have to acquire any "real" expertise, because the task was so heavily proceduralized. The soldiers claimed that what marked the real experts was being able to recall the exact page in the manual that documented the steps to be followed.

We should note that the specification of different aspects of expertise, shown in Table 2, should not be taken as a type of conclusion from a CTA study (e.g. this task requires mental models, and judgment of typicality, but not perceptual skills). Rather, the CTA study would need to fill in the depth about the structure of the mental models, the types of prototypes that are recognized, and so forth. Table 2 is a suggestion for the starting point of a CTA study, not the outcome of such a study.

DIVERSITY OF CTA METHODS

Within the past 10–15 years, a wide variety of CTA methods have emerged. Up to this point, we have been discussing CTA at an abstract level. Here, we want to get more concrete about the specific CTA methods that are available. These methods have been described in several different sources (Cooke, 1994; Crandall & Getchell-Reiter, 1993; Crandall, Klein, Militello & Wolf, 1994; Essens et al., 1995; Gordon, 1994; Gordon & Gill, 1997; Hoffman, Shadbolt, Burton & Klein, 1995; Kirwan & Ainsworth, 1993; Redding & Seamster, 1994; Schraagen, Chipman & Shalin, 2000; Vicente, 1999).

Table 3 sorts out the different methods for knowledge *elicitation*, getting the information "out of the heads" of the people performing the tasks. We have found it convenient to sort these into four categories: (a) methods that use interviews (both high and low in structure), (b) observations such as keystrokes

Table 3. Knowledge Elicitation Methods.

Interview Methods	Observation Methods	Modeling Methods	Experimental Methods
Unstructured interviews	Direct observation-questioning	MIDAS	Multi-dimensional & other types of scaling
		COGNET	
FAST	PARI		
		SOAR	Domain knowledge tests
Concept maps	Process tracing		
		ACT	
Conceptual graph analysis	Simulation- High/Low Fidelity Freeze frames		Secondary tasks
Critical decision analysis			Bruswik Lens model
	Constrained processing-		
Constructed scenarios	Missing information Time pressure		
Repertory grid			
	Expert/Novice		
Knowledge audit	comparisons		

(Kieras, 1988; Zachary, Zaklad, Hicinbotham, Ryder, Purcell & Wherry, 1991), and simulations (Woods, 1993; Gott et al., 1996), (c) computer models, and (d) laboratory tasks. Hoffman et al. (1995) have adopted a similar categorization, looking at the analysis of familiar tasks, unstructured interviews, structured interviews, and contrived tasks.) Some CTA methods focus on studies of specific incidents (e.g. Critical Decision Method, Klein et al., 1986), whereas others elicit more general information (concept maps, McFarren, 1987; conceptual graph analyses, Gordon, Schmierer & Gill, 1993; Knowledge Audit, Militello & Hutton, 1998). Hoffman et al. (1995) and Cooke (1994) have discussed the knowledge elicitation strategies in common use.

Table 4 presents different methods for knowledge *representation*, dividing these into methods that describe specific incidents, and methods that synthesize incidents (or do not work from specific incidents). Some of the methods provide representations of specific incidents. Woods, O'Brien and Hanes (1987) describe accounts of nuclear power plant control room crew members reacting to simulated accidents. Kaempf, Klein, Thordsen and Wolf (1996) present records of situation awareness shifts during navy anti-air operations.

Table 4.   Knowledge Representation Methods.

Incident-Based Methods	Generic Methods
Problem Behavior Graphs	Expert systems
Decision Flow Diagrams	COGNET
Discourse Analysis	Decision Requirements Table
Annotated Interviews	Concept Maps
Expert/Novice Contrasts	Conceptual Graph Analysis
	Critical Cue Inventory
	Knowledge Audit
	Influence Diagram
	Prototype Descriptions

Other methods provide representations of generic knowledge structures. For example, conceptual graphs (Gordon et al., 1993) provide insights into a person's mental model of a domain. Militello (2001) has described knowledge representation methods in greater detail.

CRITERIA FOR SELECTING CTA METHODS

What is the best method for doing a CTA? It should be obvious that this is a good example of a poor question. In selecting a CTA method, we need to consider the types of cognitive processes to be understood, which are a function of the type of task that is being investigated. A study of pilots flying sorties and performing the task of target acquisition needs to examine the way they control and shift their attention, and the way they perceive subtle changes in their situation. A study of librarians performing the task of recommending books to patrons, needs to examine the librarians' mental models, and can minimize the assessment of perceptual skills. (Perceptual skills might be important for a librarian performing the task of identifying books that are too badly worn to remain in circulation.)

In selecting a CTA method we also need to take into account the way the results are going to be used. If the results are going to be used to determine whether or not the job of an operator can be automated, the study has to describe all of the subtle aspects of expertise that the operator has developed, because these might no longer be available. If the results are going to be used to design a decision support system, the study has to clarify the way the operators are currently making critical and difficult decisions, so that the system will help rather than interfere with them. If the results are going to be used to build training, the CTA must uncover both high-level strategies and concepts to frame the training, as well as specific critical cues, perceptual discriminations, and contextual elements needed to make cognition visible to learners.

Some CTA methods seem to do a better job of capturing certain types of cognitive processes, such as mental models, and others appear more sensitive to different processes, such as perceptual skills, metacognitive strategies, and attentional control. In short, there is no one "best" method of CTA.

If we had a full taxonomy of CTA methods, we would be able to do a better job of matching the method to the types of expertise to be elicited, and the types of applications for the findings. As an initial step, we will present some of our beliefs about the matches between the aspects of expertise covered in Table 2, and the CTA strategies for knowledge elicitation offered in Table 3.

Mental Models

Many CTA methods concentrate on eliciting mental models – declarative knowledge and how it is organized. Concept maps (McFarren, 1987) and conceptual graph analysis (Gordon et al., 1993) fit here; both are ways of having people diagram the primary factors involved in understanding a domain, along with specifying clear linkages between the different types of concepts. Methods for multidimensional scaling (Cooke, Durso & Schwanaveldt, 1994) are another approach for eliciting mental models, by summarizing subjects' responses to paired comparisons. Layton, Smith & McCoy (1994) demonstrated the use of process tracing to describe how the level of completeness of a mental model determined a pilot's troubleshooting success in handling a malfunction.

Attention

Few CTA methods address the way people manage attentional resources. This is probably most important for dynamic, time-pressured tasks, and may be best studied using moderate to high fidelity simulations. Another way to study management of attentional resources is by using devices, such as eye movement trackers, during actual task performance. We have not found cases where eye movement trackers have been incorporated into Cognitive Task Analyses.

Perceptual Skills

These are extremely important in natural settings. The Critical Decision Method (Hoffman, Crandall & Shadbolt, 1998) and the Knowledge Audit (Militello & Hutton, 1998) are two methods for capturing perceptual skills. The Critical Decision Method does this by using a semi-structured interview to study challenging incidents, and to probe about the cues and patterns that were noticed during these incidents, particularly those that might have been missed by inexperienced personnel. The Knowledge Audit is a streamlined method for getting an overview of the types of skills, including perceptual skills, needed to perform the task.

Recognition of Typicality

The essential issue here is to identify anomalies as well as prototypes. In some natural settings, the ability to quickly identify an anomaly, in order to identify a potential problem, is important (Hoffman, 1987). It would seem that the experimental techniques for studying the way people form prototypes and categories (e.g. Kahneman & Miller, 1986; Logan, 1988) could be adapted here.

Routines and Strategies

Lesgold, Rubinson, Feltovich, Glaser, Klopfer and Wang (1988) have described the use of the Precursor, Action, Result, and Interpretation (PARI) method for describing the strategies used by skilled equipment troubleshooters. PARI relies on a structured interview procedure between pairs of experts, commenting on a simulated problem task.

Memory

COGNET (Zachary et al., 1991) is one of the few CTA methods to specifically address the limitations of working memory. COGNET consists of a computer program that is a record of the operator's performance, usually by mapping keystroke analysis into a workload framework; COGNET basically extends the Goals, Operators, Methods, and Selection (GOMS) to include workload limitations as modeled by a blackboard architecture. Few, if any CTA methods address the management of long-term memory. To the extent that mental models suggest memory organization, then the concept mapping and conceptual graph analysis methods would also be relevant here.

RESEARCH ISSUES IN CTA

Improvements in CTA will occur through continued practice and application, but this process will take time. In this section, we describe a range of topics for future research. Some of the topics are linked to the criteria for selecting CTA methods, and other topics are related to the application of CTA methods in general.

How Can We Evaluate CTA Methods?

For a practitioner trying to select a CTA method, there is not a great deal to go on other than its track record of generating discoveries and having an impact. Have boundary conditions been described? Have real-world applications been demonstrated using the method? Are there domains in which the method has been used successfully? Are there domains in which the method has been unsuccessful? Information about validity and utility of various CTA methods is not readily available. There is a critical need for such data, to allow users of various methods to make informed choices. The CTA study must accurately portray the cognitive processes of the specialists being studied. As CTA becomes more visible, demand for evidence of validity and reliability of the methods will and should increase.

How Can We Determine the Validity of a CTA Finding?

Woods (1997), personal communication) has raised the ethical question of how a CTA application will be used. He noted that in many instances, the designers of a system want to eliminate the role of the human, and are seeking to capture the human contribution to the task in a small set of rules that can be turned into an automation of a task. If a CTA application is shallow, and fails to capture the richness and subtlety of the cognitive skills, then it will be easier to dismiss the importance of the human operator, which can lead to serious consequences.

We also need to judge the comprehensiveness of the findings. A CTA project that generates valid conclusions but misses important aspects of cognitive skills, is a failure. When we study the validity of CTA methods, we need to be concerned with what the methods capture and fail to capture, and not just whether the CTA findings are accurate. There have been very few examinations of validity and reliability of CTA methods. Hoffman et al., (1998) describe the systematic attempts to assess validity and reliability of a CTA method, the Critical Decision Method. Militello et al. (1997) developed a paradigm for evaluating the adequacy of knowledge captured by CTA methods. They taught

CTA methods to one group of participants, but not to a second group, and then compared the outputs of the two groups after giving them each a chance to individually interview SMEs. The quality of the outputs (recommendations for cognitive training) were assessed by other SMEs. This type of research is labor intensive, but offers a way to determine the impact of training on the CTA methods. Although these attempts to assess validity of CTA data are encouraging, they do not address the issue of completeness.

How Can We Understand the Boundary Conditions for Specific CTA Methods?

Work here would look at ways to improve the match between the CTA method and the cognitive demands of the task. In the previous section, we offered some initial speculations about the CTA methods that appeared useful for addressing different types of cognitive demands. However, the matching of method to cognitive demands requires that we have a means to distinguish the cognitive demands of a task, and we do not. In the future, we would need a preliminary investigation of a task domain, prior to beginning the knowledge elicitation (see Hoffman, 1987). Following Roth et al. (1992), if we need to specify the cognitive demands of a domain, then that suggests that we will have to first employ some methods for capturing these cognitive demands. Boy (1998) developed a framework for a situational CTA, which he terms a cognitive function analysis. He recommends studying the task, the user, the environment, and the artifact. Vicente (1999) takes a related stance. To accomplish a cognitive work analysis, Vicente recommends that we describe the work domain, the tasks to be performed, the mental strategies needed to perform those tasks, the organizational issues that must be handled, and the operator competencies needed. Anastasi, Hutton, Thordsen, Klein and Serfaty (1997) have made a similar recommendation. They suggested using a method such as an operator function model to specify the cognitive demands, followed by the use of the appropriate CTA method. Roth et al., Boy, Vicente and Anastasi et al. would all seem to argue for an initial CTA step of depicting the task/work domain/environment as a way of understanding the cognitive demands of greatest interest. Then, the knowledge elicitation methods can be selected to match the cognitive demands. We would expect that, as methods are developed for describing the work domain, the tasks to be performed, the functions required, the organizational issues to be handled, and the features of the artifact, then these methods would be used along with CTA methods, in a more comprehensive cognitive engineering study. Work is needed to develop methods that can be used efficiently to describe work domains and environments and can connect these to CTA strategies.

A different perspective on boundary conditions is to evaluate the cost/benefit ratio of CTA methods. Most projects have limited time and money available. Often access to subject matter experts is limited. The potential interviewers or observers may lack experience. These constraints impact the CTA methods used. It will be important to articulate the amount and type of resources required by individual CTA methods. On the one hand, we would like to use a variety of CTA methods to seek converging evidence for our findings. On the other hand, most projects are necessarily limited by time and budget. To transform CTA into a technology, we need to be able to estimate the resource requirements for the methods considered. Hoffman (1987) studied the productivity of different knowledge engineering procedures. Hoffman et al. (1995) reviewed methods used to contrast the efficiency of knowledge elicitation methods. We need additional efforts like these in order to gauge relative efficiency. We appreciate that such studies may be labor intensive. However, if we could establish research paradigms, it might be possible to open the door for graduate student research projects. There are natural tasks, such as driving, playing video games, and using word processing programs, that are within reach of university research efforts and could offer platforms for comparing CTA methods in capturing expertise.

Yet another way of clarifying boundary conditions for CTA methods is by compiling and studying CTA failures to dissect what went wrong. In developing CTA approaches into a technology, one of the barriers is that there is not enough dissemination of failures. Looking at our own experience, we have had our share of CTA projects that were not successful. Sometimes, we failed to achieve the criterion of discovery. Other failures occurred when we were not successful in describing the basis for the expertise. Sometimes, this may have occurred because the so-called experts were not very skilled, as in the example discussed earlier regarding the task of assembling communications equipment. At other times, we probably used the wrong CTA methods. An example would be in trying to identify critical incidents in a situation where the participants didn't have such incidents, or could not remember them. Thus, in a study of baggage screeners (Kaempf, Klinger & Wolf, 1994) we tried to obtain critical incidents, but each screening encounter lasts at most five seconds, so the screeners had no recall of specific events. Fortunately, we were able to shift our methods and rely on observation, with subsequent probing of sample screen images. Ironically, during our observation we were present when a passenger attempted to carry a gun through the screening station, providing an unplanned critical incident. Other failures have occurred because the investigators were not sufficiently skilled. Sometimes this was related to interviewing skills, and sometimes to a lack of background knowledge.

A near failure (see Miller, Militello & Heaton, 1996) occurred when we used CTA methods to examine the way air campaign planners evaluate their plans. The preparation for the interviews identified several different potentially useful CTA strategies. Once the interviews began, one after another of the CTA strategies was applied, and found inadequate. Because of the demonstrated power of asking SMEs to recount real, lived incidents, based on the interviewees' experiences as air campaign planners, Miller et al. (1996) tried to elicit examples of such incidents that they could probe further. As the interviews progressed, the interviewers discovered that air campaign planners are in that position for only a short period of time, three to four years at most. Therefore, they do not have extensive case bases of planning incidents.

In addition, the role of the air campaign planners who were interviewed was to support the Commander in Chief (CINC) in theater. Planning support was delivered to the CINC, who would compile support from several sources. As a result, the air campaign planners received little or no feedback regarding the planning support they had provided. These elements, in addition to the fact that much of their work is highly classified, meant that the air campaign planners had a difficult time recalling and discussing real, lived incidents.

The interviewers had started with the Critical Decision Method, hoping to get the planners to talk about actual incidents. That failed. Then the interviewers used a constructive simulation exercise, asking the planners to design a difficult scenario. That was too unstructured for the planners. Then the interviewers used a probe involving a hypothetical tool that would enable the planners to identify weak links in a plan (which could be examined in greater detail), but that was still too abstract. Next, the interviewers tried a probe whereby the planners had to rely on an assistant to develop a plan; the planner's job was to evaluate the plan. Still too abstract. The fifth and last strategy was to introduce a hypothetical situation that had no plausibility, thereby avoiding concerns of security violations. The planners were asked to imagine that the U.S. had decided to invade Canada, that the planner had developed the plan, and that the plan fell through, because there were too many glitches. What were the glitches? This exercise was concrete enough to engage the planners, yet unrealistic enough to avoid their concerns about classified information.

During this project, in addition to learning about the task of air campaign planning, the CTA team learned a great deal about the boundary conditions for CTA methods that focus on real, lived experience. Had the interviewers gone in with only a single strategy, they would have failed.

How do we Calibrate the CTA Strategy Adopted with the Intended Application or Outcome?

The concern here is that the CTA findings be the appropriate type of representation, at the right level of detail, with the meaningful type of expertise covered. We need to find some way to negotiate with the sponsors and users in advance, so that they receive the product they need. For example, we can save a great deal of disappointment by preparing CTA output samples in advance, and showing these to users in order to determine their preferences. It is important to point out that direct output from knowledge elicitation sessions is rarely a useful means of communicating what has been learned. Analysis, organization, and framing are generally needed to create a meaningful representation of the knowledge captured.

Where are the Guidelines for Human Factors Professionals?

There are several ways to achieve this. We can describe exemplars of good practice. The application of CTA methods requires experience, feedback, and training, just as any type of specialized methodology does. One of the concerns facing the field of CTA is that applications will be disappointing to the sponsors, diminishing enthusiasm. This can occur because too many CTA studies result in massive documentation of irrelevant cognitive details, without making any discoveries, or having any impact. Another reason for loss of enthusiasm will be if too many system designers claimed they are using CTA methods, when they have little training or background. The resultant studies would be likely to be unsuccessful, and the blame could be placed on the methods or the approach, rather than on the analysts. But we don't know how to assess whether someone is qualified or not, or even how long it takes to become qualified on a specific CTA method.

The research questions here include the investigation of individual differences, to see if some practitioners are better or less able to conduct a CTA project than others. Are the same skills needed to use the Critical Decision Method and COGNET and Concept Mapping? Probably not. Therefore, we need to consider individual differences in using specific methods, not differences in CTA per se. For example, in training people to use the Critical Decision Method, we have obtained anecdotal evidence that some very intelligent researchers seem to be insensitive to what counts as a good story, or incident. Others seem to have difficulty in decentering, in taking the perspective of the subject matter expert. If we could demonstrate individual differences, then it would help in selecting personnel to work on CTA projects.

Another research question addresses the types of training that would facilitate competence in applying CTA methods.

Another way to support the wider use of CTA studies would be to derive methods for 'streamlining' the CTA process. Many CTA methods are relatively simple e.g. concept mapping), others can supposedly be learned in just a few hours (conceptual graph analysis) and others have been developed expressly for the purpose of helping untrained personnel get a start at tapping into cognitive skills (Militello & Hutton, 1998). The rationale of these programs is that currently, most designers do not use *any* methods to examine cognitive skills. Therefore, some methods, even simplified ones, are better than none. However, the risk is that people may use these methods carelessly, and then claim that they have captured the essential aspects of expertise needed for a design project, when they have not managed to describe the important cognitive skills. One solution might be to carefully evaluate the validity, reliability, and efficiency of streamlined CTA methods.

CONCLUSIONS

We have defined CTA as the attempt to describe three factors: the cognitive demands presented by the task and the situation, the constraints of the task itself, and the systematic interpretation of the findings. CTA typically attempts to explore aspects of expertise needed for proficient performance, but CTA methods are also used to study the cognitive processes of people who are not proficient, and may be in the process of developing competence.

Currently, a wide variety of CTA methods are being developed and used. As we learn how to define the cognitive demands presented by a task or situation, we hope we will be able to map CTA methods onto these demands, so that we can more efficiently select and apply the appropriate methods. This ability should result in more efficient studies, and greater user satisfaction. It should also help move the field of CTA into becoming more of a technology.

In considering the various steps needed to help develop CTA methods into a technology, one common theme (e.g. Hoffman, 1987) is the need for empirical evaluation of the methods, to determine validity and reliability. We need to understand what the different CTA methods capture, and what they miss. We need to understand the individual differences in analysts that might result in different findings, using the same methods in the same domain. It is not difficult to proliferate new CTA methods. It may be more important now to consolidate, by moving into a period of assessment and review. This type of support may be more available in the research community than in the practitioner community. By helping to assess the utility of different CTA methods, researchers may be able to reach better theoretical descriptions of the nature of expertise, and better descriptions of cognitive skills. The descriptions would have both basic and applied research value.

Finally, some of the greatest impacts from CTA projects occur when discoveries are made about the way complex tasks are performed. This is one of the things that sets CTA efforts apart from conventional task analyses. The exhaustive documentation of precursors and criteria and terminal conditions, the tracing of data pathways for each type of sensor, does not necessarily translate into insights. As we try to turn CTA methods into a reliable technology, we must be careful not to become too fascinated by procedures and objectivity, and lose sight of the importance of discovery. A CTA study is not an extension of hypothesis-testing methods for experimentation. One of the strengths of CTA is to provide a means for generating new hypotheses and unexpected explanations of phenomena, the way people accomplish difficult tasks in natural settings.

ACKNOWLEDGMENTS

We would like to acknowledge the effort of Beth Crandall in reviewing an earlier draft and providing many useful suggestions. We also appreciate the comments and advice of Robert Hoffman and Eduardo Salas.

REFERENCES

Anastasi, D., Hutton, R., Thordsen, M., Klein, G., & Serfaty, D. (1997). Cognitive function modeling for capturing complexity in system design (pp. 221–226). Proceedings of the 1997 IEEE International Conference on Systems, Man, and Cybernetics.

Andriole, S. J., & Adelman, L. (1993). Prospects for cognitive systems engineering, *Proceedings of the 1993 IEEE International Conference on Systems, Man, and Cybernetics* (pp. 743–747). Piscataway, NJ: Institute of Electrical and Electronics Engineers.

Barsalou, I. W. (1985). Ideals, central tendency, and frequency of instantiation. *Journal of Experimental Psychology: Learning, Memory, and Cognition, 11*, 629–654.

Boy, G. A. (1998). *Cognitive function analysis*. Norwood, NJ: Ablex Publishing Corporation.

Cannon-Bowers, J. A., & Salas, E. (Eds) (1998). *Making decisions under stress: Implications for individuals and team training* (1st ed.). Washington, DC: American Psychological Association.

Chi, M. T. H., Glaser, R., & Farr, M. J. (1988). *The nature of expertise*. Hillsdale, NJ: Lawrence Erlbaum Associates.

Cook, R. I., & Woods, D. D. (1996). Adapting to new technology in the operating room. *Human Factors, 38*(4), 593–613.

Cook, R., Woods, D., Walters, M., & Cristoffersen, K. (1996). The cognitive systems engineering of automated medical evacuation scheduling and its implication. *Proceedings from the 3rd Annual Symposium on Human Interaction with Complex Systems*. Piscataway, NJ: Institute of Electrical and Electronics Engineers.

Cooke, N. J. (1994). Varieties of knowledge elicitation techniques. *International Journal of Human-Computer Studies, 41*, 801–849.

Cooke, N. J., Durso, F. T., Schwanaveldt, R. W. (1994). Retention of skilled search after nine years. *Human Factors, 36*(4), 597–605.

Crandall, B., & Getchell-Reiter, K. (1993). Critical decision method: A technique for eliciting concrete assessment indicators from the "intuition" of NICU nurses. *Advances in Nursing Sciences, 16*(1), 42–51.

Crandall, B., Klein, G., Militello, L., & Wolf, S. (1994). *Tools for applied cognitive task analysis* (Technical Report prepared for the Naval Personnel Research and Development Center, San Diego, CA). Fairborn, OH: Klein Associates Inc.

de Groot, A. D. (1946/1978). *Thought and choice in chess* (2nd ed.). New York, NY: Mouton.

de Groot, A. D. (1986). Intuition in chess. *International Computer Chess Association Journal, 9*, 67–75.

DeMaio, J., Parkinson, S., Leshowitz, B., Crosby, J., & Thorpe, J. A. (1976). *Visual scanning: Comparisons between student and instructor pilots* (Technical Report No. AFHRL-RE-76-10 prepared for Air Force Human Resources Laboratory).

Di Bello, L. (1997). Measuring success in non-trivial ways; how we can know that a DSS implementation has really worked. *Proceedings of the 1993 IEEE International Conference on Systems, Man, and Cybernetics* (pp. 2204–2209). Piscataway, NJ: Institute of Electrical and Electronics Engineers.

Di Bello, L. & Spender, J. C. (1996). Constructive learning: A new approach to deploying technological systems into the workplace. *International Journal of Technology Management, 11*, 747–758.

Ericsson, K. A. (1996). The acquisition of expert performance: An introduction to some of the issues. In: K. A. Ericsson (Ed.), *The Road to Excellence: The Acquisition of Expert Performance in the Arts and Sciences, Sports, and Games* (pp. 1–50). Mahwah, NJ: Lawrence Erlbaum Associates, Inc.

Ericsson, K. A., & Smith, J. (1991). *Toward a general theory of expertise: Prospects and limits.* Cambridge: Cambridge University Press.

Essens, P., Fallesen, J., McCann, C., Cannon-Bowers, J., & Dorfel, G. (1995). *COADE = A Framework for Cognitive Analysis, Design, and Evaluation* (Technical Report AC/243 (Panel 8) TR/17). Brussels: Defence Research Group, NATO.

Gopher, D., Weil, M., Bareket, T., & Caspi, S. (1988). Using complex computer games as task simulators in the training of flight skills. *Proceedings of the 1988 IEEE International Conference on Systems, Man, & Cybernetics.*

Gordon, S. E. (1994). *Systematic training programs: Maximizing effectiveness and minimizing liability.* Englewood Cliffs, NJ: Prentice-Hall.

Gordon, S. E., & Gill, R. T. (1997). Cognitive task analysis. In: C. E. Zsambok & G. Klein (Eds), *Naturalistic Decision Making* (pp. 131–140). Mahwah, NJ: Lawrence Erlbaum Associates.

Gordon, S. E., Schmierer, K. A., & Gill, R. T. (1993). Conceptual graph analysis: Knowledge acquisition for instructional system design. *Human Factors, 35*(3), 459–481.

Gott, S. P., Pokorny, R. A., Kane, R. S., Alley, W. E., & Dibble, E. (1996). Development & evaluation of an intelligent tutoring system: Sherlock 2 – an avionics troubleshooting tutor (Technical Report AL/HR-TR-1996-XX). Brooks AFB, TX.

Hammond, K. R., Hamm, R. M., Grassia, J., & Pearson, T. (1987). Direct comparison of the efficacy of intuitive and analytical cognition in expert judgment. *Proceedings of IEEE Transactions on Systems, Man, and Cybernetics, SMC-17* (pp. 753–770).

Hanish, K. A., Kramer, A. F., & Hulin, C. L. (1991). Cognitive representations, control, and understanding of complex systems: A field study on components of users' mental models and expert/novice differences. *Special Issue: Cognitive Ergonomics II, Ergonomics, 34*(8), 1129–1145.

Hayes-Roth, F., Waterman, D. A., & Lenat, D. B. (1983). *Building expert systems.* MA: Addison-Wesley.

Hoffman, R. R. (1987). The problem of extracting the knowledge of experts from the perspective of experimental psychology. *AI Magazine, 8,* 53–67.

Hoffman, R. R., Crandall, B. W., & Shadbolt, N. R. (1998). Use of the Critical Decision Method to elicit expert knowledge: A case study in cognitive task analysis methodology. *Human Factors, 40*(2), 254–276.

Hoffman, R. R., Shadbolt, N. R., Burton, A. M., & Klein, G. (1995). Eliciting knowledge from experts: A methodological analysis. *Organizational Behavior and Human Decision Processes, 62* (2), 129–158.

Holding, D. H. (1985). *The psychology of chess skill.* Hillsdale, NJ: Lawrence Erlbaum Associates.

Hutchins, E. (1983). Understanding Micronesian navigation. In: D. Gentner & A. L. Stevens (Eds), *Mental Models.* Hillsdale, NJ: Lawrence Erlbaum Associates.

Kaempf, G., Klinger, D., & Wolf, S. (1994). *Development of decision-centered interventions for airport security checkpoints* (Technical Report prepared for the U.S. Department of Transportation, Cambridge, MA). Fairborn, OH: Klein Associates Inc.

Kaempf, G. L., Thordsen, M. L., & Klein, G. (1991). *Application of an expertise-centered taxonomy to training decisions* (Technical Report prepared for U.S. Army Research Institute, Alexandria, VA). Fairborn, OH: Klein Associates Inc.

Kaempf, G. L., Klein, G. A., Thordsen, M. L., & Wolf, S. (1996). Decision making in complex command-and-control environments. *Human Factors, 38,* 220–231.

Kahneman, D., & Miller, D. T. (1986). Norm theory: Comparing reality to its alternatives. *Psychological Review, 93,* 136–153.

Kieras, D. E. (1988) Toward a practical GOMS model methodology for user interface design, In: M. Helander (Ed.), *Handbook for Human-Computer Interaction.* N. Holland: Elsevier Science.

Kirwan, B. & Ainsworth, L. K. (1993). *A guide to task analysis.* London: Taylor and Francis Ltd.

Klein, G. (2000). Cognitive task analysis of teams. In: J. M. C. Schraagen, S. Chipman, & V. Shalin (Eds), *Cognitive Task Analysis* (pp. 417–430). Mahwah, NJ: Lawrence Erlbaum Associates.

Klein, G. (1998). *Sources of power: How people make decisions.* Cambridge, MA: MIT Press.

Klein, G. A. (1978). Phenomenological vs. behavioral objectives for skilled performance. *Journal of Phenomenological Psychology, 9,* 139–156.

Klein, G. A., Calderwood, R., & Clinton-Cirocco, A. (1986). Rapid decision making on the fireground. *Proceedings of the 30th Annual Human Factors Society, 1,* 576–580. Santa Monica, CA: Human Factors & Ergonomics Society.

Klein, G. A., & Crandall, B. W. (1995). The role of mental simulation in naturalistic decision making. In: P. Hancock, J. Flach, J. Caird, & K. Vicente (Eds), *Local Applications of the Ecological Approach to Human-Machine Systems* (Vol. 2, pp. 324–358). Mahwah, NJ: Lawrence Erlbaum Associates.

Klein, G. A., & Hoffman, R. (1993). Seeing the invisible: Perceptual/cognitive aspects of expertise. In: M. Rabinowitz (Ed.), *Cognitive Science Foundations of Instruction* (pp. 203–226). Hillsdale, NJ: Lawrence Erlbaum Associates.

Klein, G. A., Orasanu, J., Calderwood, R., & Zsambok, C. E. (Eds) (1993). *Decision making in action: Models and methods.* Norwood, NJ: Ablex Publishing Corporation.

Klein, H. A., Vincent, E. J., & Isaacson, J. J. (2001) Driving proficiency: The development of decision skills. In: E. Salas & G. Klein (Eds), *Linking Expertise and Naturalistic Decision Making* (pp. 305–322). Mahwah, NJ: Lawrence Erlbaum Associates.

Klinger, D. W. & Militello, L. G. (in preparation). Designing for performance: A cognitive systems engineering and cognitive task analysis approach to the modification of the AWACS weapons director interface.

Layton, C., Smith, P. J., & McCoy, C. E. (1994, March). Design of a cooperative problem-solving system for en-route flight planning: An empirical evaluation. *Human Factors, 36*(1), 94–119.

Lesgold, A. M., Rubinson, H., Feltovich, P., Glaser, R., Klopfer, D., & Wang, Y. (1988). Expertise in a complex skill: diagnosing X-ray pictures. In: M. T. H. Chi, R. Glaser & M. J. Farr (Eds), *The Nature of Expertise* (pp. 311–342). Mahwah, NJ: Lawrence Erlbaum Associates.

Logan, G. D. (1988). Toward an instance theory of automatization. *Psychological Review (95), 4*, 492–527.

McFarren, M. R. (1987). *Using concept mapping to define problems and identify key kernels during the development of a decision support system.* Master's thesis, School of Engineering, Air Force Institute of Technology, Wright-Patterson AFB, OH.

Means, B., Salas, E., Crandall, B., & Jacobs, O. (1993). Training decision makers for the real world. In: G. A. Klein, J. Orasanu, R. Calderwood & C. E. Zsambok (Eds), *Decision Making in Action: Models and Methods* (pp. 306–326). Norwood, NJ: Ablex Publishing Corporation.

Metcalfe, J., & Shimamura, A. P. (1994). *Metacognition: Knowing about knowing.* Cambridge, MA: MIT Press.

Meyer, D. E., & Kieras, D. E. (1997). A computational theory of executive cognitive processes and multiple-task performance: Part 1. Basic mechanisms. *Psychological Review, 104*(1), 3–65.

Meyer, D. E., & Kieras, D. E. (1997). A computational theory of executive cognitive processes and multiple-task performance: Part 2. Accounts of psychological refractory-period phenomena. *Psychological Review, 104*(4), 749–791.

Militello, L. G. (2001). Representing expertise. In: E. Salas & G. Klein (Eds), *Linking Expertise and Naturalistic Decision Making* (pp. 247–264). Mahwah, NJ: Lawrence Erlbaum Associates.

Militello, L. G., & Hutton, R. J. B. (1998). Applied Cognitive Task Analysis (ACTA): A practitioner's toolkit for understanding cognitive task demands. *Ergonomics, Special Issue: Task Analysis, 41*(11), 1618–1641.

Militello, L. G., Hutton, R. J. B., Pliske, R. M., Knight, B. J., & Klein, G. (1997). *Applied Cognitive Task Analysis (ACTA) Methodology* (Technical Report prepared for Navy Personnel Research and Development Center). Fairborn, OH: Klein Associates Inc.

Militello, L., & Lim, L. (1995). Patient assessment skills: Assessing early cues of necrotizing enterocolitis. *The Journal of Perinatal & Neonatal Nursing, 9*(2), 42–52. Gaithersburg, MD: Aspen Publishers, Inc.

Miller, T. E., Militello, L. G., & Heaton, J. K. (1996). Evaluating air campaign plan quality in operational settings. In: A. Tate (Ed.), *Advanced Planning Technology*. Menlo Park, CA: The AAAI Press.

Neisser, U. (1967). *Cognitive psychology.* New York: Appleton-Century-Crofts.

Newell, A., & Simon, H. A. (1972). *Human problem solving.* Englewood Cliffs, NY: Prentice-Hall.

Nisbett, R. E., & Wilson, T. D. (1977). Telling more than we can know: Verbal reports on mental processes. *Psychological Review, 84*(3), 231–259.

Pliske, R., Klinger, D., Hutton, R., Crandall, B., Knight, B., & Klein, G. (1997). *Understanding skilled weather forecasting: Implications for training and the design of forecasting tools* (Technical Report No. AL/HR-CR-1997–0003). Brooks AFB, TX: Air Force Materiel Command, Armstrong Laboratory, Human Resources Directorate.

Rasmussen, J., Pejterson, A. M., & Goodstein, L. P. (1994). *Cognitive systems engineering.* New York: John Wiley and Sons, Inc.

Redding, R. E. (1989). Perspectives on cognitive task analysis: The state of the art. *Proceedings of the Human Factors Society 33rd Annual Meeting,* 1348–1352. Santa Monica, CA: Human Factors & Ergonomics Society.

Redding, R. E., & Seamster, T. L. (1994). Cognitive task analysis in air traffic controller and aviation crew training. In: N. Johnston, N. McDonald & R. Fuller (Eds), *Aviation Psychology in Practice.* Brookfield, VT: Ashgate Publishing Company.

Roth, E. M., Woods, D. D., & Pople, H. E. (1992). Cognitive simulation as a tool for cognitive task analysis. *Ergonomics, 35,* 1163–1198.

Rouse, W. B., & Morris, N. M. (1986). On looking into the black box: Prospects and limits on the search for mental models. *Psychological Bulletin, 100*(3), 349–363.

Schraagen, J. M. C., Chipman, S., & Shalin, V. (Eds) (2000). *Cognitive task analysis.* Mahwah, NJ: Lawrence Erlbaum Associates.

Scribner, S. (1985). Knowledge at work. *Anthropology and Education Quarterly, 16*(3), 199–206.

Seamster, T. L., Redding, R. E., & Kaempf, G. L. (1997). *Applied cognitive task analysis in aviation.* Aldershot, England: Avebury Aviation.

Shanteau, J. (1992). Competence in experts: The role of task characteristics. *Organizational Behavior and Human Decision Processes, 53,* 252–266.

Simon, H. A. (1956). Rational choice and the structure of the environment. *Psychological Review, 63,* 129–138.

Sloman, S. A. (1996). The empirical case for two systems of reasoning. *American Psychological Association, Inc., 119*(1), 3–22.

Smith, E. M., Ford, J. K., & Kozlowski, S. W. J. (1997). Building adaptive expertise: Implications for training design strategies. In: M. A. Quinones & A. Ehrenstein (Eds), *Training for a Rapidly Changing Workplace: Applications of Psychological Research.* Washington, D.C.: APA.

Vicente, K. J. (1999). *Cognitive work analysis: Towards safe, productive, and healthy computer-based work.* Mahwah, NJ: Lawrence Erlbaum Associates.

Woods, D. D. (1993). Process-tracing methods for the study of cognition outside of the experimental psychology laboratory. In: G. A. Klein, J. Orasanu, R. Calderwood & C. E. Zsambok (Eds), *Decision Making in Action: Models and Methods* (pp. 228–251). Norwood, NJ: Ablex Publishing Corporation.

Woods, D. D., O'Brien, J., & Hanes, L. F. (1987). Human Factors challenges in process control: The case of nuclear power plants. In: G. Salvendy (Ed.), *Handbook of Human Factors/ Ergonomics.* NY: John Wiley and Sons, Inc.

Zachary, W. W., Zaklad, A. L., Hicinbotham, J. H., Ryder, J. M., Purcell, J. A., & Wherry, R. J. (1991). *COGNET representation of tactical decision-making in ship-based anti-air warfare* (Technical Report 911015.9009 for Naval Ocean Systems Center, San Diego, CA).

Zsambok, C., & Klein, G. (1997). *Naturalistic decision making.* Mahwah, NJ: Lawrence Erlbaum Associates.

5. THE APPLICATION OF HUMAN MODELING TECHNOLOGY TO THE DESIGN, EVALUATION AND OPERATION OF COMPLEX SYSTEMS[1]

Wayne Zachary, Gwendolyn E. Campbell,
K. Ronald Laughery, Floyd Glenn and
Janis A. Cannon-Bowers

ABSTRACT

This chapter reviews the ability of the emerging human performance modeling technologies to support the design and operation of complex systems. The ability of existing technologies to meet current application needs is analyzed, and the results are then used to assess the areas where additional research and development is most needed. Following a brief history of human performance modeling, a taxonomy of models and modeling techniques is established, as a framework for remaining discussion. The human performance modeling technology base is separately analyzed for its ability to support system design processing and to support system operation. The system design process analysis considers the various roles that human performance models may play during that

Advances in Human Performance and Cognitive Engineering Research, Volume 1,
pages 201–250.
Copyright © 2001 by Elsevier Science Ltd.
All rights of reproduction in any form reserved.
ISBN: 0-7623-0748-X

process, ranging from generating design concepts to affording simulation-based design evaluation. The system operation analysis also assesses a range of roles, from training to performance support to automation. These analyses demonstrate that human modeling technology has reached a sufficient state of maturity and has become a proven contributor of the complex systems engineering process. Challenges for further high-payoff research are also presented in five categories: cognition, knowledge management, team and organizational structure and processes, predictive models of training, and human-centered systems engineering.

INTRODUCTION

A continuing activity in behavioral and social science research has been constructing models as a means of formalizing, integrating, testing, and even developing theory. In recent years, this avenue of research has been very active, with substantial advances in the development of computer models of human thought and behavior (see Pew & Mavor, 1998). This research has begun to fuel speculation that the human modeling endeavor may have progressed to the point that the current generation of models could have immediate or near-term engineering application.

At the same time, both industry and the government (particularly the military) are facing challenges that are driving the need for human performance models. For example, DoD is requiring that future Navy ships must be built with reduced budgets *and* operated by vastly smaller crews, and must operate effectively and efficiently in mission environments that are complex, difficult to define, and changing rapidly. Thus, the human component is, more than ever, the critical component to mission success. Moreover, the sheer size and scale of complex systems such as ships (or factories, or aircraft, etc.) severely limit the opportunity for traditional experimental approaches. It is simply too costly and time consuming to build physical prototypes (or even effective mock-ups) and then empirically assess their impact on human performance. In this context, the techniques of human modeling and simulation provide perhaps the only viable option. They hold the promise of providing powerful new means to design, evaluate, and operate modern ship systems to meet, accommodate, and enhance human abilities, if the technology exists to model them appropriately and effectively. Recent successes, such as the use of human performance models in embedded Naval training (see Zachary, Bilazarian, Burns & Cannon-Bowers, 1997; Zachary, Cannon-Bowers, Burns, Bilazarian & Krecker, 1998) and in support of large scale training exercises (see Laird, Coulter, Jones,

Kenny, Koss & Nielsen, 1997), suggest that the technology may now be ready to be used in this manner.

The purpose of this chapter is to assess the ability of the state-of-the-art in modeling technology to solve pressing problems in the engineering of complex systems. On the one hand, we seek to identify the 'low hanging fruit' – obvious and immediate applications of human modeling technology. On the other hand, we seek to identify areas where additional research and development is needed, and from those to identify areas that have a high payoff potential.

The remainder of the introduction briefly establishes an historical context of human performance modeling research. The second section creates a taxonomy of modeling technologies, which will be used throughout the rest of the chapter. The third section focuses on the application of human modeling techniques to support the design and evaluation of a complex system. Specifically, the section addresses both how human models could be incorporated to support the relatively common practice of simulation-based design evaluation, and how human modeling technologies might be applied to support the generation of design concepts. The validation and maturity of the human performance models themselves are also discussed in this section. However, these are large topics in there own right, and a full discussion is beyond the scope of this chapter. The fourth section focuses on the application of human modeling techniques to support the operation of complex systems. These applications typically involve embedding the model(s) in the operational system to provide support for activities such as decision-making, embedded training, and task or workload management. The final section summarizes the current capabilities, and highlights and identifies the needs and opportunities for longer-term research based on potential application payoff.

Historical Development and Application of Human Modeling

While work on computer simulation techniques did not begin until the emergence of commercial computers in the 1950s, many of the basic quantitative models of human performance used in those simulations were actually developed much earlier, often in university research laboratories. Modern techniques for the analysis and modeling of cognitive performance can be traced back at least to the seminal work of Donders in the Netherlands in the mid-19th century. Current models for basic processes in visual and auditory perception can be related back to the late 19th century research of Helmholz, Hering, Weber, and Fechner. Work from the early part of this century on the dynamics of eye movements (Dodge & Cline, 1901) and hand movements (Brown & Slater-Hammel, 1949) continues to be relevant in contemporary models. Indeed, a very large literature has developed on models for many distinct aspects of human performance, ranging from basic features of sensation, through many kinds of perception, motor activity, information processing, and decision making. Fortunately, recent efforts have also addressed the compilation and indexing of information about this rapidly growing body of human performance models (e.g. Boff, Kaufman & Thomas, 1986).

Individual Level Human Performance Model

Formulation of the first computer simulations of human performance began in the late 1950s along two very different tracks. Beginning in the late 1950s was the work of Siegel and Wolf (1962, 1969) to construct computer simulations of the performance of individuals and teams in operating complex military systems. The Siegel-Wolf models represent the first of the class of task network models that describe the dynamics of task performance in terms of the sequence and timing of subtasks. This approach was later translated into a general purpose modeling tool for the Air Force in the form of a modeling system designated as SAINT (Systems Analysis of Integrated Networks of Tasks), which was subsequently adapted for micro-computer use and commercially distributed under the name Micro Saint (Laughery, 1998). These task network models have been applied in the analysis of a large number and variety of contexts and have been shown to provide a very efficient means for simulating such large, complex systems.

Around the same time, Allen Newell and his colleagues at Carnegie-Mellon University were taking a different approach to understanding and modeling human performance, beginning with the concepts of the logic theory machine and the general problem solver and leading through the mainstream development of artificial intelligence and cognitive modeling to the current GOMS (Card, Moran & Newell, 1983) and SOAR techniques. These models and techniques focus heavily on describing how performance is derived from knowledge, which in turn must be represented in fine detail in order to support performance predictions.

Initially, a modeler had to choose between these two fundamentally different approaches, with task network models requiring the user to provide estimates for the times and accuracies of behaviors at the finest level of model representation, and knowledge-based models affording the promise of obtaining basic performance data from general perceptual, motor, and cognitive models (Laughery & Corker, 1997). However, it wasn't long before modelers began to look for ways to integrate the two approaches. The first general purpose modeling tool which sought to integrate the task network and knowledge-based features was the Navy's Human Operator Simulator (HOS) which was initially developed in the early 1970s (Lane, Strieb, Glenn & Wherry, 1981). This tool provided a mechanism for representing the detailed configuration of displays and controls in a crewstation, the task procedures by which the user operates the crewstation, and the component "micro-models" by which the human interacts with the displays, controls, and related information.

SOAR was unveiled by Newell and colleagues in the mid-1980s (Laird, Newell & Rosenbloom, 1987) as the first major offering of a general architecture for human cognitive performance, promising to provide the capability to represent the complete range of human behavior from a knowledge-based perspective. In addition to representing both declarative and procedural knowledge, SOAR also incorporates a learning mechanism based on the use of various general problem-solving strategies and the "chunking" of successful solutions. SOAR has been widely used in university laboratories around the world and has recently been demonstrated in a large-scale application for computer-generated forces (Laird, Coulter, Jones, Kenny, Koss & Nielsen, 1997).

Since the emergence of SOAR, several other candidates have been developed as general computational architectures for representation of human cognition, such as ACT-R, EPIC, and COGNET. ACT-R was developed by Anderson (1993) as a model for higher level cognition, such as in problem solving tasks, with a principal focus on the investigation of mechanisms of learning. EPIC was developed by Kieras and Meyer (1997) to provide a detailed representation of how human task performance is dictated by the constraints imposed by perceptual, motor, and cognitive abilities, with special emphasis on defining how perceptual and motor activities interweave with other aspects of cognition. COGNET was developed by Zachary and colleagues (Zachary, Ryder, Ross & Weiland, 1992; Zachary, Le Mentec & Ryder, 1996) as a model of expert-level problem solving and task performance in real time, multiple-task environments. Pew and Mavor (1998) reviewed ACT-R, COGNET, EPIC, MicroSaint, SOAR, and several other integrative modeling architectures in detail, in the context of military simulations of human behavior.

Group and Team Level Human Performance Models

In addition to these general models and architectures for individual human cognition and performance, other types of models represent and study the performance of multiple individuals operating as teams or larger organizations.

Unlike the psychological models, which have focused on individual cognitive and behavioral processes, these social science models have tended to focus on the structure of human interactions and social systems. Whereas individual-level models have focused on processes, these group and team models have been primarily concerned with the role of constraints and structure on processes, rather than on underlying mechanisms. However, similar to the psychologically based individual-level models, the team and organizational models of current interest also come (primarily) from two distinct lines of research, which can be termed the micro and macro approaches.

The micro approaches focus on modeling interaction upward from the (atomic) level of the individual dyadic relationships. This work has been heavily mathematical and influenced by the early work of Harrary, White, and others who employed the mathematics of graph theory as a framework for modeling the networks of relationships among people. During the 1960s and 1970s, very sophisticated models were derived from this "social network as graph" simile (e.g. see White, Boorman and Breiger, 1976, or Zachary, 1977, for very different network modeling approaches, among others). This research showed how the collection of individual dyads that makes up teams, groups, and organizations has a deep structure that could often be seen to have clear effects (or at least reflections) in the activities and processes that occurred within these social units. At the same time, it became increasingly clear that collection of the data on individual dyads was a costly and time-consuming process, and a series of experimental studies, termed the "informant accuracy studies", demonstrated the difficulties in measuring the dyadic structure of social networks on an indirect (i.e. non-observational) basis (see Bernard, Killworth, Kronenfeld & Sailer, 1984). These measurement and data collection problems have continued to hamper broader development and application of the field to the present day.

The macro approach focuses on broader processes in social groups, particularly large social units such as organizations, cities, societies, etc., without reference to individuals and/or their unitary dyadic relationships. This tradition achieved prominence with the work of Jay Forrester at MIT (Forrester, 1971) and the Club of Rome (Meadows, Meadows, Randers & Behrens, 1972), who began to model the behavior of complex systems as the dynamic interactions of multiple complex sets of constraints and underlying relationships. Formulated as systems of difference and/or differential equations, the resulting system dynamics were instrumental in demonstrating how underlying relationships had long-lasting and subtle effects on the long-term behavior of the larger systems. Just as the micromodels of group structure showed how the pattern or relationships in a network led to higher level structures and constrained group processes, the dynamic models of the macromodelers demonstrated how a constant set of underlying relationships could give rise to a broad range of complex and varying processes through time.

A third, and now dominant, approach has arisen from a combination of the micro and macro approaches (see Pew & Mavor, 1998: Chapter 10 for a more detailed review). In this approach, which can be termed the agent-based approach, the individuals within a team or organization are represented in simplified fashion as agents, interconnected by networks of command, control, and communication relationships. Typically, both the agents and the network in which they are embedded are dynamic, leading both to learning and organizational changes over time.[2] A critical issue in this approach is the degree of cognitive sophistication given to the agents, and the degree of organizational sophistication of the network in which they are embedded.

Use of Human Models in System Engineering

Just as the research into modeling human behavior is not new, the current attempts to apply human models to complex systems engineering are not the first of their kind either. In the early 1970s, for example, the Navy initiated the CAFES (Computer Aided Function Evaluation Systems) program to develop simulation-based tools for assessment of workload, function allocation, and anthropometric accommodation in aircraft cockpits (Hutchins, 1974). This was followed by the Air Force CADET (Computer Aided Design and Evaluation Tools) program (Connelly, 1984) and then another larger scale Air Force program on Cockpit Automation Technology (CAT) (McNeese, Warren & Woodson, 1985). In the mid 1980s, the Army began the development of a collection of simulation-based tools to support the methods of the MANPRINT program, since designated as the HARDMAN-III tools (see Risser & Berger, 1984). At about the same time, the Navy started the Advanced Technology Crew Station (ATCS) program to develop and demonstrate the use of simulation and computer-based tools in design and development of new aircraft cockpits. More recent programs in this vein include the Air Force's OASIS program and NASA's MIDAS program. And there have been several systematic reviews and conferences in this area over the past few decades (e.g. Moraal & Kraiss, 1981; McMillan, Beevis, Salas, Strub, Sutton & Van Breda, 1989; Elkind, Card, Hochberg & Huey, 1990; Baron, Kruser & Huey, 1990). Of course, the technologies of human performance modeling and simulation are not stationary targets, and their rapid development over recent years warrant periodic reexamination of status and development needs.

In general, these DoD programs did not develop the basic human performance models, but rather sought to adapt existing models and techniques in order to produce practical tools to aid system designers and developers. For example, several of the Army's HARDMAN-III tools used the same basic human performance model (variants of Micro Saint) for distinct applications to determine system performance requirements, to evaluate workload for a team of system operators, and to assess the effects of individual differences. While these and other programs were successful at applying human performance models to some specific 'target' system or concept, they have, so far, failed at the more global task of making human modeling an accepted and standard component of complex systems engineering within DoD.

THE TECHNOLOGY BASE

Human cognition and behavior are modeled through a variety of approaches and technologies. Some of these focus on individual components of human performance (e.g. models of visual target detection), while others focus on the integration of components at the architectural level (e.g. executable cognitive architectures). The various ways in which human models can be used in complex systems design, evaluation and operation do not inherently favor either component or integrative approaches. For example, in designing a sensor display to optimize human target detection, a model of visual detection may be completely sufficient. A more integrative model that included anthropometry, auditory processing, cognitive planning, and problem solving, etc., might well be 'overkill' and too cumbersome to justify its use. On the other hand, applications such as large-scale system simulation or distributed training exercises may require highly integrated modeling approaches. To facilitate a more systematic mapping of the human modeling technology base onto the various opportunities and requirements in the complex systems domain, a simple taxonomy of the existing technology base is presented below.

The taxonomy uses two broad groupings – models and modeling techniques. *Models* includes complete formulations (or families of them) that attempt to describe, predict, or prescribe aspects of human competence or performance, either component-wise or integrative. *Modeling techniques* includes computation, mathematical, or methodological formulations that have been used to build models of human competence/performance or to apply human models to system design, operation, or evaluation problems. They differ from the first grouping in that modeling techniques are more general purpose tools for modeling (in mathematics, physics, computer science, etc.) that have been sometimes used to represent human cognition or behavior. These modeling techniques do not embody specific psychological or sociological theories, nor were they developed specifically for the purpose of human modeling.

Following the discussion of the various categories of models and modeling techniques, the next sections will consider the use of this human modeling technology in the complex system design/evaluation process, and in the complex system operation process.

Classes of Human Models

Human models, as defined, may be classified into 18 categories, which span the range from highly specialized component models (e.g. perceptual models) to highly integrative representations (e.g. computational cognitive models). These categories are (in alphabetical order):

(1) *Closed form component models.* Self-contained mathematical formulations that represent some component aspect of human performance as a self-contained closed form mathematical relationship rather than any common application or set of underlying terms. Fitts' Law (Fitts & Peterson, 1964) is a classical example of this type of model.

(2) *Computational cognitive models.* Integrative models of human cognition, perception, sensation, motor action and knowledge that embody a principled underlying theory or framework for human information processing. This class includes items such as ACT-R (Anderson, 1993), COGNET (Zachary, Le Mentec & Ryder 1996), EPIC (Kieras & Meyer, 1997), and SOAR (Laird, Newell, and Rosenbloom, 1987), among others. These models capture human knowledge in a symbolic form and allow behavior and cognition to be generated as a result of a symbolic computation process.

(3) *Critical decision models.* Domain-specific models that capture and represent the logic and situational relationships that underlie decision-making in that specific domain (Klein, Calderwood & MacGregor, 1989). These descriptive models typically focus on extracting knowledge from expert decision-makers and representing it in a combined prose/graphical notation.

(4) *Decision theory models.* A broad family of normative models that represent human behavior in choice-among-alternatives situations. Generally drawing on the terms of game theory (Von Neuman & Morgenstern, 1947), the choice process is represented in terms of outcomes, outcome-utilities, and underlying distributions of input states, together with varying parameters that include factors such as subjective value, risk, and risk preference, etc.

(5) *Finite state models.* A computational framework for relating inputs to behaviors using the notions of internal information states and the mathematics of finite state automata.

(6) *GOMS (Goals, Operators, Methods, Selection Rules).* Domain-specific models of the knowledge used in human-computer interaction that are developed using a notation created originally by Card, Moran and Newell (1983). GOMS models decompose primarily procedural knowledge into goal hierarchies, which are conditionally related to states of the interactive process and interface.

(7) *Group Training Models.* Team-level representations that could either relate collective (i.e. team) training to performance or to models that relate performance to training requirements.

(8) *Human reliability analysis.* Various models for estimating the likelihood of errors occurring on complex tasks as a function of elemental task error probabilities and other factors. These techniques are used, for example, to estimate the impact of human errors on system performance and to evaluate system designs and recommend improvements (Czaja, 1997).

(9) *Link models of anthropometry and movement.* Numerical/graphical models that represent the human body and its capability for movement and vision through an articulated set of 'links' which themselves represent lower-level body components (e.g. fingers, arms, torso, etc.). In the most sophisticated of these models, the links are represented not as simple lines but rather as complexly-interrelated solids.

(10) *Network models.* Models in which individuals, teams, groups, and/or organizations are represented as nodes and their dyadic relationships as links in a graph-theoretic mathematical representation. The degree of complexity in the dyadic representation varies greatly, and the mathematics often make recourse to higher-level systems computed on the raw graphs.

(11) *Optimal control models.* Mathematical/computational representation of decision making and/or adaptive behavior in an uncertain environment, based on the underlying mathematics of optimal control theory (Kalman, Falb & Arbib, 1969). These models include an internal model of the external world which is used to select behavior in the world based on current input, current output, current internal state, and various filters.

(12) *Perceptual models.* Various descriptions of sensation and perception for any of the human sense modalities, though primarily for vision and hearing. The possibilities range from models for detection of simple stimuli, through interpretation of complex patterns.

(13) *Recognition Primed Decision Making (RPD)*. Models of domain-specific expert human decision making that are developed using an underlying RPD framework. This framework asserts that decisions emerge from an (implicit or explicit) situation assessment process that maps situational features and understanding onto appropriate decision-options. Developed by Klein (1989), the RPD framework is related to more general modeling techniques of case-based reasoning.

(14) *Signal Detection Theory*. Models for determining the probability of detection of a stimulus (which may be very simple or quite complex) based on the assumption that the signal (i.e. stimulus) and the background noise can each be characterized by normal distributions along relevant psychological dimensions (Green & Swets, 1966).

(15) *Task Hierarchies*. Domain-specific models of task performance achieved through a conventional task analysis that simply decomposes a job into a hierarchy of tasks and subtasks.

(16) *Task networks*. Domain-specific or job-specific models which decompose human activity in the domain or job into a series of interconnected tasks, where tasks are represented as transformations of some state/variable vector, and task-connections represented as potential task transitions, often conditioned by probabilistic factors. Originating from the SAINT methodology (Wortman, Duket, Seifert, Hann & Chubb, 1978), the network is often used to simulate the behavior of the system as well.

(17) *Training taxonomy*. A structural model of generic tasks in terms of the underlying skill requirements so as to support analyses of training effects on skill retention and, hence, task performance (see Swezey & Llaneras, 1997).

(18) *Workload Models*. Models which represent residual human work or information processing capability in specific context. Typically workload models are based on an underling theory, such as Wicken's (1980) Multiple Resource Theory which represents information processing and capacity as the result of interactions among multiple lower-level capabilities or resources.

These eighteen categories represent only broad classes of human models, and even then only a subset of human models that appear particularly relevant to the complex system design and operation problems. The functional definition of the classes allows many vastly different models to be included within a given class.

Regardless of the class to which a model belongs, however, it can be described along four key dimensions:

(1) *Model goals.* Models that attempt to describe the regularities of human behavior or cognition within a specific setting that are captured in empirical data are called *descriptive models.* Other models, called *predictive models*, attempt to predict human behavior/cognition in a range of (future or hypothetical) situations described in terms of empirical data. Finally, there are *prescriptive models* which attempt to prescribe what a person should do/think in a given (future or hypothetical) situation.

(2) *Architectural focus.* A given model may focus on individual architectural aspects of human capabilities and behavior, including: (a) the characteristics of the *physical* body and the ability of the body to move and act in a given physical environment, (b) the processes of registering information from the external environment (*sensation*) and/or internalizing registered information into a form/representation used for internal information processing (*perception*), (c) the representation of information in the mind and the process of manipulating that information to yield complex behaviors such as reasoning, decision-making, or planning (*information processing*), or (d) the process by which the person acquires information and knowledge about the external world and external processes, and internalizes this information and knowledge on a long-term basis for use in future information processing (*learning*). There are also *integrative* models, which attempt to integrate all of the multiple components into a single model of human cognition and behavior.

(3) *Predictive focus.* Those models that seek to predict human behavior can differ on the aspects of human capability that they seek to predict. The most basic kind of predictive focus is on the *outcome*, or specific behaviors that a person will take and the outcomes of those behaviors in a given scenario or situation. There are also *time*-based models, which seek to predict the time it takes for activities and/or actions to be performed, and *accuracy*-based models, which seek to predict the accuracy with which activities and/or actions will be performed. *Workload* models seek to predict the workload, either total or by-component, associated with performing specific actions and/or activities. Some models seek to predict the *situation awareness* that a person will have of the internal and external situation at a specific point in a specific scenario. Finally, some models may attempt to predict the internal *structure* or organization of an activity or process.

(4) *Level of modeling.* Finally, models can address different levels of human activity, either the *individual* level, or the *organizational* level, which is taken here to include models of dyads, teams, organizations, etc. (any unit above the individual level).

There are other possible dimensions along which models could be compared, but these four are discussed here because they are relevant for the issues and assessments made in later application sections of this chapter. Table 1 shows the eighteen model categories evaluated on their ability to support the construction of models with different values along these four dimensions.

Technology Maturity

The range of human modeling technology discussed above is broad. These various technologies are not at the same stage of development, nor are they at the same point of readiness for practical application to complex systems engineering. Model maturity can be rated according to three categories:

- Applicable Now – the modeling type/technique has been used successfully or is judged to offer sufficient potential for successful application to some aspect of system design today.
- Applicable in the Short term – the modeling type/technique is at a state where several years of focused research and development coupled with supporting model validation research would probably make it applicable to system design.
- Applicable in the Long term – the technique, while offering promise, is not yet at a state of maturity where a usable, practical technique can be envisioned, but the technique still merits further research and development.

In general, all the model classes listed in Table 1 are applicable now, with two exceptions. Both Group Training Models and Training Taxonomies are in early stages of development and are applicable only in the long term. Also, Computational Cognitive Models are rapidly evolving, and substantial new capabilities are likely to be available in the short term.

Validation of Human Models

In various engineering communities, there are standards and processes for model verification, validation, and accreditation. Of course, the behavioral sciences community has independently established its own expectations as to what is meant by the term validity. These communities have not been well coordinated, and a plan for assessing human performance model validity that addresses concerns of both communities is an immediate concern.

Before any model can be used for engineering decision making, the model's validity and utility must be established. Three general criteria are commonly used to assess the validity of a given human model. *Predictive/concurrent*

Table 1. Model Classes Rated on Key Comparative Dimensions.

Model Class	Goals	Architectural Focus	Predictive Focus	Level
Closed form component models (e.g. Fitts' Law)	descriptive, predictive	various	outcome, time, accuracy	both
Computational cognitive models	descriptive, prescriptive, predictive	integrative	outcome, time, accuracy, situation awareness, workload	individual
Critical decision models	descriptive	information processing	outcome, situation awareness	individual
Decision theory models	descriptive, prescriptive	information processing	outcome	individual
Finite state models	descriptive, predictive	integrative	outcome, time, situation awareness	individual
GOMS	descriptive, prescriptive, predictive	information processing	outcome	individual
Group training models	descriptive	learning/training	outcome	organizational
Human reliability analysis (HRA)	descriptive, predictive	physical, perception	time, accuracy	individual

Table 1. Continued.

Link models of anthropometry & movement	descriptive, predictive	physical	outcome	individual
Network models	descriptive	integrative	outcome, structure	organizational
Optimal control models	descriptive, predictive	integrative	outcome, time, accuracy, situation awareness	individual
Perceptual models	descriptive, predictive	perception	outcome	individual
Recognition Primed Decision-making (RPD)	descriptive, predictive	information processing	outcome, situation awareness	individual
Signal Detection Theory	descriptive, predictive	perception.	outcome	individual
Task hierarchies	descriptive, prescriptive	behavior	process	individual
Task network	descriptive, predictive	behavior	outcome, time, accuracy, situation awareness, workload	both
Training taxonomy	prescriptive	learning/training	structure	individual
Workload	descriptive, predictive	information processing	workload	individual

validation is established by comparing the predictions of the model to actual performance data. *Construct validation* is established by demonstrating that the underlying constructs and model components are valid. *Face validation* is established by submitting the model for review by experts to assess apparent validity. These three types of validation are presented in the order of the power of the statement of validation (predictive validation makes a much stronger argument than face validation). This typically also translates into cost (e.g. predictive validation studies involving sufficient numbers and types of subjects will be far more expensive than the less-strong face validation studies).

Table 2 presents a summary of the types of validation studies that have been conducted for the human performance modeling types introduced earlier in this section. There is one important caveat regarding Table 2. The entries in the table reflect not that the modeling approach (e.g. task network modeling) has been validated, but rather that models built of specific systems using this approach have been validated. Overall approaches can not be validated per se except to the extent that the underlying scientific theory they embody or formalize can be validated. Validating a particular model (application)

Table 2.   Estimated Level of Validation Studies on Model Types.

Modeling Class	Validation Studies Conducted
Closed form component models (e.g. Fitts' Law)*	Face/construct/predictive
Computational cognitive models*	Face/construct/predictive
Critical decision models	Face
Decision theory models†	Face/construct/predictive
Finite state models	Face/construct/predictive
GOMS*	Face/construct/predictive
Group training models	Face
Human Reliability Analysis	Face/construct
Link models of anthropometry & movement	Face/construct/predictive
Network models*	Face/construct/predictive
Optimal Control Models	Face/construct/predictive
Perceptual Models	Face/construct/predictive
Recognition Primed Decision-making (RPD)*	Face/construct/predictive
Signal Detection Theory	Face/construct/predictive
Task hierarchies*	Face
Task network*	Face/construct/predictive
Training Taxonomy	Face
Workload*	Face/construct/predictive

* Varies with individual model in this class. † Models in this class have been shown to have very constrained prediction validity.

example, on the other hand, is more constrained and more possible. At the same time, if a model type or approach has been demonstrated to be valid in specific applications, it is easier to make the argument for its validity in other applications.

While the goal of validating human performance models by predictive validation (the highest standard, as noted above) is commendable, this is a high and often unachievable goal. Human performance is inherently variable which means to get stable measures of performance against which to compare model predictions requires large numbers of subjects. Also, human performance research in complex systems is expensive and, particularly for evolving systems, often impossible. It is therefore the case that lower standards than predictive validity may be adequate. In fact, typical military verification, validation, and accreditation (VV&A) does not consistently require predictive validity as part of the validation process. In addition, it is probably the case that different model types may have different requirements. For example, models such as anthropometric or perceptual models may require predictive validity to be established (in either a general or situation-specific context) before they can be reasonably used in system validation, while for other model types (particularly those that are highly descriptive, such as Critical Decision Analysis, GOMS, task network representation) the concept of predictive validation may be less meaningful and not required.

In a broader context, however, the assessment of model validity is in fact subject to different standards and processes. Specifically, academic and scientific research utilizes one set of principles and standards for establishing the validity of models, particularly as embodiments of scientific theory, while engineers and simulation analysts, particularly in the military, have very different processes for VV&A of models for use in military analysis. In the narrow sense of specific models being used in engineering applications, it is reasonable that established requirements of the military VV&A process should form a sufficient test of validity in most cases (subject to the arguments discussed in the preceding paragraph). This suggests that the human performance modeling and systems engineering communities rely on construct and face validation where these may be sufficient conditions. This will allow experience to be gained in using the models to build actual systems and will ultimately lead to empirical usage data that can be used to compare model-based predictions to actual outcomes, and thus lay the foundation for broader predictive validation.

Finally, *model usefulness* should be considered as relevant to model validity. Four dimensions related to model usefulness can be identified. First, essential to any determination of a model's utility is defining when the model is appropriate and, by inference, when it is not. Factors to be considered include the underlying assumptions and the situations under which the assumptions are met (for example, a visual model may assume high levels of ambient light, making it inapplicable in dimly lit or night-vision situations), the type of human performance outputs predicted by a model (e.g. models that do not predict performance time would be inappropriate for evaluating data through-put rates), and known limitations from prior validation studies. Models with well-defined boundaries will be more useful because their applicability will be easier to assess. Second, for a human performance modeling tool to be useful, it must be usable. During the assessment of model usefulness for a purpose, one must consider what is required of the target user in order for the tool to be usable. A modeling tool that takes months to use when only weeks are available is not useful when there are severe schedule constraints. A modeling tool that requires several years of education or can only be used by highly specialized people is limited to applications where there is a high potential payoff.

In addition to being usable, a model (or just the use of modeling) may add value beyond the narrow confines of the modeling application. For example, the analysis required to build the model may lead to other engineering, design, or conceptual insights, or results that have nothing to do with the actual model application. This kind of "value added" contributes to a model's overall usefulness. Finally, an increasingly important component of model usefulness is its interoperability, or the extent to which the model can be linked to other models of hardware, software, and even other types of human performance models. The easier it will be to get a human model into an integrated modeling environment, the more useful the model will be.

Relevant Modeling Techniques

The state of the art of human modeling has certainly not progressed to the point that there is a well-defined collection of models that can be used in all commonly occurring situations. There are still many cases where a human model has to be cobbled together ad hoc from lower-level building blocks for a specific, unique situation. A number of these "building blocks", or modeling techniques, are presented below and discussed in terms of five high-level categories, as shown in Table 3.

Knowledge Representation Techniques are methods that have been developed, typically in artificial intelligence and cognitive science, to capture and represent human knowledge in symbolic form for use by computational models of reasoning and problem solving. Three commonly used techniques for knowledge representation include blackboards (Carver & Lesser, 1994),

Table 3. Modeling Techniques Applicable to Human Model Development.

Modeling Function	Modeling Technique
Knowledge Representation	Blackboards
	Production Rules
	Semantic Nets
Decision Making and Reasoning	Bayesian Inference
	Fuzzy Logic
	Hybrid Logic
	Neural Nets
	Hidden Markov Models
	Case-based Reasoning
Design/Analysis Techniques	Early comparability analysis
	Simulation-based tutoring and authoring
	Simulation based walk-through
	Statistical models (descriptive)
	Statistical models (interpretive)
Natural Language Processing Techniques	(various methods)
General Purpose Simulation	Monte-Carlo methods
	Dynamical models

production rules (Anderson, 1976) and semantic nets (Collins & Quillian, 1969). Blackboards are hierarchical representations of primarily declarative knowledge that are used in opportunistic reasoning and open problem solving systems. Production rules, on the other hand, are abstracted representations of atomic if/then propositions, which can be applied inductively and deductively to specific sets of facts to yield new facts and inferences. This is the form of representation typically used in expert systems. Finally, semantic nets are representations of facts and the semantic relationships among them (e.g. 'part of', 'kind of', and other more domain-specific forms), typically developed using graph representations.

Reasoning Techniques are methods that have been developed to allow the computational representation of problem-solving, planning, decision-making, or other reasoning processes. These methods were not developed as models of human performance per se, but have sometimes been used to develop human cognitive/behavioral models. Commonly used techniques include Bayesian inference, fuzzy logic, neural networks, hidden Markov models and case based reasoning. Bayesian inference techniques are mathematical and computational methods to permit reasoning about uncertainty based on the underpinning of Bayes rule (that the probabilities of all disjoint events sum to unity). A particular manipulation of Bayes formula for conditional probability is of particular importance, as it allows reasoning about sequences of discrete events (i.e. data) in which (prior) estimates of underlying distributions are updated following each observed event (to yield a posterior distribution). This process has been used to model diagnostic inference processes. Fuzzy logic techniques, on the other hand, are mathematical and computational methods to permit reasoning about uncertainty without requiring the mathematical constraint of Bayes rule. Originally developed by Zadeh (1965) as an artificial intelligence method, it has been offered as an alternative (i.e. non-Bayesian) way of modeling human reasoning and decision-making under uncertainty. (Note: there are methods that incorporate multiple aspects of logic and both Bayesian and non-Bayesian inference methods into a single framework, and these are typically called hybrid logic approaches.) Neural nets are methods that simulate the processing of information by a distributed and highly intercon- nected network of (typically simulated) simple information processing devices analogous to individual neurons (see Rumelhart, McClelland et al., 1986). Hidden Markov models are processing algorithms, often used in language processing models, that provide discrete stochastic state-based representations of sequential relationships (i.e. Markov models) organized in a hierarchical manner, so that what appear to be states at one level are actually complete Markov processing models at a lower level of detail. Finally, case based reasoning methods categorize problem solving processes into alternative strategies that are indexed by archetypal examples called 'cases', and allow individual problem-solving examples to be mapped into appropriate problem- solving processes according to their similarity to the various case archetypes.

Design/Analysis Techniques are methods that have been developed to support the process of designing systems or components of systems. In many cases, though not all, these techniques either can interface with models of humans or can produce situation-specific human models. For example, one standard engineering technique, early comparability analysis, is a method in which design situations or design candidates are compared with other existing implemented systems or subsystems as a basis for estimating characteristics such as manning requirements, training requirements, complexity, etc. Another common technique, simulation can be used in a number of ways, including simulation based tutoring and authoring, a method by which rapidly constructed simulations are used to capture procedural knowledge and support the interactive tutoring of novices in those procedures. Simulation based walk- through is a method in which a simulation of a system or system design is used as a basis for visualizing or 'walking through' that design, which is typically used in conjunction with virtual prototyping technology that provides the high-fidelity simulation of the system. Finally, there are a series of classical, statistical methods which either describe the characteristics of specific populations in terms of distributions of random variables (descriptive), or model the relationships among (interpretive) groups of independent or interdependent random variables (e.g. among arm, leg, trunk length in contributing to individual height in a human population).

Natural Language Processing Techniques are a family of primarily computational techniques that model the human ability to process language in written (i.e. text) form. These techniques can allow other types of human models to interact with real humans in simulations or games, or can be used to provide model users with natural language access to the functionality of other models or techniques.

General purpose simulation methods are computer science and operations research techniques that are used to simulate systems of all types, not just human systems. Although there are many ways to categorize these methods, Zachary (1986) uses two orthogonal dimensions (mechanical vs. analytical and stochastic vs. deterministic) to create four categories. Mechanical methods are those that decompose a process into discrete events and processes and mechanistically simulate the system's behavior in terms of those events and processes. Often called discrete event simulation, mechanical models can be either stochastic or deterministic in the way they process through the event/process space. The class of human performance models termed "task networks" represents the application of mechanistic simulation methods to human modeling. Analytical methods are those that describe a system in terms of the underlying relationships, typically expressed in mathematical terms, that describe either input/output transformations or time-dependent relationships. Dynamical models, on the other hand, are analytical models which represent the changes in a system through time as a set of simultaneous differential (continuous change) or difference (discrete change) equations which are functions of time, or by dynamically interacting agents. These models can also be either stochastic or deterministic, although deterministic representations are more tractable and more common.

USING HUMAN MODELS IN SYSTEM DESIGN

Today, it is standard practice to use models of system hardware and software during concept exploration, preliminary design, and full-scale engineering development of a complex system. One of the functions of these models is to ensure that the system performance objectives, whatever they may be, are satisfied by the design. Additionally, the models ensure that the performance objectives are met within any defined design constraints, such as weight, power-consumption, etc. This use of models reflects a (often implicit) focus on the system *sans* humans, as if the human role was unimportant, imponderable, or both. Increasingly, though, this view is being called into question, often as the result of designs that have proven unusable, untrainable, or unstaffable. A new view is emerging in which the performance of the *integrated* system – hardware plus software plus people – is the explicit focus of performance objectives. In other words, the human role is explicitly viewed as important and even critical. And as the discussion above shows, the modeling of this human role is certainly no longer imponderable; a wide range of models and modeling tools exist. The question that arises, then, is what types of models should be used for what purposes in the design process?

We begin with a brief overview of the design process for complex systems, and from that discuss two major uses of human models – one traditional, and one non-traditional. The traditional application is the use of human models to validate design concepts, by assessing whether explicit design concepts can meet their performance requirements given the capabilities and limitations of their human components. This is a traditional application because the human model is used in exactly the same way that hardware and software models are now used, and there is a growing history of success at using human performance models in this way. The non-traditional application is the use of human models to support the synthesis and concept generation activities associated with the design process. This is a relatively new and somewhat exploratory area of application for human performance models.

The Complex System Design Process

The design of complex systems is a main concern of the discipline of system engineering. As any engineering discipline, it is the subject of ongoing discussion, research, and debate. There are several standards produced by various organizations, e.g. Institute of Electrical and Electronic Engineers (IEEE Standard 1220–1998), International Committee of System Engineering (INCOSE Systems Engineering Handbook), Government Electronic and Information Technology Association (EIA standard 632), and the U.S. Department of Defense (Directives 5000.1 and 5000.2-R), and competing theories of how the process should be done (cf., Blanchard & Fabrycky, 1998). Thus, there is no single commonly agreed standard for how a complex system should be designed. Still, it is possible to identify the main features from most commonly applied approaches, and distill them into an abstract representation that can guide the consideration of where and how human models might fit in.

Most approaches fall along a continuum from what is called 'waterfall' to what is called 'spiral'. Both processes proceed through a well-defined series of stages, generating concepts, evaluating them, selecting the best, developing detailed designs from it, and implementing and testing those designs. Waterfall approaches tend to go through this process only one time, building systematically from coarse granularity to fine granularity in the design and implementation. Spiral approaches tend to proceed through the process many times, each time creating a more-complete design or implementation, correcting problems from past cycles, and adding new detail in areas previously ignored. The core steps of both approaches can be seen in Fig. 1.

As a general overview, the system design process in Fig. 1 has three fundamental stages. Initially, designers deal with mission analysis and requirements analysis (WHY is this type of system needed?). Next, designers deal with functional analysis and logical design (WHAT will the system have to do?). Finally, designers deal with implementation details associated with a particular design, such as allocating functions and resources (HOW will the system accomplish that?). At each stage, there are two types of activities. *Design synthesis* activities are the tasks a designer engages in to come up with a potential requirement and logical design and detailed design. Design synthesis typically involves a high degree of art and creativity. *Design analysis* activities include systematic, thorough, and rigorous attempts to evaluate a potential requirement and logical design and detailed design. The overall cycle can be iterative in nature, as in a spiral process, or recursive as in a waterfall

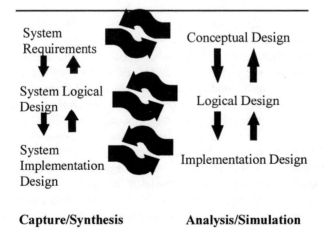

Capture/Synthesis   **Analysis/Simulation**

Fig. 1. Abstracted System Design Process.

process, where systems are broken into subsystems, which are broken into sub-subsystems, etc. Information needs to roll up and down the hierarchy, explicitly identifying the implications of a design implementation of a subsystem on a variety of measures, including cost, impact on other subsystems, ability to meet the mission needs, etc.

Of course, complex systems are rarely, if ever, built entirely de novo. Certain components are typically adapted or incorporated from pre-existing systems on a legacy basis, to limit the complexity of the design process and to limit the developmental cost of the final system. The amount of novelty in the system can and does vary, however, and this strongly affects the design process. In general, a given design problem can also be seen as falling on a continuum from evolutionary (involving an incremental moderate modification to an existing system) to revolutionary (involving a total departure from the design of existing systems). Few systems are totally revolutionary, as the cost of making everything new is prohibitive, yet few are also totally evolutionary, as new designs are rarely warranted without substantive change.

More revolutionary design problems, though, can lead to more open-ended design processes. An interesting case in point is the Navy's goal of a 70% manning reduction on future Navy ships (Carnevale, Bost, Hamburger, Bush & Malone, 1998). The realities of cost and financing dictate that it is not pragmatically possible to start designing this ship with a totally clean sheet of paper. The extreme requirement for manpower reduction, though, may require a design that is "revolutionary" in that it includes all aspects of design – function automation, consolidation, elimination, and simplification – and considers a wide variety of factors including, but not limited to, human factors. For example, improving the human-computer interface (HCI) of a system could reduce manpower requirements by allowing fewer people to accomplish more work. On the other hand, a better paint needs less repainting, which also reduces manpower requirements. It is interesting to note the revolutionary requirements may not be unidirectional. Achieving global manning reductions on this future ship may not require proportional reductions in each area, and may even require increasing manning in some areas. For example, as a consequence of the increased automation during the 'Smart Ship' project, a training department was added to the ship (see Giffen, 1997).

Revolutionary system requirements and design processes can also conflict with the more traditional life-cycle model of complex systems, in which an initial version is implemented and fielded, and then incrementally modified over a long period of time. This process minimizes the marginal cost of any modification, as (in theory) only the new functionality must be designed, implemented and integrated, rather than a whole new system. However, it has some pernicious effects, particularly with regard to the role of human components. Here again, ship design is a good example. Historically, a ship was viewed as a collection of component systems "riding side-by-side" inside a common hull. When a new weapon or sensor system was added to a ship, it was added by an incremental modification process. The new hardware was designed, squeezed onto the already crowded deck and/or hull, and a minimally invasive 'stovepipe' was created to connect this new hardware with the people who would run it and the other systems (power, data, etc.) that would supply it. The result was that a new console, job function, etc. was created for each new incremental component, which frequently required a new human role. Over time, this stovepipe strategy exploded the complexity and manning requirements of a ship, even though at each step it was the most efficient alternative.

This has led to the concept of total system design, in which the interconnections and ramifications of design decisions at all levels are taken into account, not just the marginal effects. The whole system (in this case the ship) is conceptualized as a single complex system, with the roles of humans and software/hardware components designed together. Under this approach, a top-down functional analysis for the entire ship is performed, and then design options with different allocations among hardware, software and human operators are compared and evaluated. Often this involves task-centered design, in which decisions about the design of subsystems, and about human and machine roles and the human-machine interface, are made with reference to the tasks that must be performed by the person and person-machine combination. Total system design and task-centered design both work within the overall framework pictured in Fig. 1 above, but represent customizations needed to appropriately factor in the design of human work and roles.

Human Models to Support Design Analysis

Human models can be used in the system design process in all three of the stages shown on the right-hand side of Fig. 1, primarily as a means of analyzing the design products on the left-hand side of the figure – system requirements, system logical designs, and system implementation designs. The analysis of requirements involves testing the 'why' decisions in the design process; the analysis of logical designs involves testing the 'what' decisions embedded in the iterative design; and the analysis of implementation designs involves testing of the 'how' decisions contained in engineering design.

Historically, the major use of human models has been in the later phases (e.g. Gray, John & Atwood, 1993), but there is a great potential payoff from their use in earlier design phases because they have the greatest impact on the system's likelihood of success and its life-cycle costs. The potential uses of human models in the first two design phases are discussed below together, after which the use in the last design phase is discussed.

Requirements and Logical Design Analysis

These early design phases answer such questions as "What functions will the system be able to perform" and "What general classes of components will be involved in performing these functions"? There are at least four ways in which human models might support these early stages of analysis with current or near-term technology.

The first is identifying stress points and opportunities. Human models can be used to find points in the predecessor system (i.e. the system that the new system will be replacing or supplementing) that are prone to stress or are underutilized. These points provide opportunities for improvement; for example, underutilized human operators could point to requirements for job consolidation opportunities and overloaded human operators could point to requirements for a need for automation. The second use is in identifying organizational requirements. For example, through models, limits on team size and structure can be developed, based upon the need for speed in complex decision making. A third use is in life cycle cost estimation. Human models can be used to develop estimates of the costs of various design requirements and concepts, e.g. the costs of various manpower alternatives. The fourth high-payoff use is in performance budgeting, that is, in using human models to allocate performance requirements to functions and, ultimately, to components in a way that achieves overall system performance requirements. For example, this could be used during initial function allocation exploration to assess where the expected functional requirements can be met by each component.

Table 4 presents a summary of the different kinds of human models and modeling techniques that could be used for each of these four types of concept and requirement analyses. In this and similar tables below, the reader is advised that the mapping is suggestive only. That is, the authors are aware of applications of this type or believe that applications of that type are possible.

The Use of Human Performance Models to Validate and Evaluate Engineering Designs

In Fig. 1 above, there is a natural flow in the design capture/synthesis process from the 'what' stage, where the establishment of requirements is the main issue, to the 'how' stage, where a determination of how the system will achieve these functions becomes the primary concern. But there is a reverse flow as

Table 4. Models Applicable to Concept and Requirements Analysis.

Model Class	Identify Stress Points and Opportunities	Organizational Design	Life Cycle Cost Estimation	Performance Budgeting
Closed form models			X	
Computational cognitive models	X	X		X
Critical decision analysis	X			X
Decision theory models	X			
Finite state models	X			
GOMS	X			
Group training models		X	X	
Human reliability analysis (HRA)		X		
Link models of anthropometry & movement	X			
Network models		X		X
Optimal control models	X			
Perceptual models	X			
Recognition Primed Decision Making (RPD)	X			
Signal Detection Theory		X		
Task hierarchies				
Task network	X	X	X	X
Training taxonomy			X	
Workload	X			X
Modeling Technique				
Knowledge Representation				
Decision-making & Reasoning				
Design/Analysis Techniques	X	X	X	X
Natural Language Processing Techniques				
General Purpose Simulation	X	X	X	X

well. For example, if during detailed design it becomes apparent that a requirement cannot be met or can easily be exceeded, then the requirement may change. It is largely models (on the analysis/simulation side of Fig. 1) that can be used to play "what if . . .". with a candidate design or operational concepts. The design engineer can use human performance models to determine whether requirements can or cannot be met.

In defining how human models could be used in detailed design validation, it is necessary to consider the kinds of information that would flow between the stages of the design process. Inherent in the idea of evaluating a design is the idea that it must be evaluated against some 'target', such as a performance standard or benchmark. Ideally, such standards and benchmarks should be created during concept validation (although the specific requirements could change during design iterations). While the whole system concept may include many benchmarks and data for system validation, those that are particularly relevant to the application of human models include:

- Lists of functions to be accomplished,
- Function allocations (to the extent that they have been allocated at any phase of design),
- Function level performance requirements (time, accuracy, risk),
- Manpower constraints,
- Personnel characteristic constraints, and
- Training constraints.

The *function lists* and *performance requirements* are not exclusively human functions at early phases of design when the allocation of functions among humans, hardware, and software (and even dynamic function allocation) is being considered. Indeed, much of the value of human performance models will be in assisting the tradeoffs of *function allocation* at all levels of design.

Also, in order to evaluate a design with respect to humans in the system, its constraints on the human subsystem must be known. These include *manpower constraints* (i.e. how many people), *personnel characteristic constraints* (i.e. what kind of people), and *training constraints* (i.e. how much time and resources will be available to provide the humans with the necessary skills for safe and successful system operation).

Without defining such constraints, it is impossible to reasonably validate or evaluate a design. For example, a system design might meet the manpower and personnel constraints, but it might take many years of training for the personnel to achieve the required level of performance. Therefore, all of these constraints must be defined before detailed engineering design begins.

Human models can have many uses in validation/evaluation of detailed system or component designs, such as:

• Predicting performance time,
• Predicting performance accuracy (e.g. error rates,% deviations),
• Predicting risk (e.g. probability of achieving function success),
• Predicting the satisfaction of anthropometric limitations,
• Predicting communication requirements/success,
• Predicting training requirements, and
• Integrating human performance predictions with other system performance models for integrated systems analysis.

Table 5 summarizes the models and modeling techniques that are applicable to each of these seven areas. It should be noted, however, that there are significant limitations in the capabilities of today's models in many or most of the boxes in Table 5. For example, in predicting and validating a design with respect to accuracy, there are many aspects of system accuracy that might need to be modeled, but only some can be effectively predicted using current human modeling technology.

Human Models to Support Design Synthesis

It is easy to envision the role that human performance models could play in supporting design analysis activities, as engineers and designers have been using models of hardware and software to do simulation-based system analysis for years. Design synthesis, however, includes what is often conceptualized as a creative component, and the application of human performance modeling techniques to support these types of activities is less obvious.

The total-system and task-centered design views, as described above, can be used to help frame the kind of design tools that are needed to support the design process. For example, to support task-centered design, tools are needed to help identify team/organizational structures that match task requirements. An effort to develop such a tool is currently underway, supported by the Navy. Paley and colleagues (Paley, Levchuk, Serfaty & MacMillan, 1999) are developing a design tool (the Team Integrated Design Environment, or TIDE) that facilitates the application of a mission-based organizational design methodology. The first stage in following this methodology is to apply a multi-dimensional decomposition procedure to a particular mission, and determine the mission tasks and their interdependencies and relative sequencing. This mission structure can be represented in a series of mission task dependency graphs. This mission structure provides one of the two main inputs to the modeling tool. The other main input is a set of "organizational constraints", which include the

Table 5. Models Applicable to Analysis During Detailed Design.

Human Performance Model Class	Time	Accuracy	Risk	Anthropometric	Communication	Training	Integration
Closed form component models (e.g. Fitts' Law)	X	X					
Computational cognitive models	X	X			X	X	X
Critical decision models					X	X	X
Decision theory models			X				
Finite state models	X	X			X		
GOMS	X					X	
Group Training Model						X	
Human Reliability Analysis (HRA)		X	X				
Link Models of anthropometry movement				X			
Network models					X		
Optimal Control Models	X	X					
Perceptual Models	X	X					
Recognition Primed Decision Making (RPD)						X	
Signal Detection Theory		X					
Task hierarchies					X	X	X
Task Network	X	X			X	X	X
Training Taxonomy						X	
Workload	X	X					
Modeling Technique							
Knowledge Representation					X	X	
Decision-making & Reasoning			X		X	X	
Design/Analysis Techniques	X	X			X	X	X
Natural Language Processing Techniques					X		
General Purpose Simulation	X	X	X		X	X	X

resources and technologies available to support the human team members in accomplishing the mission. Given these two inputs, the modeling tool follows a three-part allocation algorithm to produce a team structure that is optimized to perform the mission. The tool produces an optimized structure by modeling organizational performance criteria as a multi-variable objective function, and then using advanced mathematical techniques to optimize that function. Of course, as with all design activities, this tool should be used in an iterative fashion, with multiple checks being performed on its output and the results of those checks fed back into the front end definition and analysis of the mission. While the software tool itself is still being developed, the underlying algorithms are already being successfully applied in several military domains.

To further support total-system and task-centered design, other tools are needed to analyze and determine when tasks and functions should be automated (replacing the human) versus when they should be supported by aiding-automation (keeping the person involved in the task). Issues such as determining effective task allocation, the impact of automation on human performance, and the design of human-machine interfaces are addressed by practitioners in the field of Human Factors. In another Navy sponsored project, Eilbert and colleagues (Eilbert, Campbell, Santoro, Amerson & Cannon-Bowers, 1998) are currently using a cognitive computational modeling technology to capture some of the knowledge and reasoning capabilities of human factors engineers in order to develop a design decision aid. (There is more discussion on the use of models to build decision aids, below.) The modeling framework chosen, COGNET, uses a combination of software components, including demons representing perceptual processes, a blackboard structure holding declarative knowledge, and GOMS-like rules capturing procedural knowledge, to simulate the opportunistic (or context sensitive) reasoning of a human expert in a limited domain. Once complete, the model will be used during design, not to replace human factors engineers, but rather to identify and draw to the attention of the system and design engineers the human factors issues, problems and analyses that need to be addressed. If this decision aid can increase the awareness of the existence and importance of human factors issues throughout the design of a complex system, then, hopefully, the human factors engineers will be given a larger role in supporting the design process.

Human Models and Human Experimentation

Traditionally, human issues in system design have been resolved, where possible, by experimentation with human subjects interacting with prototypes

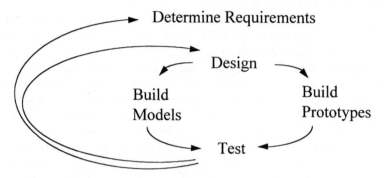

Fig. 2. Uses of Human Performance Models in Systems Validation.

or mockups or simulations of the system under design. The maturity and availability of human models will affect this practice. However, rather than reflecting an either/or relationship, these two approaches should be seen as having a complementary relationship. Figure 2 shows the roles that either human modeling or human-in-the-loop testing may play in validating either system requirements or design details.

The need for synergy between experimentation and modeling is perhaps even more important for human system components than elsewhere (e.g. hardware models) since the high degree of variability in human components of the system make them inherently less predictable. At the same time, the lower cost and logistical simplicity of models allows them to help focus the collection of empirical human performance data. A particularly important area in which this focusing could occur is risk mitigation. Models could be used effectively to focus the human-in-the-loop studies in the areas of design and operation that pose the greatest risk. Conversely, the human-in-the-loop studies could provide important calibration data for the human models, to enhance their predictive power and even to assess the validity of the models. This set of relationships is shown in Fig. 3.

Another linkage between model-based validation and human-in-the-loop testing is that the effectiveness of both techniques depends on the appropriate development and use of design basis scenarios in the validation process (a concept borrowed from the nuclear power industry). A design basis scenario is a scenario that taxes the system-under-design to the limits of its expected ability to be able to perform. Typically, several design basis scenarios are developed that push the system in different ways. To evaluate human/system performance and know when the human and system are performing acceptably,

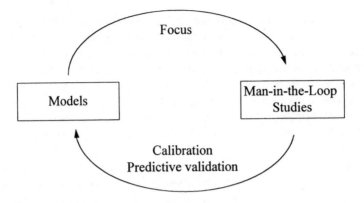

Fig. 3. Relationship between Human Performance Models and Man-in-the-Loop Studies.

there must be some human-focused design basis scenarios against which to test. Such scenarios will serve as the basis for model development *and* the conduct of human-in-the-loop experimentation.

General Issues Regarding Human Modeling Techniques to Support System Design

Regardless of whether human modeling techniques are being applied to support design synthesis or design analysis, there are three general issues that must be addressed: the level of design detail required for the application, the usability and interoperability of the modeling tool, and the maturity of the modeling technique. Each is further discussed below.

Many, if not all, variations of design process frameworks emphasize the iterative nature of design in which design details slowly emerge over time. This can lead to a concern of when there is sufficient detail to begin applying human models. For example, is it necessary to know how many missiles a hypothetical person might be coordinating before that person/role can be modeled? Or how long it takes one missile to go from warm-up to detonate? The NYNEX corporation's experience in applying models to assess a new operator workstation design is illustrative here. Gray, John & Atwood (1993) were able to build the detailed GOMS models used in the evaluation of a new workstation only *after* the design was fully specified. Unfortunately, in the complex-systems acquisition process (particularly as practiced by DoD), once design details are specified, it is essentially too late to make changes if the modeling suggests that the design is sub-optimal. However, even though most of the historical use of human performance models in design has focused on human-computer interface issues, this does not have to be the case. For example, work is currently in process (Kirschenbaum, Gray & Ehret, 1997; Ehret, Kirschenbaum & Gray, 1998) to use models of command decision-making in submarine attack center design. What is useful in this case is modeling the decision-maker's information seeking strategies and behavior at a high level, not the details of how they actually get that information through the HCI of their workstations.

In fact, the human factors community argues strongly that human engineering must be done early and often during the design process, and that modeling can be useful before the implementation details of a design are determined. Fortunately, systems engineers are comfortable using high-level models of hardware and software (with the associated level of approximation in those models' outputs) early in the design process. But the questions of: (1) how one can build human performance models before detailed system design has begun, (2) how one can estimate the amount of imprecision in those models, and (3) the degree to which different modeling techniques are amenable to supporting high level models, are still somewhat open and debatable, making this an important area for further investigation.

It is also important to consider the potential impact (or lack thereof) of providing human performance models and modeling tools to systems engineers. It is unrealistic to expect to turn system engineers into human engineers simply by handing them a modeling tool. Ideally, a good tool will help in simple, straightforward cases, but in complex situations the support of a human factors engineer or human modeling specialist will likely be needed. In addition, the adoption of human-modeling tools will ultimately require use of a broader (human engineering) design process.

Interestingly enough, the degree of tool and model maturity needed before the tool/method becomes useful is, in fact, a variable. Returning to the NYNEX example, when Gray and John (1993) applied GOMS at NYNEX, the model was not developed as a part of a mature technology, yet the model nonetheless proved very useful (although it was highly sophisticated users – Psychology PhDs – who applied the technique). In general, a still-research-level model or tool can be made useful if the consumer organization has the commitment and willingness to put time and money into the process; typically this only happens if the problem involved is big and perceived as important. For the myriad of small, mundane problems, though, special resources will typically not be available, so highly mature and usable tools will be needed.

Finally, any human performance modeling tool must conform to the same rules as any other design tool. For example, if different human-model-based tools are required or recommended, then the tools should all be able to work from common inputs, so that the design at any particular level has to be captured only once. Designs captured at different levels of detail must also be traceable to one another. Modeling will have to prove more cost effective than prototyping combined with human-in-the-loop studies, and should enable more design options to be considered. Ultimately, the key to acceptance is the ability to assess operability and relate operability to cost. Model-based approaches and tools must be able to demonstrate that doing the additional analyses required by model-based approaches can significantly increase our ability to produce long run cost savings. And, of course, the tools themselves should be usable and well human-factored.

USING HUMAN MODELS IN SYSTEM OPERATION

The applications of models of human capabilities are not limited to the design and engineering of complex systems. It is also increasingly possible to embed cognitive and other human models in components of complex systems and use those models to support the operation of those systems. Another way to view this is as using the models as part of the implementation of the system, rather than as part of the design, as considered in the previous section. Following the approach of the design discussion above, the various functional ways in which human models could be used in system operation are first reviewed, and the current technology base from Table 1 is then mapped into the functional application areas.

The use of cognitive (or other human) models in system operation places a unique constraint on the development of a model that is not necessarily present when these models are being applied to system design. This is the constraint of *embeddability*. Applying a model in system operation implies that the model must exist in some form that is embeddable directly into the system itself. Purely analytical representations in prose or other non-executable formalisms may be used to inform the design process and may suggest specific features of the system being designed, but such representations cannot be actually embedded in the system itself.

The embeddability of a model implies some aspect of executability, but that executability can take many forms. The model can represent the internal processes of the human (for example, allowing the system to gain insights into human goals and intentions), or it could merely represent behavior (for example, manipulating a watchstation in a human-like manner). The model can deal with process, representing the internal steps in a decision or analysis process, or merely represent the outcomes via input-output relationships, but the constraint of embeddability still remains. Within this bounded definition of human model, ten functional applications to system operation, and the specific capability requirements associated with each application, can be defined.

(1) *Information access, retrieval, and integration.* In this application, the model is used to automate or replace human roles in gathering information and integrating it for use by human crew-members or other automated systems. Information access problems fall along a dimension that ranges from closed ended, in which the information to be retrieved is precisely defined from the problem conditions, to open-ended, in which defining the information to be sought and integrating partial pieces into a whole solution are part of the problem. Clearly, relatively simple human models can address closed-ended problems, while more open-ended problems would require more robust models that contain substantial knowledge and problem-solving capabilities.

(2) *Performance monitoring and assessment of human operators.* A model of normative or expected human performance can be used to monitor a human crewmember's performance for adverse effects (e.g. of fatigue, extreme environmental condition, etc.) or other kinds of impairment, or it can be used to provide dynamic performance assessment of the human crewmembers for evaluation purposes, to identify training needs, etc. The relevant dimension for assessing the applicability of human models is the aspect of human performance that is being monitored or assessed. At one end is a purely behavioral monitoring/assessment (focusing on what the person is doing), and at the other end is a knowledge-oriented monitoring/assessment (focusing on what the person knows). Here again, different models are needed for different points on this dimension, depending on their focus on cognition, behavior or both.

(3) *Real-time decision support.* Cognitive or decision models, typically encapsulating the strategy or knowledge of experts, can be used to aid the decision process or decision making of human crewmembers. This is the most commonly found application of embedded human models today. This category overlaps somewhat with others enumerated here, especially information access, retrieval, and integration and also task automation. In general, however, decision support applications fall somewhere between these other alternatives, offering the human crewmember computed criterion functions and specific recommendations, but leaving the actual selection and implementation of the decision to the human.

(4) *Associates.* A model or combination of models can be used to provide a digital assistant or one-on-one associate for a specific human crewmember (often in a senior or decision-making role). These associates can be used to off-load work in an on-demand basis, to support and simplify the human-computer interaction with the watchstation, and/or to carry out other tasks when directed by the human being assisted. Operator associates is an area where substantial research has been invested to date (esp. DARPA associate systems programs), although much of the research has focused on technologies other than human models. The key constraint here is on the robustness of the associate, which must be able not only to perform many of the tasks assigned to the human, but also must be able to interact with the person in an intelligent and cooperative manner.

(5) *Embedded intelligent training.* Models of experts or instructors can be used to provide critiques of trainee actions, to define dynamically the correct or desired actions in training scenarios, and to specify the kinds of knowledge needed (or evidently lacking) for specific actions taken by trainees. The key distinction here is whether the training is knowledge based or performance based (or both). When only (behavioral) performance is being trained, then models that predict performance alone can be used. However when the goal is to diagnose the knowledge strengths/ weaknesses of the trainee and focus instruction on those areas (rather than just on behavior), then models that represent knowledge and internal reasoning processes are needed.

(6) *Cooperation and collaboration support.* Models of team level processes and organizational work can be used to enhance, structure, and support collaboration and cooperation among teams of human crewmembers, for example, by making sure that all required work gets done (i.e. nothing 'slips through the cracks') or that redundant work efforts are not being undertaken needlessly. The key dimension for assessing the applicability of human modeling technology here is the breadth of the cooperation. At one end is simple dyadic (one-on-one) collaboration, in which all work must be accomplished by that two-person team. At the other end are large organizations, in which there are many levels of restrictions concerning who can work with whom, information flows, etc. Nearer to the organizational end, models that deal with organization structures and processes (rather than individuals and roles) are needed, while nearer to the dyadic end, models that explicitly deal with individual responsibilities and characteristics are needed.

(7) *Dynamic role/function allocation.* Models of individual workload and organizational/team requirements can be used to re-allocate functions and

roles (either among people on a team or between people and automation) to level workload and avoid performance bottlenecks due to overload of some (human or machine) parts of the system. Given that this definition is based on workload management, it is critical that models used be able to assess the residual work capability of the human and machine agents involved. This assessment can occur either explicitly (e.g. through use of explicit workload models) or implicitly through a variety of other mechanisms. A secondary dimension of concern here is the ability to assess which agents are capable of performing specific functions that are candidates for re-allocation. Although lacking this facility, the dynamic reallocation process can be explicitly restricted to those functions that can be freely re-allocated to any agent within the team.

(8) *Task management.* Models of the flow of work (e.g. the flow of tasks or jobs needed to accomplish some key system-level goal) can be used to manage the efficient performance of the work under dynamic conditions, by reallocating functions, tasks, even whole human roles, as needed to get the job done. Task management differs from dynamic function allocation in that the latter, as defined here, is driven by individual workload issues (and is thus person-focused), while the former, as defined here, is driven by workflow issues, and is thus task focused. The considerations for task management are very similar to those for dynamic reallocation, with one exception. A task manager must still represent the workload and task-specific abilities of the agents (individuals or people) within its purview. However, because the task management process, as defined above, is task-flow oriented, models that can support this functional application must also have some explicit ability to represent and track the performance of tasks within an overall job-flow.

(9) *Task automation.* Models of human crewmembers that are sufficiently robust that they can perform tasks at approximately the same level (or perhaps even greater) than a human can be used as intelligent automation to replace humans for specific tasks or roles. There are relatively few restrictions on the use of models for task automation. Because task automation explicitly focuses on task performance (i.e. behavior), any model that can produce realistic and robust behavior is potentially applicable. In some cases, though, the ability to communicate about task performance may be required as well, and this would require use of models that can engage in explanation and inter-agent communication.

(10) *Knowledge management and transfer.* Finally, models can be used to act as acquirers and keepers of "corporate knowledge" and to disseminate or provide access to this corporate knowledge when needed. This emerging

area is the least well-defined. The only clear constraint is that a model or modeling technique used for this function must have a clear and explicit representation of knowledge.

Given the requirements of the various applications delineated above, only certain modeling categories and techniques are appropriate for each application. The assessments are summarized in Tables 6 and 7. Table 6 focuses on specific human model types, while Table 7 focuses on more general modeling techniques.

CONCLUSIONS

This chapter has presented an assessment of the ways in which cognitive modeling and other related human modeling technologies could be used in the design, evaluation and operation of complex systems. Specifically, it has tried to delineate and characterize the short term opportunities for human model application in complex system engineering efforts, and to identify areas where additional research and development investment are needed and can lead to high-value applications in the future. Each of these goals is addressed below.

A commonly used metaphor is that of "low hanging fruit", and this chapter tried to characterize the short-term application opportunities of human performance modeling technologies. Table 8 below summarizes these results. Using the taxonomy from Table 1, it reviews those techniques identified as ready for immediate or short-term application in each of the three areas of concern: system design, system operation, and concept and design evaluation. In addition, the current validation status of these techniques is also included.

Beyond the short-term applications, potential areas for high payoff research and development are also interesting. Many specific research needs and opportunities can be identified and classified into five general areas: cognition, knowledge management, team and organizational structure and processes, predictive models of training, and human-centered systems engineering. Each of these is further discussed below.

Research Need No. 1: Advanced Capability to Model Cognitive Processes
Research into cognition and development of models of cognition has led to many of the specific human models listed in Table 8. However, there are several areas where additional research support is needed before the technology can be applied to complex systems. These areas include:

(1) *Modeling human reading and understanding graphic-based displays.* The range of design options available today and in the future includes a

Table 6. Models Applicable to System Operation Applications.

Model Type	Inf. Access, Retrieval, & Integration	Performance Assessment	Decision Support	Associates	Embedded Intelligent Training	Cooperation/ Collaboration Support	Dynamic Function Allocation	Task Management	Task Automation	Knowledge Management
Closed Form Component Models (Fitts' Law)			X							
Computational Cognitive Models	X	X	X	X	X	X*	X	X	X	X
Critical Decision Models			X							
Decision Theory Models			X							
Finite State Models	X	X	X	X	X		X	X	X	
GOMS			X							
Group Training Models										
Human Reliability Analysis (HRA)							X	X		
Network Models						X				
Optimal Control Models		X	X							
Perceptual Models			X							
Recognition Primed Decision-Making			X							
Signal Detection Theory			X							
Task Hierarchies										
Task Network	X	X	X	X	X	X	X	X	X	X
Training Taxonomy										
Workload		X	X							

* If expanded to include cooperative issues.

Table 7. Modeling Techniques Applicable to System Operation Applications.

Model Type	Inf. Access, Retrieval, & Integration	Performance Assessment	Decision Support	Associates	Embedded Intelligent Training	Cooperation/ Collaboration Support	Dynamic Function Allocation	Task Management	Task Automation	Knowledge Management
Blackboards	X		X	X	X	X*	X		X	X
Production Rules	X		X	X	X		X		X	X
Semantic Nets	X		X	X		X*				X
Bayesian Inference	X	X	X		X			X		
Fuzzy Logic	X		X		X			X		
Hybrid Logic			X					X		
Neural Nets		X	X				X	X	X	
Hidden Markov Models		X	X							
Case-Based Reasoning	X		X	X	X	X	X			X
Early Comparability Analysis										
Simulation-Based Tutoring & Authoring					X					
Simulation-Based Walk-Through										
Statistical Models (Descriptive)	X	X	X							
Statistical Models (Interpretive)										
Natural Language Processing	X	X	X	X	X	X	X	X	X	X
Monte-Carlo Methods			X		X					
Dynamical Models							X			

* By sharing the model across individuals.

Table 8. Near-Term Application Opportunities for Human Models.

Model Class	Design	Operations	Concept & Design Evaluation	Validation status (1)
Closed Form Component	X	X		face, construct, predictive
Computational Cognitive Models	X	X	X	face, construct, predictive
Critical Decision Models	X		X	face
Decision Theory Models		X		face, construct, predictive
Finite State Models		X		
GOMS	X		X	face, construct, predictive
Group Training Models				face
Human Reliability Analysis (HRA)			X	face, construct
Link Models Of Anthropometry & Movement			X	face, construct, predictive
Network Models	X			n/a
Optimal Control Models		X	X	face, construct, predictive
Perceptual Models			X	face, construct, predictive
Recognition Primed Decision-Making (RPD)				face, construct, predictive
Signal Detection Theory				face, construct, predictive
Task Hierarchies				face
Task Network	X	X	X	face, construct, predictive
Training Taxonomy	X			face
Workload			X	face, construct, predictive

dizzying array of interface technologies. Current cognitive models (even the cognitive modeling technologies that were developed for the purpose of human-computer interface evaluation) do not provide the ability to differentiate (in a predictive sense) human responses or performance across these kinds of design alternatives, and thus cannot support the kinds of design decisions that must be made.

(2) *Extending computational cognitive architectures to provide collaborative support.* Current computational architectures lack the capabilities to model social/organizational cognition, metacognition, and discourse that are needed in truly collaborative work. These architectures need to be extended to include such capabilities so that models can be used in system operation as workflow managers or as surrogate team-members, capable of adapting to changing team circumstances as human team members would.

(3) *Cognitive models of leadership.* Current cognitive models focus on task performance and decision making, yet leadership remains a key element of military, and indeed of all complex systems. The role of leadership in complex systems can not currently be modeled, and can not therefore be factored into system design or validation in a model-based way.

Research Need No. 2: Advanced Capability to Model Knowledge Management

Knowledge management is rapidly emerging as a key area in the engineering of manned systems, both commercial and military (e.g. Nonaka & Takeuchi, 1995). As an emerging area it is less well defined than cognitive modeling, but there are two areas where research needs can be identified:

(1) *Knowledge representation for engineering use.* Human factors engineers and systems engineers need access to the existing knowledge of complex system users to support future design, implementation, and evaluation activities. Techniques for representing specific kinds of human knowledge have been developed by cognitive researchers, but these methods were either oriented toward specific application frameworks (such as computational cognitive models) or for research and/or theoretical purposes. Research is needed to identify and implement methods and tools to make the existing (and future) knowledge representation schemes accessible to the system engineering process.

(2) *Knowledge growth/transfer.* Most knowledge representation methods and knowledge acquisition schemes treat knowledge as a static set of objects, to be captured and represented once. In reality, though, the knowledge of an individual or team is constantly changing. Some changes are the result of learning, and others are the result of environmental changes that cause

some previously used elements of knowledge to become less useful (or even useless) and other elements to become more important. Organizational processes and system evolutions also constantly contribute to this process. Research is needed into means of capturing and representing these dynamic aspects of an individual or organizational knowledge base.

Research Need No. 3: Advanced Capability to Model Teams
Team/organizational research is also seriously needed in several areas. While much of the human modeling technology base developed with an individual-level focus (perhaps because of its roots in psychology), applications tend to revolve around designing and operating complex systems, for which key human behaviors frequently occur in team or organizational contexts. Three general areas can be singled out:

(1) *Team/organizational level modeling for cooperation/collaboration support.* Particularly in reduced manning systems, human teams must work together more effectively and efficiently. There will be little workload slack built into these systems, so the teams will have to collaborate more effectively, and in a much more complex and fluid environment than today, one in which roles, tasks, and even interfaces are dynamic and re-allocable. Surprisingly, there is relatively little useful research or (ideally) models concerning how teams collaborate (particularly at the cognitive level) that can be used to guide or even inform the design of collaborative environments or of automated tools such as task managers to support collaboration.

(2) *Team leadership.* Leadership is key to effective team performance, yet there are virtually no models of the leadership process, particularly in complex dynamic environments as envisioned, for example, in the future Navy ships. Models of team leadership are needed both to design and evaluate these systems.

(3) *Team level processes and training.* Cognitive research has produced useful models and architectures of individual level information processes and training. The team level analogs of these do not yet exist. Thus, the system designer has no clear reference points on the key limitations (e.g. analogous to short-term memory limits or cognitive biases) or important features in team level processes, particularly those of collaborative task performance and team training, making the design of work teams highly unstructured and subjective.

Research Need No. 4: Advanced Capability to Support Training Analyses Through Modeling

Several issues in the domain of training are also good candidates for future research. These concern not specific training methods or systems, but research into the training process itself so that training needs and costs could be better predicted during the system design and evaluation process. Specific modeling needs include:

(1) *Group training models.* Development of models of the processes by which groups or teams are trained, in terms of the underlying parameters and dependent variables such as time, cost, and effectiveness.

(2) *Training taxonomy for cost.* Research to map taxonomies of training techniques or training requirements (e.g. a skill taxonomy) into cost predictions, so that even at very early design stages, training options and cost could be estimated.

Research Need No. 5: Advanced Capability to Build Reusable, Interoperable Models

One final set of issues for future research concerns not human models per se, but the ways in which they mesh with the complex system engineering process. In many cases, these are issues associated with the transition of human modeling from a research to an engineering activity. They represent truly interdisciplinary applied research needs, and as such can easily fall into the cracks in the research funding process. However, they also represent critical problems that must be solved if the basic and exploratory research into model development is to be productively integrated into the system development process:

(1) *Model insertion.* Human models represent a new kind of tool for the systems engineering process. Even revolutionary systems such as the future Navy ships will be largely composed of legacy components, for which there are no human models, or at least for which no human models have been incorporated into the design/implementation/evaluation process. It is not clear how human models should be inserted into the life cycle of complex systems, nor what engineering and cultural issues associated with this insertion will arise.

(2) *Model integration.* Different human models must be able to be integrated with one another, and with the other models and tools used in the system development life cycle. This concern was echoed in the National Research Council report as well (Pew & Mavor, 1998). Research is needed to

identify integration frameworks, to develop standards, and even to create integration support tools.

(3) *Reusable taxonomies/task description.* The lexicon of knowledge and human activities has never been standardized, or even cross-mapped among the many idiosyncratic frameworks used by different researchers or groups. Practitioners and appliers of this technology who are not researchers will need a taxonomy or reusable set of definitions and descriptions that they can use to identify and apply the appropriate human models. Research is needed either to standardize descriptions for concepts like task descriptions or taxonomies, or, where they do not exist, to create them. (One possible model for this process is the research to create a unified medical terminology system that integrates and cross-maps the individual vocabularies among the many specialties of medicine.)

(4) *Tools to "bridge the gap" between system engineering functional decomposition tools and human-centered representations.* The tools of system engineering do not represent or decompose either structures or processes in the same way as human modeling methods such as task networks, computational cognitive models, etc. If the human models are to become part of the process, they will need to communicate with the existing system engineering decompositions, or make use of some higher-level framework that encompasses both needs. Without such a framework or translator, the cost of developing and managing dual decompositions for system and human modeling will prove too great a barrier.

(5) *Representation and modeling the evolvability/maintainability of systems & jobs.* Just as with knowledge, the jobs humans perform and the systems with which they perform them are constantly evolving, particularly during the post-deployment phase of the system life-cycle (which includes most of the life cycle, as well as most of the life-cycle costs). As the jobs and systems change, the design-phase analyses and models become increasingly irrelevant. Research is needed to find ways to incorporate this evolutionary aspect into the design phase models, and into the process of job/system evolution itself.

Of course, further follow-up is needed by design teams to make use of the available technology, and by the broader research organizations to fill the research gaps identified here. This is an exciting time for researchers and practitioners alike, as human modeling technology has now reached a state of maturity where it has proven itself able to become a contributing component to the design, evaluation, and operation of complex systems.

NOTES

1. Many of the ideas contained in this paper originally arose from a three-day workshop on Cognitive Models in Complex Systems, sponsored by the Office of Naval Research and the U.S. Naval Air Warfare Center Training Systems Division. The authors express their gratitude to the sponsors of the workshop, and to the 45 researchers, engineers, and domain experts who contributed to the workshop. The authors also gratefully acknowledge the suggestions of Kevin Bracken on earlier drafts of this paper, as well as the contribution of Christine Volk in preparation of the manuscript.

2. Thus, the concepts of individual/network are maintained from the micro approach, but the use of organization-wide dynamics and the simplification of individual representations is retained from the macro approach.

REFERENCES

Anderson, J. R. (1976). *Language, Memory, and Thought*. Hillsdale, NJ: Erlbaum.

Anderson, J. R. (1993). *Rules of the Mind*. Hillsdale, NJ: Lawrence Erlbaum.

Baron, S., Kruser, D. S., & Huey, B. M. (1990). *Quantitative Modeling of Human Performance in Complex, Dynamic Systems*. Washington, D.C.: National Academy Press.

Bernard, H. R., Killworth, P., Kronenfeld, D., & Sailer, L. (1984). The Problem of Informant Accuracy: The Validity of Retrospective Data. *Annual Review of Anthropology, 13*, 495–517. Ann Arbor: Annual Review Press.

Blanchard, B. S. & Fabrycky, W. J. (1998). *System Engineering and Analysis* (3rd ed.). Upper Saddle River, NJ: Prentice Hall.

Boff, K. R., Kaufman, L., & Thomas, J. P. (1986). *Handbook of Perception and Human Performance*. New York, NY: Wiley-Interscience.

Brown, J. S., & Slater-Hammel, A. T. (1949). Discrete Movements in the Horizontal Plane as a Function of their Length and Direction. *Journal of Experimental Psychology, 39*, 84–95.

Card, S., Moran, T., & Newell, A. (1983). *The Psychology of Human-Computer Interaction*. Hillsdale, NJ: Erlbaum.

Carnevale, Bost, R., Hamburger, T., Bush, T., & Malone, T. (June, 1998). Optimizing manning on DD 21. Paper presented at Warship '98 International Symposium.

Carver, N., & Lesser, V. (1994). Evolution of blackboard control architectures. *Expert Systems with Applications, 7(1)*, 1–30.

Collins, A. M., & Quillian, M. R. (1969). Retrieval time from semantic memory. *Journal of Verbal Learning and Verbal Behavior, 8*, 240–248.

Connelly, E. M. (1984). Empirical investigation of aids for non-programming users in developing cost-effective requirements specifications. *Proceedings of the Human Factors Society Annual Meeting*.

Czaja, S. J. (1997). Systems design and evaluation. In: G. Salvendy, (Ed.), *Handbook of Human Factors and Ergonomics* (pp.17–40). New York, NY: Wiley-Interscience.

Dodge, R., & Cline, T. S. (1901). The angle velocity of eye movements. *Psychology Review, 8*, 145–157.

Ehret, B., Kirschenbaum, S. S., & Gray, W. D. (1998b). Contending with complexity: the development and use of scaled worlds as research tools. In: *Proceedings of the Human*

Factors and Ergonomics Society 42nd Annual Meeting. Santa Monica, CA: Human Factors and Ergonomics Society.

Eilbert, J. L., Campbell, G. E., Santoro, T., Amerson, T. L., & Cannon-Bowers, J. A. (December, 1998). The role of cognitive agents in the design of complex systems. Paper presented at the 1998 Annual Interservice/Industry Training Systems and Education Conference. Orlando, FL.

Elkind, J. I., Card, S. K., Hochberg, J., & Huey, B. M. (1990). *Human Performance Models for Computer-Aided Engineering.* San Diego, CA: Academic Press, Inc.

Fitts, P. M. & Peterson, J. R. (1964). Information capacity of discrete motor responses. *Journal of Experimental Psychology, 67,* 103–112.

Forrester, Jay. (1971). *Principles of Systems.* Cambridge, Mass.: MIT Press.

Giffen, H. C., III, VADM (1997). *Smart Ship Project Assessment Report.* http://www.dt.navy.mil/smartship/assess0997.html.

Gray, W. D., John, B. E., and Atwood, M. E. (1993). Project Ernestine: Validating a GOMS analysis for predicting and explaining real-world task performance. *Human-Computer Interaction, 8,* 237–309.

Green, D. M., & Swets, J. A. (1966). *Signal Detectability and Psychophysics.* New York, NY: Wiley.

Hutchins, C. W. (1974). A computer-aided function allocation and evaluation system (CAFES). *Proceedings of the Human Factors Society Annual Meeting.*

IEEE Standard 1220–1998, IEEE standard for applications and management of the systems engineering process (1999). New York: Institute of Electrical and Electronic Engineers.

Kalman, R., Falb, P., & Arbib, M. (1969). *Topics in Mathematical Systems Theory.* New York: McGraw Hill.

Kieras, D. E. Meyer, D. E. (1997). An overview of the EPIC architecture for cognition and performance with application to human-computer interaction. *Human-Computer Interaction, 12*(4), 391–438.

Kirschenbaum, S. S., Gray, W. D., & Ehret, B. D. (1997). *Subgoaling and subschemas for submariners: Cognitive models of situation assessment* (Technical Report NUWC-NPT TR 10,764–1). Newport, RI: Naval Undersea Warfare Center Division Newport.

Klein, G. (1989). Recognition-primed decisions. In: W. Rouse (Ed.), *Advances in man-machine systems research, 5,* 47–92. Greenwich, CT: JAI Press, Inc.

Klein, G. A., Calderwood, R., & MacGregor, D. (1989). Critical decision method for eliciting knowledge. *IEEE Transactions on Systems, Man, and Cybernetics, 19*(3), 462–472.

Laird, J., Coulter, K., Jones, R., Kenney, P., Koss, F., & Nielsen, P. (1997). *Review of Soar/FWA Participation in STOW-97.* Published electronically at http://ai.eecs.umich.edu/ifor/stow-review.html. November 7, 1997.

Laird, J. E., Newell, A., & Rosenbloom, P. S. (1987). Soar: An architecture for general intelligence. *Artificial Intelligence, 33*(1), 1–64.

Lane, N., Strieb, M., Glenn, F., & Wherry, R. (1981) The Human Operator Simulator: An overview. In: J. Moraal & K.-F. Kraiss (Eds), *Manned Systems Design: Methods, Equipment, and Applications,* New York: Plenum Press.

Laughery, K. R. (1998). Modeling human performance during system design. In: E. Salas (Ed.), *Human/Technology Interaction in Complex Systems.* JAI Press.

Laughery, K. R. & Corker, K. (1997). Computer modeling and simulation. In: G. Salvendy's (Ed.), *Handbook of Human Factors and Ergonomics.* New York, NY: John Wiley & Sons

McMillan, G. R., Beevis, D., Salas, E., Strub, M. H., Sutton, R., & Van Breda, L. (Eds) (1989). *Applications of Human Performance Models to System Design*. New York, NY: Plenum Press.

McNeese, M. D., Warren, R. & Woodson, B. K. (1985). Cockpit automation technology: a further look. *Proceedings of the Human Factors Society Annual Meeting*.

Meadows, D., Meadows, D., Randers, J., & Behrens, W. W., III. (1972). *The Limits to Growth*. New York: Universe Books.

Moraal, J., & Kraiss, K. F. (Eds). (1981). *Manned Systems Design: Methods, Equipment, and Applications*. New York: Plenum Press.

Nonaka, I., & Takeuchi, H. (1995). *The Knowledge-Creating Company: How Japanese Companies Create the Dynamics of Innovation*. London: Oxford University Press.

Paley, M. J., Levchuk, Y. N., Serfaty, D., & MacMillan, J. (1999). Designing optimal organizational structures for combat information centers in the next generation of Navy ships. Paper submitted to 1999 Command and Control Research and Technology Symposium.

Pew, R. W., & Mavor, A. S. (Eds) (1998). *Modeling Human and Organizational Behavior: Application to Military Situations*. Washington, DC: National Academy Press.

Risser, D. T. & Berger, P. (1984). Army HARDMAN: Its origin, evaluation, implementation to date. *Proceedings of the Human Factors Society Annual Meeting*.

Rumelhart, D. E., McClelland, J. L., & The PDP Research Group (1986). *Parallel Distributed Processing: Explorations in the Microstructure of Cognition* (2 volumes). Cambridge, MA: MIT Press.

Siegel, A. I. & Wolf, J. J. (1962). A model for digital simulation of two-operator man-machine systems. *Ergonomics, 5*, 557–572.

Siegel, A. I. & Wolf, J. J. (1969). *Man-Machine Simulation Models*. New York, NY: Wiley-Interscience.

Swezey, R. W. & Llaneras, R. E. (1997). Models in Training and Instruction. In: G. Salvendy (Ed.), *Handbook of Human Factors and Ergonomics*. New York, NY: Wiley-Interscience, 514–577.

Von Neumann, J., & Morgenstern, O. (1947). *Theory of Games and Economic Behavior*. Princeton University Press, Princeton, NJ.

White, H., Boorman, S., & Breiger, R. (1976). Social structure from multiple networks. I. Blockmodels of roles and positions. *American Journal of Sociology, 81*, 730–780.

Wickens, C. D. (1980). The structure of attentional resources. In: R. Nickerson & R. Pew (Eds), *Attention and Performance VIII*. Hillsdale, NJ: Erlbaum.

Wortman, C. D., Duket, S. D., Seifert, D. J., Hann, R. I., & Chubb, A. P. (1978). *Simulation using Saint: A user-oriented instruction manual*. Wright-Patterson AFB, OH: Aerospace Medical Research Laboratory (AMRL-TR-77–61).

Zachary, W. (1977). An information-flow model for conflict and fission in small groups. *Journal of Anthropological Research, 33* (Winter), 452–73.

Zachary, W., Bilazarian, P., Burns, J., & Cannon-Bowers, J. (1997). Advanced Embedded Training Concepts for Shipboard Systems. In: *Proceedings of 19th Annual Interservice/Industry Training Systems and Education Conference*.

Zachary, W., Le Mentec, J. C., & Ryder, J. (1996). Interface agents in complex systems. In: C. Ntuen & E. H. Park (Eds), *Human Interaction With Complex Systems: Conceptual Principles and Design Practice*. Norwell, MA: Kluwer Academic Publishers.

Zachary, W., Cannon-Bowers, J., Burns, J., Bilazarian, P., & Krecker, D. (1998). An Advanced Embedded Training System (AETS) for tactical team training. In: *Proceedings of ITS '98*.

Zachary, W., Ryder, J., Ross, L., & Weiland, M. (1992). Intelligent Human-Computer Interaction in Real Time, Multi-tasking Process Control and Monitoring Systems. In: M. Helander & M. Nagamachi (Eds), *Human Factors in Design for Manufacturability* (pp. 377–402). New York: Taylor and Francis.

Zadeh, L. A. (1965). Fuzzy sets. *Information and Control, 8*, 338–353.

6. TRAINING TEAMS TO TAKE INITIATIVE: CRITICAL THINKING IN NOVEL SITUATIONS

Marvin S. Cohen and Bryan B. Thompson

TEAMWORK AND INITIATIVE

A U.S. Army infantry handbook published in 1939 states, "The art of war has no traffic with rules, for the infinitely varying circumstances and conditions of combat never produce exactly the same situation twice." Much the same can be said about business environments characterized by rapidly shifting technologies, markets, and competitive landscapes. The purpose of this chapter is to explore how members of military, business, and other organizations cope with uncertainty, change, and conflicting purposes. It will focus on: (1) the cognitive skills that individuals need to function effectively in such organizations, and (2) on methods for training those skills.

We will focus on skills that enable individuals or subteams to take the initiative within a team context. We can start by distinguishing two advantages that teamwork provides over an individual acting alone: (1) The first advantage is based on *bringing together complementary inputs*, and derives from the coordination of multiple hands, eyes, heads, etc. to accomplish a complex task. Increased effectiveness comes from sharing of both physical and cognitive workload and through specialization of knowledge and skills. (2) The second advantage is based on *choosing from among substitutable alternatives*, and derives from the diversity of competing solutions to the same problem that different members of a team can generate. Better decisions result if there is an

Advances in Human Performance and Cognitive Engineering Research, Volume 1,
pages 251–291.
2001 by Elsevier Science Ltd.
ISBN: 0-7623-0748-X

effective organizational mechanism for selecting from, averaging, or mixing these diverse ideas to arrive at a single decision (e.g. Kerr, MacCoun & Kramer, 1996).

Teamwork is not guaranteed to provide either of these advantages. With respect to (1) combining complementary inputs, increasing the size of an organization tends to reduce its overall efficiency unless there is also an increase in departmentalization and standardization of tasks (Blau, 1970). The latter features, however, reduce flexibility of response in a changing or novel environment (Donaldson, 1995). A related problem is *goal displacement*, in which specialized units lose sight of the larger organizational purpose, and pursue their own goals as if they were fixed ends rather than means, which should be reevaluated when conditions change (Scott, 1998). With respect to (2) better decisions, groups may be affected by socialization biases, such as "groupthink," which induce conformity rather than diversity of thought (Janus, 1972; March, 1996.). For this reason, group decisions tend to be better when individuals think about the problem independently before arriving at a group judgment (Castellan, 1993; Sniezek & Henry, 1990). Both challenges – speed of response to change and innovative thinking – can be addressed by organizational structures that emphasize *decentralization*: granting individuals or subteams the autonomy to make decisions in their own spheres (Burns & Stalker, 1961; Van Creveld, 1985). In some cases, outcomes may be better when individual team members bypass standard procedures, question the accepted beliefs or practices of the group, and act on their own responsibility.

The degree of appropriate autonomy varies. Decentralization and initiative are adaptive responses to specific organizational environments, and are not everywhere appropriate. Interdependency among team tasks heightens the importance of coordination (Thompson, 1967), whether it is achieved implicitly on the basis of shared knowledge of tasks, procedures, and other team members (Cannon-Bowers, Salas & Converse, 1993; Cannon-Bowers, Tannenbaum, Salas & Volpe, 1995; Kleinman & Serfaty, 1989), by contingency planning that begins when unexpected possibilities first become apparent (Orasanu, 1993), or by mutual monitoring, feedback, back-up, and closed-loop communication as the tasks are carried out (McIntyre & Salas, 1995). On the other hand, when the task environment is rapidly changing and uncertain, and individuals or teams are *spatially dispersed*, decentralization and initiative gain in importance. This is a not uncommon predicament in combat: Company E's job is to guard Company F's flank while Company F secures a bridge that the division intends to cross. Now, however, Company F appears to be stalled in a major firefight some distance from the bridge. Company E cannot raise either Company F or higher headquarters on the radio (and it will take too long for runners to find them and return). Should Company E sit tight until Company F is ready to seize the bridge or until communications are reestablished? Should it go help Company F in the firefight, at the risk of getting bogged down itself? Or should Company E attempt to seize the bridge now – a risky choice, but possibly the only way to accomplish the higher-level purpose of supporting the division in a timely manner?

The combination of time stress, spatial separation, and uncertainty – along with varying degrees of task interdependency – can alter the nature of teamwork, overlaying a set of qualitatively different decision tasks on the traditional ones. For example:

- *Should we communicate?* When events unfold in an unanticipated manner (*uncertainty*), advance planning and shared task understanding may fail to bring about coordination. Yet the *dynamic* character of the situation limits real-time communication. *Spatial separation* imposes a bandwidth limitation on communication, exacerbating the impact of both uncertainty and time constraints. The upshot is that real-time closed-loop communication can no longer be regarded as routine. When an unexpected, time-critical problem arises, team members or subteams must decide whether or not the potential benefits of communicating and/or waiting for a response are worth the delay.
- *What will other team members do?* In time-critical situations, subteams will sometimes be unable to communicate, or choose not to communicate, with one another. If their tasks are interdependent, however, the success of one will depend on coordination with the actions of another. In these cases, team members or subteams must make autonomous decisions that depend on plausible assumptions about concurrent decisions being made by other subteams in other locations. Shared task, team, and team member models may help support such predictions, but cannot be fully relied on in novel circumstances.
- *How good is the information?* Even when team members and subteams do decide to communicate, the combination of bandwidth and time constraints will prevent them from sharing information fully. Communications (e.g. reports, feedback, orders, or advice) from another subteam will have to be evaluated with incomplete understanding of the sources and assumptions behind them, and, conversely, with the benefit of other information that is available locally but not to the subteam that originated the message.

In the next section, we will briefly describe an empirically-based theory that addresses skills of this kind. We will argue that the skills underlying initiative involve *critical thinking about mental models* of the task and the team. We illustrate the application of the theory by means of an actual example of initiative within a team, in a context where the degree of decentralization of authority happened to be somewhat ambiguous. We then describe a training strategy that is based on the theory and which focuses on the mental models and critical thinking skills that underlie decisions about initiative. The value of such training should be quite general. Virtually every team is to some degree a *distributed* team. Even when team members are within plain sight and hearing of each other (e.g. in an emergency room, airline cockpit, or the combat information center of a cruiser), the high workload associated with uncertainty and time stress can be quite sufficient to limit the rate of communication (Kleinman & Serfaty, 1989) and make initiative essential.

AN EMPIRICAL AND THEORETICAL FRAMEWORK

Studies of expert-novice differences suggest that expertise develops along two paths over time, one leading to better performance in *familiar* situations, the other leading to improved ability to handle *unusual* situations. A considerable body of research has focused on the first path: Experts accumulate a large repertoire of patterns and associated responses, which they use to recognize and deal quickly with familiar situations (Chase & Simon, 1973; Larkin, McDermott, Simon & Simon, 1980; Klein, 1993). The difference between experts and novices, however, goes well beyond the quantity of patterns they draw on or the number of situations they regard as familiar. In fact, a key hallmark of expertise is *goal-setting*, or intentional creation of novelty. In fields such as writing and historical or scientific research, for example, experts are more likely than novices to identify opportunities for original, productive work, establish their own goals, and create challenging tasks for themselves, which cannot be solved by pattern matching alone (Ericsson & Smith, 1991; Anzai, 1991; Holyoak, 1991). Novel ideas and strategies are also important in military and business environments.

When performing a challenging task, whether self-created or externally imposed, experts and novices differ in other ways that are not fully accounted for by pattern recognition. Scardamalia and Bereiter (1991) found that expert writers, compared to novice writers, discovered more problems with their own work and struggled longer to find solutions, revising both their goals and their methods more often than novices. Patel and Groen (1991) found that expert physicians spent more time *verifying* their diagnoses than did less experienced physicians. Physics experts are more likely than novices to check the correctness of their method and result, and to actively change their representation of the problem until the solution becomes clear (Larkin et al.,

1980; Larkin, 1981; Chi, Glaser & Rees, 1982). Expert programmers pay more attention to the goal structure of a task than novices, searching first for a global program design, while novices tend to be more "recognitional," plunging rapidly into a single solution (Adelson, 1984). In foreign policy problems, expert diplomats spent more time formulating their goals and representing the problem, while students primarily focused on the options (Voss, Wolf, Lawrence & Engle, 1991). VanLehn (1998) found that less successful physics learners were more likely to solve new problems by analogy with old problems (a recognitional strategy), while more successful learners used general methods for solving new problems, drawing on analogies only when they reached an *impasse* or wished to *verify* a step in their solution. Chi, Bassok, Lewis, Reimann and Glaser (1987) found that better performing physics students were more likely to generate self-explanations and self-monitoring statements than poor students. Glaser (1996) identifies effective self-evaluation and self-regulation as key components in the acquisition of expertise.

Tactical battlefield problems tend to be viewed differently by experts and by novices. Novices often regard them as puzzles, which have "school book" solutions, while more experienced officers view them in a more challenging light, acknowledging the possibility that the enemy may not succumb so readily to a predictable course of action. Serfaty (1993) compared experienced Army planners to novice planners, and found that the experienced planners did not appear to use recognitional strategies; that is, they did not perceive more similarities with prior situations, did not generate plans more rapidly, tended to see the situation as more *complex*, were less *confident* in their solutions, and felt the need for more *time* than novices. Among the distinguishing features of experts that Shanteau (1992) identified in his research was the ability to handle adversity, to identify exceptions, and to adapt to changing conditions (Shanteau, 1992).

If expertise develops along two paths, what is the nature of the second, non-recognitional path? One view distinguishes it sharply from the first path: Experts define and deal with challenging problems by substituting formal analytical methods for pattern matching. This is the general approach urged by decision analysts (e.g. Watson & Buede, 1987), who define *normative* methods that require breaking novel problems down into component parts (e.g. options, outcomes, goals), assessing them quantitatively, then recombining them in order to calculate a recommended decision. The research reviewed above, however, suggests that this characterization of the second path is wrong. Formal methods are both too time-consuming, and too divorced from the knowledge experts have accumulated (Cohen, 1993). Dreyfus (1997) puts it well: "Usually when experts have to make such decisions they are in a situation in which they have already had a great deal of experience. The expert, however, is not able to react intuitively, either because the situation is in some way unusual or because of the great risk and responsibility involved . . . the experts draw on their context-based intuitive understanding, but check and refine it to deal with the problematic situation . . . . Deliberative rationality is detached, reasoned observation of one's intuitive practice-based behavior with an eye to *challenging and perhaps improving intuition without replacing it . . .*" [italics added].

Instead of dropping pattern recognition in novel situations, experienced decision makers learn to pause and *think critically about the results of recognition.* They ask, in effect: "What in this situation conflicts with my expectations? How can I stretch the pattern, i.e. tell a new story, to make the pattern fit? What assumptions must I accept to believe this story? What information is missing that would clarify the assumptions? How plausible is the story? What alternative patterns might apply? What story must I tell to make one of these other patterns fit, and what assumptions does it require? Which story is more plausible?" Reflective processes of this kind amplify the power and flexibility of recognitional processes without altogether throwing away their advantage in rapid access to knowledge. Moreover, critical thinking can make itself unnecessary the next time round. Decision makers sometimes handle novel situations by identifying regularities underlying exceptions to known patterns. Mental models embodying these newly discovered regularities provide patterns that can be recognized in later situations (Chi et al., 1981; McKeithen et al., 1981; Adelson, 1984; Larkin et al., 1980; Thompson, Cohen & Shastri, 1997).

Because their function is to monitor and regulate recognition, we call the reflective processes used in unusual situations *metarecognitional.*[1] and we call this framework the Recognition/Metacognition Model (Cohen, Freeman & Wolf, 1996; Cohen, Freeman & Thompson, 1998). The R/M model implies that the two paths along which expertise develops are intertwined. Reflection increases the power of recognition, but itself gains power as a base of recognitional knowledge is built.

It is reasonable to suppose that expertise in *teamwork* evolves with increasing experience in a domain along the same two paths as expertise in *taskwork* (McIntyre & Salas, 1995). Yet Orasanu & Salas (1993) note that "most current team training aims at developing habits for routine situations . . . . Habit and implicit coordination will carry people a long way in routine situations; we need to prepare them for the unusual." In this chapter we will explore how the dual nature of expertise sheds light on the tension between initiative and coordination in teamwork, and provides a framework within which both initiative and coordination can be trained.

Mental Models Underlying Initiative

Initiative means taking "the first step, or the lead; the act of setting a process or chain of events in motion" (Brown, 1993). Extending this definition, we can define *degree of initiative* in terms of *when* in a chain of events someone intervenes and the amount of influence over the chain of events that person achieves: the earlier and more influential the intervention, the more initiative the person has shown with respect to that process. Interventions are often (though not always) targeted at the decision-action-outcome cycle of other agents. In business, for example, one may try to influence, predict, or react to the actions of competitors, customers, superiors, subordinates, or co-workers. In combat, one may try to influence, predict, or react to actions of the enemy, other friendly forces, superiors, or subordinates. In all these cases, greater initiative means that the decision-action-outcome cycle of other agents has been more thoroughly shaped in accordance with your own goals or purposes. The essential questions for training are: What must people know, and how must they think about what they know, to make appropriate decisions about initiative within an organization? What are the mental models and the critical thinking processes that underlie initiative?

The following analysis is based on 25 critical incident interviews and problem-solving sessions with active duty Army officers serving on operations, planning, and intelligence staffs at a variety of organizational levels (battalion, brigade, division, and corps). The goal of our analysis was to uncover cognitive structure beneath the surface descriptions of the incidents.

Structure was extracted in three successive stages: (1) We grouped judgments and decisions within the incident that occurred at the same time or in reference to the same event. We then classified these judgments and decisions by topic, using categories relevant to the domain, such as the higher level *purpose* of an operation, enemy or friendly *capabilities*, observation or analysis of *terrain*, enemy or friendly *intent*, enemy or friendly *action*, enemy or friendly *rate of movement*, *reliability* of an information source, and so on. (2) We then identified clusters of such topics that tended to be correlated with one another within and across incidents, e.g. assessments of enemy intent were found to be based on assessments of enemy capabilities, terrain, enemy doctrine, and enemy actions. These correlated groups of concepts typically constitute a narrative, or *story*, about how certain kinds of events are expected to lead to other kinds of events (Pennington & Hastie, 1993). We call these

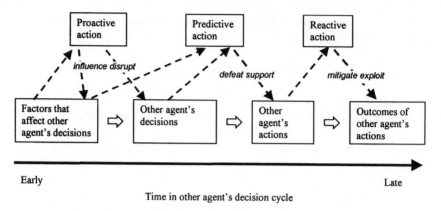

Fig. 1. Three different time orientations differ in where and how they intervene to cause changes in another agent's decision cycle.

correlated groups of concepts, together with their implicit or explicit causal relationships, *mental models*.

In addition to mental models, three degrees of initiative, or *time orientations*, were defined as shown in Fig. 1, in terms of where and how they intervened in the chain of events representing another agent's decisions, actions, and outcomes. The *proactive* time orientation represents the maximum amount of initiative. It was present if a friendly action was designed to *influence* future enemy or friendly intent (e.g. to eliminate an enemy option or lure the enemy into a trap; to degrade the enemy's decision-making process; to create an opportunity for a specific action by another friendly unit; or to influence a decision by your own commander). The *predictive* time orientation represents the next highest degree of initiative. It was present if a friendly action was adopted because a future enemy or friendly action was expected to occur (without our doing anything special to bring it about). Predictive actions include disrupting or defeating the planned enemy action; exploiting an enemy weakness or avoiding an enemy strength that will be caused by the enemy action; and preparing to provide support where and when other friendly forces are likely to need it. The *reactive* time orientation represents the least amount of initiative. It occurred when a friendly action was adopted because of an enemy or friendly action already accomplished or underway (e.g. to limit the damage from a surprise attack; to take advantage of an enemy blunder; or to rescue a friendly unit in trouble).[2] The three time orientations are not mutually exclusive. A decision-maker might be reactive at one level but proactive and/or predictive at other levels, with respect to other decision cycles that belong to the same or different agents.

(3) The third stage of analysis involved examining correlations of mental models and time orientations with one another and with other variables. We can visualize this level of structure by placing the mental models, time orientations, and other variables in a multidimensional space, as shown in Fig. 2. The closer any two items are situated in this space, the more highly correlated they were across incidents (Kruskal, 1964). In addition to mental models and time orientations, two variables are also shown: officers' experience and the degree to which an incident surprised them.[3]

Initiative is a good organizing principle for the mental models in this space. Analysis of the correlations in Fig. 2 (Johnson, 1967) reveals three basic clusters of mental models, corresponding to the three time orientations: *reactive*, *predictive*, and *proactive*. The two dimensions shown in Fig. 2 are suggestive. They are anchored on the three clusters, and provide a natural interpretation of the contribution of different mental models to initiative. One dimension reflects *when* uncertainty about another agent's action is reduced

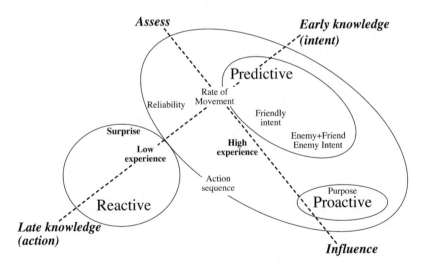

Fig. 2. Proximity in this space represents degree of correlation among mental models, time orientations, and two variables (low/high experience and surprise by the enemy). Ovals show high-level structure derived by a hierarchical clustering algorithm. Italicized labels and dotted lines are a suggested two-dimensional interpretation of this space.

(early versus late), and the other reflects *how* it is reduced (by assessment or by action).

Mental models of the *other agent's intent* and of *one's own intent* were utilized approximately equally often by decision-makers who were trying to predict intent as by decisions makers who were trying to influence it. However, proactive decision makers, who attempt to make others act in accordance with their own intent, were most likely to think deeply about their own intent, i.e. to use mental models of higher-level *purpose*. On the other hand, predictive decision makers were more likely to use the *rate of movement* mental model. Mental models of *reliability* were used both in the predictive orientation (to evaluate predictions ahead of time) and in the reactive orientation (to figure out why a prediction failed). Similarly, *alternative causes and effects* were considered most often in reactive modes, when decision makers tried to explain a failed expectation. Mental models of *action sequence*, which specify how one's own actions are to be carried out, were approximately equally important in all three time orientations.

In sum, concepts in this domain appear to be organized into a set of mental models, including *purpose, intent, action sequence, alternative causes and effects*, and *reliability*. These models in turn are organized around a set of more fundamental principles pertaining to the time and manner in which uncertainty about other agents is reduced (the axes and clusters depicted in Fig. 2). Since reactive, predictive, and proactive time orientations represent increasingly influential interventions in another agent's decision cycle, moving horizontally from left to right in Fig. 2 (which affects both how and when intervention takes place) represents increasing *initiative*. Initiative in this sense is highly correlated with experience. There was a significant correlation between experience level and being proactive, and also a significant correlation between experience level and considering higher-level purposes. As Fig. 2 indicates, when decision makers advance from low to high experience, they tend to move from the cluster of mental models associated with reacting to unexpected events, to the cluster containing both predictive and proactive strategies. It remains now to consider how these mental models are used in decision making.

Critical Thinking about Mental Models

The basis for decision making, more often than not, is recognition, and in ordinary circumstances, the recognitional responses of experienced decision makers are likely to be adequate (Klein, 1993). In such situations, perceptual inputs and goals rapidly converge within a decision maker's mind onto one, and only one, stable "intuitive" decision. In more unusual situations, however, recognition needs to be supplemented by other processes.

Recognitional learning enables humans (and other animals) to acquire adaptive responses to environmental conditions that arise with some regularity during a single lifetime, even when they have not appeared in the previous history of the species. At this scale, the effect of natural selection on inherited stimulus-response connections would be far too slow. On the other hand, recognitional skill may itself take many years to reach the expert level in a particular domain; how long it takes will depend on the extent of the environmental variability that must be mastered. *Critical thinking* provides a further gain in flexibility in rapidly changing or novel environments, where recognitional learning is itself too slow. Critical thinking enables decision makers to find adaptive responses to even finer-grained environmental variations, which may not have appeared at all in the previous experience of the decision maker. It does so by building a relatively simple layer of control over the recognitional processing that is already taking place. The simplicity of the required control processes (described below), along with their potential importance, lends plausibility to the hypothesis that such a second-order capability could have evolved, and that specific skills drawing on that capability could be shaped by individual experience.[4]

Critical thinking includes *meta-recognitional* processes that monitor and regulate recognition. As shown in Fig. 3, the Recognition/Metacognition model distinguishes three basic metacognitive functions: (1) The *Quick Test*, which is a rapid assessment of the value of taking more time for critical thinking versus acting immediately on the current recognitional response; (2) *critiquing* the current results of recognition in order to identify problems; and (3) *correcting* those problems by influencing the operation of the recognition system. Previous descriptions of the R/M model may be found in Cohen, Freeman and Wolf (1996) and Cohen, Freeman and Thompson (1998; see also Cohen, Parasuraman, Serfaty & Andes, 1997).

A fundamental meta-recognitional skill is distinguishing *grounds*, i.e. what is given in a particular situation, from *conclusions*, i.e. what is inferred or decided in that situation (Kuhn, Amsel & O'Loughlin, 1988). This must be a real-time discrimination, because the same event may serve as evidence in one situation and as a recognitional conclusion in another. For example, in one situation the observation that a missile site is active may rapidly lead to the recognitional conclusion that the enemy intends to fire a missile and also to the decision to strike the missile site. In another situation, intelligence that the enemy intends to fire at a U.S. ship might rapidly lead to a prediction that the missile site will go active.

The relationship between grounds and conclusion on a particular occasion is an *argument* (Toulmin, 1958), which may or may not be compelling. Meta-recognitional processes focus on the credibility of *recognitional* arguments (other types of arguments are based on principles other than recognition, e.g. logic, theory, or expert authority). In critiquing, the decision maker looks for *uncertainty* in the arguments composing the present recognitional conclusion. There are three ways that recognition can fall short, i.e. ways in which it can fail to produce one and only one stable conclusion. These three kinds of uncertainty correspond to situations in which: (i) *more than one* conclusion seems plausible, because of *gaps* in knowledge or values, (ii) *less than one* (that is, *no*) conclusion seems entirely plausible due to *conflicting* beliefs or values, or (iii) the conclusion is subject to *variation* over time, because of shifting, *unreliable* assumptions about beliefs or values.

Critical thinking addresses these problems by removing one major limitation on recognitional learning: that the situation and the response retrieved to handle it must have been closely associated in the individual's previous experience. The mechanisms that overcome this limitation involve relatively simple

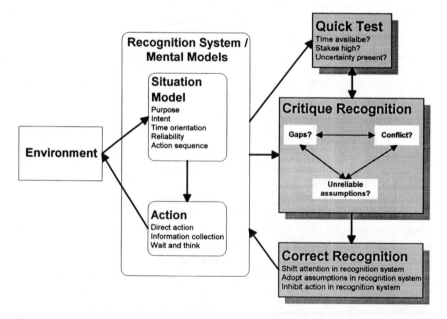

Fig. 3. Basic components of the Recognition/Metacognition model. Shaded components are meta-recognitional.

processes of controlled attention. One important meta-recognitional correcting step involves shifting attention from cues in the situation (perceptual grounds) to selected elements of the current recognitional conclusion. The result is activation of potentially relevant knowledge in long-term memory that has not yet played a role in the present argument because it is too distantly related to the situational cues. Activation of this new information may lead, via recognitional processes, to activation of still more indirectly related knowledge, to which attention may then be shifted, and so on. The newly activated information may then serve as the grounds for new arguments regarding the conclusion. Such attention shifting is equivalent to *posing queries* about the acceptability of the currently active situation model and plan (Shastri & Ajjanagadde, 1993; Thompson, Cohen & Shastri, 1997).

A more directive variant of attention shifting is to *persistently* attend to a *hypothetical* or *counterfactual* action or event. Persistent attention to such a possibility is equivalent to assuming or imagining that it is true, and posing a query about what *would* happen if the hypothesized action or event were the case (Ellis, 1995). This strategy extends the reach of recognitional processing even further, by activating relevant knowledge that is not directly associated either with cues in the actual situation or with the recognitional conclusion. This newly activated information may also serve as grounds for new arguments, e.g. for or against alternatives to the current situation model and plan.

The result of attention shifting strategies of either kind is always to increase (or at least never to decrease) the amount of knowledge brought to bear on a problem. Attention shifting, however, operates in different ways and has different consequences in response to different types of uncertainty. It is likely that experienced decision makers learn meta-recognitional strategies that reflect these differences:

- To identify and fill *gaps* in an argument (the case where more than one conclusion is consistent with the current evidence), attention shifts to one of the possible conclusions – in effect, querying its truth. The result is activation of an associated *mental model*, which indicates the types of information that have been useful in the past in determining the truth or falsity of the attended conclusion. (For example, in order to determine the *intent* of an enemy unit, it is useful to consider the *capabilities* of that unit, as well as its *opportunities*, *goals*, and *actions*.) Attention then shifts to one of the components of the activated mental model for which information is not currently active (e.g. the decision maker decides to think about the *capabilities* of the enemy unit whose intent is uncertain). The result may be retrieval of relevant information in long-term memory about that component, or, if relevant information is not retrieved, a decision to initiate external data collection.

A more directive strategy for activating relevant knowledge in long-term memory is to temporarily assume that a conclusion is correct, by persistent attention to that possibility. This and subsequent shifts of attention may activate less immediately accessible information about the likely long-term consequences of an option, or about the less obvious implications of a hypothesis.

Knowledge activated by these attentional strategies may help narrow down the set of plausible conclusions: (i) by showing that one or more of the conclusions *conflicts* with existing goals or beliefs, or (ii) by uncovering the relevance of new goals or beliefs that further *constrain* the solution. There are three possible outcomes of these correcting steps. First, if newly activated knowledge eliminates all but one plausible conclusion, the problem is solved, i.e. there is now one and only one stable conclusion. Second, the result may be a new problem, *conflict*, if *no* conclusion appears to satisfy all the newly discovered constraints. Third, the result may be another kind of problem, *unreliability*, if the elimination of options is the result of as yet unconsidered assumptions rather than firm knowledge.

• One method for identifying *conflict* is to fill gaps as just described. Newly retrieved or collected information may expose hitherto hidden conflict between a conclusion and existing goals or beliefs. Another, more directive strategy for identifying conflict is to temporarily assume (by persistent attention) that a conclusion is *wrong*, in effect tasking the recognition system to activate an account of how that could happen. This tactic heightens the salience of negative information about the conclusion, e.g. possible bad outcomes of an option or reasons why a hypothesis might not be the case. Awareness of this information may have previously been suppressed by stronger positive information.

Conflict among arguments (the situation in which there are grounds for both accepting and rejecting every conclusion) can be addressed by shifting attention to the sources of information or to the goals that are responsible for the conflict. As a result of this shift in attention (and subsequent shifts to which it leads), it may be learned, for example, that: (i) one or more conflicting sources of information are not as credible as previously supposed, (ii) one or more sources of information were misinterpreted in some way, (iii) one or more conflicting goals are not as important as previously supposed, or (iv) one or more options does not in fact conflict with a goal as previously thought. In this case, additional knowledge *removes* constraints on the recognitional conclusion, rather than adding constraints as in the case of filling gaps. Attention shifting reveals that what was previously thought to be a constraint on belief or action (e.g. a report from an information source, or a goal) was based on assumptions (Doyle, 1979; Cohen, 1986).

In the more directive version of this correcting step, the decision maker temporarily assumes (by persistent attention) that one of the conflicting conclusions is *correct* despite the information or goals that conflict with it, thus tasking the recognition system to activate an account of how this could be. Alternatively, the decision maker assumes that a specific source is not credible, or a specific goal is not important, etc., tasking the recognition system to account for how this could be. Such directive techniques can increase the chance that hitherto inactive knowledge in long-term memory about the relevant sources or goals will be retrieved.

There are three possible results of these correcting steps. First, the problem is solved if newly activated knowledge convincingly undermines the original reason for rejecting one and only one of the competing conclusions. For example, newly activated knowledge may establish that one of the conflicting information sources is not credible or that one of the conflicting goals is not important. Second, these correcting steps might resurrect more than one conclusion, by undermining the reasons for rejecting them, thus leading back to the problem of gaps in arguments. Third, these correcting steps may lead to *unreliability*, if the activation process does not actually refute the initial assumptions but simply reverses those assumptions. Acceptance of one and only one conclusion will then depend on the *possibility of imagining* that a particular information source is not credible or that a particular goal is not important. Conclusions based on possibility in this way are, of course, subject to change. A decision maker may or may not be explicitly aware of such assumptions.

- To address *unreliability*, a decision maker must first *identify* key assumptions underlying possible conclusions and then *evaluate* them. Identification of hidden assumptions is not trivial. A decision maker may have a high degree of confidence in the initial recognitional response to a situation, and yet that conclusion may turn out to depend on questionable assumptions, for example, that the present situation resembles previously experienced ones in important respects. In addition, as we have seen, when the initial recognitional response is uncertain, correcting steps to fill gaps or resolve conflict can smuggle in assumptions that are not even noticed by the decision maker. Instability of conclusions over time, or variability in the conclusions of different decision makers at the same time, are symptoms that unreliable assumptions could be playing a role. However, (a) variability per se does not indicate *what* the problematic assumptions are, and (b) variability is not always available as an indicator.

In a group context, a strategy for identifying assumptions is for decision makers to articulate *reasons* for their divergent conclusions and then to compare these justifications. Openness to such a dialogue is, of course, a natural part of a healthy group decision making process (e.g. Helmreich & Foushee, 1993). When variability does not exist, because there is a single convincing conclusion, disagreement can be induced more artificially, by assigning some individuals the task of "red-teaming" the preferred conclusion or playing the role of devil's advocate. Each potential problem discovered in this way represents an assumption implicit in the favored solution, to the effect that the relevant problem will not materialize.

Skilled decision makers use attention-shifting strategies to simulate these group processes. No matter how confident they are in a particular conclusion, one powerful approach is to assume that it is *incorrect* (through persistent attention to that possibility), in effect querying the recognition system for an explanation of how that could be. If they are persistent enough, an explanation for the falsity of the prediction or the failure of the plan will be generated. Decision makers may then imagine that this is not the correct explanation for the failure, and force the recognition system to activate another explanation, and so on. Each explanatory possibility activated in this way corresponds to an assumption. If the decision maker expects the preferred conclusion to succeed, the decision maker must be comfortable assuming that each possibility of failure that can be generated is false.

The mere fact that a conclusion depends on untested assumptions is not sufficient cause to reject it. First, we never know with certainty that we have successfully identified all the assumptions underlying any given conclusion (a constructivist view of knowledge would suggest that it is impossible in principle). Second, because of limitations on time, only a small number of assumptions can be evaluated in any depth, e.g. by shifting attention to activate knowledge that bears on their plausibility. Third, in the novel situations where critical thinking is appropriate, some crucial information will inevitably be unavailable (gaps), and no conclusion will fit all the observations or goals perfectly (conflict). If gaps and conflicts are to be resolved at all in these cases, it will have to be by means of assumptions.

In fact, real-world decision makers often use an *assumption-based correcting strategy*. They attempt to fill gaps and resolve conflicts in a recognitional conclusion, by retrieving or collecting information if possible but by making assumptions where necessary. They continue this process until they have a *complete* and *coherent* story. In effect, they ask themselves, "What is the best story I can tell to justify this inference or plan?" They then step back, take a look at the story they have created, and try to evaluate its plausibility *as a whole*. In particular, they ask, "What assumptions did I have to make to build this story? Are the assumptions I had to make credible in this situation?" If the assumptions are troubling, the decision maker may temporarily drop them, re-establishing the gaps and conflict that the assumptions were intended to handle. The decision maker may then fill the gaps and resolve the conflicts with a new story, supporting a different conclusion. The choice between competing hypotheses or actions is often made based on evaluation of the plausibility of the assumptions underlying competing stories (Pennington & Hastie, 1993).

As the preceding discussion makes clear, meta-recognitional processing is a highly iterative, open-ended, and flexible process. The solution to one type of problem (e.g. filling a gap) can lead to another type of problem (e. g., conflict), which prompts new correcting steps, leading to new problems (e.g. unreliable assumptions), and so on. In the course of this process, recognitional conclusions are improved and/or modified bit by bit through local decisions about what to do next, and an understanding of the strengths and weaknesses of alternative conclusions is developed at the same time. These improvements are accomplished across cycles of shifting attention that either activate long-term memory contents that lay beyond the reach of a single recognitional cycle or lead to external information collection. When further benefits are likely to be outweighed by the costs of additional delay, critical thinking stops, and the decision maker can act immediately on the current best solution to the problem.

In most of these respects, meta-recognitional processing contrasts with formal analytical approaches to decision making. Typically, formal methods require a problem structuring stage which specifies in advance the inputs and analytical steps that will be used to model the problem. These inputs and analytical steps are not related in any direct way to recognitional responding and the knowledge that it taps. Although some iteration of modeling may take place, along with sensitivity analysis of the results (e.g. Watson & Buede, 1987), "thinking" is largely over and a solution is available as soon as, but not a moment before, the model is finished according to the prespecified blueprint.

EXAMPLE: "ASK FORGIVENESS, NOT PERMISSION"

As we saw earlier, initiative is a matter of *time*: acting early enough to influence another agent in accordance with one's own purposes. Yet, as we have just seen, critical thinking takes more time than simple recognition. It is reasonable to ask, then, whether or not critical thinking is consistent with the tempo of decision making demanded by initiative. We argue that it is. Rapid recognitional responding can, in some situations, trap a military decision maker in a reactive mode with respect to the enemy, or trap a business decision maker in a reactive mode with respect to competitors and customers. Seizing the initiative will often be impossible in the absence of critical thinking about innovative solutions that bypass standard procedures. The following incident (based on an interview conducted as part of the Navy's Tactical Decision Making Under Stress (TADMUS) program; see Kaempf, Klein, Thordsen & Wolf, 1996) is an excellent illustration of how critical thinking about mental models can support initiative, and how the time cost of critical thinking can simply be dwarfed in comparison to the advantages of the proactive tactics to which it leads.[5]

Initial Recognitional Response

A U.S. naval officer was serving as the Anti-Air Warfare Coordinator (AAWC) on an Aegis cruiser in the Persian Gulf, when he received intelligence reports that an Iraqi Silkworm missile site had suddenly gone active. The site was a threat to a large number of U.S. surface ships assembled in the area at the start of the air war against Iraq. Unfortunately, no airborne strike aircraft were close enough to be used against the missile site. The first thing that occurred to the AAWC, i.e. his *recognitional response*, was the standard procedure for this situation: Ask the Tactical Operations Officer (TAO) on his own cruiser to call the Battle Force TAO and request that strike aircraft be launched from the carrier to destroy the newly activated missile site.

Quick Test. The AAWC was initially in a *reactive time orientation* with respect to the Iraqi missile site's turning on its fire control radar. Whatever he chose to do was designed to mitigate any advantage the enemy might derive from that surprise move. His *purpose*, however, quickly became *proactive* with respect to the enemy's launching a missile, an option that he wished to eliminate. The question, then, was: Will the standard procedure be effective and timely in destroying the missile site as quickly as possible? Rather than immediately carrying out the standard procedure, the officer paused momentarily to critically evaluate it.

Critiquing the Initial Recognitional Response

Find conflict. One problem with the recognitional response came to mind immediately, based on a mental model of *team member reliability*. The officer recalled a previous experience when carrier staff failed to take into account updated information about target coordinates. *Resolve conflict by adopting an assumption:* Rather than immediately give up the initial recognitional response, the AAWC tried to repair it as well as he could. The standard procedure would be justified if the AAWC could assume that this situation was in crucial ways different from the previous one. *Evaluate assumption:* In fact, there was a difference: He was able to provide the required targeting information earlier now than he had on the previous occasion. Despite this difference, the AAWC believed that the magnitude of the previous error indicated a strong possibility that the deck-launched intercept would not be properly targeted. He was not comfortable with the assumption.

Fill gaps by retrieving information. The AAWC was also concerned about the speed with which a missile strike could be implemented, so he decided to scrutinize the recognitional response further. He imagined that the standard procedure was adopted, stepped through the expected *action sequence* in his imagination, and looked for problems (Klein, 1993). In doing this, he drew on mental models not only of *action sequence* and *team member reliability.* He predicted that the Battle Force AAWC would pass the request to the Battle Force TAO, who would probably bring in the Commander, because the typical lieutenant commander standing TAO watch "didn't want to be responsible for . . . big decisions." If permission was granted by the commander, the Battle Force staff would then have to contact the carrier, initiating a new process that would itself take a number of minutes. Moreover, the process might take even longer than usual because the carrier was about to launch other aircraft. *Find conflict:* The AAWC's expectations regarding the standard procedure conflicted with the *purpose* of timely, proactive response to the missile site.

Resolve conflict by adopting an assumption. Even now, the AAWC was not ready to abandon the initial recognitional response. To defend the standard procedure in the face of this problem, the AAWC tried to construct the best possible story; in effect, the AAWC imagined that the standard procedure was a success, and asked how that could be. The AAWC concluded that for the standard option to be acceptable, he would have to assume that the Iraqi missile site had switched on its fire control radar without the intent to launch a missile. *Evaluate the assumption:* While this was possible (for one thing, they had previously launched a missile without turning on their radar in advance), it was certainly not guaranteed. To assume the enemy would not fire meant adopting a *predictive* time orientation, which depends on assumptions about what the enemy will do, rather than a *proactive* orientation, which influences what the enemy can do. He was not comfortable with this assumption either. *Quick test*: The AAWC chose not to consider enemy intent any further. Taking more time to think critically about enemy intent was unnecessary in this situation. [It is worth noting that this judgment contrasts sharply with the behavior we have observed in non-wartime or low intensity conflict situations, where inferring hostile intent can play a major role in the decision to engage a target. In the latter situations, officers use critical thinking to fill gaps and resolve conflicts in an *enemy intent* mental model, and often consider *alternative possible causes and effects* of an unexpected and possibly hostile enemy action. Thus, critical thinking focuses on different mental models in different circumstances. See Cohen et al., 1996.]

Resolve conflict by finding another option. The Anti-Air Warfare Coordinator voiced misgivings to his own staff, including an Air Intercept Coordinator (AIC) whom he regarded as "outstanding." The AIC suggested another option just as the AAWC was thinking of it himself: An Armed Surface Reconnaissance (ASR) plane already in the air might be able to take out the missile site. *Quick Test:* This option was also subjected to critical scrutiny, since it was a departure from standard procedure. This option, too, was not without problems.

Critiquing the New Option

Fill gap by collecting information. One problem was immediately apparent: Was the ASR well enough armed to carry out this unusual mission, and was it willing to do so? The AAWC and AIC contacted the ASR to find out, and the ASR crew responded that they could and would undertake the mission. *Find conflict:* A second problem had to do with the violation of standard operating procedures: A reconnaissance aircraft had never before been used under the control of an Anti-Air Warfare officer for a ground strike mission. *Resolve conflict by adopting assumption:* The AAWC chose to assume that he had the authority to retask the ASR, since he was the officer in control of the airspace. *Evaluate the assumption:* The AAWC was comfortable with this assumption. The Captain of his cruiser had established an atmosphere that encouraged initiative: "If I had a different kind of captain that had a different type of mentality . . . I might not have made that decision."

Find another conflict. The normal procedure would be to refer the decision regarding use of the ASR to his own TAO. Again drawing on knowledge of *team member reliability*, however, the AAWC figured that his TAO "didn't make aggressive decisions . . . if it wasn't something that had happened before." *Resolve conflict by modifying the option:* Instead, he announced what he was going to do, and his TAO "went along with it." The AAWC adopted a *proactive* orientation with respect to his superior, influencing rather than soliciting his decision.

Find another conflict. The TAO, nonetheless, called the Battle Force staff to inform them of the decision, and they said to wait. The TAO told the AAWC that Battle Force staff wanted to determine if any friendly troops were in the area of the Iraqi missile site. This created a new problem: The ASR had just radioed the AIC and AAWC that it was low on fuel and would have to strike the missile site immediately or else return to base. There was no time to wait for the Battle Force staff to close the loop. *Resolve conflict by finding another option:* The AAWC briefly considered waiting for the ASR's replacement, an S-3 aircraft, to become airborne. *Find conflict:* However, this presented similar problems that, if anything, were worse than the problems with using the ASR: Taking control of the S-3 would require too much time. Moreover, the S-3 had more explicit restrictions on its use than the ASR, which would take even more time to work around. *Quick Test:* The AAWC did not think it worthwhile to further consider this option.

Resolve conflict by modifying the option. The AAWC now considered the possibility of acting prior to receiving clearance from the Battle Force. He would again be adopting a *proactive* orientation toward a superior, by denying the Battle Force Commander the option of preventing use of the ASR. *Find conflict:* But were there friendlies in the area (i.e. was the Battle Force concern valid)? *Resolve conflict by retrieving information:* In deciding whether to use the ASR without clearance, the AAWC drew on knowledge of the *task situation.* He thought it extremely unlikely that any friendly forces would be in the area of the missile site, since he had been sending attack missions into that area all day. *Continue to resolve conflict by collecting information:* Because the cost of an error was high, the AAWC chose to verity this further by calling staff on the battleship Missouri, who confirmed that no friendlies were in the area.

Continue to resolve conflict by adopting assumption. It seemed reasonable to conclude that no friendlies were in the area, but why then was the Battle Force staff reluctant to approve use of the ASR? The AAWC drew again on knowledge of *team member reliability.* Based on past experience, the AAWC felt that the Battle Force staff was overly cautious in general. All the signs indicated that the Battle Force would eventually give its approval. He also concluded that if they did deny permission to send the ASR, that decision would be based on caution rather than on safety-related information. Acting prior to clearance was thus *predictive* with respect to his superior's eventual approval, but proactive with respect to his superior's real options. *Evaluate assumption*: The AAWC resolved the conflict by assuming that approval would eventually come, but accepting that he would have to "take the hit on being too aggressive" if permission were denied. He was comfortable with accepting this risk. By contrast, following the standard procedure required a predictive orientation to the enemy, based on assumptions he was far less comfortable with: that the enemy missile site would not fire, or that the carrier launch process would come off more accurately and quickly than before.

Taking Action

The AAWC told the TAO what he was going to do, then tasked the ASR to strike the missile site. The site was successfully destroyed. Clearance from the Battle Group Commander arrived shortly thereafter. The AAWC and TAO waited a few minutes, then reported the destruction of the missile site to the commander. They received commendation for their action, and use of the ASR in this way became a new standard operating procedure in the battle force. The Battle Force commander never knew that the AAWC had acted on his own initiative before receiving clearance.

Discussion

In this example, taking initiative with respect to the enemy required taking initiative within the organization, and both required critical thinking. Critical thinking that focused on mental models of *action sequence, team member reliability*, and *purpose* enabled the AAWC to identify problems with the standard procedure. In particular, he saw that it implied a predictive rather than a proactive stance in the face of an unexpected enemy action (turning on its radar), and thus did not sufficiently reduce uncertainty about enemy action in the future (firing a missile). The desire to be proactive toward the enemy, in turn, was the source of the time pressure that influenced the AAWC's subsequent decision making. In that decision making, he drew on critical thinking about mental models to decide: (i) whether to communicate, (ii) how to coordinate without communication, and (iii) how to evaluate communications that did occur. These are, of course, the issues identified in the Introduction as characteristic of time-stressed, novel, and spatially distributed situations. The AAWC's way of handling these issues involved each of the three time orientations:

(1) *Should we communicate?* Through critical thinking, the AAWC decided not to wait for closed-loop communication with the Battle Force commander. Waiting would have entailed an unacceptable loss of initiative with respect to the enemy. Instead, he chose to be *proactive* both with respect to the enemy and with respect to the Battle Force commander (and his own TAO). Consistent with Fig. 2, the key mental models in this critical thinking process were friendly *purpose* (to prevent damage to the battle group by the missile site), and shaping both *enemy intent* and *friendly intent* (i.e. eliminating options).

(2) *What will the others do?* On the other hand, the AAWC also used critical thinking to achieve as much coordination as possible despite the lack of full communication, through a *predictive* time orientation. For example, he predicted that the standard procedure would not accomplish a strike on the missile with the required accuracy or speed. He also predicted with some confidence that friendly forces would not be in the area of the target. He predicted that the TAO would go along with the decision presented to him, and that the Battle Force commander would ultimately approve the strike on the missile site. Again consistent with Fig. 2, the key mental models were *friendly intent*, team member *reliability* and the *rate of movement* (i.e. likely duration) of a friendly *action sequence*.

(3) *How good is the information?* Finally, the AAWC used critical thinking to evaluate the information that was communicated to him and to *react* appropriately to it. For example, he considered alternative hypotheses about the intent of the enemy in turning on the missile site radar. He interpreted the hesitation of the TAO and the Battle Force staff as indicators of habitual caution rather than as signs of actual disapproval or risk. By contrast, he assigned greater credibility to the opinions of the AIC and the staff of the battleship Missouri, both of whom he regarded as more likely to favor decisive action in regard to the enemy. Again consistent with Fig. 2, the key mental models were *alternative causes and effects* and team member *reliability*.

By means of critical thinking, the AAWC was able to develop proactive tactics both toward the enemy and toward his own organization. In doing so, he developed a mutually supporting framework of proactive, predictive, and reactive orientations toward different aspects of the task. He invested a small amount of time thinking in order to buy much more time for action. The long-term result was improved adaptation to environmental variability *at the organization level*.

TRAINING FOR INITIATIVE

How should critical thinking skills be trained? Different conceptions of decision-making skill are associated with different training strategies. For example, if decision-making skill is regarded as a small set of general-purpose techniques (Baron & Brown, 1991), critical thinking can be taught as a subject in its own right, distinct from the various specialized domains in which it is applied. The primary method of training, from this point of view, is typically explicit classroom instruction, with examples of decision problems playing a secondary role for motivation and practice (e.g. Adams & Deehrer, 1991). At the opposite extreme, if decision-making skill is regarded as pattern matching, critical thinking cannot be identified as a subject matter by itself. Training should be fully infused into the regular curriculum for each specific subject area . This training will focus primarily on practice with numerous realistic and typical examples of decision problems and their solutions, with very little explicit instruction (Means, Salas, Crandall & Jacobs, 1993).

The approach to training based on the Recognition/Metacognition model is distinct from both of these. The content of critical thinking training is not a small set of general-purpose methods nor is it a vast quantity of specialized patterns and responses. The focus is on a moderately sized set of mental model types (including time orientations) and critical thinking strategies that critique and correct them. Unlike specialized patterns, both the mental models and the thinking strategies are generalizable (in many if not all respects) from one domain to another, especially domains characterized by uncertainty about human action within and outside an organization and by time constraints. But there is a problem with *teaching* critical thinking as a general purpose methodology, even if it can be broken down into a moderately sized set of mental models and strategies. To the extent that critical thinking is *meta-recognitional*, it can be effectively exercised only within a domain that is familiar enough for there to be significant recognitional knowledge. The domain must also be familiar enough for the creative exploration of a rich knowledge base, for example, in the identification of assumptions and the development of alternative conclusions. Thus, critical thinking might best be taught as *a separate module (or set of modules)*, because there are reasonably general critical thinking principles, but *within a specific subject matter area*, because critical thinking cannot be exercised effectively without pre-existing knowledge. Training involves a combination of explicit presentation of critical thinking concepts followed by intensive practice and feedback in realistic, challenging, but not necessarily typical scenarios.

Training based on this approach has been developed and successfully tested in Navy and Army tactical decision-making environments. The training is based on empirical research, such as that described above, on differences in mental models and thinking strategies between more and less experienced decision makers in real-world problems. Most recently, we have developed a computer-based interactive training program for Army battlefield critical thinking, packaged as a stand-alone CD that runs under Microsoft Windows, and that can also be accessed by a browser on the World Wide Web. The program, which is called MEntalMOdeler, or MEMO, uses graphical interactive techniques to present concepts and provide practice and feedback. MEMO has recently been assigned and evaluated in an advanced tactics course at the Army Command and General Staff College (Center of Army Tactics), Leavenworth, KA.

The training teaches students the elements of initiative, focusing on how to think critically about *purpose, time,* and *uncertainty.* It includes four major segments. The first segment contains an introduction to the mental models that represent purpose, followed by a second segment on thinking critically about those mental models. The third segment addresses the mental models that represent time orientation (i.e. influencing, predicting, or reacting to another agent), followed by a fourth segment on how to think critically about those mental models. Each of these segments contains an introduction to the relevant concepts using both verbal and graphical methods, military examples of how the concepts apply, historical case studies that illustrate the concepts, and interactive exercises with feedback. The training increases in difficulty as it progresses through these four segments. A final, fifth segment applies the mental model and critical thinking concepts to so-called "maneuver warfare" and "attrition" tactics.

All exercises involve relatively realistic (though brief) military scenarios adapted from the Tactical Decision Games feature published monthly in the *Marine Corps Gazette* (see also Schmitt, 1994). Each of the scenarios selected for use in the exercises addresses the issue of initiative in a context of uncertainty, time stress, and limited communication.

Segment 1: Purpose

Focus on purpose increases with experience and is closely associated with the ability to adopt a proactive time orientation (see Fig. 2). This section of the training, which is the simplest, gives students conceptual and graphical tools for organizing their thinking about purpose. The main points of the section are: (i) that thinking about the situation and about one's own plans should always be guided by an understanding of purpose, and (ii) purpose is not simply the immediate mission of your part of the organization, but includes the purposes of adjacent and superior units. Purpose in this higher-level, longer range sense provides the big picture within which critical thinking takes place.

The section starts by reviewing a graphical tool, called a *nesting diagram*, that shows *why* your own unit has the purposes and tasks that are assigned to it, in terms of its relationships to purposes and tasks of adjacent units and superior units two or more levels up. A nesting diagram shows which units are assigned the main effort of their superior unit and which adjacent units are tasked to support those efforts. The training provides practical guidance on how to extract elements of the nesting diagram from an operations order received from superior headquarters, and contains exercises on constructing such diagrams in both simple and complex cases (e.g. missing information, purposes not lined up with the organizational hierarchy). Many students are already somewhat familiar with nesting diagrams, and they thus provide a good entry point for understanding mental models.

The next section generalizes the idea of a *mental model* beyond nesting diagrams. A mental model is defined as a succinct summary of events or ideas, which shows how each event or idea is linked to success or failure of your purpose. Mental models, which can be verbal or graphical, provide a tool by means of which decision makers stay focused on purpose as their thinking evolves through stages of the decision-making process. Upon receipt of the mission, the command staff creates a nesting diagram placing their own unit in the larger context of the operation. Planning starts with this nesting diagram and asks *how* the various purposes it represents can best be achieved. The initial answer to this question is the commander's guidance or intent, which states how the purposes of the unit will be achieved in the present situation. Subsequently, during course of action development, the mental model is elaborated in still more detail, to provide a concept of operations. Later, during course of action analysis, the mental model takes the form of a detailed synchronization matrix, coordinating activities of different subordinate units at different places and times. This section of the training emphasizes diagrammatically how all these stages of mental model development are linked to one another and to the unit's purposes.

The next section begins the discussion (which will continue through the rest of the training) of how mental models are used to make decisions. It emphasizes the importance of considering higher-level purposes. A plan that is designed to achieve a unit's immediate purpose may be inadequate if it does not also put the unit in a position to provide back-up for adjacent and superior units, and to assume their tasks in the case of the unexpected.

Segment 2: Critical Thinking About Purpose

This section provides an overview, examples, and exercises for the critical thinking process, called *I.D.E.A.S.* (an acronym for *Identify, Deconflict, Evaluate, Act,* and *Stop*), based on the model in Fig. 3. The first three steps (*Identify, Deconflict,* and *Evaluate*) correspond to critiquing for the three kinds of uncertainty identified in our research: gaps, conflict, and unreliable assumptions. More specifically, the first step is to identify and fill gaps in mental models, i.e. missing components of the plan or of one's situation understanding that are likely to have an impact on the achievement of purposes. The second step is to identify and resolve conflicts between information sources or goals. The third step is to find and evaluate assumptions in the current plan or situation model. *Act* represents the different correcting strategies that can be adopted to address those problems and to improve the situation model or plan. *Stop* stands for the Quick Test, which weighs the benefits of continued critical thinking against its costs and determines when it is necessary to take action based on the best current solution.

These steps are discussed by means of examples from both planning and real-time operations. Filling gaps in a plan leads to discovery of a conflict between optimal achievement of the immediate purpose of the unit and providing back-up for higher-level purposes. A variety of correcting steps are illustrated and evaluated: e.g. collecting more information to confirm or disconfirm the likelihood that other units will need back-up, adding a branch or contingency to the existing plan in case of unexpected events, changing the current plan to provide more flexibility, or accepting the risk that nothing will go wrong for other units. During the operational phase of the plan decision makers not only monitor progress in achieving their own goals, but also monitor the success or failure of other units in achieving their goals. When unexpected events during an operation occur, an immediate decision must be made on how and what to communicate, and whether to continue on the original task or to shift the focus of effort.

An interactive exercise requires students to critique and modify a plan in the face of surprising events. Feedback is given, and then a new variant of the plan is provided that addresses shortcomings of the previous option. The students must then critique and modify the new option. Feedback is again given, along with yet another variant of the plan to be critiqued and corrected. A historical example of initiative is also provided, involving U.S. Grant at Vicksburg. Attention to higher-level purposes led General Grant to abandon his line of communications, modify virtually every part of his orders, and still achieve one of the pivotal victories of the Civil War.

A final topic on critical thinking about purpose focuses on ferreting out hidden assumptions, by means of a devil's advocate strategy. This strategy involves imagining that a crucial assessment or plan will fail to achieve its purpose(s), and forcing oneself to explain how that could happen. Students learn to stimulate their imagination by picturing an infallible crystal ball that persistently tells them their explanations of the failure are wrong, and demands that they generate another one. They also learn to use their mental models in conjunction with the crystal ball to identify points where failure could occur. An interactive exercise asks that they use this technique to find and resolve problems in a tactical scenario.

Segment 3: Time Orientation

The next major segment of the training involves *time orientation*, i.e. putting purposes to work in a framework of time and action. In the first section, the training extends the graphical mental modeling tools introduced in the previous segment, by adding a horizontal time dimension to represent a sequence of events and actions (the vertical dimension continues to represent the hierarchy of purposes). *Initiative* is discussed in terms of mental models that show how friendly actions can influence, predict, or react to the decision cycle of the enemy or other friendly units. The three time orientations – proactive, predictive, and reactive – are explained in terms of how and when they reduce uncertainty about another agent's actions.

The next section of this segment introduces the use of time orientation models to make decisions. It describes the questions that need to be asked to fill gaps in reactive, predictive, and proactive mental models. To create a predictive model, for example, the decision maker asks: "What will the enemy do and what strengths or weaknesses are associated with those actions? What are the implications of those strengths and weaknesses for my purposes? And what can I do to avoid the strengths or exploit the weaknesses?" To create a proactive mental model, on the other hand, the decision maker asks: "What are my higher purposes? What do I *want* the enemy to do that will promote those purposes? And what can I do to get him to do it?" An interactive exercise requires students to identify the time orientations implicit in different strategic, operational, and tactical plans during Operation Desert Storm.

Segment 4: Critical Thinking About Time Orientation

This segment introduces students to a more sophisticated set of critical thinking strategies, and to a deeper understanding of how proactive, predictive, and reactive orientations can co-exist in a single mental model. The first section discusses how correcting one kind of problem can lead to other problems across cycles of critiquing and correcting. The primary emphasis is on how each time orientation can be used to address weaknesses in the other time orientations, as plans are gradually elaborated and improved, and that the most effective plans ultimately involve several time orientations in a mutually supporting pattern.

The next section provides a detailed example of the evolution of a plan through the I.D.E.A.S. cycle, and illustrates a simple multiple time-orientation pattern. Planning begins with a predictive model, in particular, a plan based on the expectation that an enemy unit will cross a river and be vulnerable to attack as it crosses. A devil's advocate strategy is then used to critique the plan. (An infallible crystal ball says, "The plan will fail. Explain how.") This process brings to light hidden assumptions about enemy intent upon which the plan depends. To make the plan more robust, proactive tactics are developed to lure the enemy across the river. Other proactive tactics are developed to increase the enemy's vulnerability while crossing by using artillery to prevent it from concentrating forces. To guard against the possibility that predictive and proactive tactics fail to achieve their purpose, the plan is further elaborated to include monitoring of enemy movements and a flexible, reactive orientation in case the enemy does something other than what is expected. The result is a template in which different time orientations provide mutual support: Proactive tactics are utilized to increase the chance that predictive assumptions will turn out to be true, while reactive tactics monitor for the unexpected.

In a continuation of this example, the enemy does in fact behave in a surprising manner (heading in a different direction than expected). A new template for mutually supporting time orientations is illustrated. The initial reaction is designed to mitigate any immediate threat from the enemy action. The next phase is to consider any enemy weaknesses that the action exposes or creates (e.g. failing to cross the river leaves a command post relatively undefended on the other side). These weaknesses are, ideally, independent of specific assumptions about what the enemy is up to. Predictive tactics are developed to exploit opportunities that are identified. At the same time, a way is sought to use these opportunities to *create* new weaknesses, i.e. to proactively degrade the enemy's capability to pursue *future* operations (e.g. by destroying a command post, or attacking logistics). The result of this critical thinking process is a template for reaction to surprise that shifts as rapidly as possible from reactive to predictive to proactive orientations.

Two historical examples of reaction to surprise are described, in both of which unexpected enemy action was turned to friendly advantage: U.S. Grant at Fort Donelson, and Eisenhower in the Ardennes offensive. An interactive exercise requires students to identify the combinations of time orientations represented by the small unit tactics described in James McDonough's book, *Platoon Leader.*

Segment 5: Applications to Initiative-Oriented Fighting

This segment of the training applies the above lessons to current discussion of Army tactics. It continues to focus on critical thinking about time orientation, but gives special attention to issues raised by proponents of *maneuver warfare*, which focuses on initiative (Hooker, 1993; Lind, 1985; The United States Marine Corps, 1989; Leonhard, 1991, 1994). The first section clarifies the difference between maneuver and attrition methods by the use of diagrammatic mental models depicting all three time orientations: (1) *Reactive*: Attrition emphasizes taking time to prepare, while maneuver emphasizes the ability to react quickly and flexibly to events by local commanders on the spot. (2) *Predictive*: Attrition emphasizes predicting and attacking enemy strength, while maneuver emphasizes predicting and attacking enemy weakness. (3) *Proactive*: Attrition destroys the enemy's assets in order to gradually wear down its ability to fight and limit its future options, while maneuver tries to generate moral effects, like shock and panic, which reduce the ability of enemy to make decisions at all and can lead to a sudden enemy collapse.

The next section shows how maneuver tactics draw on a highly interdependent system of mutual supports among time orientations. A series of graphical time orientation templates is presented to depict these relationships. For example, the tactics of "surfaces and gaps" involves mutual support between rapid reaction and prediction of enemy weakness. Friendly forces probe in many locations for weaknesses (or "gaps") in enemy front lines, and take initiative in order to react rapidly to any success, by sending reserves through the gaps into the enemy rear. If this *reaction* is rapid enough, the enemy will be *predicted* to be unable to repair the breach in time to prevent the exploitation. At the same time, attacking predicted enemy weakness makes speed possible by avoiding unnecessary fights. Thus, reactive and predictive orientations support one another.

Predictive and proactive orientations are even more closely intertwined in maneuver warfare. The objective of the exploitation of gaps is *proactive*: to reach the enemy rear and strike a high-leverage enemy vulnerability, typically command and control or logistics, without which the enemy cannot continue to fight. This objective is *predicted* to be relatively lightly defended by virtue of being in the rear, and the rapidity of the attack is also expected to prevent any redeployment of enemy forces for its defense. In addition, the predictive aspects of this action can provide an important *proactive* byproduct: By attacking suddenly in an area thought to be safe, friendly forces can cause the enemy to panic. This panic will proactively degrade the enemy's ability to continue the fight as much as the actual loss of command and control or logistics. These proactive effects in combination create new weaknesses that can be further exploited by predictive actions.

In short, the essence of maneuver warfare is the snowballing, positive feedback effects that it strives to create among the three time orientations. Autonomous decision making by low-level units is crucial for the required rapidity of response that gets the process going. The purpose is to win as quickly as possible, at the least cost. An interactive exercise requires students to apply maneuver warfare concepts in the process of critical thinking about courses of action.

The next section in this segment explores critical thinking about maneuver warfare tactics more closely. It examines some of the problems to which highly initiative-oriented maneuver tactics can lead. (1) Reactive and predictive orientations can conflict, for example, if speedy reactions leave units with unprotected flanks. This is an example of a more general problem with taking initiative in the absence of complete communication or advance coordination. Assumptions must be made about the actions taken, or the success realized, by other friendly units, and these risks must be weighed against the potential advantages of quick reaction. (2) Predictive and proactive orientations can conflict if normally high-leverage targets, such as command and control and logistics, are in fact not weakly defended. A greater emphasis on preparation and coordination rather than tempo and surprise may be required when this is the case. (3) Maneuver tactics use all three time orientations to compensate for lack of coordination among friendly units: by rapidly reacting to signs of existing enemy weaknesses, by exploiting them before the enemy can respond, and by creating new enemy weaknesses through high tempo and surprise and by striking high-leverage targets. Success on all these fronts depends on a number of assumptions: that rapid movement can be executed given the terrain, weather, equipment, and enemy resistance; that predictions about weakness are correct, e.g. that apparent gaps in enemy front lines are real rather than traps laid by the enemy; that shock tactics will have the intended psychological effects on this particular foe, causing them to collapse rather than hunker down; and that the enemy really does depend critically on the targeted command and control and logistics capabilities. Failure of these assumptions can turn promising initiative into disaster. Students get practice making these kinds of tradeoffs in exercises in which high levels of initiative involve a cost in communication and coordination.

LESSONS LEARNED: TRAINING INITIATIVE IN TEAMS

Lesson 1: Initiative is Vital in Team Performance

Initiative is an important but neglected topic in team decision making and team training. It is a vital ingredient in situations characterized by unexpected and rapidly unfolding dangers or opportunities, and where communication is limited by spatial separation, workload, specialization of knowledge, or other factors. In such environments, leadership initiative and responsibility devolves upon teams and individuals that are ordinarily subordinate, but who are able to act more quickly and effectively on the spot. These individuals and teams need training that enables them to discriminate situations where initiative is appropriate, from other situations where coordination and communication are more important (e.g. when many sources of information must be integrated, large-scale patterns of events must be interpreted, and actions must be coordinated across the organization). When initiative is appropriate, teams and individuals need to learn when and how to communicate, how to anticipate actions of other friendly units, and how to interpret information that is communicated by other friendly units.

Lesson 2: Training Can Be Based on Differences Between More and Less Experienced Decision Makers in Real-World Situations

Development of training content for a particular domain can be based on analysis of interviews in which decision makers describe actual experiences in challenging, real-world situations. This approach reveals important differences between more and less experienced decision makers in both the knowledge they draw upon (mental models) and the thinking strategies they employ. These differences can become the focus of effective training for initiative in that domain. Moreover, there is reason to suspect that key aspects of that training will transfer across domains, such as the importance of purpose, time, and critical thinking.

Lesson 3: Awareness of Purpose is a Key Ingredient of Initiative

An important difference between more and less experienced decision makers is focus on higher-level and longer-term purposes or general principles. In non-routine situations, experienced decision makers work to clarify goals, and to modify and elaborate them if necessary. This understanding of purpose is then used to guide attention to the most critical features of the situation and to construct or select actions. Attention to purpose correlates both with experience and with the degree of initiative shown by decision makers. Attention to purpose also plays a role in *creativity* or innovation. Creativity often involves questioning or disregarding traditional, lower level goals, habits, and constraints and focusing on new ways to achieve what the organization truly values (Ray & Myers, 1986).

Lesson 4: Appropriate Time Orientation is a Key Ingredient of Initiative

Another important difference associated with experience involves time orientation. Experienced decision makers make greater use of proactive strategies, and therefore take more initiative. Proactive decision makers influence the decisions of other agents (e.g. enemies, competitors, superiors, or colleagues) rather than simply predict or react to their actions. Time orientation in turn helps determine the knowledge or mental models decision makers draw upon. Nor surprisingly, the proactive orientation is closely associated with attention to higher-level purpose. Both proactive and predictive orientations draw on mental models of intent. Both predictive and reactive orientations draw on models of team member reliability. Finally, all three orientations draw on knowledge of the sequence of actions in a task.

Lesson 5: Critical Thinking Processes are a Key Ingredient of Initiative

Critical incident interviews and other research suggests that a variety of critical thinking strategies also develop with experience. These skills supplement and improve pattern recognition skills rather than replacing them with formal decision making methods. Experienced decision makers learn to verify their initial recognitional response when the stakes are high, time is available, and the situation is unfamiliar or uncertain. They learn to flesh out their understanding of a hypothesis or action by recalling or collecting relevant information. They learn to notice conflicts, in which observations fail to match familiar patterns, and standard responses are not likely to achieve desired purposes. When conflict is found, instead of immediately rejecting the recognitional conclusion, they tend to patch it up by generating a story that explains the conflict. They then evaluate the assumptions required by the story, and accept, modify, or reject the conclusion based on that evaluation. For decision makers armed with these skills, initiative is the result of careful scrutiny of the standard response; the decision to deviate from it is made with full awareness of the assumptions and risks involved.

Meta-recognitional processes can be understood in terms of the intelligent shifting of attention to activate additional knowledge in the recognitional system, and the persistent application of attention to hypothetical contingencies in order to conduct what-if reasoning. Here again, there is a suggestive link to research findings on creativity. Creative thinking involves inhibiting routine responses, letting attention roam beyond the immediate associations in the situation, and challenging assumptions.

Lesson 6: Training for Initiative Should Include a Focus on Purpose, Time Orientation, and Critical Thinking

A strategy method has been developed for Army battlefield decision-making skills that focuses on these three key ingredients of initiative: purpose, time orientation, and critical thinking. The strategy trains less experienced decision makers to use both the knowledge structures and decision-making strategies characteristic of more experienced decision makers. The training has five segments: purpose, critical thinking about purpose, time orientation, critical thinking about time orientation, and more advanced issues in deciding when to take initiative.

The training (in a previous, non-automated version) has been tested with active-duty officers in Army posts and schools around the country, and it works (Cohen, Freeman, Fallesen, Marvin & Bresnick, 1995; Cohen, Freeman, Wolf & Militello, 1995). A short period of training, both in Army and Navy contexts, has been consistently found to produce significantly better combat decisions, as judged by experienced officers. In addition, trained participants were able to consider a wider range of factors in making a decision, identify more evidence that conflicted with their initial recognitional response, identify more assumptions, and generate more alternative options than untrained participants.

A computer-based version of the training was enthusiastically received by the dean of the Command & General Staff College and the director of the Center for Army Tactics at the Army Command and General Staff College, Leavenworth, KA. CGSC instructors in several different courses have expressed an interest in using the material, and it has already been used in one advanced tactics course. Preliminary evaluation of the latter suggests that the training helped students identify more assumptions and adopt more robust plans in test scenarios.

Lesson 7: Training Should Combine Instruction, Examples, Practice, and Feedback

The computer-based version of the training is accessible either through CD-ROM or over the World Wide Web, and will be suitable for classroom instruction, training in the field, or distance learning. The combination of techniques utilized in this system reinforces learning and seems to successfully accommodate differing student learning styles. For example, some student comments stressed the value of the explicit instruction, while other comments stressed the value of actual examples from military history. Most students appreciated the interactive exercises and expressed a desire for more.

Future Directions

This chapter has focused on an important role of critical thinking in teamwork: how it is used to balance the benefits of initiative against those of coordination in uncertain, dynamic situations. There are many open questions and avenues for further research. Here are just a few, regarding teams, organizations, individuals, and training:

Teams. What role does critical thinking play in other aspects of teamwork, such as planning, mutual monitoring, backup, feedback, and load leveling? How are critical thinking styles and mental models related to leadership styles, such as autocratic versus consultative (Yukl, 1998), or concern for people versus concern for performance (i.e. the "managerial grid," described in Foushee & Helmreich, 1988)? Answers to these questions might lead to improved training of teamwork behaviors.

Organizations. What role does critical thinking play in larger organizations? For example, there is often a tradeoff in such organizations between risky exploration of new possibilities and the short-term certainty of building up competence and reaping the benefits of existing products and ideas (March, 1996). This is at least superficially analogous to the tradeoff between initiative and coordination in teams, and we may wish to study the role of critical thinking about mental models in decisions about allocating resources to research, decentralization versus centralization of organizational structure, receptivity to innovation, introduction of new products, and infusion of personnel from outside the organization. How do leaders and/or followers use critical thinking to adapt their organizations structurally and functionally in changing task environments? Are different critical thinking skills and types of mental models required at different levels of leadership in an organization, as suggested by Jaques & Clement (1994)?

Individuals. Individuals face an analogous tradeoff in the decision of whether or not to think critically at all. Leaders at every level must find a balance between rapid responding based on readily retrieved information and more time-consuming reflective processes that may lead to something new. Do people differ in their bias for recognition versus reflection, i.e. do people differ in *impulsivity – reflectivity* (Messer, 1976)? How do variations in this cognitive style dimension affect leadership? What variables determine the appropriate balance between impulsivity and reflectivity, and do they include organizational level? Are there more subtle individual differences in style of critical thinking? For example, can individuals who are equally prone to critical thinking differ in the emphasis they place on improving existing ideas versus finding radically new ones? Can *creativity* itself be understood at least in part as a style of critical thinking involving, for example, relatively unconstrained search for alternatives?[6]

Training. We asked earlier, How should critical thinking be trained? This issue should be revisited in light of its links to individual cognitive styles, on the one hand, and organizational variables, on the other. Can critical thinking training be made robust enough to stand on its own, as a separate subject matter, by focusing on broad cognitive styles and attitudes? Such styles and attitudes might generalize across domains and situations more readily than specific strategies (Baron, 1994; King & Kitchener, 1994). On the other hand, do cognitive styles and attitudes themselves vary significantly from one organizational context to another, as we suspect they do? If so, critical thinking might best be taught as a separate module but within a specific subject matter and organizational level. The latter is the approach illustrated in the present chapter.

   Although these questions remain open, they do not preclude tentative conclusions in the light of what is already known: There are many areas of practical life where team performance will be improved by enhancing the ability of team members to judge when, where, and how to take the initiative.

NOTES

   1. This name is by analogy to other so-called *metacognitive* skills, such as *meta-memory* (skills for monitoring and improving memory performance), *meta-attention* (skills for improving the control of attention), and *meta-comprehension* (skills for monitoring and improving the understanding of text). See Forrest-Pressley, MacKinnon and Waller (1985); Metcalfe and Shimamura (1994); Nelson (1992).
   2. The same concept of initiative could also be applied to intervention in natural chains of events, e.g. proactively preventing a hurricane by seeding a tropical storm,

predicting and preparing for the hurricane's point of impact, or reacting by declaring a state of emergency after it hits.

3. To score the presence of a mental model in the description of a particular incident, we required the explicit mention of only two or more out of the cluster of correlated topics defined as components of that kind of model (see step 2). For example, an *intent* model was scored as present if the description mentioned: (i) enemy or friendly intent, and (ii) two or more reasons to adopt that intent (e.g. an opportunity or capability) or indicators of that intent (e.g. resulting actions or outcomes). *Purpose* was scored as present if the description mentioned: (i) friendly intent that is motivated by, (ii) a higher-level goal or a longer-term objective extending beyond own unit's mission, or a general principle of warfighting. *Action sequence* involved: (i) two or more enemy actions or two or more friendly actions, (ii) with the explicit constraint that one must be performed before the other. *Reliability* involved: (i) a claim regarding the situation, a predicted enemy or friendly action, or the best friendly course of action, (ii) explicit mention of the source of the claim or recommendation, and (iii) an assessment of its reliability.

4. The hypothesis that meta-recognitional strategies can be learned through experience is being tested by experiments with a computational implementation of the Recognition/Metacognition model. The implementation utilizes a connectionist architecture with a backpropagation learning algorithm, and employs temporal synchrony of firings for consistency of object reference in relational reasoning (Thompson, Cohen & Shastri, 1997).

5. Our work on Navy decision making was supported by Contract No. N61339–96-C-0107 with the Naval Air Warfare Center Training Systems Division, as part of the TADMUS program.

6. A compelling case can be made that critical thinking and creativity are inseparable aspects of thinking. Bailin (1990) and Paul (1987) argue that critical judgment is necessary for creativity; e.g. to recognize the inadequacy of existing solutions and decide that a new approach is required (sometimes as part of an extended process of questioning and doubting authority), to determine directions for investigation, and to evaluate the products of creativity. Conversely, it has been implicit throughout this chapter that creativity is a part of critical thinking, even when it leads only to modification rather than replacement of the existing solution. As Bailin points out, critical thinking requires many non-algorithmic and non-analytic processes, such as identification of background assumptions in an argument, visualizing potential problems with your own position, empathetically imagining alternative positions, and arriving at an overall assessment.

ACKNOWLEDGMENTS

This work was sponsored by the Army Research Institute under Contract No. DASW01–97-C-0038 with Cognitive Technologies, Inc. We are grateful to the COTR, Sharon Riedel, for her many contributions, and to the important contributions of Len Adelman, Terry Bresnick, General Bill Richardson, and General Joe Mead throughout the project. Thanks to Colonel Tystad and Lieutenant Colonel Hewitt of the Command and General Staff College, Leavenworth, KA, for their cooperation, and to Lieutenant Colonel Billy

Hadfield for his active participation in the development and evaluation of the training.

REFERENCES

Adams, M. J., & Feehrer, C. E. (1991). Thinking and Decision Making. In: J. Baron & R. V. Brown (Eds), *Teaching Decision Making to Adolescents* (pp. 79–94). Hillsdale, NJ: Erlbaum.

Adelson, B. (1984). When novices surpass experts: The difficulty of a task may increase with expertise. *Journal of Experimental Psychology: Learning, Memory, and Cognition, 10*(3), 484–495.

Anzai, Y. (1991). Learning and use of representations for physics expertise. In: K. A. Ericsson & J. Smith (Eds), *Toward a General Theory of Expertise* (pp. 64–92). Cambridge: Cambridge University Press.

Bailin, S. (1990). Argument criticism as creative. In: R. Trapp & J. Schuetz (Eds), *Perspectives on argumentation*. Prospect Heights, IL: Waveland Press.

Baron, J. (1994). *Thinking and Deciding*. Cambridge: Cambridge University Press.

Baron, J., & Brown, R. V. (Eds) (1991). *Teaching Decision Making to Adolescents*. Hillsdale, NJ: Erlbaum.

Blau, P. M. (1970). A formal theory of differentiation in organizations. *American Sociological Review, 35*, 201–218.

Brown, L. (Ed.) (1993). *The New Shorter Oxford English Dictionary*. Oxford: Clarendon Press.

Burns, T., & Stalker, G. M. (1962). *The Management of Innovation*. London: Tavistock.

Cannon-Bowers, J. A., Salas, E., & Converse, S. (1993). Shared Mental Models in Expert Team Decision Making. In: N. J. Castellan (Ed.), *Individual and Group Decision Making* (pp. 221–246). Hillsdale, NJ: Lawrence Erlbaum Associates.

Cannon-Bowers, J. A., Tannenbaum, S. I., Salas, E., & Volpe, C. E. (1995). Defining competencies and establishing team training requirements. In: R. A. Guzzo, E. Salas, & Associates (Eds), *Team Effectiveness and Decision Making in Organizations* (pp. 333–380). San Francisco: Jossey-Bass Publishers.

Chase, W. G., & Simon, H. A. (1973). The mind's eye in chess. In: W. G. Chase (Ed.), *Visual Information Processing* (pp. 215–281). NY: Academic Press.

Castellan, N. J., Jr. (1993). Paradoxes in individual and group decision making: A plea for models. In: N. J. Castellan (Ed.), *Individual and Group Decision Making* (pp. 125–134). Hillsdale, NJ: Lawrence Erlbaum Associates.

Chi, M., Bassock, M., Reimann, P., & Glaser, R. (1989). Self explanations: How students study and use examples in learning to solve problems. *Cognitive Science, 13*, 145–182.

Chi, M., Feltovich, P., & Glaser, R. (1981). Categorization and representation of physics problems by experts and novices. *Cognitive Science, 5*, 121–152.

Cohen, M. S. (1986). An expert system framework for non-monotonic reasoning about probabilistic assumptions. In: J. F. Lemmer & L. N. Kanal (Eds), *Uncertainty in Artificial Intelligence* (pp. 279–293). Amsterdam: North-Holland Publishing Co.

Cohen, M. S. (1993). The naturalistic basis of decision biases. In: G. A. Klein, J. Orasanu, R. Calderwood & C. E. Zsambok (Eds), *Decision Making in Action: Models and Methods* (pp. 51–99). Norwood, NJ: Ablex.

Cohen, M. S., Freeman, J. T., Fallesen, J. J., Marvin, F., and Bresnick, T. A. (1995). *Training Critical Thinking Skills for Battlefield Situation Assessment: An Experimental Test*. Arlington, VA: Cognitive Technologies, Inc.

Cohen, M. S., Freeman, J. T., & Thompson, B. B. (1998). Critical thinking skills in tactical decision making: A model and a training method. In: J. Canon-Bowers, & E. Salas (Eds), *Decision-Making Under Stress: Implications for Training & Simulation*. Washington, DC: American Psychological Association Publications.

Cohen, M. S., Freeman, J., Wolf, S. P., Militello, L. (1995). *Training Metacognitive Skills in Naval Combat Decision Making*. Arlington, VA: Cognitive Technologies, Inc.

Cohen, M. S., Freeman, J. T., & Wolf, S. (1996). Meta-recognition in time stressed decision making: Recognizing, critiquing, and correcting. *Human Factors, 38*(2), 206–219.

Cohen M. S., Parasuraman, R., Serfaty, D., & Andes, R.. (1997). *Trust in Decision Aids: A Model and a Training Strategy*. Arlington, VA: Cognitive Technologies, Inc.

Donaldson, L. (1995). *american Anti-management Theories of Organization: A Critique of Paradigm Proliferation*. New York: The Cambridge University Press.

Doyle, J. (1979). A truth maintenance system. *Artificial Intelligence, 12*(3), 231–162.

Dreyfus, H. L. (1997). Intuitive, deliberative, and calculative models of expert performance. In: C. E. Zsambok & G. Klein (Eds), *Naturalistic Decision Making* (pp. 17–28). Mahwah, NJ: Erlbaum.

Ellis, R. D. (1995). *Questioning Consciousness*. Philadelphia: John Benjamins Publishing Company.

Ericsson, K. A., & Smith, J. (1991). Prospects And limits of the empirical study of expertise: an introduction. In: K. A. Ericsson & J. Smith (Eds), *Toward a General Theory of Expertise*. Cambridge: New York: University Press.

Forrest-Pressley, D. L., MacKinnon, G. E., & Waller, T. G. (Eds) (1985). *Metacognition, Cognition, and Human Performance*. NY: Academic Press.

Foushee, H. C., and Helmreich, R. L. (1988). Group interaction and flight crew performance. In: E. L. Wiener & D. C. Nagel (Eds), *Human Factors in Aviation*. San Diego: Academic Press.

Glaser, R. (1996). Changing the agency for learning: Acquiring expert performance. In: K. A. Ericsson (Ed.), *The Road to Excellence: The Acquisition of Expert Performance in the Arts and Sciences, Sports, and Games*. Mahwah, NJ: Lawrence Erlbaum Associates.

Halpern, D. F. (1996). *Thought & Knowledge: An Introduction to Critical Thinking*. Mahwah, NJ: Lawrence Erlbaum Associates.

Helmreich, R. L., & Foushee, H. C. (1993). Why crew resource management? Empirical and theoretical bases of human factors training in aviation. In: E. L. Wiener, R. L. Helmreich, & B. G. Kanki (Eds), *Cockpit Resource Management*. NY: Academic Press, Inc.

Holyoak, K. J. (1991). Symbolic connectionism: toward third-generation theories of expertise. In: K. A. Ericsson & J. Smith (Eds), *Toward a General Theory of Expertise*. Cambridge: New York: University Press.

Hooker, R. D. Jr. (1993). *Maneuver Warfare: An Anthology*. Novata, CA: Presidio Press.

Janis, I. L. (1972). *Victims of Groupthink*. Boston: Houghton Mifflin.

Jaques, E., & Clement, S. D. *executive Leadership: A Practical Guide to Managing Complexity*. Malden, MA: Blackwell Publishers.

Johnson, S. C. (1967). Hierarchical clustering schemes. *Psychometrika, 32*, 241–254.

Kaempf, G. L., Klein, G., Thordsen, M. L., & Wolf, S. (1996). Decision making in complex command-and-control environments. *Human Factors, 38*(2).

Kerr, N. L. MacCoun, R. J., & Kramer, G. P. (1996). "When are N heads better (or worse) than one?": Biased judgment in individuals versus groups. In: E. Witte & J. H. Davis, *understanding Group Behavior: Consensual Action by Small Groups* (Vol. 1). Mahwah, NJ: Lawrence Erlbaum Associates.

King, P. M., & Kitchener, K. S. *developing Reflective Judgment: Understanding and Promoting Intellectual Growth and Critical Thinking in Adolescents and Adults*. San Francisco: Jossey-Bass Publishers.

Klein, G. A. (1993). A Recognition-Primed Decision (RPD) model of rapid decision making. In: G. A. Klein, J. Orasanu, R. Calderwood, & C. E. Zsambok (Eds), *Decision Making in Action: Models and Methods* (pp. 138–147). Norwood, NJ: Ablex.

Kleinman, D. L., & Serfaty, D. (1989). Team performance assessment in distributed decision making. In: R. Gilson, J. P. Kincaid, & B. Goldiez (Eds), *Proceedings of the Interactive Networked Simulation for Training Conference*. Orlando, FL: Naval Training Systems Center.

Kuhn, D., Amsel, E., & O'Loughlin, M. (1988). *the Development of Scientific Thinking Skills*. San Diego: Academic Press, Inc.

Kruskal, J. B. (1964). Non-metric multidimensional scaling: A numerical method. *Psychometrika, 29*, 115–129.

Larkin, J. H. (1981). Enriching formal knowledge: A model for learning to solve textbook physics problems. In: J. R. Anderson (Ed.), *Cognitive Skills and their Acquisition* (pp. 311–344). Hillsdale, NJ: Lawrence Erlbaum Associates.

Larkin, J., McDermott, J., Simon, D. P., & Simon, H. A. (1980). Expert and novice performance in solving physics problems. *Science, 20*(208), 1335–1342.

Leonhard, R. R. (1994). *fighting by Minutes: Time and the Art Of War*. Westport, CT: Praeger.

Leonhard, R. R. (1991). *The Art of Maneuver*. Novata, CA: Presidio Press.

Lind, W. S. (1985). *Maneuver Warfare Handbook*. Boulder: Westview Press.

March, J. G. (1996). Exploration and exploitation in organizational learning. In: M. D. Cohen & L. S. Sproull (Eds), *Organizational Learning* (pp. 101–123). Thousand Oaks, CA: Sage Publications.

McIntyre, R. M., & Salas, E. (1995). Measuring and managing for team performance: Lessons from complex environments. In: R. A. Guzzo, E. Salas, & Associates (Eds), *Team Effectiveness and Decision Making in Organizations* (pp. 9–45). San Francisco: Jossey-Bass Publishers.

McKeithen, K. B., Reitman, J. S., Rueter, H. H., & Hirtle, S. C. (1981). Knowledge organization and skill differences in computer programmers. *Cognitive Psychology, 13*.

Means, B., Salas, E., Crandall, B., & Jacobs, T. O. (1993). Training decision makers for the real world. In: G. A. Klein, J. Orasanu, R. Calderwood & C. E. Zsambok (Eds), *Decision Making in Action: Models and Methods*. Norwood, NJ: Ablex Publishing Corporation, 306–326.

Messer, S. B. (1976). Reflection-impulsivity: A review. *Psychological Bulletin, 83*, 1026–1052.

Metcalfe, J., & Shimamura, A. P. (1994). *Metacognition*. Cambridge, MA: The MIT Press.

Nelson, T. O. (1992). *Metacognition: Core Readings*. Boston: Allyn and Bacon.

Orasanu, J. M. (1993). Decision making in the cockpit. In E. L. Wiener, R. L. Helmreich, & B. G. Kanki (Eds.), *Cockpit Resource Management* (pp. 137–172). NY: Academic Press, Inc.

Patel, V. L., & Groen, G. J. (1991). The general and specific nature of medical expertise: A critical look. In: K. A. Ericsson & J. Smith (Eds), *Toward A General Theory of Expertise: Prospects and Limits* (pp. 93–125). Cambridge: Cambridge University Press.

Paul, R. W. (1987). Dialogical thinking: Critical thought essential to the acquisition of rational knowledge and passions. In: J. B. Baron & R. J. Sternberg (Eds), *Teaching Thinking Skills: Theory And Practice*. New York: W. H. Freeman and Company.

Pennington, N., & Hastie, R. (1993). A theory of explanation-based decision making. In: G. A. Klein, J. Orasanu, R. Calderwood & C. E. Zsambok (Eds.), *Decision Making in Action: Models and Methods* (pp. 188–201). Norwood, NJ: Ablex.

Ray, M., & Myers, R. (1986). *Creativity in Business*. New York: Doubleday.

Scott, W. R. (1998). *Organizations: Rational, Natural, and Open Systems*. Upper Saddle River, NJ: Prentice Hall.

Schmitt, J. F. (1994). *mastering Tactics: A Tactical Decision Games Workbook*. Quantico, VA: Marine Corps Association.

Serfaty, D. (1993). *hypotheses and Recent Findings on Command Decision-Making Expertise*. Presentation at U.S. Army Research Institute Workshop on Developing Expertise in Command Decision-Making, Fort Leavenworth, KS, February 4–5.

Shanteau, J. (1992). The Psychology of experts: An alternative view. In: G. Wright & F. Bolger (Eds), *Expertise and Decision Support*. New York: Plenum Press. The U.S. Marine Corps (1989). Warfighting. New York: Doubleday.

Shastri, L., & Ajjanagadde, V. (1993). From simple associations to systematic reasoning: A connectionist representation of rules, variables, and dynamic bindings using temporal synchrony. *Brain and Behavioral Sciences, 16*, 417–494.

Sniezek, J. A., & Henry, R. A. (1990). Revision, weighting, and commitment in consensus group judgment. *Organizational Behavior and Human Decision Processes, 45*(1), 66–84.

The U.S. Marine Corps (1989). *Warfighting*. New York: Doubleday.

Thompson, B. T., Cohen, M. S., & Shastri, L. (1997). *A Hybrid Architecture for Metacognitive Learning (Hybrid Architectures for Complex Learning Program, Office of Naval Research Contract No. N00014–95-C-0182)*. Arlington, VA: Cognitive Technologies.

Thompson, J. D. (1967). *Organizations in Action* New York: McGraw-Hill.

Toulmin, S. E. (1958). *The Uses of Argument*. Cambridge: Cambridge University Press.

Van Creveld, M. (1985). *Command in War*. Cambridge: Harvard University Press.

Voss, J. F., Wolfe, C. R., Lawrence, J. A., & Engle, R. A. (1991). From representation to decision: An analysis of problem solving in international relations. In: R. J. Sternberg & P. A. Frensch (Eds), *Complex Problem Solving: Principles and Mechanisms* (pp. 119–158). Hillsdale, NJ: Lawrence Erlbaum Associates.

Watson, S. R., & Buede, D. N. (1987). *Decision Synthesis*. New York: Cambridge University Press.

Yukl, G. (1998). *Leadership in Organizations*. Upper Saddle River, NJ: Prentice Hall.

7. USE OF COMMERCIAL, OFF-THE-SHELF, SIMULATIONS FOR TEAM RESEARCH

Clint A. Bowers and Florian Jentsch

INTRODUCTION

Because of the great importance of teams in organizations, there has been an increasing need to conduct research on what determines team performance and how team performance can be improved. Over the past 15 years, a number of approaches to studying teams have been taken, including the study of actual work teams on-the-job, research involving teams in part- or whole-task simulations, and investigations of team processes and performance in laboratory settings, with real or ad-hoc teams. One of the most puzzling questions to date in this area, however, has been the development, testing, and selection of valid and reliable tasks that can be used in the study of teams.

One method that has found wide application is the use of task simulations that are run on computers and present teams with relevant task cues on sensory displays (e.g. visual, auditory, kinesthetic). In fact, today's computer and display technologies allow researchers to create and conduct team simulations for an astounding array of realistic task settings (Bowers, Salas, Prince & Brannick, 1992; O'Neil, Chung & Brown, 1997; Swezey, Streufert, Satish & Siem, 1998; Weaver, Bowers, Salas & Cannon-Bowers, 1995). Whether it is flying an aircraft (D. Baker, Prince, Shrestha, Oser & Salas, 1993), controlling complex industrial processes (Caldwell & Everhart, 1998), or making tactical decisions in the military (Fletcher, 1999), computer simulations can create

Advances in Human Performance and Cognitive Engineering Research, Volume 1, pages 293–317.
2001 by Elsevier Science Ltd.
ISBN: 0-7623-0748-X

relevant and realistic cues that teams need to perform their tasks (Crookal & Arai, 1995; Jentsch, Hicks, Sierra & Bowers, 1996). Consequently, a review of the capabilities of computerized team tasks is indicated to identify future applications.

Technical Aspects of Computer-Based Team Tasks

The technical aspects of computer-based team tasks can be organized according to three major categorizations. First, simulations can be distinguished according to their level of "fidelity," that is by the degree to which they replicate the tasks and environments that teams are confronted with in the real world. Second, one can distinguish between those simulations that were specifically developed for team research and those that were adapted from commercial, off-the-shelf (COTS) software programs. Finally, one can categorize team simulations as those that are run on single workstations (the application to teams notwithstanding) versus those that are or can be networked on multiple computers. In the following sections, we review these three sets of variables in more detail.

"High-" vs. "Low-Fidelity" Simulations

The "fidelity" of simulators, although generally described as either "high" or "low," actually has several components (cf. Jentsch & Bowers, 1998). The first of these is the physical fidelity of the simulation soft- and hardware. Physical fidelity refers to the degree to which the physical environment of the task is recreated in the simulation. For example, an aircraft simulator that faithfully recreates the location, size, feel, weight, and color of the controls and displays is said to have higher physical fidelity than a simulator that represents the controls and displays of the simulated aircraft on a two-dimensional computer monitor.

A second component of a simulation's fidelity is its functional fidelity. Functional fidelity describes the degree to which the simulation replicates the functions and behavior of the system that is being simulated. A simulation of a stove that incorporates the changes in the temperature at which water boils with barometric altitude is said to have higher functional fidelity than one that does not. Likewise, an aircraft simulator that allows the simulation of an engine failure has higher functional fidelity than one that does not.

The third and final component of simulation fidelity is the one that is most difficult to define, describe, establish, and validate. At the same time, it is probably the most important component of fidelity. This third component is the psychological fidelity of the simulation, that is, the degree to which the simulation replicates the necessary and sufficient cues and consequences of a task. In a team simulation, critical cues could be environmental data, for example, that are relevant to weather decision-making, whether or not displayed in the same format as in the real world. To the extent that a simulation provides more of these critical cues needed by team members, it possesses a higher level of psychological fidelity than one that does not. Conversely, even a simulation with a setup of high physical fidelity may not possess a high level of psychological fidelity if it lacks functional fidelity of the knobs, levers, and other controls replicated in it.

It is sometime difficult to distinguish psychological fidelity from aspects of physical and functional fidelity. A simulation of the highest physical and functional fidelity will, by definition, also have a high level of psychological fidelity. However, it may provide not only the critical cues but also a large number of irrelevant ones. If, for example, the simulation is used to study (or train) communication skills to aircrew, the accurate replication of all engine controls and displays may not be needed, especially if none of the research or training examples involve engine parameters.

The bottom-line is that psychological fidelity is as much a function of the purpose and application of a simulation as of its physical and functional fidelity (Salas, Bowers & Rhodenizer, 1998). Only when the purpose and the application of a simulation are known, can an informed decision be made about the required physical and functional fidelity. In the past, this point has been largely overlooked in the development and selection of simulations. As a result, those who buy and employ simulations have tended to "aim high" on physical and (to a lesser degree) functional fidelity for their simulations. Consequently, physical fidelity has remained at center stage for many applications in research and training.

The definition of the relevant and required psychological fidelity for a simulation is important, insofar as the cost of computer-based simulations depends largely on the simulation's physical fidelity. Full-mission simulators, such as those certified by the Federal Aviation Administration (FAA) for pilot training and testing, employ technologies that replicate the physical environment inside and outside the aircraft as much as possible. Motion systems and large, high-definition, collimated visual displays in combination with simulator cabins replicate the physical reality of the vehicle or situation that is being simulated down to the last switch and lever. This has led to very realistic, yet also comparatively expensive task simulations for team research.

In addition to these expensive, full-mission simulations with their high degree of physical fidelity, however, a number of less expensive potential test-beds for team research has become available over the past two decades. The increase in the number and quality of relatively low-cost team tasks has been a function of hitherto unimaginable improvements in the processing speed and memory storage capability of personal computers. Often lacking a high degree of physical or even functional fidelity, these PC-based simulations are frequently referred to as "low-fidelity" simulations. However, because the level of psychological fidelity is so dependent upon the purpose of a research project and the application of the simulation, we believe it is more appropriate to refer to these simulations as "PC-based."

Although PC-based simulations have been used quite extensively in team research (e.g. Weaver et al., 1996), questions have remained even within the research community whether "gaming" can ever substitute for high-fidelity simulation or observation on-the-job. Team researchers who use PC-based ("low-fidelity") simulations have therefore found themselves facing a difficult decision: "Should we create/acquire simulations of high physical and functional fidelity, with all the attendant questions of cost, training time, and performance measurement?" Or, "should we create/acquire less-expensive PC-based simulations in the hope that they have the required level of psychological fidelity – and then having to defend the decision against those that doubt its validity?" Given that the latter approach involves much lower initial cost, it is probably the more desirable one in an austere research environment. However, in doing so it is vitally important to first identify the purposes for which a simulation would be used and then to establish its psychological fidelity. Finally, after selection, testing, and application of a simulation, there are several resources which can be used to make the case for the validity of the selected PC-based simulations for research and training purposes (e.g. Bowers, Jentsch & Salas, 1994; Driskell & Salas, 1992; Jentsch & Bowers, 1998).

Custom-built vs. Commercial Off-the-Shelf (COTS)
Team simulations used in research have come from two different sources. Initially, the majority of simulations used in team research were custom-built to replicate a particular task environment (e.g. the TANDEM and DEFTT simulations for naval team decision making; cf. Johnston, Poirier & Smith-Jentsch, 1998). Most current team simulations, however, now come from the area of computer gaming, that is, from the entertainment world. Consequently, they were developed for entertainment rather than with the researcher in mind. Yet, the adaptation of these low-cost simulations for team research, initially described by Bowers, Salas, Prince, and Brannick (1992), has become an acceptable way to conduct team research (Bowers, Jentsch & Salas, 1994; Driskell & Salas, 1992; Jentsch & Bowers, 1998) and team training (Prince & Jentsch, in press).

As indicated earlier, the success of an adaptation of a commercially developed simulation or game for research purposes is less a function of the simulation's physical and functional fidelity, but rather of its psychological fidelity. Those devices and simulations that replicate the critical cues and consequences of the task in question can usually be adapted quite well to research. One example that has found widespread use in team research is "Space Fortress," a game that has been used extensively in the study of team work and skill acquisition in teams. Although having very low physical and functional fidelity with respect to any real-world team task, Space Fortress provides team members with an interesting and challenging environment that allows researchers to study critical team processes, such as team learning and decision making (e.g. Shebilske, Jordan, Goettl & Day, 1999).

While some COTS software products have been successfully adapted for the study of teams, there have also been auspicious developments of computer software applications specifically for team research and training (e.g. Hollenbeck, Sego, Ilgen & Major, 1997; Swezey et al., 1998). These simulations are not derived from COTS software. Instead, they are the products of focused development for specific purposes. In fact, it can be argued that there are occasions in which the development of an inexpensive computer program for a specific team task is beneficial. For example, the "Team Track" research project conducted at UCF between 1993 and 1996 used a very short software program written in the Quick BASIC computer language to study the effects of feedback on team performance (Jentsch, Bowers, Compton, Navarro & Tait, 1996).

Single-Workstation vs. Networked Simulations
In addition to single-workstation games and simulations, the enhanced networking capability of single-user workstations has also led to an increasing number of networked, multi-player, multi-workstation simulations for team training and team performance assessment (cf. O'Neill, Chung & Brown, 1997). Initially, multi-player simulations tended to be custom-built for team research (cf. Weaver et al., 1995). Stelling (1999), for example, developed and validated a two-person team task that was programmed in Turbo Pascal 7.0. The emergence and proliferation of large-scale computer networks, specifically of the Internet and the World Wide Web (www), however, have now created a network capability that is available to virtually everyone. Consequently, companies producing computer games and simulations for entertainment purposes have begun to offer the majority of their new simulations with a multi-player capability. Many of these computer programs can be networked

using a local area network (LAN) among individual workstations, or they can be networked via the Internet and the World Wide Web.

Since team research inherently involves the study of multiple individuals, networking capability is generally considered a positive characteristic of a simulation. At the same time, using the Internet or the World Wide Web as the networking mechanism may have its drawbacks when planning team research. Limited bandwidth, server failures, and network traffic congestion are much more likely to affect a research study that uses the open architecture of the Internet or the World Wide Web than one that uses a local area network, direct point-to-point ("head-to-head") connections, or a custom-built intranet. Also, security of data collection may be compromised in the Internet's open architecture. When selecting a simulation for team research processes, therefore, scientists should critically review whether a COTS capability for networking through the Internet or the World Wide Web is indeed preferable to other networking solutions. Nevertheless, simulations that are created with any networking capability in mind are probably better suited for research purposes than those which were created as single-user software.

Summary

Three technical aspects must be considered when reviewing computer-based team tasks and simulations. The first of these is the "fidelity" of the simulation. As indicated above, the most important determinant of a simulation's suitability for team research is its psychological fidelity, that is, the degree to which the simulation presents the team with the critical cues and consequences of their tasks. Depending upon the research question, psychological fidelity may or may not be closely related to the more obvious aspects of physical and functional fidelity. Selection of a test-bed or simulation in the absence of clearly defined research goals will thus likely lead to "wrong guesses" with respect to the required levels of physical and functional fidelity.

A second important technical aspect when selecting team simulations is the question of whether to custom-build or to acquire COTS soft- and hardware. Custom-building is costly and will likely lead to products that are either too expensive because they are intended for too many purposes, or too limited in scope to be useful across a wide range of research questions.

An alternative to custom-building is the careful selection of COTS software. Because these simulations are usually intended for the highly competitive, but also very lucrative electronic gaming and entertainment market, they tend to incorporate relatively sophisticated software solutions. These solutions would be too expensive for small series, custom-built research software, but are typically easily amortized across the large volume sold in the entertainment market.

At the same time, simulations and test-beds developed for the entertainment market may have shortcomings in terms of their usefulness for research that are a function of the characteristics desired by their intended audience. A careful delineation of requirements for research (see the following sections) and review of COTS software with respect to these requirements and in light of the research application is therefore advisable before making the decision between COTS and custom-built software.

Finally, a third technical aspect that must be considered when selecting test-beds for team research is the capability to create networked team tasks. As we indicated earlier, not all networking capabilities may be useful for research under all circumstances. A test-bed, for example, that can only be networked through the open architecture of the Internet or the World Wide Web will face limitations and vagaries with respect to bandwidth, network congestion, and data security and may thus not be suitable for many research purposes. A software system, on the other hand, that does not have any a priori networking capability may only be suitable for team research after costly custom modifications. When selecting test-beds, therefore, careful attention must be given to the research purposes, set-ups, and research requirements desired of the test-bed. With respect to the latter, the following sections review two critical research requirements, namely the manipulation of independent variables and the measurement of dependent ones.

Research Requirements: Manipulation of Variables

Researchers typically are interested in the relationship between constructs; they want to study the effects of one construct on another. For example, team researchers may want to study the effect of team size on communication efficiency in teams. This means that they must be able to define and manipulate those independent variables that represent the construct that is supposed to execute the effect (e.g. team size). Additionally, researchers must be able to define and control those extraneous variables that represent constructs which may also affect the outcome constructs but which are not the focus of the investigation (e.g. size of the workspace). Finally, they must be able to define and measure those dependent variables that represent the construct that is being affected (i.e. communication efficiency). This section is concerned with the two former issues (i.e. manipulation of independent variables and control of extraneous variables). The next section then focuses on the issues involved in the measurement of dependent variables.

Manipulation of Independent Variables
A wide variety of variables have been suggested to affect team performance, from more auspicious ones (such as team size) to less obvious ones (e.g. the climate of the organization that houses the team). One model that incorporates a number of these variables is the Team Effectiveness Model as proposed by Salas, Dickinson, Converse, and Tannenbaum (1992). It is shown in Fig. 1.

Given the multitude of potential independent variables that researchers might want to manipulate, it is difficult to imagine a low-cost test bed that allows the manipulation of all of them at the same time. Consequently, it is important to identify those variables that are most likely to represent the constructs of most interest to team researchers.

Control of Extraneous Variables
In addition to manipulating the independent variables in a team study, researchers also want to be able to control extraneous variables. As indicated

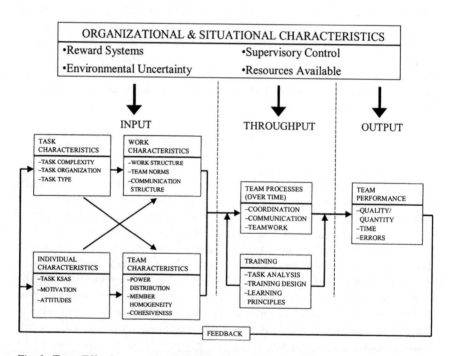

Fig. 1. Team Effectiveness Model (TEM; adapted from Salas, Dickinson, Converse, & Tannenbaum, 1992, p. 16).

earlier, extraneous variables represent all those constructs that may affect the relationship between the independent and dependent variables but which do not form the focus of the research study. Given how many constructs that can be hypothesized to affect team performance are represented in Fig. 1 above, it quickly becomes clear that control of extraneous variables is a particularly important step in team research to ensure its internal validity.

In our experience, the most important extraneous variable that must be controlled when conducting dynamic simulations (specifically with teams) is the difficulty of the task scenario the participants encounter (cf. Cannon-Bowers, Burns, Salas & Pruitt, 1998). Flights in an airplane, malfunctions in a power plant, or emergencies in the trauma center must be of comparable difficulty across study conditions. Otherwise, it will be almost impossible to disentangle the effects of the manipulations from those resulting from the differences in scenario difficulty.

Many of the early commercially available simulations and games used "canned" scenarios that were fixed with respect to the situations players would encounter. For example, the location of targets in a military simulation would be the same irrespective of how many times players engaged in a particular scenario. This made control of extraneous variables across experimental conditions and across study administrations comparatively easy. At the same time, however, the fixed nature of scenarios made it possible to learn and anticipate the challenges a scenario would provide. In the opinion of many critics, this latter effect reduced the desirability of the programs for the entertainment market that these products were intended for. Consequently, those developing software programs quickly begun to incorporate certain elements of randomness in the scenarios. In the newer products, the number of targets one will encounter in a particular scenario may be the same regardless of the scenario administration, but their location may change from administration to administration. By introducing such random variations, learning and anticipation are reduced, and the products are considered to longer remain interesting.

Unfortunately, introducing "random" changes in scenarios across administrations may have some negative side effects. Scenarios in team studies often attempt to capture such team skills as "providing backup," which is dependent upon a particular cue that must be consistently introduced at the same time and with the same strength. Random variations in the timing of a cue can quickly change the nature of a scenario so that the targeted skill is more or less appropriate. Hence, random variations that are created without careful consideration of the possible consequences for the research scenario are undesirable. When selecting COTS software for team research in particular, care must therefore be taken that the commercially attractive capability of "random scenarios" does not become a burden that may invalidate the research. Likewise, other changes across scenarios (such as external conditions like weather, day vs. night, etc.) must be carefully studied with respect to their impact on the desirable goal of controlling extraneous variables.

Summary

To study teams effectively, researchers must be able to manipulate the independent variables that form the focus of the study while controlling extraneous variables. Frameworks such as the Team Effectiveness Model (Salas et al., 1992) list a number of constructs that are of interest to team researchers. They can be used to identify both independent and extraneous variables of interest when selecting test-beds.

At the same time, the large number of variables that can be hypothesized to affect team performance makes it difficult to develop a definitive listing of required manipulations that a test-bed should allow for. Once the researchers have identified the variables they want to study, however, the selection of test-beds becomes easier. As we suggested, the decision between custom-built and COTS software will be strongly influenced by the list of variables that must be manipulated or controlled. Sometimes, when only a small set of variables must be manipulated, a custom-built test-bed of limited scope can be preferable over COTS software. Conversely, when several variables are of interest to the researcher, a selection of more than one COTS test-beds that have similar capabilities may be an appropriate solution. Having multiple test beds, whether COTS or custom-built, is in any case beneficial, as it allows researchers to conduct studies that focus on different variables and may allow the use of different populations (Johnston et al., 1998).

One major consideration during the selection of scenario-based software is the degree to which the scenario difficulty remains constant across administrations while allowing for a variety of scenarios. COTS software that promises "random" scenarios poses the danger that scenario difficulty also changes in "random" and, hence, unpredictable ways across scenario administrations. In this case, it will be very difficult to decompose the performance effects of the manipulated variables from that of varying scenario difficulty.

Research Requirements: Measurement

If the manipulation of independent variables and the control of extraneous variables are important characteristics in the selection of a test-bed, measurement of dependent variables must be considered the key characteristic without which a test-bed cannot and should not be used. Unfortunately, while the development of computers and of simulation software has made great strides in the past 15 years, it has not been mirrored by an equal advancement in the area of team performance measurement (O'Neil, E. Baker & Kazlauskas, 1992). Although there has been some progress, many questions still remain (Brannick, Salas & Prince, 1997; McIntyre & Salas, 1995). In the following sections, we review the literature on team performance measurement with respect to the lessons that can be learned for the selection of test-beds for team research.

Process vs. Outcome Measurements
One major distinction that affects team performance research more than other behavioral research is the distinction between the measurement of process and outcome variables (Cannon-Bowers & Salas, 1997). As indicated in Fig. 1 above, team processes such as communication and coordination are central to linking input and output variables. In fact, the requirement for interactions among team members is what defines teams and distinguishes them from individuals performing tasks. Consequently, team research has focused extensively on the study of team processes, and many team performance measures use team processes as critical dependent variables.

A typical, custom-built team performance test-bed that collects both process and outcome measures is the Distributed Dynamic Decision Making (DDD) paradigm, hosted on a network of SUN workstations at the University of Connecticut's CYBERLAB (Kleinman, Luh, Pattipaty & Serfaty, 1992). Outcome measures in the DDD paradigm include team reward earned, team-level accuracy, and team-level timeliness of behaviors and decisions. They can be combined into a composite measure of "team final strength" that represents the total outcome that a team achieved in the simulation.

Process measures in the DDD paradigm, on the other hand, include variables such as resource requests, resource transfers, etc. These measures can be clustered under the headings of either "strategy" or "coordination" variables.

While the DDD paradigm and comparable simulations (such as TANDEM or DEFTT) collect a number of process and outcome variables simultaneously, it is not entirely clear how close the linkage is between process and outcome in these simulations. There is thus still a need to better tie process together with outcome. One way to do this is the TARGETs methodology pioneered by NAWCTSD (Dwyer, Fowlkes, Oser & Salas, 1997). In TARGETs, perform-ance is measured by counting the number of processes a team exhibits that were a priori defined as promising the best overall outcome. Given that the link between process and outcome is established a priori, the collection of additional outcome variables may not be necessary. At the same time, even in TARGETs, the linkage between process and outcome is not firm; occasionally, even inefficient process may lead to effective results and vice versa.

Despite the progress made in improving the linkage between process and outcome measures of team performance measures, serious questions remain. It is not uncommon to find a set of results in team studies where process variables show strong effects of the manipulations under study, yet the outcome measures do not show parallel effects. In these cases, it is possible that: (a) differences in process are just not related to differences in outcomes (a rather unpleasant conclusion), or that (b) the outcome measures are not sensitive enough to pick up the effects of the manipulations. In either case, it behooves the researcher to look at both process and outcome variables when selecting a test-bed for team research.

Individual vs. Team-Level Measurements
In addition to the question of whether one should collect process or outcome measures (or both), the issue must be considered what the focus of the measurement should be. Specifically, does one want to measure at the individual or at the team level? As pointed out by Tesluk, Mathieu, Zaccaro, and Marks (1997), "the assessment of team performance within organizations requires [. . .] a consideration of individual versus collective contributions. [. . .] Yet, [. . .] this assumption is valid only for some collective work arrangements" (p. 198). For example, under pooled interdependence conditions as described by Saavedra et al. (1993), team members each contribute their efforts to the team's, without having to wait for others and their contributions. In this case, there is a direct linkage between an individual's contribution and the team's overall success; the team's collective output is merely the sum of the inputs made by individuals.

Under sequential interdependence conditions (such as is found at an assembly line), however, a team member's contribution is dependent upon a preceding team member's output. Hence, the second team member may be willing and able to put effort forth, but his/her actual contribution is limited by the output that those before him/her have generated. In this case, total output is not merely the sum of individual contributions, etc.

Since most team work situations occur under interdependence conditions that are more complex than pooled interdependence, individual-level measures cannot substitute for team-level observations. A typical Navy combat information center (CIC), for example, may contain up to 25 dedicated positions with specific roles, all of which interact in a complex and dynamic fashion (Johnston et al., 1998). In this situation, a variety of team- and individual-level process and outcome measures are needed to adequately diagnose performance (Smith-Jentsch, Payne & Johnston, 1998). For example, process and outcome measures are needed for each of the 25 positions, plus process and outcome measures that describe the team as a whole. Each of the process measures must use specific behavioral examples to be valid, and outcome measures must accurately capture the nature of the interdependence situation encountered by the team members.

As is evident from the example of the shipboard CIC, the collection of such a large number of measures involves significant effort. Currently, multiple raters are still needed to observe individuals. These raters must have had appropriate inter-rater agreement (training), and must coordinate so that critical observations are not left out while others are duplicated. As a result, researchers must resist the temptation to try and collect all possible data. Instead, a selective approach that defines what should be observed, at what level, and why, is needed. Only in this fashion will it be likely that there is a strong link between process and outcome measures, and between individual- and team-level measures.

Summary

Performance measurement in teams, regardless of the test-bed employed, remains a serious bottleneck in team research. Depending upon the team set-up, the interdependencies within the team, the team size, and a host of other variables, researchers must select an appropriate set of measures. These measures can focus on process or on outcome, and they can be collected at the individual- or team-level. Each has advantages and disadvantages, and it is therefore particularly important to match the measures to the purpose of the research. Consequently, it is unlikely that there is one set of measures available that is suitable for all research purposes.

Regardless of whether team performance measures are focussed on the individual or on the whole team, and irrespective of whether processes or outcomes are measured, however, there are a number of minimum characteristics that team performance measures must have. The following list of requirements was assembled by Cannon-Bowers and Salas (1997) for team performance measures in training. It is equally applicable to team performance measures that are used in research with team simulations.

(1) Team performance measures must consider multiple levels of measurement.

(2) Team performance measures must address process as well as outcome.

(3) Team performance measures (in training) must be able to describe, evaluate, and diagnose performance.

(4) Team performance measures must provide a basis for remediation.

While the last two criteria may initially seem to be specific only to training, they have important implications for team research as well. These implications are, first, that team performance measures must accurately describe what happens in teams, why, and what that means for the relationships among the constructs under study. Second, the measures must allow team performance researchers to make decisions how to change manipulations or levels of extraneous variables in response to study findings. Finally, all this should ideally be possible in real time, so as to avoid large gaps between studies.

The last of the criteria mentioned in the preceding paragraphs (i.e. real-time measurement capability) is one that so far has largely eluded team researchers. Most performance measures (especially those involving processes) require the transcribing and coding of video- and/or audio-taped communications and other team behaviors. A test-bed that incorporates the ability for automated, real-time measurement and analysis of team performance measures would therefore be particularly desirable.

In summary, the selection of adequate team performance measures remains a bottleneck in the development and application of test-beds for team research. While the selection of adequate dependent variables is the most critical step in the selection of a test-bed, others (such as those discussed in the preceding sections) also affect the suitability of a team simulation for research. More knowledge about the constructs team performance researchers are interested to study is therefore desirable to avoid costly mistakes in the selection of test-beds.

EVALUATION OF COTS SIMULATIONS

Approach

The goal of this effort was to review the existing COTS products to identify candidates for team research. A wide range of COTS programs were considered using magazines, demonstration disks, web sites, and actual software products.

Each product was evaluated using several criteria. These included system requirements, independent variables that can be manipulated, dependent variables that can be observed, and special considerations such a violent content. Based on this review, specific games were studied in additional detail. The overall review is provided in Table 1. Selected games are discussed afterward.

Table 1. Games Reviewed.

Name	Version	Plat-form	RAM rq.	Other Req.	Genre	Multi-player?	Sce-nario Gene-rator?	Fixed Sce-narios?	Per-formance Recor-ding?	Est. Training time	Appro-priate Sample	Other	Con-struct	Further Eval?
Harpoon	Admirals Ed.	486+	8	M	RT Strategy	No	Yes	Yes	Poor	>4 hours	novice-expert	Poor Usability	SA, DM, B	No
Sin	1	P166+	16		FPS	Net	No	Yes	Poor	1 hr	novice-expert	Poor Usability	SA	No
Operational Art of War	1	P100+	16		TB Strategy	H2H	Yes	Yes	Excel-lent	>4 hrs	novice-expert	Domain Knowl. Req.	DM, B	No
European Air War	1	P166+	32	Direct x, M,S	Sim	Net	No	Yes	Poor	1–2 hrs	novice-expert	Domain Knowl. Req.	SA, DM, B	No
Tribal Rage	1	P166+	16	M	RT Strategy	No	No	Yes	Fair	1–2 hrs	novice-expert	Very Playable	SA, DM, B, L	No
Plane Crazy	1	P166+	16	3D	Sim	H2H, Net	No	Yes	None	1 hr	novice		SA	No
Xenocracy	1	P166+	32	M, J	Sim	H2H, Net	No	No	Poor	>4 hrs	novice	Very Difficult	SA	No
MAX 2	Beta	P166+	16	M	RT Strategy	H2H, Net	Yes	Yes	Fair	5–6 hrs	novice	Compli-cated	SA, DM, B	No
Wargasm	1	P166+	16	3D	Sim	H2H, Net	No	No	Good	2 hrs	novice	Arcade-like	SA	No
Heavy Gear II	Beta	P166+	64	3D	Sim	H2H, Net	No	Yes	Good	2 hrs	novice	Arcade-like minor Violence	SA, DM	No
Settlers III	1	166+	16	M	Strategy	Net	Yes	Yes	Fair	2–3hrs	novice		DM	No
Future Cop LAPD	1	166+	16	M, 3D	FPS	Net	No	Yes	Poor	2 hrs	novice	Arcade-like	SA	No
Shogo: MAD	Beta	166+	32	M, 3D	FPS	No	No	Yes	Poor	2 hrs	novice	Arcade-like, Violence	SA	No
Recoil	Beta	133+	16	M, 3D	Sim	H2H, Net	No	Yes	Good	1–2 hrs	novice		SA, DM	No
Heretic II	1	200+	32	3D	FPS	H2H, Net	No	Yes	Poor	2–3 hrs	novice		SA	No
Descent 3	1.02	200+	32	3D, JS	RT Strategy	H2H, Net	No	Yes	Poor	3–4 hrs	novice	Very Difficult	SA, DM	No

Table 1. Continued.

Name	Version	Platform	RAM rq.	Other Req.	Genre	Multi-player?	Scenario Generator?	Fixed Scenarios?	Performance Recording?	Est. Training time	Appropriate Sample	Other	Construct	Further Eval?
Ruthless.com	1	133+	16	M	TB Strategy	Net	No	Yes	Good	2–3 hrs	novice	Business-based	DM	Yes
Half-Life Team Fortress	1.0.8	200+	32	3D, M	FPS	Net,	Yes	Yes	Fair	1–2 hrs	novice	Violence	SA, DM	Yes
Warzone 2100	Demo 1.0	166+	32	3D, M	RT Strategy	Net	No	Yes	Poor	3–4 hrs	novice	Complicated	SA, DM, P	No
Rainbow Six	1	200+	32	3D,M	FPS	Net, Team	No	Yes	Poor	3–4 hrs	novice-expert	Complicated, Violence	SA, DM	No
Quake II	1	166+	32	3D	FPS	Net, Team	Yes	Yes	Poor	1–2 hrs	novice	Very Violent	SA	No
Chron X	1	133+	16	M	Strategy	Net	No	Yes	Poor	3–4 hrs	novice	Complicated	DM	No
Delta Force	0.09.01.07D	133+	32	3D, M	FPS	Net, team	No	Yes	Poor	2–3 hrs	novice	Violence	SA	No
Commandos	Demo 1.0	166+	16	3D, M	RT Strategy	Net, Team	No	Yes	Poor	3–4 hrs	novice-expert	Mild Violence	SA, DM, B	No
Slave Zero	Pre-Demo	166+	32	3D, M	FPS	Net	No	Yes	Poor	1–2 hrs	novice	Mild Violence	SA	No
Star Trek Fleet Command	Demo 1.0	166+	32	3D,M	RT Strategy	Net	No	Yes	Poor	3–4 hrs	novice	Mild Violence	SA, DM	No
Drakan	Demo 1.0	166+	32	3D, M	Action		No	No	Poor	1–2 hrs	novice	Mild Violence	SA	No
Hidden & Dangerous	Demo 1.0	233+	32	3D, M	FPS	Team	No	Yes	Fair	1–2 hrs	novice	Mild Violence	SA, DM, C, B	No
Army Men III	Demo 1.0	166+	32	3D, M	RT Strategy	Net	No	Yes	Poor	1–2 hrs	novice	Mild Violence	SA, DM	No

Table 1. Continued.

	Platform		Speed	RAM	Other Req.	Genre	Multiplayer?				Time	Skill		Construct	
Unreal Tournament	Demo	3.32	166+	32	3D, M	FPS	Net, Team	No	No	Poor	1–2 hrs	novice	Moderate Violence	SA	No
Delta Force 2	Demo	1.1	166+	32	3D, M	FPS	Net, Team	No	No	Poor	3–4 hrs	novice	Moderate Violence	SA, DM, P	No
Rogue Spear		1	200+	64	3D, M	FPS	Net, Team	No	Yes	Poor	5+ hrs	novice	Moderate Violence	SA, DM, P	No
Antietam	Demo	1.0	166+	32	3D, M	RT Strategy	Net, Team	Yes	Yes	Very Good	1–2 hrs	novice		DM, P	Yes
Worms II		1.1	166+	32	3D, M	TB Strategy	Net	No	Yes	Poor	1–2 hrs	novice	Very Playable	DM	No
Nerf Arena Blast	Demo	1.0	200+	32	3D, M	FPS	Net, Team	No	No	Poor	1–2 hrs	novice	Very Playable	SA	No
Close Combat IV	Demo	1.0	200+	32	3D, M	RT Strategy	Net, Team	No	No	Poor	4–5 hrs	novice	Complicated	DM	No

Notes: Platform:

Processing speed in MHz

RAM req.: Random Access Memory required in MegaBytes (MB)

Other Req.: 3D (3-D accelerator card), M (Mouse)

Genre: Action, FPS (First Person Shooter), RT Strategy (Real-time Strategy), Sim (Simulation), TB Strategy (Turn-based strategy)

Multiplayer?: Team, Net (Internet, www), H2H (Head to Head)

Construct: B (Briefing), C (Coordination), DM (Decision Making), P (Planning), SA (Situation Awareness)

Examples of Games Suitable for Team Research

Sid Meier's Antietam (Firaxis Games)
Antietam is a civil war simulation. Players are assigned to either the union or
confederate armies. In multi-player mode, players are further assigned to
brigades within armies. The players are required to utilize a fixed pool to
resources to achieve victory. Unlike other traditional war games, this game
requires relatively little knowledge of civil war era weapons or tactics. Rather,
the game is designed to allow novice players to play with relatively little
training. More difficult scenarios allow for studies of skill acquisition and
transfer of training. The multiple brigade structure also affords many
opportunities to manipulate training conditions.

Several factors suggest that this game might be an effective research test bed.
First, relative to other games it has very reasonable hardware demands. It is
advertised to run on a 90 MHz Pentium with 32MB of RAM. Furthermore, it
can be played using a relatively low-end graphics card. Thus, an entire
network-based research platform could be constructed at very low cost. Game
content is generally inoffensive. Brigade casualties are represented by
horizontal soldiers, but there is no graphic violence.

This game is also effective in that in includes a tutorial. The tutorial is very
effective in teaching players how to use the controls and simple elements of
strategy. This will allow standardized training across studies.

Finally, Antietam provides performance recording that is superior to most
other games. Data are collected at the team and player level, a rarity in
computer gaming. Unfortunately, these data cannot be written to disk
automatically.

Ruthless.com (Red Storm Entertainment)
Ruthless.com is a turn-based strategy game deployed in a business setting.
Players are required to utilize their resources to bring about the greatest long-
term profit to their organization. In so doing, players may make both
investment-based and destruction-based decisions. In other words, they can
focus on building their own business or destroying their opponent's. The
decision-making requirements, therefore, are challenging enough for research
use.

The game provides several advantages for researchers. Like Antietam, it
requires only minimal hardware to run effectively. It can be used on a 120MHz
Pentium and does not require a 3D accelerator at all. Thus, it can be run

effectively on machines typically found in surplus. Multi-player capability can be established via modem or a TCP/IP network. In multi-player mode, players can work cooperatively against another team or against an artificially intelligent opponent. Game content might be offensive to some. Strategies that can be employed include sabotaging or assassinating rival players. These actions are not displayed in a graphic manner, however.

Ruthless.com provides an on-line tutorial that, along with a written text, is effective in providing the skills required to play the game. This, combined with a very intuitive point-and-click interface should keep training costs very reasonable and make it easy to provide standardized training across studies.

The game provides rudimentary data collection that is limited to individual player scores across three variables. These data would probably have to be augmented by real-time recording by observers to be useful for research. However, the game also provides a chat mode that will allow researchers to capture team processes for later analysis.

Fleet Command (Jane's Combat Simulations)
Fleet Command is a real-time naval strategy game. In single player mode, players assume the role of battle group commander. In multi-player mode, players command specific group assets in a cooperative or competitive mode. In both cases players are required to attend to both the physical position of their assets as well as resource management, engagements, and so forth.

Fleet Command is advertised to run on 200 MHz, 32 MB machines with a 2MB graphics card. However, a more powerful system (300 MHz, 64 MB RAM, and Voodoo graphics is recommended for acceptable play character-istics, especially in a networked game). Multi-player games can be deployed over an on-line gaming service or by using a TCP/IP network. Content should not be objectionable.

The key advantage of Fleet Command is its realistic warfare modeling. Game assets perform very similarly to their real-life counterparts. Experienced naval personnel should find the game reasonably realistic. However, more training will be required to use this game with novices. The game does include a tutorial that is effective in teaching game controls. However, the tutorial is not effective in teaching strategy or weapons characteristics.

Data collection in Fleet Command is fair. The game records asset loss and mission objectives. However, additional real-time data recording is probably required for effective research use. Fleet Command does include a chat option in multi-player mode for analysis of team process, but the interface is difficult to use and might interfere with performance.

Half Life: Team Fortress Classic (Valve)
Team Fortress Classic (TFC) is a modification to the popular Half Life game. TFC create a two-team game in which teams compete for a specific goal. The game is compelling because it allows players to assume one of several roles, each critical for overall team success. Thus, the game provides an excellent platform for studying planning, situation awareness, and adaptability.

The game requires fairly high-end hardware for effective performance. A 300 MHz Pentium with 32 MB of RAM and a Voodoo graphics card is recommended. The game makes excellent use of sound, so a sound card and speakers are recommended. TFC can be deployed using a modem or a TCP/IP network.

TFC provides an on-board tutorial that is effective in teaching the complicated control system. Because the game requires both keyboard and mouse inputs, players will require several practice trials to become effective. Furthermore, the on-board training must be augmented by training about the game's specific roles for effective team performance to result. Teams will probably require a reasonable amount of practice to become competent.

Data collection is this game's chief weakness. The game collects data about overall team performance but there are no data about individual players. A comprehensive rating program will probably be required to make this an effective research platform.

DISCUSSION

A number of criteria must be considered when selecting a test-bed for team research. Technical criteria include the level of fidelity, the match-up between software and (existing) hardware, and the selection of networking solutions that best address the research needs. Additionally, researcher must be able to manipulate those independent variables, control those extraneous variables, and measure those dependent variables that represent the constructs of interest to them. Matching all these criteria for a test-bed is indeed a tall order, especially in an environment of austere budgets and reduced study times. It is therefore important to identify the needs of an organization that embarks upon team performance research before making recommendations for the selection of test-beds.

CONCLUSIONS

Based on the results of the current research, the following conclusions can be drawn.

(1) Research on teams involves a large number of constructs that are of interest to researchers. Hence, it is difficult to predict which variables researchers will choose to manipulate, control, and measure. Consequently, it is unlikely that there is a single test-bed that will allow for the study of all potential variables. This reduces the probability that one, custom-built software product can be used to address the research needs of an entire organization.

(2) Commercial, off-the-shelf computer programs can provide a low-cost alternative to custom-built software for team research purposes. Because of the large and very competitive market in the computer gaming/entertainment industry, COTS products from this area tend to be relatively inexpensive while providing sophisticated stimuli and comparatively realistic task simulations. At the same time, not all features of COTS software that are of benefit in the entertainment market are also helpful to the team researcher. The introduction of "random" scenarios, for example, creates significant problems for researchers who want to use strictly controlled scenarios. Likewise, a networking capability only over the Internet or the World Wide Web may not be suitable in an environment where confidential data collection is a prime concern for the protection of human subjects.

(3) When a range of variables must be manipulated, it is sometimes possible to select a group of COTS products, each of which allows manipulation of a specific (sub-)set of variables. Occasionally, however, the differences between the products in the group may make the transfer of research results across test-beds difficult, if not impossible. In this case, the development and validation of custom software with limited purpose may be the better alternative.

(4) Among the technical and psychometric questions related to the selection of test-beds for team research (regardless of whether COTS or custom-built), performance measurement remains the major bottleneck. In particular, the definition, measurement, and validation of appropriate dependent variables for team research continues to pose problems. While great strides have been made in the capabilities of low-cost, PC-based simulations with respect to the manipulation of independent variables, equal improvements on the performance measurement side have not materialized.

(5) COTS software in particular, while usually less expensive per copy than custom-built software, is traditionally not created with the rigid requirements of performance measurement for research in mind. Performance measures in COTS software tend to be outcome-, rather than process-oriented, and they are often at the individual level, rather than at the team

level. The selection and application of COTS software in team research must therefore be handled judiciously.

(6) Finally, because performance measurement remains an issue that limits progress in team research, scarce research and development resources may be spent best on improving the theory and practice of appropriate team performance measures. Instead of attempting to build one, custom-made software product that can answer all team performance research questions, we believe it is more beneficial to apply the resources to the development of strategies and tools that improve the reliability and validity of team performance measures. The results of such a program of research could then effectively be devoted to the development of valid team performance measures that can be overlaid onto relatively inexpensive COTS software.

In summary, we believe that the development of improved performance measures, when combined with the judicious selection and application of COTS software, promises the greatest potential return on investment for team performance researchers. Because COTS simulations/games can play a significant role in future research, we offer some guidelines in the following sections regarding the appropriate selection of COTS software.

Guidelines for the Selection of COTS Software

(1) *Specify the constructs that shall be studied.* Selection of COTS software in the absence of clear specifications of the independent, extraneous, and dependent variables will likely be unsuccessful.

(2) *Create a list of key variables that would suitably represent the constructs.* Operationalization of key constructs will help in the identi-fication of alternative test-beds. It will also allow the identification of the appropriate levels of physical, functional, and psychological fidelity.

(3) *Review COTS software with respect to these key variables.* If no single software product fulfills all of the requirements, consider using a group of COTS software products in a "back-to-back" research design.

(4) *Consider the wisdom of networking capability over the Internet or the World Wide Web.* Limited bandwidth, server failures, and network traffic congestion may endanger data collection. Openness of the Internet's network architecture may compromise the confidentiality of data.

(5) *Consider the wisdom of automatic or random scenario generation.* Auto-matic or random scenario generation, while attractive for the entertainment market, may severely threaten the internal validity of team studies. Difficulty of simulation scenarios is one of the variables that strongly affect team performance processes and outcomes.

(6) *Match your software to your hardware.* When selecting COTS software, make sure to match the software needs to the existing hardware. "Minimum" requirements listed on many COTS products are truly "minimum;" using minimum hardware may lead to simulations that are so slow or cumbersome that they are unsuitable for research. It is better to use a less sophisticated COTS software product that has only 80% of the capabilities but runs reliably 100% of the time, than to have one that has 100% of the requirements but only runs 80% of the time.

(7) *Select the most appropriate (set of) COTS software product(s).* Based on the review of the critical constructs and variables, the required manipulations, as well as considering hardware, network, and scenario generation requirements, select a set of target products. Then test the products on your hardware and network setup to identify whether their technical aspects are suitable for your intended purpose.

(8) *Spend most of your effort on identifying and validating performance measures.* Performance measurement in teams is still the major bottleneck of team studies. It is better to use a less sophisticated test-bed but get valid and reliable data than to use a very sophisticated test-bed without strong performance measures.

(9) *Validate your selection through small-scale testing.* After selecting your hard- and software setup, developing your manipulations, and creating your performance measures, conduct thorough testing before fielding the test-bed. The importance of manipulation checks cannot be overstated. If you are manipulation scenario difficulty, for example, make sure to measure how difficult participants think the various scenarios are. Likewise, when manipulating cues in sensory displays, study whether these changes can be perceived by participants.

(10) *Conduct follow-up reviews. COTS software changes rapidly.* Hence, a product that is available today may not have any support tomorrow. Conversely, subsequent versions of the same software may be more, or less, suitable for research than preceding ones. Conduct periodic reviews of the available products to identify potential candidates for future test-beds.

REFERENCES

Baker, D., Prince, C., Shrestha, L., Oser, R., & Salas, E. (1993). Aviation computer games for crew resource management training. *International Journal of Aviation Psychology, 3*(2), 143–156.

Bowers, C., Salas, E., Prince, C., & Brannick, M. (1992). Games teams play: A method for investigating team coordination and performance. *Behavior Research Methods, Instruments & Computers, 24*(4), 503–506.

Bowers, C., Jentsch, F., & Salas, E. (1994). *Studying automation in the lab – Can you? Should you?* Proceedings of the 21st Conference of the Western European Association of Aviation Psychologists, March 28–March 31, 1994, Dublin, Ireland. Avebury, England: Ashgate.

Brannick, M. T., Salas, E., & Prince, C. (Eds) (1997). *Team performance assessment and measurement: Theory, methods, and applications*. Mahwah, NJ: Lawrence Erlbaum Associates.

Caldwell, B. S., & Everhart, N. C. (1998). Information flow and development of coordination in distributed supervisory control teams. *International Journal of Human-Computer Interaction, 10*(1), 51–70.

Cannon-Bowers, J. A., Burns, J. J., Salas, E., & Pruitt, J. S. (1998). Advanced technology in scenario-based training. In: J. A. Cannon-Bowers & E. Salas (Eds), *Making Decisions Under Stress: Implications for Individual and Team Training* (pp. 365–374). Washington, D.C.: American Psychological Association.

Cannon-Bowers, J., & Salas, E. (1997). A framework for developing team performance measures in training. In: M. T. Brannick, E. Salas, & C. Prince (Eds), *Team Performance Assessment and Measurement: Theory, Methods, and Applications* (pp. 45–62). Mahwah, NJ: Lawrence Erlbaum Associates.

Crookall, D., & Arai, K. (Eds) (1995). *Simulation and gaming across disciplines and cultures: ISAGA at a watershed* (Proceedings of the Meeting of the International Simulation and Gaming Association, July 1994, Ann Arbor, Michigan). Ann Arbor, MI: International Simulation and Gaming Association.

Driskell, J. E., & Salas, E. (1992). Can you study real teams in contrived settings? The value of small group research to understanding teams. In: R. E. Swezey & E. Salas (Eds), *Teams – Their Training and Performance* (pp. 101–124). Norwood, NJ: Ablex.

Dwyer, D. J., Fowlkes, J. E., Oser, R. L., & Salas, E. (1997). Team performance measurement in distributed environments: The TARGETs methodology. In: M. T. Brannick, E. Salas, & C. Prince (Eds), *Team Performance Assessment and Measurement: Theory, Methods, and Applications* (pp. 137–153). Mahwah, NJ: Lawrence Erlbaum Associates.

Fletcher, J. D. (1999). Using networked simulation to assess problem solving by tactical teams. *Computers in Human Behavior, 15*(3–4), 375–402.

Hollenbeck, J. R., Sego, D. J., Ilgen, D. R., & Major, D. A. (1997). Team decision-making accuracy under difficult conditions: Construct validation of potential manipulations using TIDE[2] simulation. In: M. T. Brannick, E. Salas & C. Prince (Eds), *Team Performance Assessment and Measurement: Theory, Methods, and Applications* (pp. 111–136). Mahwah, NJ: Lawrence Erlbaum Associates.

Jentsch, F., & Bowers, C. (1998). Evidence for the validity of low-fidelity simulation in aircrew research. *International Journal of Aviation Psychology, 8*(3), 243–260.

Jentsch, F., Bowers, C., Compton, D., Navarro, G., & Tait, T. (1996). "Team Track": A tool for investigating tracking performance in teams. *Behavior Research Methods, Instruments, & Computers, 28*(3), 411–417.

Jentsch, F., Hicks, J., Sierra, C., & Bowers, C. (1996). *Investigating low-fidelity simulations for team situation awareness research*. (Technical report submitted to the Naval Air Warfare Center Training Systems Division). Orlando: University of Central Florida.

Johnston, J. H., Poirier, J., & Smith-Jentsch, K. A. (1998). Decision making under stress: Creating a research methodology. In: J. A. Cannon-Bowers & E. Salas (Eds), *Making Decisions*

Under Stress: Implications for Individual and Team Training (pp. 39–59). Washington, DC: American Psychological Association.

Kleinman, D. L., Luh, P. B., Pattipatti, K. R., & Serfaty, D. (1992). Mathematical models of team performance: A distributed decision-making approach. In: R. E. Swezey & E. Salas (Eds), *Teams – Their Training and Performance* (pp. 177–217). Norwood, NJ: Ablex.

McIntyre, R. M., & Salas, E. (1995). Measuring and managing for team performance. In: R. A. Guzzo & E. Salas (Eds), *Team Effectiveness and Decision Making in Organizations* (pp. 9–45). San Francisco: Jossey-Bass.

O'Neil, Jr., H. F., Baker, E. L., & Kazlauskas, E. J. (1992). Assessment of team performance. In: R. E. Swezey & E. Salas (Eds), *Teams – Their Training and Performance* (pp. 153–175). Norwood, NJ: Ablex.

O'Neil, Jr., H. F., Chung, G. K. W., & Brown, R. S. (1997). Use of networked simulations as a context to measure team competencies. In: H. F. O'Neil Jr. (Ed.), *Workforce Readiness: Competencies and Assessment* (pp. 411–452). Mahwah, NJ: Lawrence Erlbaum Associates.

Prince, C., & Jentsch, F. (in press). Crew resource management training with low-fidelity devices. In: E. Salas, C. Bowers & E. Edens, (Eds), *Resource Management in Organizations*. Mahwah, NJ: Lawrence Erlbaum Associates.

Saavedra, R., Earley, C. P., & Van Dyne, L. (1993). Complex interdependence in task-performing groups. *Journal of Applied Psychology, 78*(1), 61–72.

Salas, E., Bowers, C. A., & Rhodenizer, L. (1998). It is not how much you have but how you use it: Toward a rational use of simulation to support aviation training. *International Journal of Aviation Psychology, 8*(3), 197–208.

Salas, E., Dickinson, T. L., Converse, S. A., & Tannenbaum, S. I. (1992). Toward an understanding of team performance and training. In: R. E. Swezey & E. Salas (Eds), *Teams – Their Training and Performance* (pp. 3–29). Norwood, NJ: Ablex.

Shebilske, W. L., Jordan, J. A., Goettl, B. P., & Day, E. A. (1999). Cognitive and social influences in training teams for complex skills. *Journal of Experimental Psychology: Applied, 5*(3), 227–249.

Smith-Jentsch, K. A., Johnston, J. H., & Payne, S. C. (1998). Measuring team-related expertise in complex environments. In: J. A. Cannon-Bowers & E. Salas (Eds), *Making Decisions Under Stress: Implications for Individual and Team Training* (pp. 61–87). Washington, DC: American Psychological Association.

Stelling, D. (1999). *Teamarbeit in Mensch-Maschine Systemen* [teamwork in human-machine systems; in German]. Göttingen, Germany/ Seattle, WA: Hogrefe.

Swezey, R. W., Streufert, S., Satish, U., & Siem, F. M. (1998). Preliminary development of a computer-based team performance assessment simulation. *International Journal of Cognitive Ergonomics, 2*(3), 163–179.

Tesluk, P., Mathieu, J. E., Zaccaro, S. J., & Marks, M. (1997). Task and aggregation issues in the analysis and assessment of team performance. In: M. T. Brannick, E. Salas, & C. Prince (Eds), *Team Performance Assessment And Measurement: Theory, Methods, and Applications* (pp. 197–224). Mahwah, NJ: Lawrence Erlbaum Associates.

Weaver, J. L., Bowers, C. A., Salas, E., & Cannon-Bowers, J. A. (1995). Networked simulations: New paradigms for team performance research. *Behavior Research Methods, Instruments & Computers, 27*(1), 12–24

Wellington, W. J., & Faria, A. J. (1996). Team cohesion, player attitude, and performance expectations in simulation. *Simulation & Games, 27*(1), 23–40.

8. UNDERSTANDING HUMAN PERFORMANCE IN COMPLEX ENVIRONMENTS: RESEARCH PARADIGMS AND EMERGING APPLICATION AREAS

James M. Hitt II, Steven J. Kass, Katherine A. Wilson and Eduardo Salas

INTRODUCTION

In the latter half of the 20th century we have seen technological advances take place at rapid rates not approached in any other era. Inventions such as television, jet aircraft, personal computers, and more recently, re-usable space vehicles, communication satellites, electronic banking, the internet and other innovations have had the effect of shrinking our world while at the same time permitting an expansion through increased plans for life in space. Maybe the most influential aspect of these complex systems is the nearly instantaneous electronic access and transfer of information worldwide. These changes are already having a profound effect on the world's population, from the way children are being educated to how adults carry out their banking. It is not uncommon to hear about computer-literate toddlers, while also knowing elderly individuals who struggle to use an automatic teller machine. With technological advances such as distance learning, students can acquire an

Advances in Human Performance and Cognitive Engineering Research, Volume 1,
pages 319–337.

education without ever seeing the inside of a classroom. Likewise, people can work, get paid, shop, and pay bills not only without the need for actual currency, but possibly without ever leaving home. At this rate of change it is staggering to think what this new millennium will bring.

In order to transition smoothly into the new millenium, the task of human factors scientists and practitioners will become more challenging. For example, human factors scientists will need to know the capabilities and limitations of a wider segment of the population. The users of complex systems will not only range from the very young to the very old, but as the planet continues to figuratively shrink, these people include more diverse cultures, speak a variety of languages, all with the common need to communicate.

Similarly, many questions must be addressed regarding the social impact of these technological advances on the people of the 21st century. As technology advances, our expectations increase as well. For example, ever increasing computer processing power raises the acceptable standard for student's school work, training simulation systems, personal and commercial transportation, special effects in cinematography and entertainment software, recreational activities, and even the design of common household appliances and conveniences. How will the decreased face-to-face interaction, afforded by electronic communication, affect the social skills and norms of the next generation? What effect will increased automation and computer assistance have on the cognitive, social, and motor skills we now take for granted?

In light of the above discussion, the purpose of this chapter is to highlight a number of research foci for understanding human performance in a more complex and technologically advanced world. The topics selected for discussion are neither exhaustive nor comprehensive, just illustrative. The topics we have selected represent a broad spectrum of emerging research paradigms and critical domains in need of research. Our aim is to raise awareness of how these research paradigms can contribute to our understanding of human performance in complex environments as well as how the selected application domains need research with a focus on human performance.

HUMAN PERFORMANCE AND TECHNOLOGY: A FEW OBSERVATIONS

We begin, as background, with a few (some obvious and others not so obvious) observations. First, the computer systems developed for today's industries are very complex. This complexity can be based on the system architecture, the knowledge and skills necessary for effective operation, or simply based on the usability of the system. The American Heritage Dictionary (1995) defines complex as "consisting of interconnected and interwoven parts; composite; compound." The definition is useful as it implies a certain level of connected parts as the base for complexity. Systems today may consist of thousands of small parts working in unison to complete certain tasks. The key point to share with the reader is that complex does not translate to difficult. Advances in microprocessor technology have decreased the footprint of supercomputers and mainframes from the entire space of large office floors to just a single corner in one room. We can now do more with less. For example, the first computer programming languages were difficult to use except by those who helped design the systems. The change from command-based programming to icon-based programming has provided access to a larger portion of the population. Learning curves have been shortened and retention rates are higher due to the limits of human cognition (i.e. memory) not being taxed beyond its capabilities.

Second observation. The complexity of today's systems is related to dynamic environments and the ability to multi-task activities. Each user has different requirements of their computer systems. The ability for new systems to adjust performance to help achieve the user's goals effectively and efficiently is crucial. Systems with the ability to recognize patterns of performance, adjust operating parameters, and perform this function all without the user being interrupted will become the norm and not the exception.

Multi-tasking is another great advantage of high level systems. We are observing trends illustrating work is no longer inhibited by technological flaws, only by limitations of the human. The ability to obtain, manipulate, and model information in real-time is a great advantage of high-end systems. One such example is the meteorological systems now used to track hurricanes. Previous models were less accurate in predicting a storm's path of destruction, thus providing little preparation time, while costing many lives and millions of dollars. The new systems provide both larger amounts of meteorological information coupled with an increase in the accuracy of the hurricane parameters and allow for earlier warnings.

Although the increased complexity of many systems is hidden from the user through effective and clever interface design, the fact still remains these complexities exist and often are the driving factor in user complaints. The continued increase in interface layers, as a solution to additional information is inadequate in many instances. We must design systems which will not lose the user within the layers and layers of the interface, but aid the user in achieving a more complete understanding of the interface and system operation as a whole. The importance of proper menu structuring can never be stressed enough. As additional information is made available to the user the designer must determine the most efficient manner to accomplish this task.

One can expect many trends for future complex systems. These systems will continue to become cheaper, faster, and smaller. From a designer's perspective this creates several inherent problems. Systems will need to interact flawlessly with both old and new versions of the same product as well as with other operating platforms. Users will continue to be concerned when making purchases of such products as the "half-life" for many computer systems is relatively short. This raises concerns when making system comparisons for purchasing decisions.

Third observation. Paralleling the growth of concern for the study of human-technology interaction has been the theories and applications being introduced from the human-computer interaction (HCI) community. The study of this interaction is of great importance. While we may examine both technology and human limitations independently, users never work in such a vacuum. As technologies emerge, current theories of HCI must be tested (and altered if appropriate), and new theories and research techniques proposed. The field of HCI must be viewed by the research and design community not as a solution to an already existing problem but more as a proactive and integral part of the design process. Usability procedures can drastically aid in detecting any user problems before going into production and also assist in determining such important user parameters as training requirements.

In recent years there have been many approaches to understanding the interaction between technology and humans. There are many references to proper workstation design for traditional workspaces, but there exists little guidance in the requirements for such non-traditional workplaces in which users now are using complex systems. Workplaces often are in remote and sensitive locations such as space, ocean oil platforms, tropical environments, and moving vehicles. Complex systems are requiring usage in places never dreamed of before. We must determine common standardized practices for determining the various interaction problems which might occur in these non-traditional working environments.

Our fourth observation centers around the well-established cognitive revolution. More on this later, but uncovering the mental activities and thought processes used by operators when performing a certain task is a requirement in many jobs. This information, for example, can help in designing an interface, identifying training requirements, or examining human errors. The difficulties of obtaining reliable and valid information from any cognitive analysis method is still a problem. However, several efforts have been developed to improve these cognitive techniques (e.g. cognitive task analysis, see Zsambok & Klein, 1997).

Finally, we must also state the need for both a theoretical and empirical base to any research program attempting to understand the sometimes subtle and intricate human-computer interactions which occur in systems. The research must be theoretically-driven and empirically-oriented. We also recognize the need to balance data collected in the laboratory with that on the field. Often studies lead to different conclusions when systems are tested in the field as compared to the laboratory. This is the nature of the beast of our profession. We must attempt to understand human performance in complex environments using a variety of tools, techniques, and approaches. No single method will do the job. But we need more rigorous and reliable tools and techniques. This is imperative.

As technology continues to become cheaper, faster, and smaller, the continued trend of evolving technology will proceed. The inadequacies of research and design efforts will continue to heed the need for new research paradigms. We briefly discuss three emerging paradigms that make human performance its central focus: (1) cognitive engineering, (2) naturalistic decision making, and (3) human-centered design. We selected three additional areas because they represent opportunities where proactive research can make a difference in how one designs and delivers systems that use advanced technology. These are: (4) simulation and training, (5) virtual environment, and (6) automated systems. We finally discuss two areas that are critical and timely: (7) human factors in space exploration, and (8) international/cultural ergonomics. While we probably don't do justice to the number of issues that can be addressed in these areas, we wanted to, at least, highlight their importance.

Cognitive Engineering

There has been a recent trend to further understand the cognitive nature of performance. Brought about by the shortcomings of behavioral research and the recent desire to study cognition "in the wild", a field has arisen called cognitive engineering. Woods and Roth (1988) state:

> Cognitive engineering is an applied cognitive science that draws on the knowledge and techniques of cognitive psychology and related disciplines to provide the foundation for principle-driven design of person-machine systems. Cognitive engineering does this by providing the basis for a problem-driven rather than a technology-driven approach.

In addition, cognitive engineering methods address cognitive systems which exist so as to identify those deficiencies that can be corrected by a cognitive system redesign, in addition to addressing prospective cognitive systems as a design tool during cognitive tasks allocation and joint architecture development (Woods and Roth, 1988).

This field utilizes cognitive theories and techniques to investigate cognitive processes in complex systems. Cooke, Stout and Salas (1997) state that using cognitive engineering techniques coupled with knowledge engineering techniques can aid researchers in eliciting and confirming the cognitive nature of many constructs (i.e. situational awareness). These research techniques include interviews, process tracing, and conceptual methods. Development of techniques to support cognitive engineering includes such software tools as COGNET and MacSHAPA (Sanderson, McNeese & Zaff, 1994).

Today's advanced complex systems require designers to use as much information as can be found pertaining to the designated user group. The field of cognitive engineering evolved to aid designers in understanding the information processing capabilities of humans (Woods, 1988). As system design moves from an engineering design orientation to human-centered design, the need for greater research in the area of cognition and its implications to human system integration is required.

Research Directive: Research should continue to focus the cognitive aspects of human performance, employing cognitive engineering theories and methods in order to establish human-centered design principles – as to better contribute to effective training and system design.

Naturalistic Decision Making (NDM)

Classical decision making theories are based on decisions made using logic and probability theory. Some researchers have questioned the usefulness of these theories when applied to real world settings. NDM theories differ from classical theories in that different decision strategies will be used based on several relevant variables including level of experience of the decision maker, the task, and context in which the decision must be made.

Zsambok (1997) states:

> The study of NDM asks how experienced people, working as individuals or groups in dynamic, uncertain, and often fast-paced environments, identify and assess their situation, make decisions and take actions whose consequences are meaningful to them and to the larger organization in which they operate (p. 5).

She continues by noting that decision makers are unable to depend on routine thinking or action. However, not all researchers agree with the Zsambok claim.

For example, Lehto (1997) believes that the premise of NDM is decisions are made in a manner which is routine and non-analytical. While these examples of divergent explanations of NDM might seem surprising, it is worth noting NDM is a relatively new field and different theories of its operation will do more to advance its study than to prohibit its progress. One of the most important features of NDM is that it can be applied to many domains (e.g. aviation, military, health care). Some even consider NDM to be a part of cognitive engineering.

Many theories of NDM have been proposed. The more commonly known models include the task performance model (Rasmussen, 1983), Klein's (1989) recognition-primed decision model, image theory model (Beach, 1990), the recognition/metarecognition model (Cohen, Freeman & Thompson, 1997) and the explanation-based decision model (Pennington & Hastie, 1988). These models have been tested over various domains including firefighting, juror decisions, and command and decision systems. These research efforts are to be applauded in their drive to understand decision-making processes as they occur in real world settings. The importance and popularity of this research area can be recognized in the conferences held to discuss this very topic. Each conference, held in 1989, 1994, and 1998 has led to the publication of three books, *Decision Making in Action: Models and Methods* (Klein, Orasanu, Calderwood & Zsambok, 1993), and *Naturalistic Decision Making* (Zsambok & Klein, 1997), and Salas and Klein (in press). The research testing these theories and the broad context to which NDM theory has been tested in the field lends itself to the importance of this research area. The evolution of NDM arose from insufficient methods and theories to explain the discrepancies of results between lab and field studies.

As the need to understand decision processes continues to move out of the laboratory and into real world decision environments, we must continue to exert efforts to further understand the cognitive processes that are involved in naturalistic environments. Only with a continued drive towards this goal, coupled with further development and subsequent testing of NDM-based theories and models, can we hope to extract the detailed principles deemed necessary to aid in our understanding of complex decision making performance.

Research Directive: Research must continue testing NDM-based theories, methods and applications as to generate principles and guidelines that can be used to guide the design and development of human-centered complex systems.

Human-Centered Design

Though it may seem obvious to design complex systems with the human user in mind, Norman (1993) recounts that design tends to follow a machine-centered approach. This approach gives priority to fulfilling the needs of machines, requiring humans to adapt. While it may be true that humans are highly adaptable, they are also fallible, distractible, and imprecise; all reasons why Norman suggests that 75% of commercial aviation accidents are blamed on human error. On the other hand, it is not well known how often the unique human characteristics of adaptability and creativity have been responsible for preventing accidents. While many repetitive and procedural system functions may be allocated to machines in the design process, other system features must still be designed around the capabilities and limitations of the human operator. Following the machine or technology-centered approach, the operator may become involved in the process, but at such a late stage that the resulting system is difficult to learn or incompatible with established work practices (Kontogiannis & Embrey, 1997).

The human-centered approach to design takes into consideration the information processing abilities of the user, how information should be structured and flow to maximize system efficiency, user comfort, motivation, and usability, and minimize the chance for human error. When practicing the human-centered approach, a system can be designed by human factors and ergonomics specialists knowledgeable about theories of human behavior, or the design process can involve participation by a group of users familiar with the task for which the system is being developed. While there are benefits to either user-centered approach, Eason (1995) finds that the most successful system designs result from the combination of approaches. When applied to the design of complex systems, a combined approach capitalizes on the considerable wealth of information from the human performance research literature and the task specific knowledge possessed by the targeted system user. Despite the vast amount of human performance data compiled, technology-centered design is still commonplace. Kontogiannis and Embrey (1997) suggest the problem may be that the information has not been translated into a form (e.g. design frameworks) that can be readily used by system designers. Klein, Kaempf, Wolf, Thorsden and Miller (1997) also note the difficulty of putting human or user-centered design into practice without available guidelines and recom-mendations. However, other researchers believe we need to set our goals even higher. For instance, Soloway and Pryor (1996) note that technology-centered design of computer software was driven by limitations of processing power. As more computer processing power became available in the late 1980s and escalated in the 1990s, design began focusing more on the user rather than on more efficient code. As we enter the next millennium, Soloway and Pryor suggest we aim for a learner-centered design approach that will nurture intellectual growth and creativity, and help develop expertise.

The need for methods and tools to aid human-centered design has become abundantly clear. How these instruments should be documented and used is yet to be determined, but is crucial to attaining the goal of creating software that maximizes the human potential. The first step has been to acknowledge the importance and benefits of human-centered design. We must now further these design guidelines into actual practice and make user-centered design the norm and not the exception.

Research Directive: Research focused on designing, developing and evaluating human-centered principles must be conducted. Their research should provide designers with usable tools and methods that help them make design decisions on complex systems.

Simulation and Training

The popularity of simulation is not surprising. The creation of a learning environment approximating a real-world situation provides the framework for effective training. Yet the creation or the experience within the simulation is not sufficient enough to guarantee the effective transfer of training from simulation to real-world tasks. It is this transfer which is the heart of the reason for simulation. The use of simulation has seen an increase paralleling advances in computer technology. Issues related to effective simulation are viewed through many different eyepieces. Engineers and programmers concern themselves with the ability to create the most realistic environment as possible. This may translate operationally as an increase in polygons for simulated images, a sharper picture image, or the ability to create a distributed simulation. While these issues are important in their own right, psychologists and instructors examine simulation issues through a different light. Starting with the notion simulation is but a tool to train, concerns of effective training through simulation are numerous. Scientific questions from this group might include: Is there ample opportunity for the operator to practice skilled behaviors?, does the simulation provide measurable outcomes from which performance can be accurately assessed?, are task relevant behaviors presented at an acceptable level of fidelity? This is just a sample of the cognitive and behavioral "liveware" questions.

Wickens, Gordon and Lui (1998) note several situations in which simulations can serve as effective training programs. These include the simulation of tasks with large perceptual components (i.e. pattern matching), decision-making tasks, tasks requiring teamwork skills or group problem solving, and tasks which are too dangerous or expensive to be practiced in real life. Determining the tasks characteristics which are best practiced under simulations is an important notion. For other tasks, simulation might not be the best training tool. While Wickens and colleagues have worked towards determining task characteristics effective for simulator training, Salas, Bowers and Rhodenizer (1998) have stated the existence of several assumptions relating simulation to training. These authors state these false assumptions are prevalent in the area of aviation simulation. The assumptions are the existence of simulation is sufficient for training, the greater the level of fidelity or the longer the time spent in the simulator equates to better training, and the notion if aviators subjectively like the simulator it must be effective. A special issue of *The International Journal of Aviation Psychology* in 1998 was dedicated to Simulation and Training and presents articles refuting each of these notions from both a theoretical and empirical viewpoint.

Another important facet of simulation over the last decade is the distributed simulation. In these simulations (e.g. SIMNET), many operators can participate in the same simulation from the same or remote locations. Not only does this increase the potential to train on a large scale, it provides an opportunity to measure simulation performance from a team (large or small) perspective.

In summary, simulated systems must be designed with the cognitive and behavioral aspects of the operator in mind. The most expensive, highest fidelity simulator is completely useless from a training standpoint if there are not valid and reliable methods from which to measure performance. Effective training has the best chance for success when the content, performance measures, and instructional strategies have been determined in advance.

Research Directive: Research must continue to focus on designing and developing theoretically designed instructional features that can be incorporated into simulator systems for learning purposes.

Virtual Environment

Virtual reality (VR) seemed to be the buzzword of the 1990s. The actual definition of what constitutes VR may be debated, but generally it refers to a high fidelity simulation using head-tracked visuals and may include other sensory inputs such as auditory, tactile and/or kinesthetic. References to VR are difficult to escape. It is now part of our common vocabulary, numerous science fiction books have been written and movies produced about it, and video game manufacturers and video arcades are selling it as entertainment. Despite all the commotion over VR, the technology is only in its infancy.

Though we have taken science fiction and made it a reality, or virtual reality, extensive work needs to continue. The use and misuse of virtual reality is widespread in the training community. Training device customers often demand that their training simulators are state of the art, which often means VR. The potential of VR appears limitless, but the key research questions are yet to be adequately addressed. Before a trainee straps on a pair of virtual reality goggles, or slips on a pair of data gloves, the researchers and developers should ensure the appropriateness of the device for skills training. Simply immersing an individual deeper into the simulation does not guarantee more effective training. Virtual reality's potential for training has not even come close to being fulfilled. One reason for its unfulfilled potential is that no one is really sure what virtual reality can and cannot accomplish. A use for VR that has shown some promise is in its ability to allow individuals to form a cognitive map of a space never physically experienced. For example, Wilson, Foreman and Tlauka (1997) and Witmer, Bailey, and Knerr (1996) demonstrated that spatial information experienced in a virtual environment can readily be transferred to the actual environment. That is, individuals were able to orient themselves in an actual building after experiencing the building in VR. This application may be important for professions ranging from architect to surgeon. In the not-to-distant future, surgeons will receive force feedback simulating the feel of a cut or a firefighter can experience the sight, sound, feel, and smell of a raging fire while in the safety of a VR.

Developers continue to make great strides in improving the graphics capability of VR. Faster computer update rates have allowed simulations to move smoothly eliminating much of the lag prevalent in the systems of the early 1990s that led to cyber sickness or other side effects. Despite the faster update rates, VR cyber sickness is still problematic. What side effects can be expected when the other senses are incorporated into a simulation and how do these added sensory inputs aid or hinder learning? What level of immersion is required to train particular skills? As researchers struggle in their search for answers, the developers continue to rapidly improve the technology.

Research Directive: Research must focus on determining the potential of VR in a training environment.

Automated Systems

As computer technology increases, product users have seen an increase in the amount of automated systems we encounter everyday. Many fields such as aviation (i.e. autopilot and flight management systems), manufacturing (i.e. robotics used on assembly lines), medicine (i.e. monitoring devices), banking (i.e. ATM's), and automotive (i.e. cruise control) have all been drastically affected by automated systems. Designed to replace manual tasks typically performed by humans, automation (in most cases) has led to increased safety and effectiveness, reduced workload, and increased proficiency with regard to system usage. As scientists we must be concerned with how automation affects various aspects of human performance and how the role of the human in the human-machine interface has been altered. This question is further complicated by the continuous changing nature of automation as stated originally by Sheridan (1980) (i.e. levels of automation), the strong desire to adhere to a human-centered design approach, and the rapid incessant introduction of new automated systems into society.

Research has uncovered several effects automation has on human performance. Automation, by removing the manual operation of a task from the user, has changed the role of the system operator to that of a system monitor. We have long known of the limitations of the human as a monitor (Fitts, 1951). Sarter and Woods (1994) have discussed the potential problems of automation when the user is not informed of the current state of the automated system. Work by Parasuraman and colleagues (e.g. Parasuraman, Mouloua & Molloy, 1994; Parasuraman, Mouloua, Molloy & Hilburn, 1996), supply evidence to support the poor ability of humans in the monitoring role. Based on these studies Parasuraman, Mouloua and Molloy (1996) tested the use of an adaptively automated system to combat the monitoring problem with some success. They found performance measures (i.e. detecting automation failures) could be improved if the automated system was periodically reverted to manual control. Other concerns with automated systems include trust (Muir, 1988; McClumpha & James, 1994), reliability (Sorkin, 1988; Parasuraman, Molloy & Singh, 1993; Riley, 1994), confidence in manual skills (Lee & Moray, 1992), and reduction vs. altered levels of mental workload (Wiener, 1988; Harris, Hancock & Arthur, 1993). A recent review of automation concerns with respect to human performance can be found in Parasuraman and Riley (1997).

These research areas related to automation are important and efforts should be continued to further understand the nature of human performance when humans interact with automated systems. This interaction is not to be limited to users as automation issues must be addressed in the design stage. Insufficient research has also been conducted in the areas of team performance in automated systems as well as training issues related to automation. As automated systems, and their subsequent use, continue to grow and evolve we as scientists must design systems with the human interface as the focus.

Research Directive: Research should focus on determining the effects of automated systems on individual and group performance and must uncover what are the requisite competencies to manage such systems.

Human Factors in Space Exploration

With the building of the International Space Station (ISS) the United States, as well as 15 contributing countries, have laid a foundation from which space travel and habituation can become commonplace. The human factors issues relating to space travel are enormous. Issues such as the ergonomics (or the "decor" as NASA researchers call this issue) of the space vehicles, working in zero gravity environments, human physiological reactions to a new environment, and the basic design of the ISS have become common discussion topics among researchers. With each additional launch into space, more experiments are conducted, more data is collected, and more scientific questions arise. How are we as designers to address these issues based in a world of which we have relatively little first hand experience, few large databases, and many unanswered questions? With the successful space program of the U.S. (over 1000 launches) and countries around the globe (over 3500 successful launches) many efforts have begun to examine human-technology interactions in space. Space travel has changed the nature of work, the roles of humans in space, and the relationships between the two. NASA is leading the research efforts along with industry and university partners.

One of the best sources of information about life in space comes directly from interviews and comments made by the astronauts. We need to understand and prepare our astronauts better for the varied living conditions in space. Our lack of addressing this issue is evident by a comment made by an anonymous astronaut in 1995 after being aloft for 115 days. He stated NASA neglected to prepare him for the psychological aspects associated with the isolation and confinements he experienced while in orbit (Harris, 1996). We are constantly discovering how human physiology is affected by prolonged space flight. Although not completely knowledgeable in the effect of space flight on human health, we have learned several compensations to help reduce or mediate the negative consequences on performance. Through research and experience we have learned space nausea can be relieved by medication and decreasing exercise before flight. During space flight, vestibular system balance is lost due to lack of gravity affecting the inner ear. After two days in the zero-g environment, astronauts become visually programmed and the body accepts information from the visual system only, ignoring the contradictory vestibular information from the inner ear. Once humans reenter a gravity environment the body goes through a process of gaining back vestibular balance from information from both the inner ear and the eye. We have discovered blindfolds can help to reduce this adaptation period. Decompression sickness is often encountered prior to a space walk (caused by pressure change in spacesuit). This can be reduced by having the astronaut breathe pure oxygen for several hours to purge the body of nitrogen or by lowering the pressure in the environment (spacesuit or in the module) slowly (Harris, 1996). Another major concern during space flight is physical space. Each shuttle contains many compartments filled with supplies, laboratory and computer equipment, electrical devices, emergency equipment, as well as communication devices. The design of a shuttle module must take into account such features as frequency of use of a component, its importance, as well as the constraints dictated by the size of the module itself.

With the planned ISS leading the drive towards prolonged space flight, we have addressed only a small variety of the important issues in this chapter. As space modules become a prolonged temporary home for space travelers, the need to examine the human-machine interaction associated with space flight will become ever increasingly significant. Such issues as orbital teamwork and the effect of human resource development for crews have been listed as important issues but insufficiently researched. As scientists concerned with space flight, we must always remember that we are dealing no longer with Homo Sapiens but with Homo Cosmonautics (spacefaring man).

Research Directive: Research must uncover the variables that may affect individual and group performance in space. Tested and valid principles need to emerge.

International/Cultural Ergonomics

Some measures must be taken to help prepare us for the changes coming in the 21st century. Operating standards that cut across cultures, languages, and educational levels will have to be developed and applied, but must be carefully balanced with the flexibility of allowing preferences to be set by the users. Never before has it been so important for engineers and behavioral scientists to work together to keep abreast of the changing world culture and design systems accordingly. A strong understanding of the user population (e.g. human limitations) coupled with a human-centered design approach is no longer desired but imperative for the successful introduction of new systems and products.

As technology has increased our domain of communication via electronic mail, internet access, and data/information capabilities (file transfer protocols), the need to examine cultural factors affecting performance in complex systems has never been so high. As researchers and system designers we must continue the search for cultural models so that data from various cultures can be empirically and reliably compared with a high rate of validity. The scientific community must define cultural data types as seen common among various themes such as national cultures, corporate cultures, and international markets. Users can share multiple languages, differing customs, novel environmental cues, as well as high levels of diversity within a group (nationality).

Systems must be designed and constructed with many cultural factors incorporated. We must learn to fit the job to the culture as well as to the person (Kaplan, 1995, 1997). As nations continue to collaborate in international markets, the understanding of cultural issues remains critical. We, as a nation, are constantly providing and acquiring goods and services from other nations and cultures. Without cultural knowledge of these countries and cultures how can we expect to continuously provide quality service and merchandise? An example of how cultural factors can play a major role in performance would be the recent problems encountered at the Russian space station Mir.

A recent U.S. astronaut to board Mir recently discovered that the emergency space suit (Russian) would not fit him. This safety hazard is clearly rooted in the lack of recognizing the cultural factors (i.e. physical dimensions) that differ between the U.S. astronauts and Russian Cosmonauts. Luckily, the problem was solved with minor modifications to the suit.

Industry as well as academia has recognized the need for additional scientific inquiries in the field of cultural ergonomics. Evidence of such collaboration can be found between the International Center of Cultural Ergonomics (ICOCE) and the International Ergonomic Association (IEA). This group, called the International Cultural Ergonomic Advisory Programme provides assistance to underdeveloped nations and deprived locations within the United States at no cost. Assistance may include providing advise, technical expertise, training, and addressing safety issues. Collaborative efforts such as these are needed to address the multinational and multicultural issues across the globe. Therefore, as technology decreases the boundaries between nations, we must remain cognizant of the role of cultural factors in examining the design, delivery, and use of technological-based systems.

Research Directive: Research aimed at determining the cultural factors which facilitate or hinder the optimal use of technology-based systems must be conducted.

CONCLUDING REMARKS

The purpose of this chapter is to highlight some of the important areas in human performance which will confront human factors specialists of the new millenium with the greatest challenges. We are not professing to have "a crystal ball" to set a focus on these areas but rather just use recent history to add credibility to our directives. The chapter focuses on three emerging research paradigms – cognitive engineering, naturalistic decision making, and human-centered design. We feel these paradigms will have a great focus for science into the next decades. We strengthen our claims through examination of three application areas – simulation and training, virtual reality, and automated systems. The chapter ends with a focus on two areas critical to the increase in human communication both here and away from earth – human factors in space exploration and international/cultural ergonomics.

To reiterate, we acknowledge there are other research areas which are just as important as the ones we have chosen to address here. But regardless of the topics chosen to be discussed within this chapter, there are several themes which the reader should take away from its reading. The first is that we must become proactive in our approach to system design. The cost of fixing human factors problems after the fact is enormous. We need to move our place in the design process directly to the front and not remain as an afterthought once errors are discovered.

The second theme to take away from the chapter is the necessity of multiple methodologies to solving problems. Very rarely does the use of one approach reach the desired solution. We have developed many methodologies within our "toolbox" which we take to work each day. The ability to examine issues from multiple perspectives can lead to novel and unique solutions. This type of action can only be achieved through an understanding of various methods for problem solving as there are no "canned" answers to any practical problem.

The final theme to be stressed in the new millenium is to approach problems through systematic investigation. While both laboratory and field studies each have their respective place in the scientific arena, without solid systematic techniques of investigation the findings cannot be related to what we already know and understand. The days of conducting research for the sake of research are over. The human population will need our help to solve many complex problems in the future, problems we cannot even foresee at this time. Our best chance to solve such problems is through the use of multiple methodologies, proactive research directions, and systematic investigation.

REFERENCES

American Heritage Dictionary (1995). Boston: Houghton Mifflin Company.

Beach, L. R. (1990). *Image Theory: Decision Making in Personal and Organizational Contexts.* Chidster, U.K.: John Wiley.

Cohen, M. S., Freeman, J. T., & Thompson, B. B. (1997). Training the Naturalistic Decision Maker. In: C. E. Zsambok & G. Klein (Eds), *Naturalistic Decision Making* (pp. 257–268). Mahwah, NJ: LEA.

Cooke, N. J., Stout, R., & Salas, E. (1997). Broadening the measurement of situational awareness through cognitive engineering methods. In: *Proceedings of the Human Factors and Ergonomics Society 41st Annual Meeting* (pp. 215–219). Santa Monica, CA: HFES.

Eason, K. D. (1995). User-centered design: for users or by users? *Ergonomics, 38,* 1667–1673.

Fitts, P. M. (1951). Engineering Psychology and Equipment Design. In: S. S. Stevens (Ed.), *Handbook of Experimental Psychology.* New York: Wiley and Sons.

Harris, P. R. (1996). *Living and Working in Space: Human Behavior, Culture, and Organization.* New York: Wiley and Sons.

Harris, W., Hancock, P. A., & Arthur, E. (1993). The effect of task load projection on automation use, performance, and workload. In: *Proceedings of the 7th International Symposium on Aviation Psychology* (pp. 890–897). Columbus: Ohio State University.

Kaplan, M. (1995). The culture at work: Cultural Ergonomics. *Ergonomics, 38,* 606–615.

Kaplan, M. (1997). *Culturelink: The electronic exchange vehicle of the International Center of Cultural Ergonomics [on-line].* Available: http://pegasus.cc.ucf.edu/~kaplanm1/ICOCE.

Klein, G. A. (1989). Recognition Primed Decisions. In: W. Rouse (Ed.), *Advances in Man-Machine System Research* (pp. 47–92). Greenwich, CT: JAI Press.

Klein, G., Kaempf, G. L., Wolf, S., Thordsen, M., & Miller, T. (1997). Applying decision requirements to user-centered design. *International Journal of Human-Computer Studies, 46,* 1–15.

Klein, G., Orasanu, J., Calderwood, R., & Zsambok, C. (Eds) (1993). *Decision making in action: Models and methods.* Norwood, NJ: Ablex.

Kontogiannis, T., & Embrey, D. (1997). A user-centered design approach for introducing computer-based process information systems. *Applied Ergonomics, 28,* 109–119.

Lee, J. D., & Moray, N. (1992). Trust, control strategies, and allocation of function in human-machine systems. *Ergonomics, 35,* 1243–1270.

Lehto, M. (1997). Decision Making. In: G. Salvendy (Ed.), *Handbook of Human Factors and Ergonomics* (2nd ed.). New York: Wiley & Sons.

McClumpha, A., & James, M. (1994). Understanding automated aircraft. In: M. Mouloua & R. Parasuraman (Eds), *Human Performance in Automated Systems: Recent Research and Trends* (pp. 314–319). Hillsdale, NJ: LEA.

Muir, B. M. (1988). Trust between humans and machines, and the design of decision aids. In: E. Hollnagel, G. Mancini & D. D.Woods (Eds), *Cognitive Engineering in Complex Dynamic Worlds* (pp. 71–83). London: Academic.

Norman, D. A. (1993). Toward human-centered design. *Technology Review, 96,* 47–53.

Parasuraman, R., Mouloua, M, & Molloy, R. (1994). Monitoring automation failures in human-machine systems. In: M. Mouloua & R. Parasuraman (Eds), *Human Performance in Automated Systems: Recent Research and Trends* (pp. 45–49). Hillsdale, NJ: LEA.

Parasuraman, R., Mouloua, M, & Molloy, R. (1996). Effects of adaptive task allocation on monitoring of automated systems. *Human Factors, 38,* 665–679.

Parasuraman, R., Mouloua, M, Molloy, R., & Hilburn, B. (1996). Monitoring automated systems. In: R. Parasuraman & M. Mouloua (Eds), *Automation and Human Performance: Theory and Applications* (pp. 91–115). Hillsdale, NJ: LEA.

Parasuraman, R., Molloy, R., & Singh, I. R. (1993). Performance consequences of automation-induced "complacency". *International Journal of Aviation Psychology, 3*, 1–23.

Parasuraman, R., & Riley, V. (1997). Human and automation: Use, misuse, disuse, abuse. *Human Factors, 39*(2), 230–253.

Pennington, N., & Hastie, R. (1988). Explanation-based decision making: Effects of memory structure on judgement. *Journal of Experimental Psychology: Learning, Memory, and Cognition, 14*, 521–533.

Rasmussen, J. (1983). Skills, rules, knowledge: signals, signs and symbols and other distinctions in human performance models. *IEEE Transactions on Systems, Man and Cybernetics, SMC-13*(3), 257–267.

Rasmussen, J., Pejtersen, A-M., & Goodstein, L. (1995). *Cognitive Engineering: Concepts and Applications.* New York: Wiley.

Riley, V. (1994). A theory on operator reliance on automated systems. In: M. Mouloua & R. Parasuraman (Eds), *Human Performance in Automated Systems: Recent Research and Trends* (pp. 8–14). Hillsdale, NJ: LEA.

Sanderson, P. M., McNeese, M. D., & Zaff, B. S. (1994). Handling complex real-world data with cognitive engineering tools: COGNET and MacSHAPA. *Behavioral Research Methods, Instruments, and Computers, 26*(2), 117–124.

Sarter, N., & Woods, D. D. (1994). Pilot interaction with cockpit automation II: An experimental study of pilots' model and awareness of the flight management system. *International Journal of Aviation Psychology, 4*, 1–28.

Salas, E., Bowers, C. B., & Rhodenizer, L. G. (1998). It is not how much you have but how you use it: Toward a rational use of simulation to support training. *The International Journal of Aviation Psychology, 8*(3), 197–208.

Salas, E., & Klein, G. (Eds) (in press). *Application of Naturalistic Decision Making.* Hillsdale, NJ: LEA.

Sheridan, T. (1980). Theory of man-machine interaction as related to computerized automation. In: E. J. Kompass & T. J. Williams (Eds), *Man-machine Interfaces for Industrial Control.* Barington, IL: Technical Publishing Company.

Soloway, E., & Pryor, A. (1996). The next generation in human-computer interaction. *Communications of the ACM, 39*, 16–18.

Sorkin, R. D. (1988). Why are people turning off our alarms? *Journal of the Acoustical Society of America, 84*, 1107–1108.

Weiner, E. L. (1988). Cockpit automation. In: E. L. Weiner & D. C. Nagel (Eds), *Human Factors in Aviation* (pp. 433–461). San Diego: Academic.

Wickens, C. D., Gordon, S. E., & Lui, Y. (1998). *An introduction to human factors engineering.* New York: Addison Wesley.

Wilson, P. N., Foreman, N., & Tlauka, M. (1997). Transfer of spatial information from a virtual to a real environment. *Human Factors, 39*, 526–531.

Witmer, B. G., Bailey, J. H., & Knerr, B. W. (1996). Virtual spaces and real world places: Transfer of route knowledge. *International Journal of Human-Computer Studies, 45*, 413–428.

Woods, D. D. (1988). Commentary: Cognitive engineering in complex and dynamic worlds. In: E. Hollnagel, G. Mancini & D. D. Woods (Eds), *Complex Engineering in Complex Dynamic Worlds.* New York: Academic Press, pp. 115–129.

Woods, D. D., & Roth, E. M. (1988). Cognitive Engineering: Human Problem Solving with Tools. *Human Factors, 30*(4), 415–430.

Zsambok, C. E. (1997). Naturalistic Decision Making: Where Are We Now? In: C. E. Zsambok & G. Klein (Eds), *Naturalistic Decision Making* (pp. 3–16). Mahwah, NJ: LEA.

Zsambok, C. E., & Klein, G. (1997). *Naturalistic Decision Making*. Mahwah, NJ: LEA.